THE SOLE VOICE

THE SOLE VOICE

Character Portraits
From Shakespeare
by Philip Burton

THE DIAL PRESS
New York
1970

Library of Congress Catalog Card Number: 70-120470

Printed in the United States of America

Book design by Jacqueline Schuman

First Printing, 1970

To my students
at the American Musical and Dramatic Academy,
and my audiences
throughout North America.

FOREWORD

I HAVE BEEN prompted to write this book by the people to whom it is dedicated: my actor-students and those audiences throughout North America to whom I have spoken about Shakespeare. It is an attempt to bring some of his characters alive, as I see them. Much scholarly criticism divorces Shakespeare from the theatre where he rightly belongs, and tends to make his characters symbolic abstractions, but an actor has to breathe a vivid and recognizable humanity into those characters, and my aim is to help him to do so, and also to help the reader of Shakespeare to put flesh on his words.

Without planning it, I find that the female characters have captured only three chapter titles out of twenty-one, but a look at the dramatis personae of any of the plays will show that that is a fair ratio. The strange anomaly is that Shakespeare's England was very much a man's world but dominated by an astonishing woman, Queen Elizabeth I. Shakespeare's players were solely male, which was another reason for keeping the number of women's parts to a minimum, though they often dominate the plays they are in, as the Queen did her country.

I start with the Histories, since they deal with actual people and actual events; consequently in them the strain of credibility is relaxed; there are no transvestite complications and pounds of flesh. Having found our feet on the comparatively firm ground of history, however plowed up it may be to serve the author's artistic purposes, it should be easier to launch into the wild seas of fiction and fantasy. I end with the Tragedies, since they are the ultimate expression of man at his best and worst, and of his world at its most awe-inspiring and terrifying. In the case of the English kings I have dealt with them in their historical order, but in the other two parts the characters appear in the probable order in which Shakespeare wrote them.

More than once I find that I have quoted or referred to what I have written "elsewhere." In every case the "elsewhere" is a chapter on Shakespeare in my book, *Early Doors*.

Of making many books about Shakespeare there is no end, and here is yet another, but at least this one is not primarily aimed at academic shelves. In order to preserve its non-academic appearance, I have deliberately eschewed footnotes, appendices, and even a bibliography. To prepare a complete bibliography would have been difficult in any case, for this book is the outcome of some fifty years of reading. It is not written for scholars, though it is hoped that even they may find some points of interest in it, if they are prompted only to challenge the presumptuous arrogance of some of my judgments. Not that I wish to belittle Shakespearean criticism; I owe an immeasurable debt to it; immeasurable in that it has become an organic part of me, and I can no longer separate what I owe to others from what comes from my own insight.

Contents

PART I

Introduction to the Histories   3

   1:   Joan La Pucelle   15
   2:   Richard II   28
   3:   Henry IV   49
   4:   Hotspur   64
   5:   Falstaff   78
   6:   Henry V   95
   7:   Richard III   111

PART II

Introduction to the Comedies   133

   8:   Portia   145
   9:   Shylock   159
   10:   Jacques   175
   11:   Malvolio   188
   12:   Angelo   201
   13:   Leontes   217
   14:   Prospero   233

PART III

Introduction to the Tragedies   251

   15:   Romeo   263
   16:   Hamlet   281
   17:   Othello   313
   18:   King Lear   334
   19:   Macbeth   356
   20:   Cleopatra   380
   21:   Coriolanus   405

Postscript   431

THE SOLE VOICE

Shakespeare

Others abide our question. Thou art free.
We ask and ask: Thou smilest and art still,
Out-topping knowledge. For the loftiest hill
That to the stars uncrowns his majesty,
Planting his steadfast footsteps in the sea,
Making the Heaven of Heavens his dwelling-place,
Spares but the cloudy border of his base
To the foil'd searching of mortality:
And thou, who didst the stars and sunbeams know,
Self-school'd, self-scann'd, self-honour'd, self-secure,
Didst walk on Earth unguess'd at. Better so!
All pains the immortal spirit must endure,
  All weakness that impairs, all griefs that bow,
  Find their sole voice in that victorious brow.

Matthew Arnold

PART I

INTRODUCTION TO

THE *Histories*

SHAKESPEARE was not the most learned man of his day, but his instinctive understanding of man has never been surpassed. Today's knowledge is tomorrow's ignorance, but wisdom endures. An ever-growing army of scholars down the centuries have proved to their own satisfaction that Shakespeare was consciously propagating religious and political beliefs, though they don't agree about what beliefs he was propagating. By a careful selection of passages it is possible to prove almost anything; as the Devil the Scriptures, the scholar can quote Shakespeare to his own advantage. In much the same way, many productions of the plays set out to prove a point, to illustrate a thesis, and, to do so, excise the passages that don't fit.

Shakespeare was not a scientist, a political philosopher, or a theologian, but he lived in an age when science, political philosophy, and theology were such vital matters that men died for their beliefs. Shakespeare, like all other intelligent men of his time, was exposed to passionately espoused ideas, but he was primarily a dramatist, and, as such, was much more interested in the man who held the idea than in the idea itself. The only safe rule in reading

3

his plays is to accept a speech as expressing the character's point of view, and not necessarily Shakespeare's.

Even Bernard Shaw, who was a dedicated socialist and was first drawn to write plays because of the immense power of the theatre for propaganda, warns us of ascribing to a playwright the ideas of his characters. "They are all right from their several points of view, and their points of view are, for the dramatic moment, mine also. This may puzzle the people who believe that there is such a thing as an absolutely right point of view, usually their own. It may seem to them that nobody who doubts this can be in a state of grace. However that may be, it is certainly true that nobody who agrees with them can possibly be a dramatist, or indeed anything else that turns upon a knowledge of mankind. Hence it has been pointed out that Shakespeare had no conscience. Neither have I, in that sense."

Some people think of Bertolt Brecht as primarily a communist, but even in him the playwright sometimes insists on being heard to the confusion of the committed political theorist. Thus in *Mother Courage* he wanted us to despise the leading character as the personification of all those base elements in society which batten on war, but it is almost impossible for the actress playing Mother Courage not to move us to admiration for her will to survive in spite of everything; her ironic name becomes a true one.

This introductory caution is very necessary in approaching Shakespeare. He was no theorist about man's relation to man, the state or God. Theories of human behavior change, but fundamentally man doesn't, and it is this unchanging essence that Shakespeare reveals. Whatever psychology will learn about man in the next millennium, Hamlet will still be on the dissecting table. Shakespeare knows us all, even in our most private moments, better than we know ourselves. Remote in time and status though his characters may be, they are always immediate and universal. Herman Melville said:

> No utter surprise can come to him
> Who reaches Shakespeare's core;

That which we seek and shun is there—
Man's final lore.

Shakespeare wrote ten plays about authentic kings of England. Eight of them form a continuous chronicle of the years from 1399 to 1485, but he did not write them in the order of their events. I think his failure to do so, or what I take to be his avoidance of doing so, has significance. The eight plays form a single story covering the reigns or partial reigns of seven kings—eight if we include the young boy, Edward V, who was murdered before he could be crowned—from the deposition of Richard II to the emergence of Henry VII. The deposition and subsequent murder of Richard II led to nearly a century of unrest and bloodshed until the rival claims to the throne of the Houses of York and Lancaster were finally united by the marriage of Henry VII, and the remarkable Tudor dynasty was born which, with some short-lived exceptions, was to bring peace, prosperity, and stability to the England in which Shakespeare was born, at a time when the rest of Europe was a prey to fierce dissension and open conflict.

Why did Shakespeare not tell the story in its chronological order? He starts with three plays about Henry VI, follows those with Richard III, and only then goes back to the beginning of the story with Richard II, and follows it through to its mid-point with Henry V. Why, too, in the last of the series, and for the only time, did he apologize for the inadequacies of his theatre?

> . . . But pardon, gentles all,
> The flat unraised spirits that hath dared
> On this unworthy scaffold to bring forth
> So great an object. Can this cockpit hold
> The vasty fields of France? Or may we cram
> Within this wooden O the very casques
> That did affright the air at Agincourt?
> Oh, pardon! . . .

The cockpit had held the vasty fields of France more than once before, and the scaffold had provided a stage whereon a company of players that was anything but flat and uninspired had brought forth many a great deed. And since the expert swordplay of the actors had furnished an enduring excitement to the audience for years, why should Shakespeare suddenly deprecate it?

> . . . —Oh, for pity!—we shall much disgrace
> With four or five most vile and ragged foils,
> Right ill-disposed in brawl ridiculous,
> The name of Agincourt. . . .

The answer, of course, is Henry V, the hero enshrined in the national memory, and his greatest victory, Agincourt, described by Sir Winston Churchill, who knew what he was talking about, as "a feat of arms which, however it may be tested, must be held unsurpassed." I have a feeling that Shakespeare put off, as long as he could, measuring up to his audience's inherited idealization of the hero-king, Henry V. The roistering young Prince Hal was one thing, but the kingly paragon was quite another. The first preserved lines of Shakespeare are a lamentation for the death of the young king—he was only thirty-four—whose reign had brought a nine-year halt in the long and sorry story of bloodshed at home and failure abroad.

> Hung be the heavens with black, yield day to night!
> Comets, importing change of times and states,
> Brandish your crystal tresses in the sky,
> And with them scourge the bad revolting stars
> That have consented unto Henry's death!
> King Henry the Fifth, too famous to live long!
> England ne'er lost a king of so much worth.

Shakespeare lived in dangerous days. He grew to manhood in a land under the constant threat of foreign invasion, riddled with spies, and torn by the religious passions of Catholics and Puritans. In the two brief reigns that preceded his birth, hundreds of people had been executed for their beliefs, Catholics in the reign of young Edward VI, and Protestants in that of "Bloody Mary." Elizabeth, the brilliant compromiser, who was in the eighth year of her reign at the time of Shakespeare's birth and was to reign for another thirty-nine years, had restored the religious settlement of her father, Henry VIII, and in so doing had gathered to herself the grateful and enduring devotion of the vast body of her subjects. She wooed the generality of her people with consummate skill; even many of those who opposed her views remained personally loyal to her. Her love of power and her love of England were one, and she would allow nothing to touch either. Her courage in the face of constant threats upon her life, her defiance of the foreign enemy, her shrewd diplomacy, her delight in the theatricality of pomp and ceremony, her care of the public purse, her enjoyment of physical pleasures and broad humor, all made her the object of popular adulation and devotion, and in this, as in other matters, Shakespeare was one of the people. He accepted the beliefs of the majority of his countrymen, as they were expressed by their Queen. For him history was the record of men, not theories; if the monarch was good and strong, all was well, and Elizabeth was good and strong. She was the focus of the reasonable and pragmatic, and of all that abhorred the dangers of fanaticism. Loyalty to her was essential to the unity of the country, and if any theme runs through Shakespeare's Histories it is a plea for unity, by stressing the horrors of civil strife.

There are those who say that Shakespeare differed from the generality of her subjects in his attitude to his Queen. Their chief argument is that he seems to have been silent at the time of her death in 1603, an omission apparently referred to in a contemporary poem by Henry Chettle. They dispose of the eloquent tribute to the Queen in *Henry VIII*, almost the last words attributed to the playwright, as having been written by John Fletcher, an all too prevalent scholarly gambit: when you don't like it, say he didn't write it. Here are the lines, written several years after her death, and so in no way attributable to dutiful sycophancy, as might be those that follow to James I. The lines, written with hindsight knowledge, are spoken by Archbishop Cranmer, as he blesses the babe who was to become Queen Elizabeth.

This royal infant—Heaven still move about her!—
Though in her cradle, yet now promises
Upon this land a thousand thousand blessings,
Which time shall bring to ripeness. She shall be—
But few now living can behold that goodness—
A pattern to all princes living with her,
And all that shall succeed. Saba was never
More covetous of wisdom and fair virtue
Than this pure soul shall be. All princely graces,
That mould up such a mighty piece as this is,
With all the virtues that attend the good,
Shall still be doubled on her. Truth shall nurse her,
Holy and heavenly thoughts still counsel her.
She shall be loved and feared. Her own shall bless her,
Her foes shake like a field of beaten corn,
And hang their heads with sorrow. Good grows with her.
In her days every man shall eat in safety
Under his own vine what he plants, and sing
The merry songs of peace to all his neighbours.
God shall be truly known; and those about her
From her shall read the perfect ways of honour,
And by those claim their greatness, not by blood.

As for Shakespeare's silence about Elizabeth's death in 1603, those were dark and tormented days for him, the time that produced his tragedies and bitter comedies; and it is probable that he was still deeply disturbed about the execution of the Earl of Essex two years before, an event which had had a profound effect on all the admirers of that fascinatingly dangerous man. But no one would have been more aware than Shakespeare of the agony of the Queen's necessary decision to preserve the safety of her realm by reluctantly agreeing to the beheading of the man she loved. And what of Francis Bacon, a near friend of Essex? It had been his lot to be the prosecuting attorney, and to write the subsequent justification of the verdict. I like to think that in the lines just quoted Shakespeare had come to his final summation of the Queen, and to the realization that her terrible decisions were part of the price she and her subjects had to pay for the good of England.

It was assumed by most of her subjects that the ultimate sanction for the Queen's authority was that she was the anointed of God, and not the appointed of man. Even in these days of limited and constitutional monarchy, the most solemn moment of the coronation is still the anointing with holy oil, and the same spoon was used for Elizabeth II as for Elizabeth I; it has been used for nine hundred years. Elizabeth I was very happy that some idea of the divine right of kings was taken for granted and not spelled out. The two kings who followed her had it spelled out, and it resulted in the beheading of the second of them, and in England's becoming a republic for eighteen years. Time and again Shakespeare insists on the divine source of kingship as a warning against regicide, for the Queen's life was constantly in danger, and with her life that of England. The murder of Duncan in *Macbeth* is not merely the assassination of a head of state, but

> Most sacrilegious murder hath broke ope
> The Lord's anointed temple, and stole thence
> The life o' the building.

In *Hamlet*, even the king who had gained the throne by the murder of his brother could say with confidence

> There's such divinity doth hedge a king
> That treason can but peep to what it would,
> Acts little of his will. . . .

In this case of Claudius we have the basic dilemma that Shakespeare faced in his Histories. If an anointed king is removed by force, is the authority of the king who removed him sacred too? This, in an extreme form, is the basic dilemma of all political life, the relation between the ideal and the practical. This is what Shakespeare saw in the torment of Brutus, the young idealist caught in the web of political necessity. Compared with Richard II, whom he deposed, Henry IV was a good king, and Shakespeare's Richard pathetically takes comfort in the belief that God will defend His own anointed. The Duke of York in that play seems to sum up the attitude of the average Englishman, of whom again in this matter Shakespeare was one. York opposes as best he can the seizure of the throne by Bolingbroke, but, once Bolingbroke is enthroned and anointed as Henry IV, he takes the oath of allegiance to him, and in fulfillment of that oath even denounces his own son to the new king for treason. "The King is dead. Long live the King." That is true, even if the first king has been murdered by the second. Such brutal pragmatism seems necessary to the life of the state.

There is a sense in which Shakespeare's whole eight-play cycle is a reminder to his countrymen of the dire consequences of regicide. The Bishop of Carlisle in *Richard II* proclaims the theme:

> The blood of English shall manure the ground
> And future ages groan for this foul act.
>
> .   .   .   .
>
> Oh, if you raise this house against this house,
> It will the woefullest division prove
> That ever fell upon this cursed earth.
> Prevent it, resist it, let it not be so,
> Lest child, child's children, cry against you "woe!"

It is a warning against the perils that threatened Elizabeth's life. A house was being raised against a house in her time also, in the person of Mary, Queen of Scots, who had been executed not ten years before Shakespeare wrote *Richard II*. That execution had given Elizabeth her greatest dilemma, for Mary was an anointed queen too. But the Catholic monarch's rash ambitions were a dangerous threat to Episcopalian Elizabeth, whose advisers urged her to get rid of the menace to herself and her kingdom's security, but for fifteen long years Elizabeth hesitated to do so, and even at the last tried to disclaim her part in the beheading of God's anointed Queen of Scotland.

Much has been written to prove that Shakespeare had a deeply held belief that order in society—every man, from king to commoner, in his place and function—was divinely determined, and was a reflection of an immutable order in the heavens and in

Heaven; angels, planets, and men all joining in a wondrous harmony, as shown in the "music of the spheres," to sing the praises of the Creator. The passages so often quoted to prove this thesis are mouthed for a very pragmatic purpose, like generally accepted texts quoted for dubious purposes; the Bible is often quoted in defense of unrighteous acts. In *Henry V*, the windily oratorical Archbishop of Canterbury indulges in a professional parenthesis on the honeybees,

> Creatures that by a rule in nature teach
> The act of order to a peopled kingdom,

merely to defend, in a most circuitous way, the policy of sending a military expedition to France. In *Coriolanus*, the patrician Menenius attempts to placate the rebellious mob by an amusing tale based upon comparing the body politic with the human body. In *Troilus and Cressida*, that most cynical play which Shakespeare's fellows called a tragedy but which we now consider a comedy, a very black one, it is the wily Ulysses who delivers the brilliant speech on "degree" in human society, as a respectable front for a devious plan to get Achilles to bestir himself; his practical purpose is much more succinctly phrased: "Blunt wedges rive hard knots." In every instance Shakespeare's primary interest in the idea is that it reveals the speaker's character, mind, and purpose.

Again, many of Shakespeare's explicators see his ruthlessly ambitious characters as derived from a reading of Machiavelli's *The Prince*, in much the same way that certain modern playwrights have concocted their plays from reading Freud rather than observing man in themselves and others. This, to me, is nonsense. I am sure that in sixteenth-century Europe Machiavelli was bandied about in much the same way that Darwin was in the nineteenth and Freud and Marx in the twentieth. Most of the people who confidently quote their ideas have never read their books; "survival of the fittest," "dialectical materialism," "Oedipus complex" have become cocktail chatter. In much the same way

Shakespeare's Richard says that he will "set the murderous Machiavel to school." No one has suffered more from distorting popularization than Machiavelli. He would heartily condemn those characters in Shakespeare that have been claimed as inspired by him; they lack the personal probity on which he placed such a high value, and their object is not effective government but selfish aggrandizement; it's one thing to be ruthless for the good of the state and quite another to be ruthless for private ambition. Shakespeare's so-called Machiavellian characters would have been the same had *Il Principe* never been written; they come from his understanding of the evil in the heart of man.

Coleridge said: "Let no man blame his son for learning history from Shakespeare." In the sense that Shakespeare brought historical characters and events vividly to enduring life it is true, but in the sense that he reproduced the events as he learned them from his books it is not always true. His object was the revelation of the abiding truths of humanity, not the fleeting facts of the chronicler; a dramatic unity, not a slice of rehashed journalism. Even his chief sources themselves, Holinshed and Hall, are now very suspect. They were scarcely historians in the modern sense at all. They did not distinguish between medieval rumors and medieval documents, between folktales distorted by constant repetition and eyewitness accounts, between supernatural wonders and verifiable facts. Sometimes Shakespeare followed the basic and undoubted line of a story very closely, as for instance in *Richard II*, but at other times his instinct for the significantly and colorfully dramatic led him to put two and two together to make a million. Thus, for instance, all he learned from Holinshed was this:

> The dead corpse [of Henry VI] on the Ascension even was conveyed with bills and glaves pompously—if you will call that a funeral pomp—from the Tower to the Church of Saint Paul, and there, laid on a bier or coffin bare-faced, the same in the presence of the beholders did bleed, where it rested the space of one whole day. From thence he was carried to

the Blackfriars and bled there likewise: and, on the next day after, it was conveyed in a boat, without priest or clerk, torch or taper, singing or saying, unto the monastery of Chertsey, distant from London fifteen miles, and there was it first buried.

It was an age-old belief that a corpse would bleed afresh in the presence of its murderer, so the dramatist must confront Richard with the telltale body of his victim. Furthermore, Shakespeare knew that Richard married the Lady Anne, widow of the Prince of Wales and daughter-in-law to Henry VI. What an exciting challenge to the young playwright—he was not yet thirty—to arrange things so that Richard would woo the Lady Anne over the corpse of her father-in-law, which suddenly spouts blood to accuse the murderer!

Of necessity Shakespeare's plays reflect the time and the place in which he lived. To the Englishman of his day life was a heady wine. There seemed no limit to man's possibilities, particularly if he were English, for "England—like little body with a mighty heart—" bid fair to rule the world. On September 26, 1580, Francis Drake arrived back in England after three years at sea, sailing ever westward. The impact of this achievement upon Englishmen is hard for us to imagine. It is true that the Portuguese Magellan had performed the feat nearly sixty years before; at least, his ship with the remainder of his crew had, for he himself had died during his extraordinary leap into the unknown. But Drake's return was wholly triumphant, and the holds of his *Golden Hind* were filled with priceless Spanish loot. Elizabethan adventurers rifled the coffers of the world to the applause of their Queen and country. Merchants brought back the stolen wealth of the Indies and the riches of the exotic East. Far-off countries with strange inhabitants were explored in much the same way that the twenty-first century will explore far-off worlds. Desdemona's credulity about "the Anthropophagi, and men whose heads do grow beneath their shoulders" matches that of some people today about visitors from outer space; in a sudden burst of knowledge there seems no limit to the possible. In Shakespeare's England wealth was abundant and found expression in beautiful Tudor mansions, richly furnished. Music and poetry were an integral part of life. There was no division between the artist and the man of action; the adventurers were poets too. Even the old barriers of aristocracy were breaking down; success in trade was rewarded with titles as well as success in battle.

There was a newfound pride in being English—Shakespeare has many a tilt at people who ape foreign manners—and this was reflected in a newfound pride in the language. Men exulted in speaking and writing English; they used it with exuberance and bravado, and none more than Shakespeare. Englishmen became hungry for news of their heritage, and there was an insatiable demand for plays about English history. It was the first demand that the young Shakespeare supplied, for there was a ready market.

There was another side to the richness of Elizabethan life. Outside the doors of the gorgeous palaces and wealthy mansions were plague, pestilence and poverty. (It is a commendable fact that during the reign of Elizabeth the first Poor Law was enacted, making each parish responsible for its indigent.) Death always threatened from babyhood onwards. It was an age in which to thank God if the baby lived, and in which the psalmist's three-score years and ten was rarely attained. Plague was as frequent in London as an influenza epidemic now. In his plays Shakespeare looks the everyday fact of death straight in the face; it is only our modern reluctance to do so which finds this morbid.

We are about to consider some of Shakespeare's kings and queens, not as remote phenomena or as illustrations of political philosophy but as men and women in whom we see ourselves, intensified and magnified, but deeply recognizable. Shakespeare's mission is to plumb the depth of the mystery of man, his glory and his shame, his ecstasy and misery, his awareness and delusion, his success and failure, his love and hate. His interest in history is the men who made it.

1   Joan La Pucelle

THE TITLE of this chapter will probably come as a surprise to most readers. Those whose acquaintance with Shakespeare is limited to the better-known plays will be surprised to learn that his first female character was Joan of Arc, "la Pucelle," "the Maid." Those who are aware of that fact will wonder, if space restricts us to consideration of only one female character from the Histories, why Joan was the chosen one; she seems such an incompletely realized character in a mishmash of a play. Why not choose Constance, from *King John*, that part to tear a cat in, or the admirable and victimized Katharine from *Henry VIII*, or "Captain Margaret," she with "tiger's heart wrapped in a woman's hide," the forceful and frustrated wife of the saintly Henry VI? Any of those characters would be richly rewarding to study, but in Joan it is peculiarly fascinating and revealing to watch the immature and apprentice playwright at work on a very difficult problem. He failed to solve it because something in him stood in the way, and that something was the essence of his future greatness.

First there is the problem of the play itself. Did Shakespeare write it? By that I do not mean was it written by one of the fifty-seven people—yes, fifty-seven is the latest count—who have been claimed as the author of all his plays by zealots specializing in the arcane. Let me say, in passing, that I have little patience with these misguided and misbegotten endeavors. They are fundamentally motivated by academic snobbishness: How could anybody who had not been to the university write Shakespeare's plays? It is conveniently forgotten that Shakespeare had more formal schooling than Bernard Shaw, that most knowledgeable of all dramatists, and that Sean O'Casey, a master of the English language, had virtually no schooling.

But there are scholars, as impatient as I with the fifty-seven varieties of authorship espoused by ardent cultists, who still find trouble with *Henry VI, Part I*. Various of them have, with skill and persuasiveness, found in it the hands of Marlowe, Kyd, Greene, Peele and Lodge. It is certain that there is a confusion of styles in the play, but I prefer to consider this to be the result of imitative attempts of the fledgling author in search of a style of his own, and—I hasten to add—I am not alone in this belief. After all, Heminge and Condell, the editors of the First Folio, who knew both Shakespeare and his plays, included it in *The Workes of William Shakespeare . . . Truely set forth, according to their first originall.*

Henry VI, Part I was written a couple of years after the defeat of the Spanish Armada, when England was drunk with victory and deliverance, and so the play was a paean of praise for a former English soldier whose feats of arms were legendary, Lord Talbot, "the great Alcides of the field." If Talbot is the hero, Joan must be the villain, and most unhistorically Shakespeare lets them meet in armed and single combat, the result of which is a draw, and subsequently lets Joan view the corpse of Talbot. Actually Talbot survived her by more than twenty years, and Shakespeare knew this, but even in his first grappling with history, considerations of drama are dominant. Shakespeare was not content to paint the portrait of Joan necessitated by his story, a girl possessed by devils and finally burned for witchcraft after a thorough examination by the Church. Already his divine compassion refuses to accept the stereotype and he sees such true greatness in the Maid that he actually foretells her official sainthood for which she had to wait more than three hundred years after he was dead: "Joan la Pucelle shall be France's saint." More than once in his subsequent career Shakespeare was going to find his sense of humanity at odds with a received portrait of villainy, notably in the case of Shylock, but in this apprentice play of *Henry VI, Part I* he lacks the skill to reconcile the contrary qualities in a unified character. Bernard Shaw says of the play:

> The impression left by it is that the playwright, having begun by an attempt to make Joan a beautiful and romantic figure, was told by his scandalized company that English patriotism would never stand a sympathetic representation of a French conqueror of English troops, and that unless he at once introduced all the old charges against Joan of being a sorceress and a harlot, and assumed her to be guilty of all of them, his play could not be produced.

Shakespeare found some of this ambivalence about Joan in Holinshed's Chronicles. This is what he read:

> Of favour was she counted likesome, of person strongly made and manly, of courage great, hardy, and stout withal; an understander of counsels though she were not at them; great semblance of chastity both of body and behaviour; the name of Jesus in her mouth about all her businesses; humble, obedient; and fasting divers days in the week. A person (as their books make her) raised up by power divine, only for succour to the French estate then deeply in distress.

Notice Holinshed's caveats: her chastity was but a "semblance," and this is an account of her culled from unreliable and prejudiced French books. He has no reservations whatsoever in his calumnious account of her trial, and his final summation is: "These matters may very rightfully denounce unto all the world her execrable abominations, and well justify the judgement she had, and the execution she was put to for the same."

Now let us examine Shakespeare's Joan as she is progressively revealed to us in the play. We first hear of her from the Bastard of Orleans who seeks to introduce her to the court of Charles, the Dauphin. He says:

> Be not dismayed, for succour is at hand.
> A holy maid hither with me I bring,
> Which by a vision sent to her from Heaven
> Ordained is to raise this tedious siege
> And drive the English forth the bounds of France.
> The spirit of deep prophecy she hath.

Then follows the scene in which, "to try her skill," a substitute is put in the place of the Dauphin, and she gains the ear of the Dauphin by penetrating the deception. Shaw too uses this scene but makes it clear beforehand how the trick will be accomplished. "She will know what everybody in Chinon knows: that the Dauphin is the meanest-looking and worst-dressed figure in the Court, and that the man with the blue beard is Gilles de Rais."

Bernard Shaw will have nothing to do with the supernatural. Joan's voices are a worry to him; he will allow them no objective reality. For him, Joan is one of those critical embodiments of the Life Force who periodically appear in the development of man to show the way to the next step in his evolution; in the case of Joan, she unwittingly proclaimed the values of nationalism and protestantism to lead man out of the social, political, religious, and philosophical ideas of the Middle Ages. I am reminded of what John Galsworthy said in comparing his plays with those of Shaw: "Shaw's characters express ideas they cannot possibly have; my characters have ideas they cannot possibly express." I must add that Galsworthy's plays are virtually dead, while Shaw's have an abiding life.

Shaw's Joan has an electrifying sense of mission, but all her actions are based on sound common sense. When this is pointed

out to her, she answers "crossly": "Well, I have to find reasons
for you, because you do not believe in my voices. But the voices
come first; and I find the reasons after: whatever you may choose
to believe." Shakespeare's Joan too, as we shall see, was richly endowed with sound common sense, but he did believe in her supernatural voices, even though ultimately he had to acknowledge
that they came from Hell and not from Heaven. Shaw stacks the
cards in his argument in the Court scene by making the substitute
for the Dauphin the blue-bearded Gilles de Rais, whose identi-
fication was easy. Holinshed gave Shakespeare no hint of the
identity of the substitute, and so he makes him Reignier, thus
bringing to our attention a character who was to have later im-
portance; he was the father of Margaret, whose marriage to Henry
VI was to be part of the final settlement of the Hundred Years
War, and who was to provide Shakespeare with a most vivid and
forceful character for three of his plays.

In Shakespeare, as in Shaw, Joan has no difficulty in seeing
through the deception with which she is confronted. Without
any preliminary, her opening words come straight to the matter:

> Reignier, is 't thou that thinkest to beguile me?
> Where is the Dauphin? Come, come from behind.
> I know thee well, though never seen before.
> Be not amazed, there's nothing hid from me.

She immediately has a private conference with the Dauphin and
in her speech, which is devoid of artifice and decoration, we see
the essential dramatist in the young Shakespeare adapting his style
to the necessities of the character. Our first impression of Joan is
of a forthright, uneducated, country girl.

> Dauphin, I am by birth a shepherd's daughter,
> My wit untrained in any kind of art.
> Heaven and our Lady gracious hath it pleased
> To shine on my contemptible estate.
> Lo, whilst I waited on my tender lambs,
> And to sun's parching heat displayed my cheeks,
> God's Mother deigned to appear to me,

And in a vision full of majesty
Willed me to leave my base vocation
And free my country from calamity.
Her aid she promised and assured success.
In complete glory she revealed herself;
And, whereas I was black and swart before,
With those clear rays which she infused on me
That beauty am I blessed with which you see.
Ask me what question thou canst possible,
And I will answer unpremeditated.
My courage try by combat if thou darest,
And thou shalt find that I exceed my sex.

Charles immediately accepts her challenge to single combat and is overcome. And here we must disabuse our minds of the picture of the Dauphin so brilliantly painted by Shaw. His Charles could scarcely lift a sword, much less wield it. The Charles of Shakespeare is a soldier. He goes into battle with the words:

Him I forgive my death that killeth me
When he sees me go back one foot or fly.

His defeat by Joan is necessary; she must be established as a redoubtable fighter to explain Talbot's later failure to vanquish her. But to retain our belief in Joan as a maid not a monster, Shakespeare is quick to have her explain her victory over Charles: "Christ's Mother helps me, else I were too weak." And Shakespeare's Talbot is not physically formidable. The Countess of Auvergne is amazed by his appearance, that accords so ill with his valiant reputation:

Alas, this is a child, a silly dwarf!
It cannot be this weak and writhled shrimp
Should strike such terror to his enemies.

And so Joan is given the command of the French forces to raise the siege of Orleans. The English messenger who brings the news to Talbot is unequivocal in his description of Joan; to him she is "a holy prophetess." When under Joan's leadership the French defeat the English, Talbot can only account for it by ascribing it to "baleful sorcery." When two sides are equally confident that God is on their side, the victory of the enemy must be ascribed to the Devil. The French are equally certain, when he is victorious, that Talbot is "a fiend of Hell."

When the tide turns and the French are defeated, Charles immediately rounds on Joan:

> Is this thy cunning, thou deceitful dame?
> Didst thou at first, to flatter us withal,
> Make us partakers of a little gain,
> That now our loss might be ten times so much?

Joan retorts that she is powerless against the laxity of the French sentries. Straight away the French nobles fall to assigning the blame and establishing alibis, but Joan cuts across their bickering with words of true leadership:

> Question, my lords, no further of the case,
> How or which way. 'Tis sure they found some place
> But weakly guarded, where the breach was made.
> And now there rests no other shift but this:
> To gather our soldiers, scattered and dispersed,
> And lay new platforms to endamage them.

But before her words can take effect, a fresh attack causes them to fly, "leaving their clothes behind."

There follows an interlude in England which emphasizes the dissension out of which sprang the Wars of the Roses. This, surely, is the theme of the play. The English defeats in France are due to disunion at home. The young King expresses it in words which are a unifying motif throughout the Histories:

> Civil dissension is a viperous worm
> That gnaws the bowels of the commonwealth.

The same dissension is carried overseas by the Dukes of York and Somerset, and their failure to unite their forces causes the final defeat and death of Talbot. At that time the theme receives explicit expression in a speech by Sir William Lucy:

> Thus, while the vulture of sedition
> Feeds in the bosom of such great commanders,
> Sleeping neglection doth betray to loss
> The conquest of our scarce cold conqueror,
> That ever living man of memory,
> Henry the Fifth. Whiles they each other cross,
> Lives, honours, lands, and all hurry to loss.

By implication, the strength of the French forces is due to their temporary unity, brought about by the leadership of Joan.

Shakespeare read in Holinshed of a stratagem by which six English soldiers entered a castle to release some prisoners. This he transfers to Joan to enable her to gain access to the walled city of Rouen. She and four soldiers disguise themselves as peasants taking corn to market. Here Joan is neither saint nor witch, but just a clever leader, and this down-to-earth ability of Shakespeare's Joan is a dominant feature in her. It is reflected too in her sarcastic wit. When her stratagem has succeeded in allowing the French army to enter and capture the city, she stands on the walls and addresses Talbot and his army who are outside:

> Good morrow, gallants! Want ye corn for bread?
> I think the Duke of Burgundy will fast
> Before he'll buy again at such a rate.
> 'Twas full of darnel. Do you like the taste?

Talbot taunts her with a new accusation, that the French nobles are her "lustful paramours." He tries to provoke her and the French to take the field again, but Joan's common sense is unruffled:

> Belike your lordship takes us then for fools
> To try if that our own be ours or no.

And her farewell from the walls is delightful:

> God be wi' you, my lord! We came but to tell you
> That we are here.

The tide of battle turns again, and again Joan has to deal

with her dispirited generals. Her practical optimism soon has them pleading to her for guidance, for she says:

> Care is no cure, but rather corrosive
> For things that are not to be remedied.
> Let frantic Talbot triumph for a while
> And like a peacock sweep along his tail.
> We'll pull his plumes and take away his train
> If Dauphin and the rest will be but ruled.

And this time they are ruled to a policy of shrewd diplomacy, aimed at inducing the Duke of Burgundy to change sides. This Joan accomplishes by appealing to Burgundy as a Frenchman; this is a Joan that foreshadows Shaw's. She says:

> Look on thy country, look on fertile France,
> And see the cities and the towns defaced
> By wasting ruin of the cruel foe.
> As looks the mother on her lowly babe
> When death doth close his tender dying eyes,
> See, see the pining malady of France!
> Behold the wounds, the most unnatural wounds,
> Which thou thyself hast given her woeful breast.
> Oh, turn they edged sword another way;
> Strike those that hurt, and hurt not those that help.
> One drop of blood drawn from thy country's bosom
> Should grieve thee more than streams of foreign gore.
> Return thee therefore with a flood of tears,
> And wash away thy country's stained spots.

This patriotic appeal works, but Joan with canny skill reinforces her argument by appealing to Burgundy's self-interest. She says that, once he has served the English purpose, he will "be thrust out like a fugitive." As proof, she points out that his old enemy, the Duke of Orleans, long a prisoner of the English, has been freed "without his ransom paid." Here again Shakespeare has distorted the facts he learned from Holinshed for dramatic advantage. The Duke of Orleans had been captured at the battle of Agincourt and had been held a prisoner for twenty-five years, largely to oblige the Duke of Burgundy, for there was a bitter feud between the two families. Orleans had been held prisoner because he could not pay the extravagant ransom deliberately demanded for his freedom. The irony was that Burgundy finally paid the ransom himself to ensure the friendship of Orleans. But both Shakespeare and Joan knew that for feudal lords self-interest was stronger than patriotism, and so the facts are twisted. Joan has a supremely cynical comment on Burgundy's change of side, which her own eloquence has brought about. In an aside, she says: "Done like a Frenchman. Turn, and turn again!"

Helped by Burgundy, and also by the dissension among the English forces, the French defeat and slay the valiant Lord Talbot, and with him his son. Joan talks about the young boy admiringly, and with almost comic detachment:

> Once I encountered him, and thus I said:
> "Thou maiden youth, be vanquished by a maid."
> But, with a proud majestical high scorn,
> He answered thus: "Young Talbot was not born
> To be the pillage of a giglot wench."
> So, rushing in the bowels of the French,
> He left me proudly, as unworthy fight.

Joan's realism is shown in her reaction to Lucy's full-flowered praise of Talbot, whom he acclaims with some dozen or more high-sounding titles. She cuts down all such pompous apostrophes thus:

> Here is a silly stately style indeed!
> The Turk, that two and fifty kingdoms hath,
> Writes not so tedious a style as this.
> Him that thou magnifiest with all these titles
> Stinking and fly-blown lies here at our feet.

In the same vein, when Lucy begs the bodies of the slain, Joan says:

> For God's sake, let him have 'em. To keep them here,
> They would but stink, and putrefy the air.

So far, the picture Shakespeare has painted of Joan is of a

remarkable young woman with astonishing gifts of brilliant, clever, and courageous leadership, who remains likably human by virtue of her wit and down-to-earth realism. Her claim to divine guidance was only invoked to gain her initial acceptance by Charles. To the Elizabethans, cowardice was the most contemptible of all human failings, and Shakespeare puts a finishing touch to this portrait of Joan when he gives her the words: "Of all base passions, fear is most accursed."

Right up to the last act there has been no suggestion that Joan was a witch, and now suddenly we find her conjuring up "fiends" to help her once more for, with yet another turn of the wheel, the English forces are again in the ascendant. She refers to previous sacrifices of blood and offers more:

> Where I was wont to feed you with my blood,
> I'll lop a member off and give it you
> In earnest of a further benefit,
> So you do condescend to help me now.

But even here Shakespeare insists on the unselfish, patriotic spring of Joan's actions:

> Then take my soul, my body, soul and all,
> Before that England give the French the foil.

And when the supernatural agents of evil refuse their help and depart, it is not her own imminent downfall that she bewails, but that of France: "Now, France, thy glory droopeth to the dust."

Shakespeare retains our sympathy for the abandoned Joan, even though she has suddenly been revealed as a witch—in much the same way that Marlowe did for Dr. Faustus—and as he was to do so preeminently in the case of Macbeth. Captured, she still retains her withering wit. When York taunts her by saying that, like Circe, she is trying to change him into an animal, she replies: "Changed to a worser shape thou canst not be."

There yet remains the strange scene of Joan's final condemnation. Why did Shakespeare omit Peter Cauchon, the Bishop of Beauvais, and leave her examination entirely to the English? Was he putting the popular English assessment of Joan on trial? Is this the meaning of the powerful words he puts into Joan's mouth?

> But you, that are polluted with your lusts,
> Stained with the guiltless blood of innocents,
> Corrupt and tainted with a thousand vices,
> Because you want the grace that others have,
> You judge it straight a thing impossible
> To compass wonders but by help of devils.

Remembering what wily stratagems Joan employed as a military leader, we should not be surprised that she tries desperately to lie her way out of destruction. Shakespeare confronts Joan with her father, but she denies him, claiming royal parentage and thus royal privileges. Let us not forget, too, that Christ denied his parents. To gain time, she asserts that she is pregnant, claiming as a father first Charles, then the Duke of Alençon, and lastly Reignier. All is in vain, but the Englishmen do not break her spirit. She makes her final exit with a proud curse for her captors:

> May never glorious sun reflex his beams
> Upon the country where you make abode,
> But darkness and the gloomy shade of death
> Environ you till mischief and despair
> Drive you to break your necks or hang yourselves.

It is usual to dismiss Shakespeare's Joan la Pucelle, and almost the whole of the play in which she appears, as unworthy of him; at best, a sorry apprentice effort. But to me his Joan is a compellingly vivid human being, for whom his compassion gave him affection and admiration. He leaves the obligatory witchcraft scene to the last possible moment, and does not let even that dull his picture of the woman.

Although it is unlikely that any actress reading these pages will get a chance to play la Pucelle, if it should ever occur, I should like to give her a word of advice. Don't play Joan consciously as a witch. Try to portray the extraordinary young woman I have tried to outline, and don't worry about the source of her power. When you have to acknowledge the fiends, do so as reluctantly as, I believe, Shakespeare did. Better still, try to persuade your director to cut the single witchcraft scene. Rarely indeed will I give this counsel, but in this instance I think Shakespeare would approve with a smile of relief.

2   Richard II

"I AM RICHARD the Second, know ye not that?" So said Queen Elizabeth to William Lambarde, the keeper and student of the musty records in the Tower of London, when he presented her with a digest of his labors of research. She personally accepted the old man's gift with exceptional graciousness and questioned him with delight. His reply to her reference to Richard II showed that he clearly understood the implication of the analogy. He said: "Such a wicked imagination was determined and attempted by a most unkind gentleman, the most adorned creature that ever your Majesty made." The Earl of Essex had been executed for treason some six months before, and the Queen had been persuaded that he had finally aimed at deposing her, as Bolingbroke had deposed Richard II.

The meeting between the Queen and Lambarde took place on August 4, 1601. The old man died two weeks later. Although it has no immediate pertinence, I cannot refrain from quoting this contemporary account of the cause of his death: "The unwholesome air of the records, not well aired, and the pains he took in that unwholesome place, brought him that sickness and consumption which was an end of him, and he take it principally through his nose into his head."

The comparison between Richard II and Elizabeth was widely whispered long before she herself acknowledged it to William Lambarde. In January of 1599, a book had been published under the title of *The First part of the life and reign of King Henry the 1111*. It was written by a Dr. John Hayward, who had been born in the same year as Shakespeare. It dealt chiefly with the deposition and death of Richard II, and was widely circulated in several editions. What gave it its significance was the dedicatory epistle to the Earl of Essex, in which he was addressed, in Latin, as "great, both in present judgment and in future expectation."

Two years later and two weeks before the Essex rebellion, the Queen was "mightily incensed against Dr. Hayward's book." The poor man was imprisoned in the Tower and subjected to exhaustive examination. The Queen was convinced that Hayward was but a front for a more important and seditious author and angrily demanded that he be forced on the rack to disclose the name of the real author. Sir Francis Bacon counseled caution and he prevailed. Throughout, Hayward maintained the innocence of his intentions, and added, moreover, that he had not received a penny for his writing. Caveat scriptor!

The day before the Essex uprising, some of his noble followers came to Shakespeare's company of players and

> would have them play that play of the deposing and killing of King Richard II, promising to give them 40s. more than their ordinary to play it. The players answered that the play of King Richard was so old and so long out of use that they should have little or no company at it. Nevertheless at their request, and in consideration of 40s., they played it this afternoon at the Globe, when many of my Lord of Essex's followers were present.

Too much has been made of this incident in an attempt to prove the political involvement of Shakespeare and his company. It is clear from the quoted account that they were reluctant to accede to the request, even with the inducement of a good fee, and subsequently they were completely exonerated of any complicity.

One thing is surprising in the above quotation from the Domestic State Papers: that the play was "so old and so long out of use." That smacks of an evasion because there is little doubt that the play was initially popular; within two years, 1597 and 1598, three Quarto volumes of it were published, a distinction gained by no other play of Shakespeare. But it was not until the fourth Quarto, published in 1608, after Elizabeth had been dead for five years, that the Deposition scene was included in the text. And the Queen had complained in her interview with Lambarde that, at the time of the Essex rebellion, "this tragedy was played forty times in open streets and houses." It must not be assumed that Elizabeth was implying that Shakespeare's play had been performed on all, or even any, of these occasions; there is wide evidence of other plays on the subject.

For much of the foregoing I am indebted to G. B. Harrison's fascinating and illuminating *Elizabethan Journals*. It would seem from these contemporary references that if any play of Shakespeare's was written with deliberate political intention, that play would seem to be Richard II, and yet I believe he was not vitally interested in the political principle involved, namely that a bad king could be removed by the will of the people. His whole feeling towards the monarchy as the symbol of national unity would have been revolted by such a suggestion. He was fascinated by Richard II as a person, for in him he found his first truly tragic hero. Richard II is the perfect exemplar of the theme of purification through suffering, a theme which Shakespeare was to deal with most transcendently some ten years later in *King Lear*. Here I find myself in basic disagreement with Coleridge who thought Richard to be the same in Act V as in Act I. "I perceive the utmost consistency of character in Richard: what he was at first, he is at last, excepting as far as he yields to circumstances: what he shewed himself at the commencement of

the play, he shews himself at the end of it." Coleridge wrote this
to express his own disagreement with Dr. Johnson on the subject
of Richard II, so I have the wise Samuel on my side.

Before we examine Shakespeare's Richard in some detail, two
common misconceptions about him must be dealt with: that he
was a self-conscious poet and a self-dramatizer, an exquisite of
sorrow, a masochist who delighted in playing a succession of roles,
each prompted by circumstance, and in improvising beautiful
threnodies to give vent to his deliciously tormented soul.

First, the lyricism of Richard. Shakespeare was the poet, not
Richard. By the time he came to write this play, he had already
written nine others, and was a master of the theatre. Now the
poet threatened to take command. Already he was the highly successful author of *Venus and Adonis* and *The Rape of Lucrece*
and was at work on his "sugared sonnets." At this time, and possibly all within one year, his poetic exuberance resulted in his
three most lyrical plays, a history, a tragedy and a comedy:
Richard II, in which there is not one line of prose, *Romeo and
Juliet*, and *A Midsummer Night's Dream*. His subjects were unerringly chosen to give the poet the scope he needed at that point
in his development: the magic of an enchanted forest, the ecstasy
of young love, and a young king whose mercurial instability was
coupled with a self-awareness which made him realize that his
downfall was due to his own deficiencies—"I wasted time, and
now doth time waste me"—and who, having failed in this world,
strives to prepare for the next—"Our holy lives must win a new
world's crown."

As for the poseur, the player of parts, Richard II is surely
no more than a dramatically heightened personification of the
Pirandello theme that we are the sum total of the masks we wear.
There are times when we all catch ourselves in the act of playing
a part, when the expression we give to an emotion is bigger than
the actual feeling, whether it be of love or anger, compassion or
disgust, strength or weakness. Richard is always doing this. Perhaps his most symbolic act in the play is when he calls for a

mirror and looks in it to examine himself at the moment of his downfall.

It sometimes seems to me that in this play Shakespeare, exulting in his dramatic power, is almost deliberately setting himself a challenging task: to win our sympathy and even admiration for a man whom we at first find to be despicable. To play the game fairly, he allows no redeeming features for our initial impressions of Richard. Thus, it comes as a surprise to many people who see the play that in his last scene Richard shows great physical strength and courage, seizing an axe from one of the men sent to murder him in prison, and slaying two of them before he is himself struck down. But Richard exists in the annals of English history as one of the models of bravery, for, when he was only fourteen—he had come to the throne at the age of ten—he had ridden out to meet an angry and violent mob, which had already burnt the Savoy palace of John of Gaunt and had murdered the Archbishop of Canterbury, and the royal youngster had quelled them by appealing to their leader, stirrup to stirrup. Shakespeare omits any reference to this. Again, we are told nothing of the long-standing debt of revenge which Richard owes to Bolingbroke and Mowbray, and which at least gives some human justification for his exiling of them. They were the last of five "Lords Appellant" who, twelve years before, had secured judicial murder for five of Richard's friends. Further, the chief Lord Appellant had been Richard's uncle, the Duke of Gloucester, and, by cleverly playing one faction against another, Richard had induced Thomas Mowbray, Duke of Norfolk, to murder Gloucester, which he did in this manner, according to Holinshed: ". . . he caused his servants to cast featherbeds upon him, and so smother him to death; or otherwise to strangle him with towels (as some write)." We are given no reason in the play for Richard's hostility to the nobles, and are left with the impression that he was particularly harsh to Mowbray, who had been his faithful henchman.

In his first scene Richard seems the embodiment of regal and judicial detachment. He seems personally uninvolved in the case he is arbitrating, and in an apparent desire to reconcile the "wrath-kindled gentlemen," he is wittily wise:

> Let's purge this choler without letting blood.
> This we prescribe, though no physician.
> Deep malice makes too deep incision.

In the next scene we are shocked to learn from honest Gaunt, the Duke of Lancaster and another uncle of the king, that the seemingly impartial Richard had been responsible for the murder of Gloucester, and the wise judge is suddenly revealed as a crafty schemer.

So much is Richard the focus of Shakespeare's interest that all the other characters are depicted in such a way as to highlight the author's conception of the central figure. Thus Gaunt, in order to highlight all the weakness and wickedness of Richard, is seen as a patriotic paragon of virtue; Mowbray engages our sympathy by his reaction to the decree of perpetual banishment:

> A heavy sentence, my most sovereign liege,
> And all unlooked for from your Highness' mouth.
> A dearer merit, not so deep a maim
> As to be cast forth in the common air,
> Have I deserved at your Highness' hands.
> The language I have learned these forty years,
> My native English, now I must forgo.
> .   .   .   .
> What is thy sentence, then, but speechless death,
> Which robs my tongue from breathing native breath?

The patriotism which prompts this lament of Mowbray is going to be a trump card for Shakespeare, which he will use throughout the play whenever he needs to win our sympathy for a character. Bolingbroke's exit from the scene is equally patriotic:

> Then, England's ground, farewell. Sweet soil, adieu—
> My mother, and my nurse, that bears me yet.
> Where'er I wander, boast of this I can,
> Though banished, yet a trueborn Englishman.

Most notably, patriotism is the essence of the appeal of Gaunt, to whom Shakespeare gives one of the best-known speeches he ever wrote, in which the dying man apostrophizes his beloved land with a series of immortal epithets, beginning with "This royal throne of kings." And, as we shall see, he ultimately uses it with consummate effect to change our attitude to Richard.

In the private scene after the public banishment, we see a very different Richard, the true one without mask, and he is a despicable person. He is with his favorites, and one of them, Aumerle, is reporting on Bolingbroke's departure from England, and, in so doing, indulges in the kind of sycophantic snide wit which he knows will please the king. He says he did not even return Bolingbroke's "Farewell:"

> And, for my heart disdained that my tongue
> Should so profane the word, that taught me craft
> To counterfeit oppression of such grief
> That words seemed buried in my sorrow's grave.

When they have finished with the subject of Bolingbroke, Green brings up the urgent subject of rebellion in Ireland, and we hear from his own lips about Richard's extravagance; this was the main cause of his subjects' discontent, for he spared no one unprecedented taxation, and they all complained—nobles, bishops, yeomen and peasants. The King says that he will himself lead an expedition to Ireland,

> And, for our coffers, with too great a Court
> And liberal largess, are grown somewhat light,
> We are inforced to farm our royal realm,
> The revenue whereof shall furnish us
> For our affairs in hand. If that come short,
> Our substitutes at home shall have blank charters,
> Whereto, when they shall know what men are rich,
> They shall subscribe them for large sums of gold
> And send them after to supply our wants.

In his resort to the system of farming out taxes, by which, in return for ready money, men were empowered to extort what return they could get from a given district, Richard was shame-lessly unprincipled, and gave free rein to cruelty and corruption. He himself implies that he has impoverished the country for his indulgence in panoply, rich living and lavish gifts to his friends.

A word about the King's friends, before we complete the consideration of this scene. Was the King's attachment to them homosexual? Bolingbroke, in his final denunciation of them prior to their execution, is explicit about it:

> You have in manner with your sinful hours
> Made a divorce betwixt his Queen and him,
> Broke the possession of a royal bed
> And stained the beauty of a fair Queen's cheeks
> With tears drawn from her eyes by your foul wrongs.

I suppose it is possible to interpret those lines without a specific homosexual connotation, but I think that would be a prudish evasion. On the other hand, it must be noted that it is Boling-broke who makes the accusation at a moment when he is meting out summary justice, and it is one to which male friendship lends ready credence in the eyes of ill-wishers. There is considerable contrary evidence in the play. Thus, the mutual love of Richard and his Queen is a strong thread in it, and to use this thread Shakespeare had to distort history. The Queen whom Richard loved was Anne of Bohemia, and she had been dead five years before the play opens. Her death had affected him profoundly. One year after it, he had married, for diplomatic purposes, Isabella, a daughter of the King of France. She was a seven-year-old child, and it was this child who was his queen at the time of the play. But it was the beloved Anne whom Shakespeare saw as the Queen, so he makes a composite figure of her and Isabella. One word of praise should be given to the favorites too: those who were con-demned remained loyal to Richard and defiant to Bolingbroke to the grisly end.

And now to return to the end of the scene with the favorites. News comes that "Old John of Gaunt is grievous sick." The callous cleverness of Richard's reaction is unforgivable:

Now put it, God, in the physician's mind
To help him to his grave immediately!
The lining of his coffers shall make coats
To deck our soldiers for these Irish wars.
Come, gentlemen, let's all go visit him.
Pray God we may make haste, and come too late!

To which the "gentlemen" chorus an amused "Amen."

While the dying Gaunt awaits the King in the hope that his last words of admonition may have some effect upon him, he talks with his brother, the Duke of York, who is the father of Aumerle, a favored member of the King's clique. York has no hope that any words can restrain the King, whom he accuses of listening to flattery and the "venomous sound" of "lascivious meters," and of always following the latest fashions from Italy. He also tells us that Richard is capable of hot temper, and he begs Gaunt to "deal mildly" with him, "For young hot colts being raged do rage the more."

When the King arrives with four of his intimates and two other noblemen, he is also accompanied by the Queen. The tone of the encounter is immediately set. In sharp contrast to the Queen's sympathetic enquiry, "How fares our noble uncle Lancaster?" the King says with a brusque suggestion that age is the time for dying, "What comfort, man? How is't with aged Gaunt?" There follows a battle of wits until Gaunt is exasperated, probably by the presence and attitude of the favorites, into saying:

Thy deathbed is no lesser than thy land,
Wherein thou liest in reputation sick.
And thou, too careless—patient as thou art,
Commit'st thy anointed body to the cure
Of those physicians that first wounded thee.
A thousand flatterers sit within thy crown,
Whose compass is no bigger than thy head,
And yet incaged in so small a verge,
The waste is no whit lesser than thy land.

The King is provoked into a fiery outburst:

A lunatic lean-witted fool,
Presuming on an ague's privilege,
Darest with thy frozen admonition
Make pale our cheek, chasing the royal blood
With fury from his native residence.
Now, by my seat's right royal majesty,
Wert thou not brother to great Edward's son,
This tongue that runs so roundly in thy head
Should run thy head from thy unreverent shoulders.

Taunted by this, Gaunt with his final words openly accuses Richard of being responsible for the Duke of Gloucester's death. As the old man is borne off to die, the angry king calls after him:

And let them die that age and sullens have,
For both hast thou, and both become the grave.

The Duke of York, ever the peacemaker, tries to calm Richard by assuring him of the love of Gaunt and of his exiled son, Bolingbroke, the Duke of Hereford. Richard retorts with a completely realistic assessment of the situation, which prepares us for his later penetration through the loyal words of Bolingbroke to his disloyal intentions:

Right, you say true. As Hereford's love, so his.
As theirs, so mine, and all be as it is.

The Earl of Northumberland, he who was to help Bolingbroke to the throne and then lead a conspiracy to dethrone him, enters to tell the King that Gaunt is dead. Richard reacts by perpetrating the worst of his criminal blunders; taking advantage of the exile of the son and heir, he says:

Towards our assistance we do seize to us
The plate, coin, revenues and moveables
Whereof our uncle Gaunt did stand possessed.

This is too much even for the gentle and ineffectual York, but after a spirited yet apologetic protest, his sole and characteristic action is to leave so as not to countenance the King's action by his presence. So little is Richard affected by his uncle's outburst and so unaware is he of impending danger that he leaves England in York's hands while he is away in Ireland:

> And we create, in absence of ourself,
> Our uncle York Lord Governor of England
> For he is just and always loved us well.

With those words Shakespeare subtly begins the transformation of our attitude to Richard, for York had denounced the seizure of Bolingbroke's rights with all the power of which he was capable, and yet Richard acknowledges that he is just.

No sooner has the royal party left than Northumberland sounds out the two remaining lords about their attitude to the King. They join in repeating the old complaints against Richard— the undue influence upon him of the favorites, the grievous and unending taxation, his failure to press English claims in France— and then Northumberland discloses that the exiled Bolingbroke, abetted by some powerful and dissident lords, is only waiting for the King's departure for Ireland to set sail from Brittany and land at Ravenspurgh, on the coast of Yorkshire; all three noblemen vow to meet him there. Thus does Shakespeare begin to enlist our sympathy for Richard, the unknowing underdog, who up to now we have seen as arrogantly self-willed, an exploiter of his power to satisfy his extravagance, lacking in judgment and excelling in cruel vindictiveness.

In the next scene we find two of the King's favorites with the Queen. She is sad at being parted from her "sweet Richard," and oppressed by a sense of some impending sorrow. Her patent love for Richard is another mark in his favor, and the sincere attempts of Bushy and Bagot to comfort her do much to remove the stigma of sycophancy and the imputation of homosexuality from them; they are not only the King's spoiled favorites but the Queen's privileged friends. Green, another of the favored ones, brings the news that Bolingbroke has landed at Ravenspurgh and that many powerful nobles have gone to join him. The Queen's foreboding was justified, and she counters Bushy's urging not to despair with words that foreshadow a similar reaction by Richard later:

> I will despair, and be at enmity
> With cozening hope. He is a flatterer,
> A parasite, a keeper-back of death,
> Who gently would dissolve the bands of life,
> Which false hope lingers in extremity.

York arrives to confirm the bad news and bewail his own inadequacy to deal with the situation. The King's friends sense their own doom, as we do that of the absent Richard.

While we wait for the King's return we are given three scenes that mark his declining power, and so, when we see him again, we know the truth still hidden from him, and this is an ever-effective dramatic gambit to ensure our sympathy for the unwitting victim. In the first scene York confronts Bolingbroke with nothing but powerless words; in the second, the King's loyal Welsh followers disperse because omens have led them to believe that the King is dead; in the third, two of the King's friends are condemned to death, which they face bravely, an attitude which gains our admiration.

When the King does land in Wales, his first sentiment is one of simple joy at treading his native soil again. This is the first evidence of his ordinary humanity, which will receive immortal expression before the end of the scene. He feels what an American soldier might feel when he returns by sea from a foreign war and catches his first glimpse of the Statue of Liberty. Richard is so overwhelmed by the emotional experience of his return that he feels that the very soil will help to put down rebellion, though his mind tells him this is but a "senseless conjuration." He still believes, and not without foundation, that when he comes face to face with Bolingbroke,

> His treasons will sit blushing in his face,
> Not able to endure the sight of day,
> But self-affrighted tremble at his sin.

> Not all the water in the rough rude sea
> Can wash the balm off from an anointed king.
> The breath of worldly men cannot depose
> The deputy elected by the Lord.

No one is more aware of this than Bolingbroke, and he will do his utmost to give the deposition the appearance of a voluntary abdication. With the news that the Welsh, hearing that the King was dead, have dispersed, Richard gets a foretaste of defeat, and his first reaction is that it is a judgment upon him: " . . . time hath set a blot upon my pride." But it is only a passing shadow. He is easily prompted to fresh confidence, but alas! in what a broken reed:

> . . . Are we not high?
> High be our thoughts. I know my uncle York
> Hath power enough to serve our turn. . . .

Sir Stephen Scroop brings more bad news, and Richard plunges headlong into despair. This time his frustration vents itself in fury against his favorites, who he assumes have made their peace with Bolingbroke. His horrible curses make us wince because we know that they are dead and that they died loyal to their patron.

> Oh, villains, vipers, damned without redemption!
> Dogs, easily won to fawn on any man!
> Snakes, in my heartblood warmed, that sting my heart!
> Three Judases, each one thrice worse than Judas!
> Would they make peace? Terrible Hell make war
> Upon their spotted souls for this offence!

The all too human weakness of this outburst strengthens Richard's credibility as a character. Suddenly chastened by the news that they are dead, the King is brought face to face with his own mortality, and he realizes that the life of kings is the most fragile of all lives:

> For God's sake, let us sit upon the ground
> And tell sad stories of the death of kings—
> How some have been deposed, some slain in war,

> Some haunted by the ghosts they have deposed,
> Some poisoned by their wives, some sleeping killed,
> All murdered. . . .

Two things need to be noted in that quotation: "For God's sake" is not the empty oath it has become in our day, but a conscious evocation of a religious mood; and the first kind of death that comes to his mind is that which follows deposition; it is a fleeting acceptance of the fate which he will help to bring about. This beautiful and astonishing speech ends with a very moving acknowledgment of the humanity of a king:

> Cover your heads and mock not flesh and blood
> With solemn reverence. Throw away respect,
> Tradition, form, and ceremonious duty,
> For you have but mistook me all this while.
> I live with bread like you, feel want,
> Taste grief, need friends. Subjected thus,
> How can you say to me I am a king?

Once more the Bishop of Carlisle and Aumerle try to cheer the King, but all their hopes are dashed by Scroop's final news, in which, incidentally, he is not quite fair to York:

> Your uncle York is joined with Bolingbroke,
> And all your northern castles yielded up,
> And all your southern gentlemen in arms
> Upon his party.

Richard's last thought is for the safety of his followers:

> Discharge my followers. Let them hence away,
> From Richard's night to Bolingbroke's fair day.

Our eager expectation now is of the confrontation between Richard and Bolingbroke. It takes place at Flint Castle in North Wales. The King from the walls looks down upon the threat of massed forces. Both Bolingbroke and York comment on the majesty of his appearance.

> Yet looks he like a king. Behold, his eye,

> As bright as is the eagle's, lightens forth
> Controlling majesty. . . .

The Earl of Northumberland, the envoy of Bolingbroke,
approaches the walls to talk with the King, but deliberately omits
the customary obeisance, a gesture of defiant hostility which belies
the fair words he has come to speak. Richard, infuriated by
Northumberland's lack of respect, does not wait for his words, but
impetuously reveals his knowledge of Bolingbroke's real intentions
and truly prophesies their dire result:

> Tell Bolingbroke—for yond methinks he stands—
> That every stride he makes upon my land
> Is dangerous treason. He is come to open
> The purple testament of bleeding war.
> But ere the crown he looks for live in peace,
> Ten thousand bloody crowns of mothers' sons
> Shall ill become the flower of England's face,
> Change the complexion of her maid-pale peace
> To scarlet indignation, and bedew
> Her pasture's grass with faithful English blood.

Northumberland disclaims any sinister purpose in Bolingbroke's
return:

> His coming hither hath no further scope
> Than for his lineal royalties, and to beg
> Enfranchisement immediate on his knees.

Richard manages to contain himself sufficiently to send a conciliatory message back to Bolingbroke, but he is so maddened by
Bolingbroke's hypocrisy and his own helplessness that, when
Northumberland returns, he blurts out the brutal truth which lies
beneath the polite form:

> What must the King do now? Must he submit?
> The King shall do it. Must he be deposed?
> The King shall be contented. Must he lose
> The name of king? O' God's name, let it go.

There follows a beautifully bejeweled speech of an imaginary sacrifice of the pomp and panoply of kingship, but beneath the glitter is a new element in Richard's thinking: the royal magnificence is to be replaced by a religious simplicity—"a set of beads," "a hermitage," "an almsman's gowns," "a palmer's walking staff," "a pair of carved saints;" this religious motif will be developed to the end of the play. But he ends his ornate musings and returns again to his unblinking directness, now colored with heavy sarcasm, in speaking to Northumberland:

> Most mighty prince, my Lord Northumberland,
> What says King Bolingbroke? Will His Majesty
> Give Richard leave to live till Richard die?

The King descends from the walls to meet Bolingbroke face to face. Again Richard refuses to be fooled by the fact that Bolingbroke kneels to greet him:

> Up, Cousin, up. Your heart is up, I know,
> Thus high at least, although your knee be low.

For the last line, of course, Richard points to his crown. Bolingbroke protests, "I come but for mine own," but Richard's cryptic reply again tears off the mask: "Your own is yours, and I am yours, and all." There is an affecting moment when Richard turns to York, who is weeping; he senses York's deep loyalty as clearly as Bolingbroke's hypocrisy:

> Uncle, give me your hands. Nay, dry your eyes.
> Tears show their love, but want their remedies.

The long-offending Deposition scene was largely Shakespeare's invention. The actual abdication took place in private, but to assure the Commons of its legitimacy, Bolingbroke called a parliament in the name of King Richard so that all might hear of it from Richard's own lips. In Holinshed we read: "The King with glad countenance said openly that he was ready to renounce and resign all his kingly majesty in manner and form as he before had promised." Shakespeare's Richard behaves very differently. He is moved to anger and contempt by the treachery of his erstwhile subjects and to torment of soul by his own treacherous abdication of his God-given authority. His denunciation of the assembled parliament finds expression in a daring, almost blasphemous, analogy, but its scriptural reference is significant of his new turn of thought. We shall not be surprised to find him studying the Bible in prison.

> . . . Yet I well remember
> The favours of these men. Were they not mine?
> Did they not sometime cry "All hail!" to me?
> So Judas did to Christ. But He in twelve
> Found truth in all but one; I in twelve thousand, none.

His "Here, Cousin, seize the crown" makes it publicly clear that the resignation is not an act of "tired majesty" as Bolingbroke had described it. Even now he hesitates to go through with the abdication—"Aye, no—no, aye"—and when he finally relinquishes the crown, he torments himself for his perfidy by an elaborate and improvised ceremonial of divestiture. Holinshed says that Richard willingly read over "the scroll of resignation," but in the play he refuses to do so, even though persistently pressed by Northumberland, and in his refusal again calls upon the Christian analogy:

> Nay, all of you that stand and look upon
> Whilst that my wretchedness doth bait myself,
> Though some of you with Pilate wash your hands,
> Showing an outward pity, yet you Pilates
> Have here delivered me to my sour cross,
> And water cannot wash away your sin.

He plainly states his sense of the double treachery:

> Nay, if I turn mine eyes upon myself,
> I find myself a traitor with the rest;
> For I have given here my soul's consent
> To undeck the pompous body of a king,
> Made glory base and sovereignty a slave,
> Proud majesty a subject, state a peasant.

In this spirit of public self-abasement he asks for a mirror, that he
might read

> . . . the very book indeed
> Where all my sins are writ, and that's myself.

He looks at his image in the glass and is so disgusted by the
smoothly lying mask which hides the sorrow within that he angrily
throws the mirror down, and smashes it. I am reminded of a passage by Pirandello in which he seeks to explain his dramatic conceptions: "When someone lives, he lives and does not watch
himself. Well, arrange things so that he does watch himself in
the act of living, a prey to his passions, by placing a mirror before
him. Either he will be astonished and dismayed by his own appearance and turn his eyes away so as not to see himself, or he will
spit at his image in disgust, or will angrily thrust out his fist to
smash it."

Bolingbroke, in a clumsily cryptic sentence, tries to expose the
empty theatricality of the breaking of the mirror:

> The shadow of your sorrow hath destroyed
> The shadow of your face.

Richard turns the phrase to make it express the reality of his grief:

> Say that again.
> The shadow of my sorrow! Ha! Let's see.
> 'Tis very true, my grief lies all within.
> And these external manners of laments
> Are merely shadows to the unseen grief
> That swells with silence in the tortured soul.

The Queen stands in wait for Richard when he is taken,
under escort, to the Tower. She tries to stir him to some action,
but he is in a mood of solemn resignation to "grim Necessity," and
that mood is a spiritual one:

> . . . Hie thee to France
> And cloister there in some religious house.
> Our holy lives must win a new world's crown,
> Which our profane hours here have stricken down.

But the fire in the old Richard is by no means extinguished; it is readily fanned into flame by the approach of Northumberland, who comes to say that Richard is to be taken to Pomfret Castle, not the Tower of London. We are humanly relieved to see the old spark in Richard, especially as it kindles a spirit of true prophecy that comes from his understanding of the dire results of corrupt ambition:

> The time shall not be many hours of age
> More than it is, ere foul sin gathering head
> Shall break into corruption. Thou shalt think,
> Though he divide the realm and give thee half,
> It is too little, helping him to all.
> And he shall think that thou, which know'st the way
> To plant unrightful kings, will know again,
> Being ne'er so little urged, another way
> To pluck him headlong from the usurped throne.

The parting of Richard and his Queen is very moving, because they sense that it is their final farewell, and they are torn by the conflicting desires to prolong it and to cut it short.

The Duke of York gives the Duchess an account of another progress of Richard through the streets of London, in the train of the triumphant Bolingbroke; it is a via dolorosa:

> . . . men's eyes
> Did scowl on gentle Richard. No man cried "God save him!"
> No joyful tongue gave him his welcome home.
> But dust was thrown upon his sacred head,
> Which with such gentle sorrow he shook off,
> His face still combating with tears and smiles,
> The badges of his grief and patience,
> That had not God, for some strong purpose, steeled
> The hearts of men, they must perforce have melted,
> And barbarism itself have pitied him.

Our last sight of Richard is in prison where he is reading the New Testament and trying to reconcile apparently contradictory texts. There is, for a moment, a new simplicity in his speech, as

though he were consciously stripping it of decoration to match his
loss of panoply and elegance:

> I have been studying how I may compare
> This prison where I live unto the world;
> And for because the world is populous,
> And here is not a creature but myself,
> I cannot do it; yet I'll hammer it out.

The torment of his abdication is still strong within him, and he
realizes that death alone will bring him peace:

> Nor I nor any man that but man is
> With nothing shall be pleased till he be eased
> With being nothing. . . .

He hears some music that is being played for his solace, but it is
badly played and this infuriates him, and then a newfound wisdom
checks his anger:

> This music mads me, let it sound no more,
> For though it have holp madmen to their wits,
> In me it seems it will make wise men mad.
> Yet blessing on his heart that gives it me!
> For 'tis a sign of love, and love to Richard
> Is a strange brooch in this all-hating world.

We hear so much in the play of the hostility of the common
people to Richard that Shakespeare takes care to balance this
picture. Previously two gardeners had shown their deep concern
for him, and now, in his last moments, a groom from his own
stable, after much difficulty, gets permission to visit him. Richard
calls him "gentle friend." When the keeper comes to tell him to
"give place," Richard urges him to leave, for his own safety. The
groom's last words are: "What my tongue dares not, that my heart
shall say."

Sir Pierce of Exton, thinking to ingratiate himself with the
new king, arrives with armed men to murder Richard, who dies
fighting bravely, killing two men before he is himself struck down
by Exton. This detail Shakespeare got from Holinshed, though

there Exton came with eight men, four of whom Richard slew. With his last words, the old and the new Richard are revealed; he dies, first cursing Exton and then commending his soul to heaven. Exton is immediately smitten with remorse, and later earns condemnation from the new king, Henry IV, whom he sought to please.

Richard II dies fighting like Macbeth; he achieves wisdom in his downfall like King Lear. He lacks the power and stature of those tragic heroes of Shakespeare's complete maturity, but he comes from the same mind and spirit and pen, and he has a human significance all his wondrous own. Furthermore, as in all the great Shakespearean tragedies, with the exception of *Romeo and Juliet*, his character is his destiny.

3 Henry IV

HENRY BOLINGBROKE, Duke of Hereford, and after his father's death Duke of Lancaster, and finally King Henry IV, is a key figure in three of the Histories, two of which are named for him, but he doesn't dominate one of them, in spite of being a strong character. But strength is a quality which invokes admiration rather than compassion and affection, and for Shakespeare, and so for us, those warmer feelings are reserved for other people in the Bolingbroke story—Richard II, Prince Hal, Hotspur, and, above all, Falstaff. This does not mean that Shakespeare's Henry IV is a lifeless block of granite; indeed, he is very human, and as his ruthless and successful ambition gives way to remorse and un-happiness, and sickness gradually moves him from the throne to the deathbed, our sympathy is awakened. First we see him as an irresistible rebel, then as a troubled king, having to deal with open rebellion and inner guilt, and finally as a tormented father, faced with what he considers to be an irresponsible, loose-living and un-loving son. These three threads in his life are clearly seen in *Richard II*.

It has already been pointed out that in *Richard II* all the other characters are depicted as they relate to the central one. Thus, Bolingbroke is the antagonist, and as such is given qualities exactly opposite to those of Richard. Whereas the King is a man of many words, unstable, indecisive, prejudiced and partial in his government, the rebel is a man of few words, resolute, decisive, and judicial and impartial in his government. But in the light of what we gradually learn about Bolingbroke—and Shakespeare is always revealing surprises in this man, even on his deathbed—we must be careful not to take him at his face value; indeed, while Richard is the man of many moods, it is Bolingbroke who is the man of many masks.

As for the troubled king, it is a notable dramatic irony that at the end of the Deposition scene, before Henry IV is even safely on the throne, there is a plot afoot to put him off it. Recurrent plots to dethrone him were to be the story of his reign. In summing up his life, Holinshed says of him: "he had reigned thirteen years, five months, and odd days, in great perplexity and little pleasure." The theme of his inner guilt is the last sentiment he expresses in *Richard II*:

> I'll make a voyage to the Holy Land
> To wash this blood off from my guilty hand.

Trouble at home was to prevent him from making his pilgrimage of expiation, and when, at last, it seemed safe for him to leave his country, sickness overcame him on his way to set sail, and he died. The ambitious man whose guilty conscience prevents him from enjoying his ill-gotten gains is a subject for true tragedy—it reminds us of Macbeth—but in the case of Henry IV it is muted by natural death. The effect is almost domesticated, but this very element makes Henry a more immediately identifiable figure. Many a man has gained his prominence by employing means of which he is secretly ashamed, and this secret gnaws at his enjoyment of power to the end. What is more, he ironically sees himself in those who, in turn, are seeking to displace him by equally shameful means. This is Henry IV.

The third thread, of the tormented father, has no dramatic significance for *Richard II*, but Shakespeare deliberately introduces it as a foretelling of a major theme in his next play, which he already has in mind. (It is unlikely that he, at this time, envisaged the Second Part of *Henry IV*; that probably resulted from the success of the First Part, and particularly the success of Falstaff.) Bolingbroke says:

> Can no man tell me of my unthrifty son?
> 'Tis full three months since I did see him last.
> If any plague hang over us, 'tis he.

But with a tolerance and faith he was rarely to show again, he goes on to prepare us for the wonderful end of the story:

> As dissolute as desperate, yet through both
> I see some sparks of better hope, which elder years
> May happily bring forth. . . .

The theme of the son who rebels against his father's values is a particularly pertinent one today. Many a father shares Henry's problem, but to few comes the certainty, as it did to the dying king, that after his death all will be well.

Holinshed well outlines the shape of Henry's life, and Shakespeare faithfully follows that shape:

> In his latter days he shewed himself so gentle, that he gat more love amongst the nobles and people of this realm, than he had purchased malice and evil will at the beginning. But yet to speak a truth, by his proceedings, after he had attained to the crown, what with such taxes, tallages, subsidies, and exactions as he was constrained to charge the people with; and what by punishing such as, moved with disdain to see him usurp the crown (contrary to the oath taken at his entering into this land, upon his return from exile), did at sundry times rebel against him; he won himself more hatred, than in all his life time (if it had been longer by many years than it was) had been possible for him to have weeded out and removed.

Bolingbroke's first appearances in *Richard II* are conventional and ceremonious and we have no opportunity to judge what kind of man he is; it is only in the light of later knowledge that we sense the man behind the mask. All we see is the bold and outspoken challenger of Mowbray, the faithful courtier loud in protestations of loyalty to his King, the aggrieved son and Englishman bidding farewell to his father and his country. Our first glimpse of the future rebel comes in Richard's description of his wooing sympathy from the ordinary populace:

> Ourself and Bushy, Bagot here, and Green
> Observed his courtship to the common people—
> How he did seem to dive into their hearts
> With humble and familiar courtesy,
> What reverence he did throw away on slaves,
> Wooing poor craftsmen with the craft of smiles
> And patient underbearing of his fortune,
> As 'twere to banish their affects with him.
> Off goes his bonnet to an oyster wench.
> A brace of drayman bid God speed him well
> And had the tribute of his supple knee,
> With "Thanks, my countrymen, my loving friends,"
> As were our England in reversion his,
> And he our subjects' next degree in hope.

Of course, this is a prejudiced speech, which, in its tone, reflects more unkindly upon Richard than on Bolingbroke, but the comment on calculating ambition is a true one.

In the first scene of the returned Bolingbroke, there is considerable dramatic irony in the fact that Northumberland speaks to him with such fulsome flattery as outdoes the sycophancy of Richard's favorites, but Bolingbroke's reaction to all the flattery in the scene is courteous, conventional and brief. He is not deceived, for we learn later that he trusts no one. There seems more genuine warmth in his response to the young Hotspur, who makes him a simple and direct vow of service. All the time he sees Hotspur as the man he would have liked his son to be. His steely but polite resolve is shown clearly in the scene with his uncle, the

Duke of York. He patiently listens to the powerless tirade against his act of treachery in breaking his exile without permission, and, when York's fury peters out in an offer of hospitality for the night, he graciously accepts it, but adds, with words that will not be denied, however gentle they may sound,

> But we must win your Grace to go with us
> To Bristol Castle, which they say is held
> By Bushy, Bagot, and their complices,
> The caterpillars of the commonwealth,
> Which I have sworn to weed and pluck away.

Bolingbroke throughout strives to give his acts the appearance of legitimacy. Thus, when he executes Bushy and Green, he says:

> . . . Yet, to wash your blood
> From off my hands, here in the view of men
> I will unfold some causes of your deaths.

In the confrontation with Richard at Flint Castle, Bolingbroke skillfully veils the threat of his unbiddable power with words of submission. It is characteristic of his subtlety that, during the parley, he wants the extent of his forces to be clearly visible from the castle walls, but "Let's march without the noise of threatening drum."

Richard makes Bolingbroke's task all too easy, for he cannot hide his instinctive awareness of his cousin's ambition. He even spares him the next move by saying that he supposes he must now go to London. All Bolingbroke has to say is, "Yea, my good lord."

In the preliminary to the Deposition scene, and before he has "ascended the regal throne," Bolingbroke is already acting as king, and we already see the king he means to appear—dignified, authoritative and impartial. In a scene of confused accusations and counter-accusations, challenges and counter-challenges, he remains calmly judicial. This scene seems to be a deliberate parallel to the scenes in which Richard had to deal with the quarrel between Bolingbroke and Mowbray, but we cannot imagine Bolingbroke ever saying, as did King Richard II,

> We were not born to sue, but to command,
> Which since we cannot do . . .

Moreover, Bolingbroke exhibits statesmanlike clemency, for he promises to recall from exile his old enemy, the Duke of Norfolk:

> . . . Repealed he shall be
> And, though mine enemy, restored again
> To all his lands and signories. . . .

But he hears that Norfolk has died in exile, after doing valiant service in the Crusades. It is one of the many ironies that mark the life of Bolingbroke that his enemy did what he wanted to do but was prevented from doing—fight for Christianity in the Holy Land. Bolingbroke's final words to the quarreling lords shows his self-sufficient strength:

> Little are we beholding to your love,
> And little looked for at your helping hands.

The public display of the Deposition scene is essential to Bolingbroke's claim to the legitimacy of his reign as Henry IV, and all the unpleasant confrontations on his way to the throne are performed by his chief mouthpiece, the Earl of Northumberland. Even when the Bishop of Carlisle makes his eloquent and moving denunciation of the rebellion, Bolingbroke can maintain an impassive silence, while Northumberland arrests the Bishop for "capital treason." (As one of his last acts in the play, the new king spares the Bishop his life.

> For though mine enemy thou hast ever been,
> High sparks of honour in thee have I seen.)

It is Northumberland too who harries Richard to get him to read aloud a list of the "grievous crimes" committed by him and his favorites, but Richard steadfastly refuses to do so until Bolingbroke says, "Urge it no more, my Lord Northumberland."

Richard's hostile and accusing stance throughout the scene

has been a big surprise to Bolingbroke, who had been led to expect a meek acceptance of the situation. "I thought you had been willing to resign." In his striving for legitimacy, he dare not publicly refer to or imply his power; he tries to reason with Richard, whose skill with words is much greater than his; he appears to be considerate and anxious to meet Richard's wishes, and this must be, at least in part, a genuine impulse to ease Richard's agony, for Bolingbroke is no monster of conscienceless evil, and his guilt must be deeply stirred by this painful spectacle of a king's involuntary abdication.

In what might be termed the York Interlude we see in Bolingbroke both the merciful judge and the relentless enemy. The Duke of York discovers that his son, Aumerle, is party to a plot to kill the new king at Oxford. He spurs in haste to warn Henry of the plot and to demand the punishment of treason, death, for Aumerle. The Duchess of York arrives to plead for her son's life, and her pleas win the day. The sight of a mother pleading for her son must have been poignant for Henry IV. His wife had died before his first appearance in the Histories; there is no reference to her in the plays. York's wife was a keen reminder to Henry of his loneliness, and that his son had no mother to plead for him. He spares Aumerle, but for the others the King is implacable:

> They shall not live within this world, I swear,
> But I will have them, if I once know where.

Shakespeare, in order to maintain a picture of Bolingbroke as a strong, unimpassioned and even merciful king, is careful not to let us hear him say the words which led to Richard's murder. Exton reports them and takes his cue from what he gleans from a look of Henry. And Henry's reaction to the murder is honest in summing up the conflict in himself which was to be his for the rest of his life:

> . . . Though I did wish him dead,
> I hate the murderer, love him murdered.

At the end of *Richard II* Bolingbroke spoke of going on a

pilgrimage. At the beginning of *Henry IV, Part I*, it is a year later, and news of fresh rebellions again prevents him from going to the Holy Land. Thus the theme of the troubled king is immediately announced, as is that of the disappointed father. Incidentally, we notice that the king is much more loquacious than the rebel, for his taciturnity is no longer needed to offset the volubility of Richard.

Never was Shakespeare more cavalier in juggling with dates, and to more good purpose, than in the case of Henry IV, Prince Hal and Hotspur. It is necessary to the playwright's design that Hal and Hotspur be the two antagonists and so we sense them to be both mature young men, but in fact Hotspur was older than Hal's father. Henry IV, in the opening scene, expatiates on the contrast between the two sons:

> . . . thou makest me sad and makest me sin
> In envy that my Lord Northumberland
> Should be the father to so blest a son—
> A son who is the theme of honour's tongue,
> Amongst a grove the very straightest plant,
> Who is sweet Fortune's minion and her pride—
> Whilst I, by looking on the praise of him,
> See riot and dishonour stain the brow
> Of my young Harry. . . .

Northumberland could have told the King that Hotspur too was a thorn in the flesh, for the cautious father found the hotheaded son dangerously hard to handle.

The Northumberland faction, disappointed in their share of the spoils that resulted from their helping Bolingbroke to the throne, move towards open revolt, and do so on behalf of another claimant to the throne, Edmund Mortimer. (Here both Holinshed and Shakespeare simplify history by combining two Edmund Mortimers in one; the real claimant was a nephew of the one who is the claimant in the play.) The King confronts the faction and forces them into action; he completely drops the role of merciful ruler, and warns them not to misjudge his former clemency as weakness:

> My blood hath been too cold and temperate,
> Unapt to stir at these indignities,
> And you have found me; for accordingly
> You tread upon my patience. But be sure
> I will from henceforth rather be myself,
> Mighty and to be feared, than my condition,
> Which hath been smooth as oil, soft as young down,
> And therefore lost that title of respect
> Which the proud soul ne'er pays but to the proud.

Hotspur, angered by Henry, taunts his father and his uncle for having helped "this subtle king" to seize power from Richard, "that sweet lovely rose." The dead has become lovely, and the living loathsome. But there is truth in the epithets Hotspur applies to Henry: "subtle" and "proud" and, his ultimate deprecation, "vile politician." Now he adjudges Bolingbroke's initial courtesy as that of a "king of smiles" and "fawning greyhound."

We learn much of the real Bolingbroke in his first scene with his son, even though, as fathers tend to do, he magnifies his own virtues in order to magnify his son's faults. But we find he had deliberately sought for a contrast with Richard, had purposefully maintained an austerity and aloofness,

> That men would tell their children, "This is he;"
> Others would say, "Where, which is Bolingbroke?"
> And then I stole all courtesy from heaven,
> And dressed myself in such humility
> That I did pluck allegiance from men's hearts.

The King works on the Prince very skillfully. He exasperates him by extravagant praise of Hotspur, "Mars in swathling clothes," and then angers him into furious denial by an outrageous accusation:

> Thou that art like enough, through vassal fear,
> Base inclination, and the start of spleen,
> To fight against me under Percy's pay,

> To dog his heels and curtsy at his frowns,
> To show how much thou art degenerate.

Henry's ploy works to such good purpose that he feels confident in placing the army in Hal's charge. This is no impulsive emotional decision, for Henry is not that kind of man. In *Richard II* he had seen in Hal "some sparks of better hope," and he has skillfully fanned those sparks into flame.

In the parleys that the King has with the rebels prior to the Battle of Shrewsbury, ironic parallels with his own rebellion abound. Thus, for example, what he says about the Northumberland faction, in reply to their list of grievances, could have been said by Richard about him with even more truth:

> These things indeed you have articulate,
> Proclaimed at market-crosses, read in churches,
> To face the garment of rebellion
> With some fine colour that may please the eye
> Of fickle changelings and poor discontents,
> Which gape and rub the elbow at the news
> Of hurly-burly innovation.
> And never yet did insurrection want
> Such water-colours to impaint his cause.

But the King, to avoid the horrors of war, offers the rebels complete reconciliation. When the Earl of Worcester hears this—he is in charge in the absence of his brother, the Earl of Northumberland, from real or feigned sickness—he fears he dare not trust the King's word:

> It is not possible, it cannot be,
> The King should keep his word in loving us.
> He will suspect us still, and find a time
> To punish this offence in other faults.
> Suspicion all our lives shall be stuck full of eyes;
> For treason is but trusted like the fox.

Worcester is probably true in his assessment of the offer of the enigmatic king, and he is probably equally true in thinking that

Hotspur, his nephew, might be forgiven, for there is no doubt of the King's admiration for him:

> My nephew's trespass may be well forgot;
> It hath the excuse of youth and heat of blood.

As for Henry's conduct in the battle, Shakespeare makes much of one hint from Holinshed and ignores another. Several noblemen were disguised in the King's armor and colors, and this seems to be yet another example of Henry's wily tactics, but we find no evidence in the play of the King's own doughty deeds that day, which Holinshed records: "he slew that day with his own hands six and thirty persons of his enemies." But here it is the glory of the son that Shakespeare wishes to emphasize, and that of the father must not be allowed to pale it. Even when the King is in combat with the redoubtable Earl of Douglas, he is rescued by Hal. On the battlefield Shakespeare reduces Henry to an appealingly identifiable ordinariness, neither hero nor coward.

In the Second Part of the play whose title is his, King Henry IV does not appear until the third act, and indeed the historical action plays a much smaller part than it did in the First Part; the play belongs to Falstaff. But to prepare us for a more sympathetic attitude towards the King, we learn, before we see him, that he is sick, and it is his wayward son, who has returned to the stews after his victory at Shrewsbury, that tells us so: ". . . my heart bleeds inwardly that my father is so sick." When we do see the King, he is suffering from insomnia and delivers a lyrical invocation to sleep, ending with the famous line: "Uneasy lies the head that wears a crown." His triumph over Richard has proved empty, for his kingdom is still torn by rebellion. He recounts the past, quoting a prophecy of Richard he is unlikely to have heard (though Shakespeare makes a case that he might have had it reported to him); it foretold the disaffection of Northumberland. In bitter and moving words he sums up the past:

> O God! that one might read the book of fate
> .   .   .   .

> . . . how chances mock,
> And changes fill the cup of alteration
> With divers liquors! O, if this were seen,
> The happiest youth, viewing his progress through,
> What perils past, what crosses to ensue,
> Would shut the book, and sit him down and die.

This bleak summation of an outwardly successful life is a faint sketch for much greater words to be spoken by Macbeth.

There is yet another rebellion, this time led by one of those notable medieval clerics-in-armor, the Archbishop of York, and another parley, but with what a different conclusion! No battle of Shrewsbury this time with heroic feats of arms, no hand-to-hand climactic fight between two brave opponents, but a victory by stratagem and deceit, engineered by Prince Hal's younger brother, Prince John of Lancaster. The rebel leaders are persuaded to disband their army on assurance of the young prince's word that their presented list of grievances will be granted; then the leaders are arrested and condemned to summary execution.

Yet another bitter irony of the King's reign is that, when the news comes that the last rebel has been vanquished and all energies can now be given to the crusade, he is stricken by an attack which will prove fatal. He is deeply aware of the irony:

> Will Fortune never come with both hands full,
> But write her fair words still in foulest letters?
>
> .   .   .   .
>
> I should rejoice now at this happy news;
> And now my sight fails, and my brain is giddy.
> O me! come near me; now I am much ill.

There remains the truly great scene of the last meeting of father and son. Hal, thinking his father to be dead, puts on the crown and leaves the room unobserved. The King awakes to find the crown gone, and immediately assumes that Hal has been eager to wear it. He speaks for all disillusioned fathers who find their sons too eager for the family property:

. . . See, sons, what things you are!
How quickly nature falls into revolt
When gold becomes her object!
For this the foolish over-careful fathers
Have broke their sleep with thoughts, their brains with care,
Their bones with industry;
For this they have engrossed and piled up
The cankered heaps of strange-achieved gold;
For this they have been thoughtful to invest
Their sons with arts and martial exercises;
When, like the bee, culling from every flower
The virtuous sweets,
Our thighs packed with wax, our mouths with honey,
We bring it to the hive, and, like the bees,
Are murdered for our pains. . . .

But the King was wrong. The Prince had been deeply grieved by
the sight of what he thought was his dead father, but, before he
can explain his motives in picking up the crown, the dying king has
delivered his last tirade against his son's wild ways and expressed
his fears for the future of his land,

For the fifth Harry from curbed license plucks
The muzzle of restraint, and the wild dog
Shall flesh his tooth on every innocent.
O my poor kingdom, sick with civil blows!
When that my care could not withhold thy riots,
What wilt thou do when riot is thy care?
O, thou wilt be a wilderness again,
Peopled with wolves, thy old inhabitants!

Whether this was completely a cry from the heart, or partially a
tactic to prompt the King-to-be to give some comforting assurance
to the deathbed-King, it has the same effect as did the accusation
of possible treachery just before the Battle of Shrewsbury. There
is no doubt about the overwhelming sincerity of Hal's response, or
of the King's acceptance of his explanation of the taking of the
crown:

> O my son,
> God put it in thy mind to take it hence,
> That thou mightst win the more thy father's love,
> Pleading so wisely in excuse of it!

Henry prefaces his last advice to his son by acknowledging the evil of his seizure of power and the resulting troubles of his reign:

> . . . God knows, my son,
> By what bypaths and indirect crooked ways
> I met this crown; and I myself know well
> How troublesome it sat upon my head.

He dies, as he had lived, with craft upon his lips. We had thought that at least his desire to go on a crusade had been spiritually altruistic, but now we learn, in the last revelation of this complicated man, that it too had had some political motivation:

> And all my friends, which thou must make thy friends,
> Have but their strings and teeth newly ta'en out,
> By whose fell working I was first advanced
> And by whose power I well might lodge a fear
> To be again displaced; which to avoid,
> I cut them off; and had a purpose now
> To lead out many to the Holy Land,
> Lest rest and lying still might make them look
> Too near unto my state. . . .

His characteristic advice to the young man about to be Henry V is that he should distract possible troublemakers at home by leading them into foreign adventures:

> . . . Therefore, my Harry,
> Be it thy course to busy giddy minds
> With foreign quarrels, that action, hence borne out,
> May waste the memory of the former days.

A final irony awaits Henry IV. It had been prophesied that he should die in Jerusalem; he finds that the chamber in which his deathbed lies bears the name of Jerusalem.

When the Lord Chief Justice asked the Earl of Warwick,

"How doth the King?" he answered: "Exceeding well; his cares are now all ended." This could be said of all who die in high office, but it was especially true of Henry IV, who never enjoyed the power he so doubtfully seized. He was a strong, enigmatic, unlovable man, suspicious of everybody and calculating even in his virtues, but increasingly sad and lonely. If he had had the ruthless enjoyment of the manipulation of men for his own purposes, coupled with a wicked sense of humor and witty observation, characteristics of some of Shakespeare's villains, he would have been a more vivid character, and, strangely enough, a more likeable one. But his crooked ambition was crippled by a strong conscience; he had too much respect for the law to be a happy and successful breaker of it. Yet this very ambivalence gives him almost more human identifiability than any other of Shakespeare's kings of England. After all, Mr. Selfmade Everyman tends to be dull company, for he does not wear his heart upon his sleeve, but he is a fascinating if forbidding creature when you probe the secrets of his complex soul.

❦ 4 ❦   Hotspur

Wʜᴀᴛ'ꜱ ɪɴ ᴀ ɴᴀᴍᴇ? In the case of "Hotspur" everything, for Shakespeare had no other hint on which to base his brilliant portrait of a single-minded man of action, lovable and exasperating, the quintessence of honor and yet a turncoat, alternately charming and boorish, and always invigoratingly energetic in fight and play. He is so captivating a character that actors usually prefer to play him rather than the more important character of Hal, just as most young actors prefer Mercutio to Romeo. Henry Percy's nickname, "Hotspur," probably refers to his restless passion for action, which kept his spurs ever hot, but it could also refer to the fact that he himself was hot to the spur, quick to anger; both qualities are true of him.

Some notable actors have given their Hotspur a quirk of speech. Michael Redgrave assumed a thick Northumbrian accent— though, in the same production, his father, the Earl of Northumberland, spoke impeccable English. Laurence Olivier made an unforgettable moment of the death by giving his Hotspur a speech impediment; he had difficulty with "w" so that his dying utterance became "food for w—" which Hal completed with "For worms, brave Percy." The excuse for these inventions is what I take to be a misreading of a remark made about Hotspur by his widow, in a speech which shows him to have been "the glass of fashion and the mould of form":

> . . . by his light
> Did all the chivalry of England move
> To do brave acts. He was indeed the glass
> Wherein the noble youth did dress themselves.
> He had no legs that practised not his gait;
> And speaking thick, which nature made his blemish,
> Became the accents of the valiant;
> For those that could speak low and tardily
> Would turn their own perfection to abuse
> To seem like him; so that in speech, in gait,
> In diet, in affections of delight,
> In military rules, humours of blood,
> He was the mark and glass, copy and book,
> That fashioned others. . . .

"Speaking thick," all scholars are agreed, means "speaking fast," the work "thick" being used as in "thick and fast"; the words tumble out of him, a natural expression of his extraordinary energy. From the same passage it is obvious that his speech is the opposite of "low and tardy;" in other words, it is loud and fast. The fact that "low" means "quiet" is shown in Lear's description of Cordelia's voice as "ever soft, gentle, and low," and in the frequent injunction to "speak low." Loud and fast speech is a characteristic expression of uninhibited vitality. One can imagine that his gait was an equal expression of his energy; he was the kind of man who bounces out of a chair when he stands, and strides when he walks.

Before we trace Hotspur's historical path through the two plays in which he appears, fleetingly in *Richard II* and substantially in *Henry IV, Part I*, it might be well for us to complete our picture of the man by watching him in more relaxed circumstances, though relaxation is only a comparative term in the case of this dynamo. He is naturally most relaxed with his wife, Kate, the sister of Edmund Mortimer. (Her real name was "Elizabeth," but

Holinshed had it wrong too; he called her "Eleanor." Shakespeare liked the name "Kate.")

Eager for the fray, Hotspur has been unable to sleep for two weeks, and so has not shared a bed with his wife. She has heard him, in fitful slumbers, cry out terms of war; his dreams of battle have caused beads of sweat to appear on his forehead. He has kept all news of forthcoming rebellion from her, but she senses that something desperate is afoot:

> Some heavy business hath my lord in hand,
> And I must know it, else he loves me not.

As a result of a letter he has received, he has decided to leave forthwith, and is impatient to be gone. In his preoccupation with his departure he scarcely hears his wife until she forces him to listen and tell her what it is that "carries him away." With evasive lightness, he replies, "Why, my horse, my love, my horse." The letter he had received had infuriated Hotspur, but it had also released him to decision, and now the prospect of action has lifted his spirits to gaiety. His relationship with his wife is delightful. He teases her almost past bearing, but only to stop her from sensing the danger of the unknown enterprise; for her peace of mind she must not know it, but he covers this with exasperating banter:

> . . . Constant you are,
> But yet a woman; and for secrecy,
> No lady closer; for I well believe
> Thou wilt not utter what thou dost not know.

His final solace for her is that she shall follow him on the morrow. There is the feeling of a deep love between these two people, which is expressed in a lively and witty relationship; when Hotspur is around, life is never dull.

There is another delightful set of exchanges between husband and wife when they are the guests of Glendower, and now his quips are bawdy; one feels Hotspur is as valiant in bed as on the battlefield. His initial invitation to her is "Come, Kate, thou are perfect in lying down;" and later follows this exchange:

> KATE: Now God help thee!
> HOTSPUR: To the Welsh lady's bed.
> KATE: What's that?

We are led to believe that in their private brain-battles, her oaths become as lusty as his, for when she lets slip a mild "in good sooth," he takes her amusingly to task for it:

> Swear me, Kate, like a lady as thou art,
> A good mouth-filling oath, and leave "in sooth,"
> And such protest of pepper-gingerbread
> To velvet-guards and Sunday-citizens.

Hotspur is an outspoken philistine, in Matthew Arnold's sense of the word; music and poetry are foreign and distasteful languages to him, but he is amusingly hearty in his dislike of them:

> I had rather be a kitten and cry mew
> Than one of these same metre ballad-mongers.
> I had rather hear a brazen canstick turned,
> Or a dry wheel grate on the axle-tree,
> And that would set my teeth nothing on edge,
> Nothing so much as mincing poetry.
> 'Tis like the forced gait of a shuffling nag.

When Kate tells him to be quiet and listen to Mortimer's wife sing in Welsh, he answers that he would rather hear his dog "howl in Irish."

He will have nothing to do with magic and mystery. When Glendower says that he can "call spirits from the vasty deep," Hotspur replies:

> Why, so can I, or so can any man;
> But will they come when you do call for them?

Even at the moment of his death he remains consistently earthy and realistic; there is no thought of an afterlife for his soul:

> But thoughts, the slaves of life, and life, time's fool,
> And time, that takes survey of all the world,
> Must have a stop. O, I could prophesy,

But that the earthy and cold hand of death
Lies on my tongue. No, Percy, thou art dust.

Hotspur had a directness and a chivalric code of honor that
sorted ill with conspiracy, and which was in sharp contrast with
his father's crafty deviousness. The father in excess of caution
abandoned his son to his death at the Battle of Shrewsbury, and
the widowed Kate berates him for it with a spirit worthy of Hotspur's wife:

The time was, father, that you broke your word
When you were more endeared to it than now;
When your own Percy, when my heart's dear Harry,
Threw many a northward look to see his father
Bring up his powers; but he did long in vain.
Who then persuaded you to stay at home?
There were two honours lost, yours and your son's.
For yours, the God of Heaven brighten it!
For his, it stuck upon him as the sun
In the grey vault of heaven, and by his light
Did all the chivalry of England move
To do brave acts . . .
    .   .   .   .   .   .
. . . O wondrous him!
O miracle of men! him did you leave,
Second to none, unseconded by you,
To look upon the hideous god of war
In disadvantage; to abide a field
Where nothing but the sound of Hotspur's name
Did seem defensible: so you left him.

In his own way Hotspur was as much a thorn in the flesh of
Northumberland as Prince Hal was in that of King Henry, for
caution finds it hard to live with impulsiveness. Hotspur's uncle,
the Earl of Worcester, a diplomatic schemer, had much right on
his side when he castigated his hotheaded nephew for his boorish
conduct to Glendower, whose help they were seeking:

In faith, my lord, you are too wilful-blame;
And since your coming hither have done enough

To put him quite beside his patience.
You must needs learn, lord, to amend this fault.
Though sometimes it show greatness, courage, blood,—
And that's the dearest grace it renders you,—
Yet oftentimes it doth present harsh rage,
Defect of manners, want of government,
Pride, haughtiness, opinion, and disdain.

There we have it. Hotspur's vices have the same source as his virtues, a simple and brash directness and honesty, which shines bright in a dark world of craft and deception.

And now to trace his path through the plays. We first see him in *Richard II* when he comes to join Bolingbroke's invading forces. We are immediately struck by his unsubtle directness. When his father asks him why the Earl of Worcester, the Lord Steward of the King's household, had "broken his staff of office," he replies bluntly: "Because your lordship was proclaimed traitor." And when the new would-be king is pointed out to him as someone he should already know—"Have you forgot the Duke of Hereford, boy?"—he is not at all embarrassed, but replies:

No, my good lord, for that is not forgot
Which ne'er I did remember. To my knowledge,
I never in my life did look on him.

His pledge of allegiance to Bolingbroke is simple and honest, and completely lacking in fulsome praise of his new leader:

My gracious lord, I tender you my service,
Such as it is, being tender, raw, and young;
Which elder days shall ripen and confirm
To more approved service and desert.

In his second brief appearance in the play he brings the news that King Richard is in Flint Castle, and again he speaks simply and to the point, and this is noteworthy in a play of such lyrical exuberance. In the scene of all the challenges, we should expect Hotspur to be there, throwing down his gage with the rest, and so he is, and speaking with his customary directness: "Aumerle, thou liest." Not once in this play is the nickname, "Hotspur," mentioned. All we have seen is the very straightforward young Harry Percy; but he is introduced as "the gallant Hotspur" in the opening scene of *Henry IV, Part 1,* and he is given the complimentary epithet in a report to the King, by the Earl of Westmoreland, on his prowess in the fight against the rebellious Scots. But the King, in reply, has to refer to "this young Percy's pride," for he has refused to surrender to the King the valuable Scots prisoners he has captured. Immèdiately Westmoreland excuses him:

> This is his uncle's teaching; this is Worcester,
> Malevolent to you in all aspects;
> Which makes him prune himself and bristle up
> The crest of youth against your dignity.

It says much of Hotspur that even the men whom he has made his enemies to the death speak well of him. Never once is a really derogatory word said of him, and the man who finally kills him says,

> . . . Fare thee well, great heart!
>
> .   .   .   .
>
> . . . This earth that bears thee dead
> Bears not alive so stout a gentleman.

The conduct of Hotspur when he is called before the King and his Council needs careful examination, for he defends himself with brilliant evasion, and that is unlike him. Perhaps he has been coached by Worcester; certain it is that the King dismisses Worcester before Hotspur begins his defense, which he blurts out before he is questioned. He begins, most uncharacteristically, with a downright lie: "My liege, I did deny no prisoners." Only in this speech is Hotspur the wily conspirator, and it ill becomes him. The defense is based upon his well-known reputation for quick temper; he says that the King's messenger, who came to ask for the prisoners, had been "a certain lord, neat, trimly dressed,/Fresh as a bridegroom," and this fastidious and perfumed "popinjay" had been so upset by the sights and smells of the battlefield that he had made Hotspur mad, especially as he was exhausted and wounded after the battle, and he had

> Answered neglectingly I know not what,
> He should, or he should not. . . .

Sir Walter Blunt is impressed by the speech, which probably had some basis of truth in the "popinjay," but the King, ever practical, points out that Hotspur has still made no promise to hand over the prisoners; nor does he do so. Instead he reacts angrily to the King's suggestion that Edmund Mortimer is a willing prisoner of Owen Glendower, and that he had "wilfully betrayed" the army he had led to fight against the Welshman. The unceremonious and disrespectful anger of Hotspur kindles the usually cold King to comparable heat, and he stalks out with a threat: "Send us your prisoners, or you will hear of it." But Hotspur is so enraged now that he is quite beyond the control of his cautious father:

> An if the devil come and roar for them,
> I will not send them. I will after straight
> And tell him so; for I will ease my heart
> Albeit I make a hazard of my head.

As his father says, he is "drunk with choler." The King forbade him to speak of Mortimer, and so this becomes his new theme:

> Speak of Mortimer!
> 'Zounds, I will speak of him; and let my soul
> Want mercy if I do not join with him.
> Yea, on his part I'll empty all these veins,
> And shed my dear blood, drop by drop in the dust
> But I will lift the down-trod Mortimer
> As high in the air as this unthankful King,
> As this ingrate and cankered Bolingbroke.

Both father and uncle take advantage of this wild rage of Hotspur to tell him that Richard II, when he went to Ireland, had proclaimed Edmund Mortimer heir to the kingdom. This was neces-

sary to transmute the anger of the soldierly man of simple honor
into a whole-hearted dedication to seizure of the throne from the
usurper and restoration of it to its rightful owner. Hotspur's anger
now turns against Northumberland and Worcester, for by "murderous subornation" they had helped "this canker Bolingbroke"
to power. Worcester breaks in on Hotspur's voluble anger to tell
him that a plot is afoot, and, knowing his man, speaks of danger
not deviousness:

> I'll read you matter deep and dangerous,
> As full of peril and adventurous spirit,
> As to o'erwalk a current roaring loud
> On the unsteadfast footing of a spear.

Hotspur responds with a heady eagerness for the fray, since now
he feels that he is assuredly on the side of honor:

> Send danger from the east unto the west,
> So honour cross it from the north to south,
> And let them grapple. O the blood more stirs
> To rouse a lion than to start a hare.

Such high-sounding bravado exasperates his father, who is more
at home with subtle strategy than strong blows:

> Imagination of some great exploit
> Drives him beyond the bounds of patience.

But Hotspur's spirit is soaring too high with imagination of
doughty deeds to be brought down so easily to earth:

> By heaven methinks it were an easy leap
> To pluck bright honour from the pale-faced moon,
> Or dive into the bottom of the deep,
> Where fathom-line could never touch the ground,
> And pluck up drowned honour by the locks,
> So he that doth redeem her thence might wear
> Without co-rival all her dignities.

Yet again father and uncle try to harness the headstrong Hotspur.
Worcester threatens to break off the conference:

> Farewell kinsman; I'll talk to you
> When you are better tempered to attend.

This provokes Northumberland into a testy criticism of his son, and one that has been often earned:

> Why what a wasp-stung and impatient fool
> Art thou, to break into this woman's mood,
> Tying thine ear to no tongue but thine own!

But it is still a full minute before Hotspur is reduced to temporary listening with "I have done i'faith."

Worcester's instructions to Hotspur are explicit: to release the Scottish prisoners in order to secure an alliance with the Scots. The instructions to Northumberland are suited to that nobleman's serpentine ways; he "shall secretly into the bosom creep" of the Archbishop of York. Hotspur is immediately convinced of victory; not so his father, who chides his son with "Before the game's afoot thou still let'st slip." Worcester, worried by the possible results of his nephew's impatience, warns him:

> . . . No further go in this
> Than I by letters shall direct your course.

But Hotspur has the last word, and it can carry little assurance to the two older plotters:

> Uncle adieu. O let the hours be short,
> Till fields, and blows, and groans, applaud our sport!

Northumberland's and Worcester's doubt of Hotspur's control of his impatience was well justified, for the incautious rebel disclosed the plot to a nobleman whose aid he sought; that gentleman's reply was that the enterprise was much too dubious to admit of success. Suddenly Hotspur realizes that this "frosty-spirited rogue," to ensure his own safety, might betray the plot to the King, but this spurs him to action, not fear: "Hang him, let him tell the King; we are prepared. I will set forward tonight." This same soliloquy in which Hotspur reads the letter of reply from the "shallow cowardly hind," contains words to which Sir Winston Churchill was to lend fresh immortality: "Out of this nettle, danger, we pluck this flower, safety." In moments of peril, Shakespeare has often given England its clarion call.

The comic view of Hotspur is beautifully caught in Prince Hal's cartoon of him:

> I am not yet of Percy's mind, the Hotspur of the North, he that kills me some six or seven dozen of Scots at a breakfast, washes his hands, and says to his wife, "Fie upon this quiet life, I want work." "O my sweet Harry," says she, "how many hast thou killed today?" "Give my roan horse a drench," says he, and answers, "Some fourteen," an hour after, "a trifle, a trifle."

There is admiration for a worthy foe in this exaggeration. There is much more disdain in Hotspur's reference to Hal:

> But that I think his father loves him not,
> And would be glad he met with some mischance,
> I would have him poisoned with a pot of ale.

This springs from the common and mistaken view of Hal, which saw in him most despicable vices, and made him a figure of contempt to Hotspur, who could not, when he said those words, ever envisage the possibility that the dissolute Prince would face him in battle.

Hotspur is at his most tiresomely boorish in the rebels' conference with Glendower, a redoubtable soldier and an extraordinary man. It is the Welshman's claim to magic powers that exasperates Hotspur, as he explains when he is taken to task by Mortimer for crossing his father-in-law:

> I cannot choose; sometimes he angers me
> With telling me of the moldwarp and the ant,
> Of the dreamer Merlin and his prophecies,
> And of a dragon and a finless fish,
> A clip-winged griffin and a moulten raven,
> A couching lion and a ramping cat,
> And such a deal of skimble-skamble stuff,

As puts me from my faith. I tell you what,—
He held me last night at least nine hours
In reckoning up the several devils' names
That were his lackeys. I cried, "hum," and, "well, go to,"
But marked him not a word. O he is as tedious
As a tired horse, a railing wife,
Worse than a smoky house. I had rather live
With cheese and garlic in a windmill far,
Than feed on cates and have him talk to me,
In any summer house in Christendom.

In his impatience, Hotspur even dares to make fun of Glendower's military triumphs against Bolingbroke whom he had thrice driven from the Welsh borders "Bootless home, and weather-beaten back;" to this Hotspur caustically remarks:

Home without boots, and in foul weather too!
How 'scapes he agues, in the devil's name?

Glendower behaves with astonishing dignity and forbearance in the face of Hotspur's skeptical taunts. As Mortimer says:

I warrant you that man is not alive
Might so have tempted him as you have done,
Without the taste of danger and reproof.

And Glendower himself says: "Cousin, of many men/I do not bear these crossings;" the fact that he does tolerate Hotspur's provoking gibes shows that the older and wiser man respects the true qualities of the discourteous and immature young soldier. It is always Glendower who seems to give in, and finally Hotspur is shamed by his magnanimity. They have been planning the carving up of the land, when once they have defeated King Henry. Childishly Hotspur avers that he is being cheated, but as soon as Glendower has agreed that the river Trent shall be straightened according to Hotspur's wishes, with equal childishness he does not want it any more:

I do not care. I'll give thrice so much land

> To any well-deserving friend;
> But in the way of bargain, mark ye me,
> I'll cavil on the ninth part of a hair.

Again, Hotspur's conduct is both reprehensible and endearing.

Hotspur's dislike of smooth-tongued flattery is so deep and well known that a word of praise from him to a soldier is praise indeed. Such commendation does he give to his erstwhile prisoner, the Scottish Earl, whom Falstaff had described as "that sprightly Scot of Scots, Douglas, that runs a horseback up a hill perpendicular." Hotspur says of him:

> . . . if speaking truth
> In this fine age were not thought flattery,
> Such attribution should the Douglas have,
> As not a soldier of this season's stamp
> Should go so general current through the world.
> By God, I cannot flatter, I do defy
> The tongues of soothers, but a braver place
> In my heart's love hath no man than yourself.

Then comes the news that Northumberland and his forces are not coming to the rendezvous. Worcester is dismayed and suspects correctly that his brother has been scared of the gamble at the last minute, and his sickness is but an excuse:

> This absence of your father's draws a curtain,
> That shows the ignorant a kind of fear
> Before not dreamt of.

But Hotspur's reaction to the news is very different. It is that of Prince Hal before the Battle of Agincourt: "The fewer men the greater share of honour." With the further news that Glendower will be too late for the rendezvous and that the King's forces come on apace in powerful numbers, defeat begins to loom, but even this only prompts Hotspur, that "king of honour," to a bold despair:

> Come, let us take a muster speedily.
> Doomsday is near; die all, die merrily.

In the parley with the Earl of Worcester before the battle, Prince Hal pays eloquent tribute to Hotspur:

> . . . Tell your nephew,
> The Prince of Wales doth join with all the world
> In praise of Henry Percy. . . .
> .   .   .   .
> I do not think a braver gentleman,
> More active-valiant or more valiant-young,
> More daring or more bold, is now alive
> To grace this latter age with noble deeds.

As we have already seen, Worcester decides not to transmit to Hotspur "the liberal and kind offer of the King," and so the Battle of Shrewsbury is inevitable. Hotspur who says, "I profess not talking," still has some eloquent words to inspirit his men:

> An if we live we live to tread on kings;
> If die, brave death when princes die with us.
> Now for our consciences, the arms are fair
> When the intent of bearing them is just.

In the ultimate encounter with Hal, Hotspur is chivalric to the end, because he deplores the fact that it promises to be an unequal fight:

> . . . the hour is come
> To end the one of us, and would to God
> Thy name in arms were now as great as mine;

and in the moment of dying it is his heroic reputation he regrets losing more than his life:

> I better brook the loss of brittle life
> Than those proud titles thou hast won of me;
> They wound my thoughts worse than thy sword my flesh.

Shakespeare has a particular affection for the valiant daredevils of the Elizabethan age whose lives were given for causes not always worthy of them, and the personification of their spirit is Henry Percy, known to history as "Hotspur."

5 Falstaff

OF SHAKESPEARE's characters, only Hamlet has had more written about him than Falstaff, and both have provoked bewilderingly diverse opinions. Some have tried to defend the fat knight from the obvious charge of cowardice; this is because they are so fond of the old man that they must make him worthy of their affection, and Shakespeare, as we shall see, gives grounds for the defense, for he loves him too. Dr. Johnson feels that Falstaff causes his corrupt and despicable faults to be glossed over by reason of his "perpetual gaiety, by an unfailing power of exciting laughter," and from this the worthy doctor draws a cautionary tale: "No man is more dangerous than he that, with a will to corrupt, hath the power to please; . . . neither wit nor honesty ought to think themselves safe with such a companion."

The main modern tendency seems to be to regard the relationship between the young prince and his old boozing companion as having allegorical significance, either political or religious. In the political interpretation Falstaff represents those lawless elements, so essential a part of Elizabethan England, which served the state but yet had to be controlled by it and, on occasion, to be disavowed and destroyed. Personally I find it hard to trace any similarity between Sir John Falstaff and Sir Francis Drake. The religious allegory is an extension of the Johnson view, and finds its origins in the medieval morality plays; Falstaff is Hal's beguiling devil whom he finally has the power to reject, thus saving his soul. To me, Falstaff is too complex and vivid a human being to be confined within a theological abstraction. In W. H. Auden's ingenious reflections on Falstaff, he becomes almost a saint,

> a comic symbol for the supernatural order of charity as contrasted with the temporal order of Justice symbolized by Henry of Monmouth. . . . [Falstaff] is never tired, never bored, and until he is rejected he radiates happiness as Hal radiates power, and this happiness without apparent cause, this untiring devotion to making others laugh becomes a comic image for a love which is absolutely self-giving.

All I am concerned with here is trying to discover Shakespeare's conscious intentions in Falstaff, and let us first consider the dramatic necessity for the character.

The hero of the Falstaff plays is Prince Hal, he who was destined to become "the mirror of all Christian kings." One of the most warmly cherished folk traditions and chronicled stories in English history was that of the wayward Prince Hal who was transformed into the great soldier-king, Henry V. Scandal concerning the great is always endearing, and when that scandal is limited to youth, it forms a colorful background against which the later halo shines more brightly. But Shakespeare was confronted with a very difficult problem. Why would a Prince of Wales behave so abominably? Why would he prefer the tavern and the stews to the Court? Above all, how could Shakespeare retain our sympathy for the dissolute young man? The solution was to personify the attractions of the low life in someone who would seduce the prince and, at the same time, us, and whose company we would long for as much as did Hal. He should be the antithesis of all that the court stood for—duty, honor, valor—

but so that he should not be too derelict in his duty at the time of his sovereign's need, he should be an old man so that little would be expected of him, and a fat man whose body was not made for speed and action. His sole weapon should be his wit, with which to defend himself and to lay about him, but he should never do an action which would hurt anyone so that we would cease to like him. He should have such a deep enjoyment of life that he would always see death as the enemy, and he should see through the humbug of much of the chivalric mouthings of the warlike lords. "Rare words! Brave world!" he mutters, as the call to action comes. In some such way, and out of simple dramatic necessity, Falstaff was born.

In his reading for his first play, *Henry VI, Part I*, Shakespeare had come across a character called Sir John Fastolfe, and he was sufficiently intrigued by Holinshed's hint about him that he brought him into the play, once by reference and once in person, though his appearance was gratuitous. This is what he read: "From this battel departed without any stroke stricken Sir John Fastolfe; the same year for his valiantness elected into the order of the garter." There was the germ of Falstaff, a cowardly knight who somehow managed to get himself elected into the highest order of chivalry. But the young Shakespeare felt that such a stain on nobility had to be removed, and so Fastolfe is caught in a second act of cowardice at the battle of Patay, his garter is torn from his "craven's leg" by the valiant Talbot and his "doom" is proclaimed by King Henry VI: "Henceforth we banish thee, on pain of death." Some eight years later Shakespeare's pen was to write these words for Henry V to speak of Falstaff: "I banish thee, on pain of death."

When Shakespeare had decided on the necessary companion for Prince Hal, he could not call him "Fastolfe" because his new creation had to be an old man a generation earlier than the time of the cowardly acts of Fastolfe. At first he called him "Sir John Oldcastle" and unwittingly landed himself in a deal of trouble. He had found the name in a hotchpotch of a play called *The*

Famous Victories of Henry the Fifth where a minor and colorless character who makes two brief appearances as a companion of the madcap prince had that name. But there had been a real Sir John Oldcastle, who through his marriage had become Lord Cobham. He had been a leader of the Lollards, early fifteenth-century precursors of the Reformation, and had been burned as a heretic in the reign of Henry V. He is one of the heroes in Foxe's *Book of Martyrs*. At the time when the fat knight made his first stage appearance under the name of "Oldcastle," the title "Lord Cobham" had descended to a self-important young man who was a Lord Chamberlain at the Queen's court. He had also inherited the puritanical tendencies of his famous ancestor and was bitterly opposed to the Earl of Essex and his followers; they in turn made much fun out of comparing the priggish Cobham with the rascally Oldcastle in the new play. Strenuous objection was made to Shakespeare, and he changed the name of his character to "Falstaff;" it was clearly suggested by "Fastolfe," but I feel sure that Shakespeare was not unaware of the sexual implications of the new name, a suggestion of Falstaff's old-age impotence; Falstaff, in all things, was mighty in words and girth, but small in actions. Shakespeare, in the Epilogue to *Henry IV, Part II*, made a public disavowal of Falstaff's having any relation to Sir John Oldcastle—". . . for Oldcastle died a martyr, and this is not the man"—but Lord Cobham's enemies continued their sport by referring to him as "Sir John Falstaff." The rival company to Shakespeare's players performed a play, *Sir John Oldcastle*, which may have been deliberately written to vindicate the reputation of the man who had been a brave soldier but had been burned for heresy in 1417, and deliberately performed to capitalize on the trouble Shakespeare found himself in.

It is essential to Shakespeare's purpose that we first see Falstaff in Hal's company. Their first scene introduces both of them, and we are treated to a delightful set of exchanges between them. They are a pair of well-matched wits and thoroughly enjoy the game. From the outset Falstaff's later apothegm is abundantly evidenced: "I am not only witty in myself, but the cause that wit is in other men." It is noteworthy that, even in this first scene, Falstaff has a momentary fit of guilty melancholy; such fits will recur but are easily dispelled by the prospect of some new piece of profitable or amusing wickedness. He half-humorously blames the Prince for his state of corruption, and there is some truth in this, although it is usual to think of Falstaff solely as the seducer. After all, the Prince for his own amusement encourages Falstaff in his enormities, as now, when, to get rid of the fit of the blues, he suggests a highway robbery. In blaming the Prince, Falstaff indulges in characteristic exaggeration, which makes the pill of truth deliciously palatable:

> Thou hast done much harm upon me, Hal; God forgive thee for it! Before I knew thee, Hal, I knew nothing; and now am I, if a man should speak truly, little better than one of the wicked. I must give over this life, and I will give it over. By the lord, an I do not, I am a villain. I'll be damned for never a king's son in Christendom.

A king's son; in this first scene Falstaff makes several references to his high hopes of the time when the king's son will be king; there is a beguiling honesty in his expectations of the profits that will accrue. In this scene too we get an interesting comment on Falstaff's brand of cowardice. When Poins outlines to Hal the trick that is to be played on Falstaff and the other members of the gang, by which the robbers are in turn to be robbed, he distinguishes between the cowardice of the others and that of Falstaff: "Well, for two of them, I know them to be as true-bred cowards as ever turned back; and for the third, if he fight longer than he sees reason, I'll forswear arms." To fight no longer than he sees reason is another version of Falstaff's famous aphorism: "Discretion is the better part of valour." This is not the counsel of cowardice, but of reasonableness; don't fight if defeat is certain. The fact that Falstaff improvises elaborate fictional accounts of impossible deeds of valor means that he pays lip service to the code of the dauntless fighter against mighty odds, but it does

not mean that he is a complete coward; he is an eminently reasonable man to whom life is very precious. When he is attacked
by the formidable Douglas, he knows he stands no chance, and
so he immediately falls down and feigns death; let us never forget
that he is an old and fat man.

The distinction between total cowardice and that of Falstaff
is made clear in a stage direction in the Quartos. This is the description of the robbing of the robbers: "As they are sharing,
the Prince and Poins set upon them. They all run away; and
Falstaff, after a blow or two, runs away too, leaving the booty
behind them." That "after a blow or two" is significant.

In the initial attack on the merchants, Falstaff is at his most
amusingly absurd, and no one is more aware of it or gets more
enjoyment from it than he; since he is one in spirit with the
young highwaymen, he ignores the size of his own body and
condemns the merchants as "gorbellied knaves," "bacons," and
"fat chuffs"; he also ignores the fact of his own age with his
comments, "They hate us youth. . . . Young men must live."

The scene of confrontation between Falstaff and the Prince
after the highwaymen adventure must be one of the most brilliantly comic in all dramatic literature, and it builds to a wonderful climax. First, Falstaff is disgruntled about the loss of the booty,
and cries out against the cowardice of his companions; even the
cup of sack tastes adulterated. Then he is drawn into a detailed
account of his valiant fight against odds which mount with every
sentence. When he is trapped by his lies, he maintains a dignified
refusal to explain. There follows a pyrotechnical battle of name-
calling between him and the Prince, which they indulge in like
a pair of young boys wrestling. All the time we wait for Falstaff's
reaction to the truth, when he is told that they had been robbed
so easily by the Prince and Poins. "What trick, what device,
what starting hole, canst thou now find out to hide thee from this
open and apparent shame?" There is a pause, while they and we
wait for Falstaff's evasion; there is no doubt that it will come and
that it will be outrageous. Poins has to repeat Hal's question.

"Come, let's hear, Jack. What trick hast thou now?" And then it comes, outdoing expectation and beautifully inventive.

> By the Lord, I knew ye as well as he that made ye. Why, hear you, my masters. Was it for me to kill the heir-apparent? Should I turn upon the true prince? Why, thou knowest I am as valiant as Hercules; but beware instinct; the lion will not touch the true prince. Instinct is a great matter; I was now a coward on instinct.

Falstaff is a consummate improvisational actor; he gets and gives joy by performing, whether it be in an attempt to deceive his hearers, as in his description of his single-handed fight against the band of robbers, or in a deliberate piece of clowning, as when he pretends to be first the King and then the Prince in a mock confrontation of father and son. It seems probable that Falstaff was first played by Thomas Pope; we know that he was subsequently played by John Lowin after Pope had left the company, and it is reasonable to assume that Lowin inherited Pope's roles. There is a contemporary reference to "Pope, the clowne," but T. W. Baldwin, in his conjectural assignment of parts to the original players, assumes he was the quick-witted clown as opposed to Thomas Kemp's slow-witted one; Baldwin even gives Pope the part of Mercutio. A gift of mimicry was part of the clown's equipment, and in the comic arraignment of Hal by the "King," Falstaff speaks in "King Cambyses' vein," making fun of the broader, melodramatic style of the leading rival company of players, led by Edward Alleyn. It is an intriguing suggestion that, if *Sir John Oldcastle* had been played by Alleyn's company to capitalize on the notoriety that Falstaff's first name had gained from Lord Cobham's objections, this parody of Alleyn may have been Shakespeare's sly retort. There is no doubt that Hamlet's criticism of "robustious periwig-pated fellows" who "tear a passion to tatters" referred to Edward Alleyn and his fellow-players in the company whose name changed with their patronage but which is generally referred to as the Admiral's Men, just as Shakespeare's company is usually referred to as the Chamberlain's Men.

Falstaff is a born life-and-soul-of-the-party, and, like all such people, has private moments of doubt and despondency, and the results of those private moments peep out at the most unlikely times. Thus, when the comic interlude is interrupted by the arrival of the Sheriff in search of the highway robbers, his last words before hiding are funny, but ruefully so. The Prince, settling his face to meet the Sheriff, says: "Now, my masters, for a true face and a good conscience;" to which Falstaff says, as he goes behind the arras, "Both which I have had; but their date is out, and therefore I'll hide me." But it is only a fleeting regret, for two minutes later he is found to be fast asleep and snoring. Peto, with professional skill, picks his pockets, but finds "nothing but papers." The Prince reads the top one; it is a bill, chiefly for sack, the wine on which Falstaff seems largely to live. "O monstrous!", comments the Prince, "but one half-pennyworth of bread to this intolerable deal of sack."

Falstaff redeems even his stupendous drinking by his wit. In the Second Part of *Henry IV* he delivers a long soliloquy on the virtues gained from drink, ascribing the differences between Hal and his younger brother entirely to their respective indulgence in and abstention from "sherris-sack."

> Good faith, this same young sober-blooded boy doth not love me, nor a man cannot make him laugh; but that's no marvel, he drinks no wine. There's never none of these demure boys come to any proof; for thin drink doth so over-cool their blood, and making many fish-meals, that they fall into a kind of male greensickness; and then, when they marry, they get wenches. They are generally fools and cowards; which some of us should be too, but for inflammation.

In contrast, Hal is a sack-drinker.

> Hereof comes it that Prince Harry is valiant; for the cold blood he did naturally inherit of his father, he hath, like lean, sterile, and bare land, manured, husbanded, and tilled with excellent endeavour of drinking good and good store of fertile sherris, that he is become very hot and valiant. If I

had a thousand sons, the first humane principle I would teach them should be, to forswear thin potations and to addict themselves to sack.

Churches are filled in time of trouble and many a worldly man becomes religious in old age. Falstaff is a wonderfully amusing comment on such fear-driven goodness, and we like him all the better for it in that the impulse is fleeting. When he is in one of his passing fits of the doldrums, he even thinks he is losing weight and this, to him, is a sign of losing life, and prompts him to say, "Well, I'll repent, and that suddenly, while I am in some liking. I shall be out of heart shortly, and then I shall have no strength to repent. An I have not forgotten what the inside of a church is made of, I am a peppercorn, a brewer's horse." The last two metaphors may need explication. A "peppercorn" is a dried pepper berry, and in Shakespeare's time, as opposed to today's practice, a brewer's horse was one in the final stage of employment before he went to the knacker's-yard; so Falstaff is swearing by the impossibility of regarding himself as dried-up and old!

One of the most engaging qualities of Falstaff is his witty observation of himself, as now when he unerringly pins the self-justification of Mr. Average-Man whose comfort is that he is no worse than his neighbor: "I was as virtuously given as a gentleman need to be; virtuous enough; swore little; diced not above seven times a week; went to a bawdy-house not above once in a quarter—of an hour; paid money that I borrowed—three or four times." The humor and the truth lie in the comic exaggeration. Poins's double appellation for Falstaff when he first sees him in the play, "Monsieur Remorse" and "Sir John Sack-and-Sugar," reveal the warring moods of Falstaff, and to our infinite and abiding delight, in every battle between fear of death and love of life, it is his fleshly enjoyment of life that wins.

Money is an everlasting problem for Falstaff. He has a title but nothing to sustain it, an unquenchable thirst for sack and nothing with which to pay for satisfying it. This doesn't trouble him. As of royal right, he assumes the world is there to look after his appetites. A tailor who demands security for his wares is "a rascally yea-forsooth knave!" Falstaff owes money to everybody —Hal, the Hostess of the Tavern, even Bardolph—and they continue to supply him, even though they complain, for the joy of his company. But his need for money is insatiable: "I can get no remedy against this consumption of the purse. Borrowing only lingers and lingers it out, but the disease is incurable." He steals when opportunity offers with safety, and, when he is drafted to raise a company for the war, turns even that to his pecuniary advantage; but again, instead of exulting in his nefarious cleverness, he hypocritically and humanly deplores his wickedness. "I shouldn't have done it" rarely stops a man from doing it or prompts him to undo what he has done. Falstaff is a monument to human casuistry. Having collected a company of the poorest dregs—everyone who could do so had bought his freedom, to the enrichment of Falstaff's purse—he is ashamed of the result: "If I be not ashamed of my soldiers, I am a soused gurnet [i.e. a pickled seafish of a repellent appearance]. I have misused the King's press damnably. I have got, in exchange of a hundred and fifty soldiers, three hundred and odd pounds." When the Prince upbraids him with having collected "such pitiful rascals," his superb answer sharply defines the quintessential tragedy of war, especially before these modern days in which it metes out destruction indiscriminately, and that is that it wipes out the young and healthy to protect the old and infirm. Falstaff defends his choice of "scarecrows" with "Tut, tut; good enough to toss; food for powder, food for powder; they'll fill a pit as well as better."

The battlefield is the last place that Falstaff would seek, being a reasonable man. Falstaff speaks for all normal soldiers when he says, "I would 'twere bedtime, Hal, and all well." There follows his immortal speech on honor. It should be noted that his first reaction to the inevitability of battle is "Honour pricks me on." As with most men, his reaction to crisis is the conventional one of high-sounding words. It is only when Falstaff faces honestly and in detail the implications of his conventional utterance that he comes to the opposite conclusion; "Therefore I'll none of it. Honour is a mere scutcheon." Falstaff always hears through the thrilling march played by the glittering band the lonely death rattle on the battlefield. In his pistol case he carries no pistol but a bottle of sack. Three hundred years later Bernard Shaw was to shock the romantically minded with his anti-heroic professional soldier, Captain Bluntschli, whose cartridge case is filled not with bullets but with chocolates. After World War I the ex-soldiers welcomed the irony of *Arms and the Man* but were openly derisive about the battle heroics of *Cyrano de Bergerac*. Falstaff's battlefield philosophy is that of Private John Doe everywhere: "Give me life, which if I can save, so; if not, honour comes unlooked for, and there's an end."

The only truly distasteful action of Falstaff is to stab the dead Hotspur, to make sure of him and to claim a reward. There is nothing sadistic or vindictive in the act; it is just another device for getting money, and it says much for Hal that he is so fond of the old man as to support him in his arrant lie. Perhaps it is as well that we should be revolted by some action of Falstaff; it would be dangerous for society if we were all completely seduced by this lovably anti-moral mountain of flesh. There comes a time when we must forswear him, as Hal had to do.

If, as is likely, Shakespeare intended Falstaff for the one play only, he is careful to let his last words be another avowal of reformation: ". . . I'll purge, and leave sack, and live cleanly as a nobleman should do." But now we laugh at that because we know that Sir John Sack-and-Sugar will soon silence Monsieur Remorse.

In the Second Part of *Henry IV*, Shakespeare knows from the beginning that Hal must part from Falstaff, and he prepares us for it throughout the play. Only once and briefly and with other people present do they meet for a battle of wits as in their old roistering days. In the new war against the rebels Falstaff is deliberately parted from the Prince. The Lord Chief Justice, the soul of rectitude, tells Falstaff, "Well, the King hath severed you

and Prince Harry. I hear you are going with Lord John of Lancaster against the Archbishop and the Earl of Northumberland."
The Lord Chief Justice, who had actually had the Prince arrested
for hitting him, is utterly hostile to Falstaff and all he stands for.
Falstaff's first scene in the play becomes one of a long reproof
by the Justice; Falstaff counters, as ever, with brilliant wit, but
he might as well be shadowboxing for all the effect it has. The
Chief Justice is appalled by the old man's affectation of youth.

> Do you set down your name in the scroll of youth, that are
> written down old with all the characters of age? Have you
> not a moist eye, a dry hand, a yellow cheek, a white beard,
> a decreasing leg, an increasing belly? Is not your voice
> broken, your wind short, your chin double, your wit single,
> and every part about you blasted with antiquity? And will
> you yet call yourself young? Fie, fie, fie, Sir John!

But Sir John's reply only compounds his fault; he cannot resist his
wit, even if he is the only person around to enjoy it. "My lord,
I was born about three of the clock in the afternoon, with a white
head and something a round belly. For my voice, I have lost it
with hallooing and singing of anthems. To approve my youth
further, I will not. The truth is, I am only old in judgement and
understanding." Falstaff has no way of dealing with such an admirably incorruptible a paragon as the Lord Chief Justice. He is
even foolish enough to try to get money out of him, but that is
a natural reflex action in him. "Will your lordship lend me a
thousand pound to furnish me forth?" He can't be very surprised
by the answer: "Not a penny, not a penny."

From Falstaff's first words in this second play we are made
aware of his physical deterioration. His tiny page brings a urine
report from the doctor: "He said, sir, the water itself was a good
healthy water; but, for the party that owed it, he might have
more diseases than he knew for." And at the end of the same
scene, we are again reminded of Falstaff's physical condition, but
now he sees it as a chance to earn a pension for war-service: "A
pox of this gout! or a gout of this pox! for the one or the other

plays the rogue with my great toe. 'Tis no matter if I do halt; I have the wars for my colour, and my pension shall seem the more reasonable. A good wit will make use of anything. I will turn diseases to commodity."

To prepare us in yet another way for Hal's rejection of Falstaff he even has the tavern Hostess turn against him. He has exploited her so long and to such good purpose that she is reduced to pawning her plate and tapestry. She can bear it no more, and gets the Sheriff's officers, Fang and Snare, to arrest her fat debtor. "A hundred mark is a long one for a poor lone woman to bear; and I have borne, and borne, and borne, and have been fubbed off, and fubbed off, and fubbed off, from this day to that day, that it is a shame to be thought on." The poor woman is particularly vindictive because she had been promised marriage by Sir John, but he even talks himself out of this predicament to such good effect that she promises to pawn her gown to furnish him with more money.

To compensate the tavern scenes for the almost complete loss of Hal, and to make the place more sordidly realistic, Shakespeare invents two vivid new characters—a harlot, Doll Tearsheet, and a supreme example of the "miles gloriosus," the boastful coward, Pistol, the man who wears his tatters like rich robes, a fearsome lion without and a frightened lamb within. Once more, to show the difference between Falstaff and a true coward, in a sword fight the old man readily chases the younger one out of the room. The Prince and Poins, disguised as potboys, are in hiding to observe Falstaff so that they can tease him afterwards with what he said about them in their absence. The sight of Doll on Falstaff's knee provokes Poins to say, "Is it not strange that desire should so many years outlive performance?" But Falstaff does not even affect youth with Doll; in reply to her kisses he says sadly, "I am old. I am old." When Hal and Poins reveal themselves, Falstaff is genuinely glad to see the Prince, but the resulting banter lacks its old spontaneity and the Prince soon leaves with a curt "Falstaff, good night." And it is good night indeed. When next they meet, Hal will be King, and will say those words which our reason may accept but which our hearts will reject: "I know thee not, old man; fall to thy prayers." Now, as Falstaff departs for the wars, the whore and the Hostess cry warm tears, the insults and the hurts forgotten; all is always forgiven the lovable old reprobate, except by King and Justice, the one who has to hide the weakness of humanity and the other who has none to hide.

A fundamental problem in the writing of the second play about Henry IV was that the historical ingredients had to be the same, a rebellion by the same faction and its defeat, though this time by subterfuge and without the climactic excitement of a battle. Shakespeare overcomes this difficulty by emphasizing, on the historical side, the gradual emergence of King Henry V from Prince Hal, and giving an even greater part of the play to Falstaff. Yet, even for Falstaff, the action must largely consist of recruiting for the war once more, but here Shakespeare decides to expand what he did before. All we saw in the First Part were the pitiable results of the corrupt recruiting; now we see the detailed process, and this will take us to Shakespeare's own countryside, which he was always most happy in recreating. Less likely soldiers could not be found than Mouldy, Shadow, Wart, Feeble and Bullcalf, and the best of the bad bunch, Mouldy and Bullcalf, manage to buy themselves off in a side deal with Bardolph. The recruits had been gathered by that most egregious of garrulous old dotards, Justice Shallow, and his attendant death's-head, dismal Silence, and it is these that claim our attention. Shallow lives in his old age on memories of youthful exploits that never happened. He had been a law student at a time when Jack Falstaff had been page to Thomas Mowbray, Duke of Norfolk. (Not that it bothers Shakespeare or any spectator of the play, but this is absurd chronologically. The date is 1405, and, even supposing Falstaff to be only the sixty years of age that he confesses, he would have had to be born in 1345. Now Thomas Mowbray was not born until 1366, so that Falstaff was too old to be his page even before

Mowbray was born.) Shallow calls on Falstaff to corroborate his tales of a wild youth, and the wily one, sensing an old sheep to be fleeced, agrees: "We have heard the chimes at midnight, Master Shallow." But when he is alone, Falstaff anatomizes him devastatingly: "I do see the bottom of Justice Shallow. Lord, Lord, how subject we old men are to this vice of lying! This same starved Justice hath done nothing but prate to me of the wildness of his youth, and the feats he hath done about Turnbull Street, and every third word a lie." Shakespeare often thinks in terms of sharp physical contrast, particularly that of fat-thin (Dogberry-Verges, Sir Toby Belch-Sir Andrew Aguecheek) and this contrast is wonderfully used in the case of Falstaff-Shallow. How amusingly the grossly fat one describes the grimly thin one!

> I do remember him at Clement's Inn like a man made after supper of a cheeseparing. When a' was naked, he was for all the world like a forked radish, with a head fantastically carved upon it with a knife. A' was so forlorn that his dimensions to any thick sight were invisible. A' was the very genius of famine.

We have one more sight of Falstaff on a battlefield, and strangely enough there is no taint of cowardice about what we see. He challenges and takes prisoner Sir John Coleville, whom Prince John describes as "a famous rebel." It is true that they never come to blows, and even this Falstaff is oddly honest about: "He saw me, and yielded, that I may justly say, with the hook-nosed fellow of Rome, 'I came, saw, and overcame.'" What is the point of this Coleville episode? Is Shakespeare deliberately balancing the picture of Falstaff on the battlefield of Shrewsbury, when he feigned death before Douglas and stabbed the corpse of Hotspur? If so, it is a very subtle balancing, because Coleville yields to Falstaff's words and to his reputation. Had Falstaff been made to triumph in a fight, it would have been hard to reconcile with our previous conception of him.

And now to the rejection of Falstaff by the new and metamorphosed king. Its sad inevitability is not to be gainsaid, but one or two features need to be noted. The whole base expectation of preferment through Falstaff's presumed influence with the new King is epitomized in Justice Shallow who had entertained Sir John well and even lent him a thousand pounds on the promise of such expectation. "I will use him well. A friend i' the Court is better than a penny in purse." Falstaff, too, is warned before the King appears in procession that a new severity is abroad, for Pistol brings him the news that the Hostess and Doll Tearsheet are "in base durance and contagious prison." Finally, in noting the harsh rejection we must not forget the generous thought of the King that accompanies it:

> For competence of life I will allow you,
> That lack of means enforce you not to evil.
> And as we hear you do reform yourselves,
> We will, according to your strength and qualities,
> Give you advancement. . . .

That these are not empty words is affirmed by Prince John in conversation with the Lord Chief Justice who has just had Falstaff and his companions committed to prison until he can examine them:

> I like this fair proceeding of the King's.
> He hath intent his wonted followers
> Shall all be very well provided for,
> But all are banished till their conversations
> Appear more wise and modest to the world.

Now Shakespeare faced the writing of *Henry V*, a task which I believe, as I have previously noted, he had postponed as long as possible. And now he has a complication he had not originally envisaged. Originally there was the problem of presenting a picture of the legendary hero, both worthy and human, but now there is Falstaff. In the Epilogue to *Henry IV, Part II*, he promises that Falstaff shall be in the new play, but even then his instinct told him that the fat knight would be an embarrassment: "If you be not too much cloyed with fat meat, our humble author will continue the story, with Sir John in it . . . where, for anything I know, Falstaff shall die of a sweat." When the new play appears, Falstaff is not in it, and his death is reported by the Hostess most movingly; even to the last, God and sack were still battling in his thoughts and words. Shakespeare could not let the presence of Falstaff dim the glory of Henry as it most certainly would have done, for as the Hostess reports, "The King has killed his heart."

Reluctantly for my part, some consideration must be given to the Sir John Falstaff of *The Merry Wives of Windsor;* reluctantly, because this Falstaff is but a pale shadow, in all but bulk, of the great creation. He may be "the cause that wit is in other men," though it is the wit of crude jokes played against a massive target, but as a wit in himself compared with his original he is but a flickering candle to a blazing sun. This second edition of Falstaff says: "Have I lived to be carried in a basket, like a barrow of butcher's offal, and to be thrown in the Thames?" Alas, indeed, Sir John, indeed! Not that *The Merry Wives of Windsor* is not a joy in the theatre; I only wish the fat man in it had been given some other name.

There is an old and credible tradition that Queen Elizabeth was so disappointed by Shakespeare's failure to keep his promise that Falstaff would be in *Henry V* that she commanded him to write another play about the fat knight, and even suggested the theme of Falstaff in love. The tradition is that Shakespeare fulfilled her behest in a fortnight and that the result was *The Merry Wives of Windsor*. Her delight in Falstaff tells us much about Queen Elizabeth; I feel that Queen Victoria would heartily have disapproved of him. I hope the Queen was pleased by the result of her command, but, however much she laughed, I feel she must have known that the real Falstaff had died before the play was written, and he could not be resurrected.

6　Henry V

IN THIS anti-heroic age it is hard to elicit sympathy for Henry V, but in the heroic age of Elizabeth he was the legendary quintessence of that spirit of valor and adventure which fired the soldiers and sailors of the Queen. Shakespeare had no desire to debunk the legend—he shared his fellow-countrymen's admiration of the heroic virtues—but he wanted to breathe humanity into the hero without detracting from his stature, and this he succeeded triumphantly in doing. Too often is Henry V dismissed, even by the most notable critics, as a lifeless statue of military magnificence, and sometimes even much worse. Thus to Hazlitt he is at best "a very amiable monster, a very splendid pageant," and he sees no difference between Henry's highwayman escapade at Gadshill and his action in "the affair of Agincourt." This is grossly impercipient and prejudiced, and my purpose is to show that Shakespeare not only admired and portrayed the legendary hero, but also liked, sympathized with and revealed the man beneath the royal armor.

To a playwright seeking the common humanity in the uncommon king, Holinshed was deeply discouraging, for his Henry

V is an impossibly perfect king, judge, athlete, stoic, soldier and general. He begins his long description of the paragon with these words:

> This Henry was a king of life without spot; a prince whom all men loved and of none disdained; a captain against whom fortune never frowned, nor mischance once spurned; whose people him so severe a justicer both loved and obeyed (and so humane withal), that he left no offense unpunished, nor friendship unrewarded; a terror to rebels, and suppressor of sedition; his virtues notable, his qualities most praise-worthy.

And Holinshed sums up thus: "For conclusion, a majesty was he that both lived and died a pattern in princehood, a lode-star in honour, and mirror of magnificence; the more highly exalted in his life, the more deeply lamented at his death, and famous to the world alway."

To begin with, Shakespeare makes it clear from the outset that Hal came to power reluctantly. His was a destiny he could not avoid. Never once is he prompted by personal aggrandizement. Duty calls and he obeys. Even after his victory at Shrewsbury he goes back to the tavern. At the end of his first sparring scene with Falstaff he sets the whole problem of his life in a soliloquy which many an actor has been reluctant to deliver because it seems to be so cold-blooded about the tavern company he has just been enjoying:

> I know you all, and will a while uphold
> The unyoked humour of your idleness.
> Yet herein will I imitate the sun,
> Who doth permit the base contagious clouds
> To smother up his beauty from the world,
> That, when he please again to be himself,
> Being wanted, he may be more wondered at
> By breaking through the foul and ugly mists
> Of vapours that did seem to strangle him.

That seems to me a very human speech; not admirable perhaps, but human and true. There is no doubt of Hal's genuine enjoyment of his wild oats, but he would be a monster if he did not feel guilty about it. Falstaff's remorse comes from the approach of the grave, Hal's from the approach of the crown. With typical youthful casuistry he vows to compensate for his delinquencies when the time comes.

> So, when this loose behaviour I throw off
> And pay the debt I never promised,
> By how much better than my word I am,
> By so much shall I falsify men's hopes.

"The debt I never promised." Uneasy lies the head not only that wears a crown, but is destined to wear one. And Hal is not completely reckless in his mad escapades. They are only the expression of youthful exuberance. He is careful that nobody shall be hurt by them. Thus he sees to it that the robbed travelers are paid back with interest, much to the disgust of Falstaff who likes not "that paying back."

There is a poignant and revealing moment in the comic interlude in which Hal plays his father castigating the Prince in the person of Falstaff. The old man playing the young man makes his wonderful plea on behalf of Falstaff, ending with words which gradually acquire an undercurrent of seriousness, as though he sensed the danger to him that lay ahead when Hal would be King:

> No, my good lord. Banish Peto, banish Bardolph, banish Poins. But for sweet Jack Falstaff, kind Jack Falstaff, true Jack Falstaff, valiant Jack Falstaff, and therefore more valiant, being, as he is, old Jack Falstaff, banish not him thy Harry's company. Banish plump Jack, and banish all the world.

The Prince replies, not wholly in the assumed person of his father, but partly as himself, "I do, I will." In those words too there is an undercurrent of seriousness. Actors are often concerned with the sub-text, the truth beneath the words, and in those words of the Prince there is a sad foretelling of the inevitable rejection of Falstaff.

The ambivalence of Hal towards Falstaff and all the guilt-stained fun which association with him implies is exemplified in Hal's farewell to him when he thinks him dead:

> What, old acquaintance! Could not all this flesh
> Keep in a little life? Poor Jack, farewell!
> I could have better spared a better man.
> O, I should have a heavy miss of thee
> If I were much in love with vanity!

Our first sight of Hal in the Second Part of *Henry IV* parallels that of Falstaff in the First Part. Now it is the Prince who is melancholy, though not so far gone but that he plans mischief against Falstaff by the end of the scene. Yet Shakespeare is at pains in this first entrance to let us know that the Prince is changing before our eyes; the destined king is aborning. "Doth it not show vilely in me to desire small beer? . . . Belike then my appetite was not princely got, for, by my troth, I do now remember the poor creature, small beer. But indeed these humble considerations make me out of love with my greatness." He is concerned too with the reformation of Falstaff, though he realizes that is unlikely. "Marry, the immortal part needs a physician, but that moves not him. Though that be sick, it dies not."

The King, Henry IV, in advising his younger sons how to deal with the future king, their brother, draws a perceptive character study of the Prince, stressing that his changing moods must be "observed," that is, "allowed for":

> For he is gracious if he be observed,
> He hath a tear for pity, and a hand
> Open as day for melting charity.
> Yet notwithstanding, being incensed, he's flint,
> As humorous as winter, and as sudden
> As flaws congealed in the spring of day.
> His temper, therefore, must be well observed.
> Chide him for faults, and do it reverently,
> When you perceive his blood inclined to mirth.
> But, being moody, give him line and scope,
> Till that his passions, like a whale on ground,
> Confound themselves with working. . . .

But the King is deeply disturbed about the state of the country when the wild young Prince becomes its king. It is the Earl of Warwick who points out what good use he may make of his youthful experiences:

> The Prince but studies his companions
> Like a strange tongue, wherein, to gain the language,
> 'Tis needful that the most immodest word
> Be looked upon and learned; which once attained,
> Your Highness knows, comes to no further use
> But to be known and hated. So, like gross terms,
> The Prince will in the perfectness of time
> Cast off his followers; and their memory
> Shall as a pattern or a measure live,
> By which his Grace must mete the lives of others,
> Turning past evils to advantages.

Later we learn that Warwick had not really believed this. Like the King, he feared the worst.

In the final scene between father and son, the Prince speaks the truth when he says how reluctant he is to wear the crown:

> If any rebel or vain spirit of mine
> Did with the least affection of a welcome
> Give entertainment to the might of it,
> Let God forever keep it from my head.

The Prince is well aware of "what bypaths and indirect crooked ways" his father had used to get the crown. Two years later, in his prayer before the battle of Agincourt, he is to remember the crime of deposition and to declare that all his works of vicarious penance cannot undo it:

> . . . Not today, O Lord,
> Oh, not today, think not upon the fault
> My father made in compassing the crown!
> I Richard's body have interred new,
> And on it have bestowed more contrite tears,
> Than from it issued forced drops of blood.
> Five hundred poor I have in yearly pay,

> Who twice a day their withered hands hold up
> Toward heaven, to pardon blood; and I have built
> Two chantries, where the sad and solemn priests
> Sing still for Richard's soul. More will I do;
> Though all that I can do is nothing worth,
> Since that my penitence comes after all,
> Imploring pardon. . . .

But at his father's deathbed the Prince's one thought is to bring peace to the dying King with assurance that he will defend the stolen crown worthily:

> My gracious liege,
> You won it, wore it, kept it, gave it me.
> Then plain and right must my possession be,
> Which I with more than with a common pain
> 'Gainst all the world will rightfully maintain.

The first appearance of the new King, Henry V, is filled with suspense. One of the princes, immediately before the King's entrance, says to the upright and incorruptible Lord Chief Justice that now he will have to "speak Sir John Falstaff fair." He is surely in dire jeopardy because on one occasion, when he had reproved the Prince, that impetuous young man had struck him, and the Lord Chief Justice had immediately had him arrested. Nevertheless the Justice is determined to remain his own man:

> Sweet princes, what I did, I did in honour,
> Led by the impartial conduct of my soul;
> And never shall you see that I will beg
> A ragged and forestalled remission.
> If truth and upright innocency fail me,
> I'll to the King my master that is dead,
> And tell him who hath sent me after him.

Will the new King refer to the treatment he had received as Prince? He does, and makes much of it, but merely to test the quality of the Justice:

> How might a prince of my great hopes forget
> So great indignities you laid on me?

> What! rate, rebuke, and roughly send to prison
> The immediate heir of England? Was this easy?
> May this be washed in Lethe, and forgotten?

The Lord Chief Justice makes an eloquent defense of his action but with no regret or apology. The King is deeply satisfied:

> . . . You did commit me;
> For which I do commit into your hand
> The unstained sword that you have used to bear,
> With this remembrance, that you use the same
> With the like bold, just, and impartial spirit
> As you have done 'gainst me. There is my hand.
> You shall be as a father to my youth.
> My voice shall sound as you do prompt mine ear,
> And I will stoop and humble my intents
> To your well-practised wise directions.

The new King has made a good beginning. It is to this most honorable Justice that Henry commits Falstaff, and we know that the letter of the King's intentions for the old man will be strictly carried out, including the "competence of life," which means, in Falstaff's case, that he will not want for sack.

But now for the play, *Henry V*. Is there humanity to be found in "the warlike Harry?" I think so, and in abundance.

First, the great soldier has no romantic illusions about war. He knows it releases the worst as well as the best in man. In his speech to the Governor of Harfleur he tries to stop further bloodshed by describing the horrors of the sacking of a town:

> . . . Therefore, you men of Harfleur,
> Take pity of your town and of your people,
> Whiles yet my soldiers are in my command,
> Whiles yet the cool and temperate wind of grace
> O'erblows the filthy and contagious clouds
> Of heady murder, spoil, and villainy.
> If not, why, in a moment look to see
> The blind and bloody soldier with foul hand
> Defile the locks of your shrill-shrieking daughters;
> Your fathers taken by the silver beards,

> And their most reverend heads dashed to the walls;
> Your naked infants spitted upon pikes,
> Whiles the mad mothers with their howls confused
> Do break the clouds, as did the wives of Jewry
> At Herod's bloody-hunting slaughtermen.

Henry's charge to the Archbishop of Canterbury before he expounds the legality of the King's claim to the French throne is not that of an adventurer but of a leader fully aware of the consequences of the decision to go to war:

> We charge you, in the name of God, take heed;
> For never two such kingdoms did contend
> Without much fall of blood, whose guiltless drops
> Are every one a woe, a sore complaint
> 'Gainst him whose wrongs gives edge unto the swords
> That makes such waste in brief mortality.

Shakespeare doesn't glamorize the motive for the French campaign. He makes it clear that the Church is urging it to take the King's eyes off Church property; for several years there had been a proposal to seize a goodly part of it. To disguise the real motive the Archbishop has already promised, for the outfitting of the expedition, that he will give to the King

> . . . a greater sum
> Than ever at one time the clergy yet
> Did to his predecessors part withal.

But Henry must first be convinced that his claim is legal and just. Granting the right of succession through the female, it was valid, because his great-great-grandmother had been the daughter of Philip IV of France. We should always remember that the English royal house was French in origin, ever since William, Duke of Normandy, conquered the land in 1066; Henry had a particular obsession to recover Normandy. The Archbishop's disquisition is now a great bore to us but it was essential to Shakespeare that Henry should be clear in his claim, and that the audience in the theatre too should be satisfied that their hero was

no mere adventurer. But Henry's vow to reign in France still
sounds crude and vainglorious to our ears—

> . . . Or there we'll sit,
> Ruling in large and ample empery
> O'er France and all her almost kingly dukedoms,
> Or lay these bones in an unworthy urn,
> Tombless, with no remembrance over them—

but it did not sound so to Shakespeare's audience, and Shakespeare
makes the expedition more palatable even to us by reinforcing it
with an angry reaction to the insult of the Dauphin, who accompanies a present of tennis balls to the King as more appropriate
to his dissolute youth with the warning:

> . . . be advised there's naught in France
> That can be with a nimble galliard won.
> You cannot revel into dukedoms there.

But on the eve of the departure to France a plot to kill the
King is unearthed. The would-be assassins are three noblemen,
one a relative of the King and another a dear friend. The apparent
motive, though it may have been complicated in the case of the
relative by some faint hope of the crown, was lavish bribery by
France. The King prefaces his disclosure of the treachery by
pardoning a man who in his drunkenness had railed against him;
ironically the traitors beg for the death penalty for the man.
Henry is saddened to the soul by the treachery of his friends,
particularly by that of Lord Scroop of Masham:

> What shall I say to thee, Lord Scroop? Thou cruel,
> Ingrateful, savage, and inhuman creature!
> Thou that didst bear the key of all my counsels;
> That knew'st the very bottom of my soul,
> That almost mightst have coined me into gold
> Wouldst thou have practised on me for thy use.
>
> . . . .
>
> . . . I will weep for thee;
> For this revolt of thine, methinks, is like
> Another fall of man. . . .

There is not anger here, but the deep sadness of disillusionment. Their fate is inevitable, but it is meted out with a dignified grief:

> Touching our person seek we no revenge;
> But we our kingdom's safety must so tender,
> Whose ruin you have sought, that to her laws
> We do deliver you. Get you therefore hence,
> Poor miserable wretches, to your death,
> The taste whereof God of his mercy give
> You patience to endure, and true repentance
> Of all your dear offences! . . .

In all this I sense the anguish of a very real man, not the judgment of an inhuman paragon.

In his final message to the French Court, Henry, as he would at Harfleur, pictures the general horrors of war and not the effects upon the King, Dauphin and courtiers. It is to be no heroic encounter between a Hotspur and a Hal. He bids the French King

> Deliver up the crown, and to take mercy
> On the poor souls for whom this hungry war
> Opens his vasty jaws; and on your head
> Turning the widows' tears, the orphans' cries,
> The dead men's blood, the pining maidens' groans
> For husbands, fathers, and betrothed lovers
> That shall be swallowed in this controversy.

Of course it is Henry who is precipitating the war, but he is doing so for what he thinks is a just cause, for which his ancestors had fought before him, and on the unanimous advice of his counselors. For my purpose the important thing is that he is aware of the terrible suffering war brings to the innocent, and this was at odds with the mood of the country. The young men who eagerly followed him saw only the adventure and the reward:

> For now sits Expectation in the air,
> And hides a sword from hilts unto the point
> With crowns imperial, crowns, and coronets
> Promised to Harry and his followers.

Shakespeare is consummate in his command of an audience, and *Henry V* affords an excellent example of what I mean. In dramatizing a famous life the playwright has the problem of the obligatory scene, that which springs to the mind whenever the name is mentioned—for example, in the case of Julius Caesar or Abraham Lincoln, the assassination—and for Henry V this was the battle of Agincourt. How could Shakespeare satisfy the expectation of his audience in this matter? As was pointed out in the introductory chapter, the first Chorus warns them of the difficulty, and so does the fourth. But he cannot evade it. His solution is brilliant. He gives them an unforgettable battle scene before they are expecting it, not Agincourt, but the siege of Harfleur, and, when the battlefield of Agincourt at last appears, the first scene upon it is a comic one. Indeed, the surprising gambit throughout is the amount of comedy in the battle scenes. Henry's astonishing battle-cry of a speech, "Once more unto the breach, dear friends," can still make the spine tingle if it is delivered with the right abandon, but it is one of the most difficult tasks that any actor has to face, because it starts at the top and has to end even higher. From our present point of view the most important phrase in it is "dear friends." This was the secret of Henry's appeal, the genuine common touch which we shall note several times in his leadership. This was what his youth had taught him, what he had learned in the tavern. Antony affected it in his skillful funeral oration when his first appeal was to "Friends"; the first word of the idealistic Brutus had been "Romans."

Shakespeare uses an incident he found in Holinshed to remind us of Henry's complete break with his past. He read: "A soldier took a pix out of a church, for which he was apprehended, and the king not once removed till the box was restored, and the offender strangled." Shakespeare made the unfortunate looter Falstaff's tavern companion and butt, Bardolph. Henry's comment is a model for the conduct of occupying troops:

We would have all such offenders so cut off. And we give

express charge, that in our marches through the country, there be nothing compelled from the villages, nothing taken but paid for, none of the French upbraided or abused in disdainful language; for when lenity and cruelty play for a kingdom, the gentler gamester is the soonest winner.

The Duke of Orleans in vauntingly describing the situation of the English troops before Agincourt seemed to be saying the simple truth: "Foolish curs, that run winking into the mouth of a Russian bear and have their heads crushed like rotten apples." The English forces, decimated by disease and weakened by hunger, were trying to get to Calais to sail home, as their descendants did from Dunkirk in 1940. Their way was blocked by a fresh and confident French army which outnumbered them by five to one; some historians rate the odds even higher. The fourth Chorus movingly describes the state of the English army on the night before the battle:

> . . . The poor condemned English,
> Like sacrifices, by their watchful fires,
> Sit patiently and inly ruminate
> The morning's danger; and their gesture sad,
> Investing lank-lean cheeks and war-worn coats,
> Presenteth them unto the gazing moon
> So many horrid ghosts. . . .

Then follows a description of the inspiriting effect Henry has on his men,

> For forth he goes and visits all his host,
> Bids them good morrow with a modest smile,
> And calls them brothers, friends, and countrymen.

Shakespeare sums up the effect of Henry's human contact with his men in a line of miraculous simplicity; they all felt "A little touch of Harry in the night."

Henry has not lost his pleasing sense of humor. He can even moralize lightly, for, in commenting on the fact that the imminent battle has got them early out of bed, he says:

> There is some soul of goodness in things evil,
> Would men observingly distil it out;
> For our bad neighbour makes us early stirrers,
> Which is both healthful and good husbandry.

From the beginning, Henry has been deeply aware of his responsibility in the coming bloodshed, but, to emphasize it, Shakespeare contrives a scene in which the King, incognito as a soldier, discusses it with a group of soldiers, one of whom puts the matter in words which harrow the King's soul:

> But if the cause be not good, the King himself hath a heavy reckoning to make when all those legs and arms and heads chopped off in a battle shall join together at the latter day and cry all "We died at such a place"; some swearing, some crying for a surgeon, some upon their wives left poor behind them, some upon the debts they owe, some upon their children rawly left. I am afeard there are few die well that die in a battle; for how can they charitably dispose of anything, when blood is their argument? Now, if these men do not die well, it will be a black matter for the King that led them to it.

Henry points out in a passionately reasoned reply that a man's total life is at stake in his death: "Every subject's duty is the King's; but every subject's soul is his own."

Henry is left alone to meditate and prepare himself for battle by prayer. It is true that the real Henry seemed to experience a kind of religious conversion at the time of his accession. The night after his father's death he spent in prayer and meditation with a holy man. After his wild whoring days he seems to have been sexually continent until his marriage. He strictly forbade any victory celebrations after Agincourt. He was largely responsible for making the mythical St. George the patron saint of England. When a certain Frenchman saw him, he thought he looked more like a priest than a soldier. In his lonely vigil before the battle begins, and mindful of the soldiers' comments on the King's responsibility, he deplores the agony of great authority. It is significant in both men that this soliloquy of Henry, as indeed the whole character, was a favorite of President Kennedy; at one of his last entertainments at the White House it was this speech he wanted to hear, whose theme is:

> . . . What infinite heart's-ease
> Must kings neglect, that private men enjoy!

Henry has once more to instill courage into fearful men, and this time not ordinary soldiers, but his leading noblemen. He does so with his stirring "St. Crispin" speech. Once again he profits from his tavern days. Many a time had he, and Shakespeare, heard old soldiers tell of their exploits "with advantages," that is, with fanciful exaggeration and addition, and speak familiarly of the exalted ones, as veterans of World War II speak of "Ike" and "Monty."

> He that shall live this day and see old age
> Will yearly on the vigil feast his neighbours,
> And say, "Tomorrow is Saint Crispian."
> Then will he strip his sleeve and show his scars,
> And say, "These wounds I had on Crispin's day."
> Old men forget; yet all shall be forgot,
> But he'll remember with advantages
> What feats he did that day. Then shall our names,
> Familiar in his mouth as household words,
> Harry the King, Bedford, and Exeter,
> Warwick and Talbot, Salisbury and Gloucester,
> Be in their flowing cups freshly remembered.
> This story shall the good man teach his son;
> And Crispin Crispian shall ne'er go by,
> From this day to the ending of the world,
> But we in it shall be remembered,
> We few, we happy few, we band of brothers.

At one stage in the battle Henry, seeing the French massing for another assault, gave the order that all prisoners were to be killed. Shakespeare does not avoid this black mark against Henry; he accepts it as a necessity of the desperate moment. Holinshed gave him an excuse to turn the black mark into a grey one, for there he read that some Frenchmen had attacked and slain some servants and boys who had been left in charge of the royal tents and pavilions; and the King's ruthless order to kill the prisoners could have come in a fit of vengeful anger at the news; indeed I have seen productions of the play in which the text has been rearranged to furnish the King with that motivation. But Shakespeare wanted to show, in Henry, the single-mindedness of all successful soldiers; war is not a nice matter, and its great decisions spell death to the helpless.

There is a sense in which the battle of Agincourt was another stage in the passing of the chivalric conception of war, according to which foes, equal in status and equipment, fought honorably hand-to-hand. Large numbers of the mounted French nobility were slain by the well-directed arrows of English yeomen. Technology resulting in death at a distance has progressively killed the knightly ideal of warfare; first there were arrows, then bullets, cannonballs, high-explosive bombs, until finally we have arrived at the hydrogen bomb. From his leadership at Agincourt, Henry has been called "the first modern general." There was an incredible disparity between the losses of the two sides. Shakespeare, following Holinshed, gives the figures of ten thousand French dead to the English twenty-five. The highest subsequent estimate of the English losses was six hundred, which still leaves an astonishing ratio.

With the certain knowledge that victory has been won, the mischievous Hal is again released in the soldier-hero. In his disguised encounter with the soldiers in the night before the battle, he had accepted a challenge to be settled later, if they should survive the day. Being the king, he cannot himself accept the challenge, but asks the fiery Welshman, Fluellen, with whom the King is proud to acknowledge kinship of country, to wear the challenger's glove; but, after Fluellen has left, Henry is quick to forestall injury: "Follow, and see there be no harm between them."

It is in this same relaxed and playful mood that Henry conducts his courtship of the Princess Katharine, in which the fun flows from their near ignorance of each other's language. Conversations with women like Doll Tearsheet have not fitted Henry for the courtly wooing of a Princess; he talks "plain soldier," but with eloquence and the wit which he had sharpened against that of Falstaff. Thus, when Katharine asks if it is possible that she should love the enemy of France, he replies:

> No, it is not possible you should love the enemy of France, Kate. But, in loving me, you should love the friend of France; for I love France so well that I will not part with a village of it; I will have it all mine; and, Kate, when France is mine and I am yours, then yours is France and you are mine.

And so Shakespeare brings to an end his chronicle of "This star of England." As I have pointed out already, I think he postponed writing it as long as possible. Just as Henry V was a man caught in the toils of inherited duty and could not avoid the throne, so Shakespeare was caught in the toils of theatrical necessity and could not avoid the subject. Both Henry and his chronicler acquitted themselves nobly.

7 Richard III

LIKE HENRY V, the character who was to be Richard III appears in three plays—*Henry VI, Parts II* and *III*, and *Richard III*—and for almost two hundred years the play called *Richard III* that was seen in the theatres was a concoction made by Colley Cibber from all three plays. So popular was it that when some actor-managers in the nineteenth century tried to perform Shakespeare's own *Richard III*, popular demand made them revert to Cibber's version, or to a new amalgam of Cibber and Shakespeare. One of the most oft-quoted lines from the play was by Cibber and not Shakespeare: "Off with his head; so much for Buckingham." The reason for the popularity of Cibber's version was that it gave the audience even more of the fascinating character of Richard.

To what extent Shakespeare's character is the historical Richard is the matter of a debate which has been going on for more than 350 years. There is even a society which is dedicated to the purpose of vindicating Richard and rehabilitating his name. There seems little doubt that the majority of reputable historians would hold Richard responsible for the murders of Henry VI and the two Princes in the Tower. But the historical truth does not concern us here; only the extraordinary vividness of Shakespeare's creation. In his defense it must be said that he took the basic facts from Holinshed; it was the only version of them extant; and Holinshed's main source had been a life of Richard written some fifty years before Shakespeare was born by the "Man for All Seasons," Sir Thomas More; the function of that book had been to emphasize the black deeds of Richard in order to justify the accession to the throne of the new king, Henry VII, who had defeated Richard III at the battle of Bosworth Field.

Shakespeare received all the lineaments of villainy from Holinshed, who said:

> Richard . . . was . . . little of stature, ill-featured of limbs, crook-backed, his left shoulder much higher than his right, hard favoured of visage; . . . he was malicious, wrathful, envious. . . . He was close and secret, a deep dissembler, lowly of countenance, arrogant of heart, outwardly companionable where he inwardly hated, not letting to kiss whom he thought to kill; despitious and cruel, not for evil will alway, but ofter for ambition . . . he spared no man's death whose life withstood his purpose. . . . He was of ready, pregnant and quick wit, wily to feign, and apt to dissemble.

It was that last sentence that Shakespeare seized on to make his first great study of villainy captivating. He made of Richard a brilliant liar, an outrageous dissembler, who never lied to himself. There is a modern tendency to treat Shakespeare's great villains as victims oozing self-pity, Richard for his malformed body, Edmund for his bastardy. Nothing could be further from Shakespeare's conception; if they are outside the pale physically or socially or for whatever reason, this also to their minds puts them outside the moral law, and gives them incredible power over ordinary mortals. Richard is not pitying himself but glorying in his freedom from moral restraints when he says:

> I have no brother, I am like no brother;
> And this word "love," which greybeards call divine,

Be resident in men like one another
And not in me. I am myself alone.

The completely immoral and conscienceless man has a power denied to others, and it is this power he rejoices in. However we may be horrified by the results of that power, we stand in awe of it, because it is as far beyond the reach of ordinary mortals as is sainthood, and is somehow more attractive to us. It doesn't say much for our mortal nature, but it is always easier to believe in a wholly evil character than in a wholly good one. Milton had much more success with Satan than he did with God.

It is usual in discussions of *Richard III* to trace the influence of Senecan tragedy in the play and of the medieval figure of Vice from the morality plays in the character, but neither consideration will help us much in assessing Richard as a human being, which is our sole concern. It is amazing that Shakespeare could take such a monster of iniquity and make him much more than the stock villain of a gory melodrama. It is also usual to point out, and I believe magnify, the influence of Marlowe upon Shakespeare's conception of Richard; the occasional echoes of the mighty line, the centrality of the character, yes, but the monster made man, no; that is only and could only be Shakespeare's own.

No character of Shakespeare's has so divided the critics as Richard III. The moralists must condemn him and go on to belittle the play. Thus James Russell Lowell could at best believe that Shakespeare "may have retouched or even added to a poor play which had already proved popular; but it is not conceivable that he should have written an entire play in violation of those principles of taste which we may deduce more or less clearly from everything he wrote." To Bernard Shaw the play was an enjoyable Punch and Judy show, not to be taken seriously.

> Shakespear [sic] revels in it with just the sort of artistic un-
> conscionableness that fits the theme. Richard is the Prince
> of Punches: he delights Man by provoking God, and dies
> unrepentant and game to the last. His incongruous conven-
> tional appendages, such as the Punch hump, the conscience,

the fear of ghosts, all impart a spice of outrageousness which leaves nothing lacking to the fun of the entertainment, except the solemnity of those spectators who feel bound to take the affair as a profound and subtle historic study.

Even Shaw in the same review of a performance by Sir Henry Irving had to admit that in the Lady Anne scene Richard "is Punch on the Don Giovanni plane." Here, by way of contrast, is an excerpt from a review of a performance of Edmund Kean in 1814. It was written by a Thomas Barnes.

> The great characteristics of Richard are a daring and comprehensive intelligence, which seizes its object with the grasp of a giant,—a profound acquaintance with the human soul, which makes him appreciate motives at a glance,—a spirit immoveably fearless, because, how can a mighty being tremble among animals who are but as atoms to his towering superiority?—Besides this, he is a villain; that is, he moves onward to his purpose careless of ordinary duties and ordinary feelings; and yet, when we observe his horrid march, we neither shudder with disgust nor overwhelm him with execrations. Why is this? because he seems to belong to a class above mankind: he is the destroying demon whom we regard with awe and astonishment, and not the mere murderer whose meanness and vulgarity almost rob crime of its horrors.

William Winter, in a review of a performance by Richard Mansfield, said:

> Shakespeare's Richard is a type of colossal will and of restless, inordinate, terrific activity. The objects of his desire and his effort are those objects which are incident to supreme power; but his chief object is that assertion of himself which is irresistibly incited and steadfastly compelled by the overwhelming, seething, acrid energy of his feverish soul, burning and raging in his fiery body. He can no more help projecting himself upon the affairs of the world than the malignant cobra can help darting upon its prey. He is a vital, elemental force, grisly, hectic, terrible, impelled by volcanic heat and electrified and made lurid and deadly by the infernal purpose of restless wickedness.

After that spate of forbidding words, it is surprising that Mr.
Winter found that Mansfield's Richard "was shown as a creature
of the possible world of mankind and not as a fiction of the stage."

The critics who emphasize the stature of Richard lose sight
of his own enjoyment and our fun, and those, like Shaw, who
emphasize the fun lose sight of the stature. Our purpose is to
look for the man.

I feel that from the first the character of Richard captured
the imagination of Shakespeare, and that he zestfully looked forward to the play he would soon write about him. Richard first
appears in the last scenes of *Henry VI, Part II*, and certain dominant qualities of his are immediately made apparent. He and his
elder brother, Edward, are merely there to support their father,
the Duke of York, in his parley with King Henry VI and Queen
Margaret, and subsequently in the battle of St. Alban's. Altogether
he speaks but two dozen lines, but he makes a vivid impression.
His opening line reveals the man who trusts his sword more than
words: "And if words will not [serve], then our weapons shall."
It has often been remarked that animal images are frequent in
speeches by and about Richard to suggest that his were the ways
of the cunning and ruthless animal, and much is made of the fact
that his own standard contained the figure of the head of a wild
boar, with mouth agape and cruel tusk rampant. It is noteworthy
that his first substantial speech is based on the metaphor of the
bear-pit. In replying to Clifford's taunt, "We'll bait thy bear to
death," Richard cleverly retorts:

> Oft have I seen a hot o'erweening cur
> Run back and bite, because he was withheld;
> Who, being suffered with the bear's fell paw,
> Hath clapped his tail between his legs and cried.

Clifford retorts with the first of many denunciations of Richard's
twisted body:

> Hence, heap of wrath, foul indigested lump,
> As crooked in thy manners as thy shape!

But it should be here remarked that Richard's body could not have been so grossly malformed as appears from Shakespeare's dialogue, or he would have been incapable of his many valiant feats on various battlefields. The scene ends with a battle of wits between Richard and Lord Clifford's son. In it we notice for the first time a characteristic ploy of Richard's wit, an irreverently profane use of religious ideas:

> CLIFFORD: And so to arms, victorious father,
> To quell the rebels and their complices.
> RICHARD: Fie! charity, for shame! speak not in spite,
> For you shall sup with Jesu Christ tonight.
> CLIFFORD: Foul stigmatic, that's more than thou canst tell.
> RICHARD: If not in heaven, you'll surely sup in hell.

One thing remains for Shakespeare to make clear in this quick lightning sketch and that is that Richard is as valiant with the sword as with his tongue. First, in hand-to-hand combat he kills the Duke of Somerset, and significantly he ends his ironic epitaph on the slain man with an aphorism which denies the Christian ethic: "Priests pray for enemies, but princes kill." But there is a warmer side to his bravery in the field; he uses it to defend the old Earl of Salisbury, "that winter lion," and his admiration for the old warrior is sincere:

> Three times today I holp him to his horse,
> Three times bestrid him; thrice I led him off,
> Persuaded him from any further act:
> But still, where danger was, still there I met him;
> And like rich hangings in a homely house,
> So was his will in his old feeble body.

A new element in Richard appears early in the next play, the wily casuist, when he persuades his father that his oath to the King is not valid since no "lawful magistrate" was present, and in the same speech, although he is talking of his father's imminent kingship, he reveals the value he himself places on the crown:

> How sweet a thing it is to wear a crown,
> Within whose circuit is Elysium
> And all that poets feign of bliss and joy.

His cry in the next battle is no appeal to God or a saint or honor or any chivalric ideal but an honest gambler's cry:

> A crown, or else a glorious tomb!
> A sceptre, or an earthly sepulchre!

Richard embodies the Elizabethan love of bravery, and there is a touching expression of it when he praises his father's conduct in battle, made more touching because we know, but he doesn't, that the father is already dead: "Methinks, 'tis prize enough to be his son."

When the news comes that their father has been slain, the differing reactions of the two sons, Edward and Richard, is very revealing. Edward is overwhelmed by grief, but Richard wants to hear all the details, and finds that "after many scorns, many foul taunts," his father had really been stabbed to death by Lord Clifford and the Queen while he was a prisoner, a circumstance he vows to revenge. While Edward weeps, he says:

> I cannot weep, for all my body's moisture
> Scarce serves to quench my furnace-burning heart,
> Nor can my tongue unload my heart's great burden,
> For self-same wind that I should speak withal
> Is kindling coals that fires all my breast
> And burns me up with flames that tears would quench.
> To weep is to make less the depth of grief.
> Tears then for babes; blows and revenge for me.

When, in the next parley, Richard confronts Clifford, it is no longer a fight for the throne but a simple one of revenge:

> Are you there, butcher? O, I cannot speak!
> .   .   .   .
> For God's sake, lords, give signal to the fight.
> .   .   .   .

> Break off the parley; for scarce I can refrain
> The execution of my big-swoln heart
> Upon that Clifford, that cruel child-killer.

The child referred to was the Duke of Rutland, an elder brother of Richard, but Shakespeare, to blacken Clifford's deed still more, makes him an "innocent child" and even provides him with a tutor on the battlefield!

In the battle of Towton, when Edward and Warwick the "King-maker" lose heart, it is Richard who inspirits them again. In all this action there is no hint of villainy. He is the loyal and valiant son seeking revenge for the foul murders of his father and brother, and when he finally confronts Clifford hand-to-hand, he will not allow Warwick to share in the revenge:

> Nay, Warwick, single out some other chase;
> For I myself will hunt this wolf to death.

But we do not see the fight to the death. When next Clifford enters, mortally wounded, we must assume that he has received his death from Richard. Why are all Richard's doughty deeds done offstage or reported? Is it that Shakespeare is worried by Richard's deformity and doesn't want to strain credulity? But Richard is his witty, sardonic self when he comes upon the corpse of Clifford whom he assumes to be dead because he does not swear:

> What, not an oath? Nay, then the world goes hard
> When Clifford cannot spare his friends an oath.
> I know by that he's dead. . . .

It is this sardonic humor which serves as the bridge between the bravely vengeful son and the power-hungry unscrupulous brother of the new king, Edward IV. Warwick is in France to secure a dynastic marriage for Edward, but in his absence Edward, a lustful man, desires Lady Elizabeth, the widow of an enemy who had been killed in the civil war; he can only secure her by marriage, a situation which prompts a sarcastic commentary by Rich-

ard and leads to his first and longest soliloquy, in which his
ambition, his self-appraisal and his calculated ruthlessness are laid
bare:

> Then, since this earth affords no joy to me
> But to command, to check, to o'erbear such
> As are of better person than myself,
> I'll make my heaven to dream upon the crown,
> And, whiles I live, to account this world but hell
> Until my mis-shaped trunk that bears this head
> Be round impaled with a glorious crown.

Then comes his enjoyment of the power his lack of scruple and
convincing array of false faces give him over lesser mortals:

> Why, I can smile, and murder whiles I smile,
> And cry "Content" to that which grieves my heart,
> And wet my cheeks with artificial tears,
> And frame my face to all occasions.
> I'll drown more sailors than the mermaid shall;
> I'll slay more gazers than the basilisk;
> I'll play the orator as well as Nestor,
> Deceive more slily than Ulysses could,
> And, like a Sinon, take another Troy.
> I can add colours to the chameleon,
> Change shapes with Proteus for advantages,
> And set the murderous Machiavel to school.
> Can I do this and cannot get a crown?
> Tut, were it farther off, I'll pluck it down.

The monster has made a startling entrance; from now on our
search will be for the man.

The marriage of the King to the Lady Elizabeth caused much
dissension at Court, and the preferment of her relatives to high
estate was to cause much trouble during his reign and afterwards.
When appealed to by the King for his opinion, Richard, now
Duke of Gloucester, replies with characteristic and comic ambiguity, for he finds man's pious justification for his fleshly lusts
endlessly amusing:

> No, God forbid that I should wish them severed
> Whom God hath joined together; ay, and 'twere pity
> To sunder them that yoke so well together.

The sudden marriage of the King led to one of the most cynical moves in the game called The Wars of the Roses. Warwick, in France to arrange the marriage of Edward to the French King's daughter, is humiliated and the French King himself is insulted by Edward's marriage to Lady Elizabeth Grey. Warwick changes sides and joins with King Louis and the exiled Queen Margaret to restore Henry VI to the throne, and, most cynical move of all, Clarence, Edward's brother, abruptly joins the invading forces; but he had married Warwick's daughter. Richard too was to marry a daughter of Warwick, but that's another and later story. In this new phase of the game, Richard remains loyal to his brother. Edward is defeated and captured, but Richard rescues him from a careless guard. When Edward is refused admittance to the walled city of York, he persuades the Mayor to let him in on the grounds that, though he be no longer king, yet he is at least Duke of York. Richard comments on this with relish:

> But when the fox hath once got in his nose,
> He'll soon find means to make the body follow.

Here it is Edward's stratagem he is commenting on. Richard recognizes the villainy in all men; he is just more honest about it.

The wheel of fortune turns again and Henry VI is once more captured and imprisoned. Edward and Richard bring the news to Warwick who, from the walls of Coventry, answers their trumpet's call to parley. Richard breaks the news with typical mockery:

> Alas, that Warwick had no more forecast,
> But, whiles he thought to steal the single ten,
> The king was slily fingered from the deck!
> You left poor Henry at the Bishop's palace,
> And, ten to one, you'll meet him in the Tower.

Clarence, apparently from motives of conscience but more probably because he senses a shift of wind, changes sides again and rejoins his brother. Richard's comment is simple, but we now know what a cynical judgment it covers: "Welcome, good Clarence; this is brotherlike." In the battle of Tewkesbury, Warwick is killed and Queen Margaret and her son, Prince Edward, are captured. The Prince taunts the three Yorkist brothers until they are provoked to stab him to death before his mother's eyes. Richard feels Margaret should be killed too—"Why should she live, to fill the world with words?"—but Edward intervenes, and Richard abruptly leaves for the Tower. As Edward comments, "He's sudden, if a thing comes in his head."

There follows the dastardly murder of Henry VI by Richard. Nothing can excuse it, but it is the result of the remorseless logic of the power struggle, and Richard is ruthlessly logical. How can one king sit safely on the throne while another is alive? In the frightening soliloquy which follows the deed, Richard describes himself as having "neither pity, love, nor fear," and plans to clear away another obstacle to the throne, his brother, Clarence, but this time he will work by subterfuge:

> Clarence, thy turn is next, and then the rest,
> Counting myself but bad till I be best.

He has introduced this soliloquy with a mordant example of his anti-religious wit. Commenting on the saintly nature of his victim, he says:

> What, will the aspiring blood of Lancaster
> Sink in the ground? I thought it would have mounted.

Another obstacle suddenly appears in Richard's path. The new Queen Elizabeth gives Edward a son, he who was to be so briefly Edward V. Edward IV calls upon his brothers to kiss the new Prince. Richard does so, but can't resist a private comment on his hypocrisy:

> And, that I love the tree from whence thou sprang'st,
> Witness the loving kiss I give the fruit.

> [*Aside*] To say the truth, so Judas kissed his master
> And cried, "All hail!" whenas he meant all harm.

At least the monster never blinks to himself the truth of his own evil.

Richard is the personification of those destructive impulses which are to some extent in all men, and so his natural habitat is the battlefield. In the "weak piping time of peace" this urge expresses itself in murder by violence or plotting. At the beginning of the play which bears his name, he has already laid the snare to catch his brother, Clarence. The famous soliloquy which opens the play contains one phrase that needs comment. He says he plays the villain because his deformity has made it impossible for him to play the lover, and on this and similar statements some critics have concluded that Richard is evil in protest against his birth defects. But this is not so. He accepts his difference and rejoices in the power it has given him. Even as he says, "I cannot prove a lover," he must have tongue in cheek, because he is soon to prove the most consummate wooer in all literature, winning to his bed the widow of a man he has murdered and after she has spat at him over the corpse of her father-in-law whom he has also murdered.

In contemplating the possibility of marriage with Anne, Richard says:

> . . . not all so much for love
> As for another secret close intent
> By marrying her which I must reach unto.

What other "secret close intent" did Richard—and Shakespeare—have in mind? For both there was the challenge of making the wooing credible. What else? Was it the final revenge against the perfidy of Anne's father, Warwick? Did Shakespeare deliberately leave the phrase unexplained because there are depths in Richard's motives that nobody can probe?

The Lady Anne was kin to Richard; her grandfather was Richard's uncle. But the bar of consanguinity was to Richard but another law of man to be broken. After the death of Anne he sought to marry his niece, his brother's daughter.

The aspect of Richard most apparent in *Richard III* is his protean gift; he has the convincing skill of a fine actor and can indeed frame his face to all occasions. The most dazzling display of this gift is the wooing of Anne. It is a challenge for the actors too. I have seen it played in such an ambiguous way by the Richard, who was having a joke with the audience all the time, that the Anne is reduced to an idiot or worse. The truth is that Richard acts with such apparent sincerity and exudes such charm that any woman would find it hard to deny him.

Shakespeare seems to stack the cards against himself. He makes the widowed Anne sole mourner at the funeral procession of the saintly Henry VI, and makes her a spirited denouncer of the murderer:

> More direful hap betide that hated wretch
> That makes us wretched by the death of thee
> Than I can wish to wolves, to spiders, toads,
> Or any creeping venomed thing that lives!
> If ever he have child, abortive be it,
> Prodigious, and untimely brought to light,
> Whose ugly and unnatural aspect
> May fright the hopeful mother at the view;
> And that be heir to his unhappiness.

There is a grim irony in those last lines, for Anne was to bear Richard a son, but he was to die while still a child.

First Richard asserts his natural dominance over men by stopping the cortege and daring the bodyguard to proceed. Anne is naturally moved to a fury of frustrated anger which he counters with a surprising appeal to her for charity:

> Lady, you know no rules of charity,
> Which renders good for bad, blessings for curses.

He quickly follows this with a compliment to her beauty, "divine perfection of a woman," and begs:

> Fairer than tongue can name thee, let me have
> Some patient leisure to excuse myself.

Excuse himself? How? First he says he had not killed her husband, which had the partial truth that all three brothers had stabbed him, and Richard's dagger had not been the first. He admits the murder of Henry VI and relies on his wit for a defense. Henry was a good man more fitted for heaven than this wicked world:

> Let him thank me, that holp to send him thither,
> For he was fitter for that place than earth.

Anne replies with commendable force and wit; Shakespeare has by no means made her an easy conquest. Richard with supreme impudence makes a direct request that she lie with him. Anne is so taken aback that she is almost speechless for a moment and Richard siezes the chance to tell her why he committed the murders:

> Your beauty was the cause of that effect;
> Your beauty, that did haunt me in my sleep
> To undertake the death of all the world
> So I might live one hour in your sweet bosom.

Anne is but further incensed by this astonishing piece of news, and, when he harps on his love for her, she spits in his face. He then subtly reminds her that his family too had been the victim of violence, and her own father had wept in recalling the sad tale of his father's death. But he does this tangentially in saying that no sorrow had ever been able to move him to tears, but her beauty had; at which point he probably called upon the power of which he had boasted in secret, to wet his cheek with artificial tears. Then follows the trick that Mark Antony was to use to the crowd, when, after a thrilling oration, he pleads that he is no orator; so Richard now:

> I never sued to friend nor enemy;
> My tongue could never learn sweet smoothing words;

> But, now thy beauty is proposed my fee,
> My proud heart sues and prompts my tongue to speak.

Anne is moved to listen and not retort; the most she can manage is a scornful look. Richard thinks the moment is ripe for his most audacious move. He offers her his sword to kill him. She makes a hesitating move to do so. Certain that she can't complete the thrust, he urges her to do so, as he confesses the murders, but quickly adds that her beauty was the cause. Anne drops the sword, but makes it clear that she still cannot believe him:

> Arise, dissembler! Though I wish thy death,
> I will not be thy executioner.

But her tone is no longer angry, so he knows it is safe to tell her that he will kill himself at her command, but her command now, not when she was angry. Anne is understandably confused, and she says, "I would I knew thy heart." He presses a ring upon her and begs a favor of her. To her surprise, and as apparent proof of a sincere change of heart, he wants to take her place in the funeral cortege that he, "that hath most cause to be a mourner" of "this noble king," may "wet his grave with my repentant tears." What woman could resist such flattery, that an evil man had been converted to repentance by love of her? She grants his request:

> With all my heart; and much it joys me too,
> To see you are become so penitent.

Left to himself, Richard cynically glories in his triumph:

> Was ever woman in this humour wooed?
> Was ever woman in this humour won?

No; and both he and Shakespeare deserve their triumph; but outrageous as the scene is, it is but a magnification of a frequent happening. Most people have manipulated others by exaggerated protestations, and when their point is gained, they tend to be

somewhat cynical about the weakness in their victims which made
it possible. The chief difference between Richard and lesser dis-
semblers is that his triumph is unadulterated by conscience. Later,
after she has become Richard's unhappy wife, Anne recalls the
strange wooing:

> . . . my woman's heart
> Grossly grew captive to his honey words
> And proved the subject of mine own soul's curse.

Richard maintains the pose of the simple, slandered man in
the atmosphere of uncertainty and scheming for power which
envelops the Court at the sickness and approaching death of
Edward IV:

> Cannot a plain man live and think no harm
> But thus his simple truth must be abused
> With silken, sly, insinuating Jacks?
>
> . . . .
>
> The world is grown so bad
> That wrens make prey where eagles dare not perch.
>
> . . . .
>
> I am too childish-foolish for this world.

The utter impudence of these protestations is beguiling. They
are delivered to the Queen and her relatives who have been favored by the King. In the wrangling scene, Richard has strong
arguments on his side, for he had been steadfastly loyal to Edward
while they had belonged to the opposing faction, but to remind
us of the other truth, Shakespeare uses as an observer of the scene
the widow of Henry VI, who pours down maledictions on Richard. When she makes her presence known she calls down curses
on all her enemies, but with special vehemence upon Richard:

> Thou elvish-marked, abortive, rooting hog!
> Thou that wast sealed in thy nativity
> The slave of nature and the son of hell!

When she leaves, Buckingham says, "My hair doth stand on end
to hear her curses," but Richard, to complete the picture he has

painted during the first part of the scene of a maligned honest man, says:

> . . . By God's holy mother,
> She hath had too much wrong, and I repent
> My part thereof that I have done to her.

Again he is so persuasive that he is believed, which gives him great joy when he is alone:

> And thus I clothe my naked villainy
> With odd old ends stol'n forth of holy writ,
> And seem a saint when most I play the devil.

Richard gains a sufficient modicum of public support to seize the throne as a result of the skillful advocacy of Buckingham, and his own clever portrayal of unwillingness, but once he has gained the crown a change takes place. The joy of evil disappears and remorse begins to take its place. He even begins to sound like Macbeth for he says:

> . . . But I am in
> So far in blood that sin will pluck on sin.

Shakespeare has subtly prepared us for this change by a phrase of Anne's in the previous scene; she says:

> For never yet one hour in his bed
> Did I enjoy the golden dew of sleep,
> But with his timorous dreams was still awaked.

The Richard we have known has given no hint that he would have suffered from "timorous dreams."

There is only a slight trace of the old wit when he takes stock privately after the murder of Edward IV's two sons:

> The son of Clarence have I pent up close;
> His daughter meanly have I matched in marriage;
> The sons of Edward sleep in Abraham's bosom,
> And Anne my wife hath bid this world good night.
> Now, for I know the Breton Richmond aims
> At young Elizabeth, my brother's daughter,

> And by that knot looks proudly on the crown,
> To her go I, a jolly thriving wooer.

Richard attempts to woo the young Elizabeth through her mother, Queen Elizabeth, whose sons and brother he has murdered. It is a situation comparable with the audacious wooing of Anne, but oh! the difference. He has a powerful argument, the future peace of the realm, but his brilliant persuasiveness has gone; the fun of the game has gone. Only in his comment after she leaves, apparently to win her daughter to his will, do we hear a faint echo of the old Richard: "Relenting fool, and shallow changing woman!" But he was wrong; the Queen had gone to arrange the marriage of her daughter to Richard's enemy and nemesis, the Duke of Richmond. In his prior encounter with the three cursing women, Queen Margaret, Queen Elizabeth and his own mother, Richard had been reduced to calling on the trumpets to drown their clamor.

This is an unsure, unhappy and distracted Richard. He tells Catesby to hurry to the Duke of Norfolk, and is angry to find him still there a moment later, waiting for the message he has omitted to give; and on another matter he reverses himself within a minute to Ratcliff. On the eve of the climactic battle with Richmond he notes the change in himself:

> I have not that alacrity of spirit
> Nor cheer of mind that I was wont to have.

Remorse is desirable in the villain but it makes him a sad companion. It reduces his stature to that of more ordinary men.

The ghosts of eleven of Richard's victims come to trouble his dreams and encourage those of Richmond, and, when he wakes, Richard makes a last unavailing attempt to recover his former jaunty self-confidence:

> O coward conscience, how dost thou afflict me!
> . . . .
> What! do I fear myself? There's none else by.
> Richard loves Richard; that is, I am I.

Is there a murderer here? No. Yes, I am.
Then fly. What, from myself? Great reason why,
Lest I revenge. What, myself upon myself?
Alack, I love myself. Wherefore? For any good
That I myself have done unto myself?
O, no! alas, I rather hate myself
For hateful deeds committed by myself!
I am a villain: yet I lie, I am not.
Fool, of thyself speak well; fool, do not flatter.

"Alack, I love myself." His good opinion of his villainous self had been the source of his zestful enjoyment, but now it is soured by guilt into an "Alack."

In the end, Richard is true to his original self. Richmond, in his oration to the troops before the battle, calls upon God and St. George, and Richard might have been expected to put on a final mask of piety to do likewise, but he does not mention God at all, and St. George only to invoke the spirit of St. George's enemies:

Our ancient word of courage, fair Saint George,
Inspire us with the spleen of fiery dragons!

Richard's superior forces are routed because most of them desert to Richmond in the midst of battle:

He hath no friends but what are friends from fear,
Which in his dearest need will fly from him.

But Richard himself fights like a man possessed, as indeed he is:

The King enacts more wonders than a man,
Daring an opposite to every danger.

When he is advised to flee, he says:

. . . I have set my life upon a cast
And I will stand the hazard of the die.

Like Macbeth, cornered and deserted, he dies with harness on his back.

It is the gleeful wickedness in us that responds to Richard, though we condemn him and our response at the same time, and, when his remorse sets in, we are shamefully unhappy about it. He is man, wicked man in excelsis, a sort of awesome sublimation of the destructive urges in all of us, but his enjoyment of evil is destroyed by one of the seeds of goodness in all of us, remorse. His story is a reversal of that of Adam, for Richard is blissfully happy in a Garden of Evil until he is banished by guilt. But Adam is an abstraction that speaks to our thought, while Richard is a man who speaks to that sum of contradictions in all of us which constitutes a human being.

PART II

INTRODUCTION TO

THE *Comedies*

O F T H E thirty-seven plays now found in a volume of Shakespeare, seventeen are usually labeled "Comedies," but this can be
a very misleading label for anyone approaching the plays with a
preconception of a comedy as something mildly amusing at its
most genteel or downright hilarious at its most robust. When
Shakespeare uses the word "comedian," he does not mean "funny-
man;" he means "player" and so "comedy" means "play." Two
of the plays now called comedies have these titles in the First
Folio: *The Tragedie of Troylus and Cressida* and *The Tragedie
of Cymbeline*. When a play like *Measure for Measure*, that dark
masterpiece about sexual passion and morality, is made to wear
upon the stage the straitjacket of "comedy," in its modern sense,
it is brutally misshapen, and I have seen an important production
in which this happened.

Nor is it only in the bitter comedies that we find elements
that are sombre and heavy-hearted. The whole first scene of *The
Comedy of Errors*, which for the most part is a knock-about
farce, reads almost like the beginning of a dire tragedy and ends
with the couplet:

> Hopeless and helpless doth Aegeon wend,
> But to procrastinate his lifeless end.

Lysander's description of the hazards of "true love" in *A Midsummer-Night's Dream* might seem more at home in *The Tragedy of Romeo and Juliet*.

> War, death, or sickness did lay siege to it,
> Making it momentary as a sound,
> Swift as a shadow, short as any dream,
> Brief as the lightning in the collied night,
> That in a spleen unfolds both heaven and earth,
> And ere a man hath power to say "Behold!"
> The jaws of darkness do devour it up:
> So quick bright things come to confusion.

The reverse kind of apparently misfitting elements are found in the Tragedies, where they are excused as "comic relief," but to a classicist, like Voltaire for instance, they are equally inexcusable. The fundamental truth is that Shakespeare's plays do not fit academic formulae, any more than life does. His theatrical roots are deep in his native medieval soil rather than in the foreign soil of Greek classicism. His lack of sense of strict form, or perhaps we should say of "good form," derives directly from the tradition of the English mystery and miracle plays, a genuine folk growth, in which solemn religious scenes were interspersed with scenes of farcical and earthy clowning. It is a still vital tradition, both in the legitimate theatre and the music-hall. Sean O'Casey's plays, like Shakespeare's, are essentially a tapestry of tears and laughter, awe and ridicule. And in the music-hall, Gracie Fields could sing "The Biggest Aspidistra in the World" and then "The Lord's Prayer" with no sense of incongruity, in much the same way that Shakespeare follows the murder of Duncan in *Macbeth* with the comic Porter scene, or the death of Antigonus in *The Winter's Tale* with the scene of the Shepherd and the Clown. The amalgam of grave and gay is peculiarly fitted to express Shakespeare's warm and tolerant view of human sorrow and folly, which cannot be bound by the strict classical unities. On the other hand, Ben

Jonson's comedies, which are classical, are equally expressive of his critical intelligence. Speaking very generally, Shakespeare looks at human absurdities and smiles, while Jonson looks at them and frowns.

Every scene in a Shakespearean play must be looked at for its own value; it must be approached with an open and receptive mind, and not prejudged to fit some formula. Of course, the whole play has an overall atmosphere and feeling and purpose, and nothing attests to Shakespeare's genius more than his dexterity in weaving together apparently diverse strands: the courtiers, the fairies, the "rude mechanicals" in *A Midsummer-Night's Dream* are a particularly brilliant instance of this. A director who stages a play of Shakespeare must have a unifying conception of the meaning and significance of the whole, but must beware of distorting for the sake of "comedy" a scene which is not intended to be funny; very often the feeling to be derived from a scene of "high comedy" is one of exquisite pathos. If "high comedy" were always funny there would be no need for "low comedy" to relieve it. A director's overall point of view about a play must be derived from the total text; he must not distort or even excise parts of the play to make it fit an arbitrary attitude. What sins are committed in the name of making Shakespeare relevant to our times! The simple fact is that though he belonged deeply to his own time, he also transcended it and thus became relevant to all times. A good guide for a director is to have Shakespeare's own faith in the story and to tell it as truly as possible. In the case of a production of *Much Ado About Nothing*, for instance, one test of its success, I feel, is the effect upon the audience of Beatrice's request to Benedick that he "Kill Claudio." In the best production I ever saw of this play—Sir John Gielgud's in London —the effect was electrifying in its surprise and seriousness; for some reason the moment was considerably diminished when I saw the Gielgud production on Broadway. In another American production I saw of the play, a misguided attempt had been made to broaden the high comedy so that the "Kill Claudio" incident became an embarrassment to actors and audience alike. When Shakespeare's plays are acted truthfully, it will be found, as in the best of Sean O'Casey's plays, that the tragic, the pathetic, the wistful, the fanciful, the ironic, the comic, the farcical, all reinforce one another, and hold the mirror up to the complexities of nature.

Not only do Shakespeare's comedies contain very varied elements, but considered as a body of work they are extraordinarily diverse. Written over a period of approximately twenty years, and a twenty years during which England and the theatre underwent profound changes, they run the gamut from bright sunlight to stormy darkness, from optimism to disillusionment, from boisterous fooling to delicate sentiment, from brilliant wit to bawdy back-chat. And, of course, Shakespeare's technical development was extraordinary, as, for instance, in his command of blank verse; one has only to compare the jog-trot of the iambic pentameters in the opening of *The Comedy of Errors*, probably his first comedy, to their smooth fluidity in Miranda's first speech in *The Tempest*, his last comedy, to see the difference between the apprentice and the master.

Shakespeare's first three comedies are amazingly different; already the playwright seems capable of anything. In trying to find his own métier, he wrote three different kinds of comedy, and all with astonishing skill and success. Following the fashion of the day, he began with a farce derived from the Latin and based upon the mistaken identities of long separated twins, which he complicated by giving them as servants another pair of long separated twins; this was well named *The Comedy of Errors*. Clearly he found it an uncongenial world, for never again did he go to Plautus and Terence for a plot. Then he seemed deliberately to challenge the university wits at their scintillating game of wordplay and affectation, in that feast of exuberant language and high spirits, *Love's Labour's Lost*. Shakespeare had and gave great fun in the play with

> Taffeta phrases, silken terms precise,
> Three-piled hyperboles,

and, even though his object may have been a warm-hearted satire, he found much to enjoy and cherish in the exercise, and echoes of the play and its characters were to linger in other plays for a long time. But it was in the third of his apprentice comedies, *The Two Gentlemen of Verona*, that Shakespeare found his richest vein. Immature though it is, it is one with the three great romantic comedies of his glorious noonday in atmosphere, source, story, setting, and characters: *Much Ado About Nothing*, *As You Like It*, and *Twelfth Night*. Roughly eight fecund years separate the promise of *The Two Gentlemen of Verona* from its fulfillment in *Twelfth Night*, and in those years, in addition to six histories and two tragedies, Shakespeare had written four other comedies of astounding diversity: that flawless jewel, *A Midsummer-Night's Dream;* that disturbing play, *The Merchant of Venice*, which changed times and altered values have made difficult of total acceptance in its original terms; that high-spirited, rough-and-tumble battle of the sexes, *The Taming of the Shrew;* and that strictly domestic and bourgeois comedy, the only one Shakespeare ever wrote, *The Merry Wives of Windsor*.

In his late thirties, and in the new century when James I, "the wisest fool in Christendom," succeeded the great Elizabeth, the mood of the times changed, and with it that of Shakespeare. Many writers have speculated on the causes of this "black period" in Shakespeare's life. It may have been that some sadness in his personal life coincided with the feeling of disillusionment that almost inevitably follows a great age, but, whatever the cause, we should be grateful for it, because out of it came four great tragedies, *Hamlet, Othello, King Lear* and *Macbeth*, and three bitter comedies, all seven plays being written within a period of four or five years, and Shakespeare's coverage of the human experience is immeasurably widened and deepened. The first of the three bitter comedies is *Troilus and Cressida*, a brilliant and searing examination of the romantic values of love and war, which has found little acceptance in the theatre down the centuries. Indeed, it is probable that it was too strong meat even for Shakespeare's audience, and may never have been performed during his lifetime. There were some performances during the eighteenth century, but of a version by John Dryden, who sugar-coated the pill by making Cressida remain faithful to Troilus. It would seem that the spirit of the play would find ready acceptance in our own faithless times, and indeed it has received some noteworthy productions since World War I shattered the last chivalric notions of war, but the play still awaits the public and critical acclaim it so richly deserves. The second of the bitter comedies is *All's Well That Ends Well*, which again upset a romantic convention, for in it a wonderful woman pursues a worthless man. Bernard Shaw had a particular fondness for this play because he saw its heroine, Helena, as Shavian, not only because she was the hunter and not the hunted, but because she foreshadowed the modern woman in that she possessed professional skill in medicine! The third of the bitter comedies, *Measure for Measure*, to which I shall return in the chapter which considers Angelo, is an unsparing and profound study of a lustful puritan.

Pericles did not find acceptance in the Shakespearean canon until 1664, a fitting celebration of the first centenary of his birth. In that year a Third Folio was published which contained seven plays attributed to Shakespeare in addition to the thirty-six contained in the First Folio. Of the seven, *Pericles* alone has gained general acceptance as being indeed, at least for the most part, the authentic work of Shakespeare. It is a bridge between the bitter comedies and the last three, which were to close Shakespeare's career, and which were to be of yet another kind.

At the end of his professional career, as at the beginning, Shakespeare followed a theatrical fashion set by others, and became the supreme master of it. In his last three comedies there is no tiring of his genius, but instead a surprising and extraordinary will to experiment. He used the new kind of play, the dramatic romance, made popular by John Fletcher principally, to express his ultimate and mature view of man. These three plays contain the elements of tragedy, which in lesser hands of the period degenerate into crude melodrama—treachery, suffering, death—but the resolution in all three of them is calm and peaceful. To parody the title that could serve as a generic one for Shakespeare's happy comedies, these might be called *Much Ado About Much*. Two of the titles indicate the harsh and stormy components of the plot—*The Winter's Tale* and *The Tempest*—and it has already been noted that *Cymbeline* made its first appearance in print as a "Tragedie." The resolutions of the plots seem even to echo one another. Thus in *Cymbeline* we hear:

> The power that I have cn you is to spare you,
> The malice towards you to forgive you.

This is the same note as Prospero's in *The Tempest:* "The rarer action is in virtue than in vengeance."

While it is true that every play script, whatever abiding literary value it may have, was originally a blueprint for a production in a theatre, relying upon actors to bring it to its intended life, it is particularly true of those parts which Shakespeare wrote for the clowns and fools, and those rare beings are not quite the same as actors. A natural clown has an indefinable quality which causes us to laugh; even when he suffers we laugh. Shakespeare's company contained some great clowns, and he wrote some parts to fit their particular qualities. While William Kemp was in the company we get the lovable oafs like Bottom and Dogberry; when Robert Armin succeeded him we get the quick-witted fools like Touchstone and Feste. Clearly these players were eagerly awaited "acts" in themselves, and Hamlet's critical comment undoubtedly came from Shakespeare's own unhappy experience:

> And let those that play your clowns speak no more than is
> set down for them; for there be of them that will themselves
> laugh to set on some quantity of barren spectators to laugh

too, though in the mean time some necessary question of the
play be then to be considered. That's villainous, and shows
a most pitiful ambition in the Fool that uses it.

It is useful to maintain a distinction between clowns like
Kemp, who largely relied on physical characterization and bum-
bling ineptness, and fools like Armin, whose stock-in-trade was
verbal wit and irrepressible vitality; it is this latter kind of comic
that Hamlet is most objecting to, the kind who laughs more at
his own jokes than anybody else does; television abounds in them.

It has been well said that comedy derives from three sources:
situation, witty dialogue, and character, and undoubtedly the
greatest of these is character. Situation is contrived, wit is artful,
but character is universal; and both situation and wit are at their
best when they flow naturally from characters, as they do most
transcendently in the case of Falstaff. One of the basic reasons
for the diminished impact of the Falstaff of *The Merry Wives of
Windsor* is that he is trapped in contrived situations.

The physical form of the Elizabethan playhouse was well
adapted to the much-used comedy situation of unobserved observers. While the main action took place on the open stage, spies
could look on and comment from the balcony or the backstage;
it is very difficult to make this sufficiently credible in a proscenium
theatre. The example of this kind of scene that springs to mind
is the gulling of Malvolio in the garden, but the device is used
plentifully throughout the Comedies.

One of the problems of Shakespeare's comedies is the salty
wit that has lost its savor. The Elizabethans delighted in the verbal
fun of cross-talk. It derives directly from the exchanges of the
Devil and his Vice in the old morality plays, and was well preserved in the music-hall, and it has recently been given a new
lease on life in television series depending upon a pair of cross-
talkers. But there are elements in wit that do not wear well. Very
often it depends upon a reference to a contemporary event, and
when the event is forgotten the clever remark becomes an im-
penetrable riddle. Then there are fashions in wit. Nowadays, for

instance, it is fashionable to groan at puns, but Shakespeare's audience delighted in them; and even now, if the pun is outrageous and clever enough, the groan it provokes is a cover for admiration of the perpetrator's verbal dexterity. Here it should be pointed out that there are certain comic passages in Shakespeare which have lost their Elizabethan nuances but which can still raise legitimate laughter; for instance, this exchange in *Twelfth Night* between Sir Toby and Sir Andrew:

> SIR ANDREW: I would I had bestowed that time in the tongues that I have in fencing, dancing, and bear-baiting. O, had I but followed the arts!
> SIR TOBY: Then hadst thou had an excellent head of hair.
> SIR ANDREW: Why, would that have mended my hair?
> SIR TOBY: Past question, for thou seest it will not curl by nature.

Here the joke for the Elizabethans lay in the fact that "tongues" was pronounced "tongs," (*i.e. curling irons*). We know the Shakespearean pronunciation because, for instance, in Sonnet XVII "tongue" is rhymed with "song" and in Sonnet LXXXIX with "wrong." But even without the value of this original pun, the passage rarely fails to make a modern audience laugh; the character of Sir Andrew is enough, combined with his hair, which "hangs like flax on a distaff."

On the other hand, such a scene as the first one between Speed and Proteus in *The Two Gentlemen of Verona* tends to make hard going today, for it depends on the facts that in Elizabethan England "sheep" was pronounced "ship" and "mutton" was a euphemism for whore.

The exact sources of the plots of Shakespeare's comedies are not always known and the resulting riddles have provoked many scholarly and intriguing suggestions; for instance, could Shakespeare read Italian? The story of the basic plot of *Much Ado About Nothing* is nearest to an Italian original of Bandello which at that time had not been translated into English. Some possible answers to the riddle are: (1) Shakespeare read enough Italian to get the gist of the story, and that was certainly all he took from it; his basic grounding in Latin would soon have given him the necessary skimming knowledge of Italian. (2) Somebody who had read the story in Italian told it to Shakespeare; he could have done so in a couple of sentences to give the playwright all he used. (3) There was another adaptation of the story into English, which has since been lost. The glories of the play, Beatrice-Benedick and Dogberry-Verges, are entirely Shakespeare's own. There is no source for the Comedies to the extent that Holinshed was for the Histories. There were direct translations of stories from Italian and French, new versions of the same stories by contemporary English writers, both in prose and verse, original romantic tales by Elizabethan authors, and the common heritage of English literature dating from Chaucer. But what matters is Shakespeare's use of the material, and the only really useful object in studying his source material is to note the changes he made in his use of it, for this is frequently a revealing guide to his purpose in the play. Often Shakespeare brilliantly interweaves several stories from various sources into one play; thus in a *Midsummer-Night's Dream* he took a hint from Chaucer for the Theseus-Hippolyta strand; the Pyramus-Thisbe strand from Ovid, probably in a 1567 translation by Arthur Golding; the lovers' complications possibly from his own *Two Gentlemen of Verona;* as for Puck and the fairies, to assign a particular source for them would be like saying that Bernard Shaw's source for *Pygmalion* was Perrault's seventeenth-century tale of Cinderella, which was in turn derived by various stages through various languages from a Chinese tale of the ninth century. Shakespeare's audience liked to be told stories full of color and action, and to be told three or four for the price of one was so much the better.

All Shakespeare's comedies deal with love, and in almost all of them the more wonderful being in the pair of lovers is the woman, but they are never idealized to the point of abstraction; they are all credible human beings in their complexities, and though they share a capacity for wholehearted love, they differ in all else. It is hard to believe that these consummate revelations of the feminine were originally played by boys; this, of course, accounts for the facts that there are no scenes of explicit passion in any of the plays and that the female character is often called upon to disguise herself as a man or a boy, which I'm sure was a great relief to the young actors. In the modern theatre the strain on credibility is reversed, especially when some well endowed actress masquerades as a boy, but the advantages of having Shakespeare's women played by women are enormous, and sometimes the advantage is subtle. Thus, for instance, since so many of the plots are complicated tangles of love which at the end have to be quickly untangled, somewhat arbitrarily on occasion, and retied as marriage knots so that

> Jack shall have Jill;
> Nought shall go ill;
> The man shall have his mare again and
>   all shall be well,

it is a great aid to belief to know that the female character disguised as a boy is in fact a woman; subconsciously we can approve of Orsino's attraction to Cesario and their ultimate mating, not because Cesario is really a female character called Viola, but because in our theatre she is actually a woman.

The disguise convention is only one of many incredibilities involved in the plots of the Comedies. How can such absurd stories hold the mirror up to nature? How can they tell us about ourselves? Because the motives that impel the characters are real and true. Viola and Helena reveal the torment of forbidden love, whatever the obstacle be; the ridiculous gambit of the pound of flesh does not impair the reality of Shylock; the fairy-tale quality of the coming to life of Hermione does not dull the wonder of forgiveness and reconciliation. And, as throughout this book, it is the revelations of humanity we are concerned with, and which we shall discuss in the following chapters.

8 # Portia

It MAY SEEM strange that, with seventeen plays to choose from and an arbitrary limit of seven subjects, two chapters should be devoted to characters from one play, *The Merchant of Venice*. Shylock could not be omitted, but why Portia? Why not Rosalind or Beatrice or Viola or Isabella or Helena or the wondrous and neglected Imogen? Because Portia urgently demands restitution to her central position in the play from which she has been displaced by Shylock.

What is *The Merchant of Venice* about? Of no play is it more important to have an overall conception of Shakespeare's purpose, and in no play is it easier to get it wrong, particularly when considerations of anti-Semitism intrude. The title, I think, gives the essential clue; it belongs not to Shylock, as some people misguidedly assume, but to Antonio, yet he appears but briefly in five scenes. (Shylock appears in five, Bassanio in six, and Portia in nine. For those who are interested, the approximate apportionment of their lines is as follows: Portia, 590; Shylock, 370; Bassanio, 330; Antonio 180.) It is clear from the dialogue in the Trial scene that Antonio is the merchant of the title, and, to reinforce this, the first Quarto of the play bears this description: "The most excellent Historie of the Merchant of Venice. With the extreme crueltie of Shylocke the Jewe towards the sayd Merchant, in cutting a just pound of his flesh, and the obtaining of Portia by the choyse of three chests." Why, then, is a relatively minor character given the title role? Because, I believe, he is Shakespeare's ideal hero in the play.

In *The Merchant of Venice* Shakespeare is examining the values people place on money. From this point of view, Shylock is a man obsessed by love of it, Portia is a wealthy lady who gladly gives her possessions away for love, Bassanio is a blatant fortune-hunter who is rescued by love from his pecuniary ambitions, and Antonio is a wealthy man to whom his wealth means nothing. In the value he places upon money, Antonio is the antithesis of Shylock, and it is in this context that they become respectively the hero and the villain of the play.

Antonio opens the play as a textbook melancholic, and Salarino and Salanio immediately assume, as most people would, that he is worried about his shipping enterprises, but Antonio is suffering from an unaccountable malaise of the soul. Dramatically this is necessary because it makes more credible his readiness to sacrifice his life for his friend. In this, too, he enshrines a Renaissance ideal, which placed a higher value upon male friendship than on sexual love. After all, sexual love springs from a physical necessity, whereas normal male friendship doesn't. A recent tendency to ascribe Antonio's sadness to a frustrated homosexual love for Bassanio betrays a complete ignorance of Renaissance thought, and debases the significance of Shakespeare's hero.

To begin with, Portia is very wealthy. The first thing Bassanio says about her is that she is rich. He adds that she is both beautiful and good, but there is no doubt about which of her attributes is the most important to him initially. To win her fortune is a business gamble for which he seeks a capital loan; his own pocket is always empty because he confesses to living a life beyond his slender means. The wealth of Portia is so great that even princes, rich in their own right, come to seek her hand in marriage. At this point in the play Bassanio seems neither a likely nor desirable winner, and yet, from a previous visit, he senses that Portia found him attractive:

> . . . Sometimes from her eyes
> I did receive fair speechless messages.

It is surely significant that Portia's first line in the play links her in spirit with Antonio: "By my troth, Nerissa, my little body is aweary of this great world." Having everything, she has nothing, for material possessions are not enough. Nerissa, the practical, passes the world's judgment on her mood: time for you to grumble, lady, "if your miseries were in the same abundance as your good fortunes are." But, unlike Antonio, Portia knows the root cause of her depression; she wants to get married but is bound in her choice by her father's will, which imposes on her would-be husbands the casket test; and indeed, in spite of its fairy-tale quality, it has a considerable logic, certainly, in my opinion, not less than that contained in some of today's much vaunted intelligence tests. Her father knew that Portia's wealth would be much sought after, and so, to protect her from irresponsible men, he established the prior condition that all suitors who chose to undergo the test must first vow never to marry if they chose the wrong casket; the three caskets of gold, silver, and lead, with their challenging inscriptions, are a real test of one's values. They are still questions against which man can measure his ambition:

(1) "Who chooseth me shall gain what many men desire."
(2) "Who chooseth me shall get as much as he deserves."
(3) "Who chooseth me must give and hazard all he hath."

Nerissa, the perfect companion, knows how to jockey Portia out of her doldrums; it is to prompt her to exercise her brilliant and lethal wit, to which Nerissa will play the "straight man." In the light of what is to happen, it is very important to establish that Portia is not a sentimental romantic. No one in the whole Shakespeare gallery has a quicker insight into the comedy of human frailty or a sharper wit in depicting it. Nerissa mentions six suitors and asks Portia to pass judgment upon them. They are wide-ranging, having come from Italy, Germany, France, England, and Scotland, which enables Portia (and Shakespeare) to have fun about some national characteristics too. Portia's wit is not of the kind of which Queen Victoria would have approved, though it would have delighted Queen Elizabeth I. She says of the Neapolitan Prince, ". . . he doth nothing but talk of his horse, and he makes it a great appropriation to his own good parts that he can shoe him himself;" and then she adds, "I am much afeard my lady his mother played false with a smith." The County Palatine "doth nothing but frown" (Oh! those German philosophers!); the French lord is so volatile that "he is every man in no man;" Baron Falconbridge of England is handsome but he can speak no language but English, and, as if to compensate for that, imitates continental fashions and manners (verbum sapienti Americano, and, still more, Americanae). Here is her full reply to Nerissa's question as to how she liked the Duke of Saxony's nephew:

> Very vilely in the morning, when he is sober, and most vilely in the afternoon, when he is drunk. When he is best, he is a little worse than a man, and when he is worst, he is little better than a beast. An the worst fall that ever fell, I hope I shall make shift to go without him. . . . Therefore, for fear of the worst, I pray thee set a deep glass of Rhenish wine on the contrary casket, for if the Devil be within and that temptation without, I know he will choose it. I will do anything, Nerissa, ere I'll be married to a sponge.

It should be noted that both women know the right casket, as they must by this time from a process of elimination. Portia sums up the present batch of suitors with "there is not one among them but I dote on his very absence, and I pray God grant them a fair departure." Nerissa then impishly mentions Bassanio; she had obviously noted Portia's previous reaction to him. We learn that he had not himself been a suitor on that occasion, but had just come in the entourage of another noble suitor, the Marquis of Montferrat. Nerissa describes Bassanio as "a scholar and a soldier." As to the first of those appellations, it is noted that an early speech of Bassanio contains two elementary Greek and Roman references, but it is to be hoped that it also implies a lively intelligence, not always a concomitant of simple scholarship, for Portia's corruscating wit will take some living with.

Portia is not compounded of saintly virtues; for instance, where a husband is concerned, she is color-prejudiced. The Prince of Morocco expects to find her so, for he begins his suit with "Mislike me not for my complexion," and in the courtesy of fair speech she says:

> Yourself, renowned Prince, then stood as fair
> As any comer I have looked on yet
> For my affection;

but when he makes the wrong choice and makes his dignified exit with the words:

> Portia, adieu. I have too grieved a heart
> To take a tedious leave. Thus losers part,

she says the truth which lay beneath her courteous mask:

> A gentle riddance. Draw the curtains, go.
> Let all of his complexion choose me so.

When we first see Portia and Bassanio together, he is ready to undergo the test of the caskets, and already the fortune-hunter has been displaced by the lover. To me it is a weakness of the play that we have no scene in which we might see the transformation being accomplished. We are given some hint of what that scene would have contained because we learn that Bassanio had been honest enough to declare that his show of wealth was a sham; the mere fortune-hunter would have been careful to maintain the fiction until the marriage contract was safe, but, when he receives the news of Antonio's peril, Bassanio says:

. . . Gentle lady,
When I did first impart my love to you,
I freely told you all the wealth I had
Ran in my veins, I was a gentleman,
And then I told you true. And yet, dear lady,
Rating myself at nothing, you shall see
How much I was a braggart. When I told you
My state was nothing, I should then have told you
That I was worse than nothing; for, indeed,
I have engaged myself to a dear friend,
Engaged my friend to his mere enemy,
To feed my means. . . .

In the casket scene there is the most subtle graduation in Portia from the wit of sophistication to the simplicity of love. She immediately acknowledges her love, and is therefore reluctant to let Bassanio submit himself to the hazard of the test, but there is a teasing quality in her reasoning:

There's something tells me, but it is not love,
I would not lose you, and you know yourself,
Hate counsels not in such a quality.

She is unequivocal in her determination not to guide his choice:

. . . I could teach you
How to choose right, but then I am forsworn.
So will I never be; so may you miss me;
But if you do, you'll make me wish a sin,
That I had been forsworn. . . .

There have been productions of the play in which Bassanio's choice of the leaden casket is guided by an attention-getting emphasis on the rhyme in the first three lines of the song, "Tell me where is fancy bred." This is a gross degrading of Portia's character and a total distortion of what I take to be the significance of Bassanio's choice; in choosing

. . . meager lead,
Which rather threatenest than dost promise aught,

he comes as near as he can, without open and embarrassing confession, to saying that the fortune-hunter has given way to the lover.

Portia retains an occasional teasing tone as long as she can. As soon as he says that the delay she has urged puts him on the rack, she plays with the word:

> Upon the rack, Bassanio! Then confess
> What treason there is mingled with your love.

And again:

> Aye, but I fear you speak upon the rack,
> Where men enforced do speak anything.

But when the inevitable moment of decision comes, there is no banter in her words:

> Live thou, I live. With much much more dismay
> I view the fight than thou that makest the fray.

Although Portia will not guide his choice, she has previously dared to suggest that, if he makes the wrong choice, she may ignore the result, and so dare Hell for broken faith and filial disobedience. The lines in which she hints at this are complicated, as becomes the state of mind that prompts them:

> One half of me is yours, the other half yours,
> Mine own, I would say, but if mine, then yours,
> And so all yours. O, these naughty times
> Puts bars between the owners and their rights!
> And so, though yours, not yours. Prove it so,
> Let fortune go to hell for it, not I.

To paraphrase those last few lines: I am yours by my will, but may be barred from becoming legally yours by your failing the test of the caskets; but if you do, let the test go to hell, not I; the implication being that she will ignore the result and thus merit the punishment of Hell. This is a much more admirable frame of mind than if she stooped to cheating by guiding Bassanio's choice.

Once the choice is correctly made, what a change comes over Portia! She speaks with moving simplicity that poignantly reveals the inexperienced virgin in the sophisticated woman. The brilliantly satirical observer of her numerous suitors is now moved to say:

> . . . But the full sum of me
> Is sum of nothing; which, to term in gross,
> Is an unlessoned girl, unschooled, unpractised;
> Happy in this, she is not yet so old
> But she may learn; happier than this,
> She is not bred so dull but she can learn;
> Happiest of all is that her gentle spirit
> Commits itself to yours to be directed,
> As from her lord, her governor, her king.

But there is even more significance in this beautiful speech than Portia's self-revelation. A woman of such perspicacity as she revealed in her first scene could not have been blind to the initial fortune-hunting motive of Bassanio. She knows too, by his choice of the leaden casket, that he has tried to disavow his original mercenary impulse, and, with heart-warming subtlety, she proves to him that she has no reservation about the quality of his love by reminding him that as part of the normal marriage settlement she will be giving him everything:

> Myself and what is mine to you and yours
> Is now converted. But now I was the lord
> Of this fair mansion, master of my servants,
> Queen o'er myself, and even now, but now,
> This house, these servants, and this same myself
> Are yours, my lord. . . .

And for him she wishes she were "ten thousand times more rich." Portia finishes the declaration of her love with a charming return to her playful teasing, for she gives him the betrothal ring with the warning that, if he parts with it for any reason, she will take it as a sign that he no longer loves her, and she will seize the opportunity to tell him off.

When the news comes of Antonio's dire straits, Bassanio describes him in these words:

> The dearest friend to me, the kindest man,
> The best-conditioned and unwearied spirit
> In doing courtesies, and one in whom
> The ancient Roman honour more appears
> Than any that draws breath in Italy.

Portia immediately assumes that money will solve the problem:

> . . . You shall have gold
> To pay the petty debt twenty times over;

but she does more than that. Seeing Bassanio's deep concern, she says that they will be married immediately but will postpone their nuptial night,

> For never shall you lie by Portia's side
> With an unquiet soul. . . .

There is no hint of jealousy in Portia's attitude to Antonio. Lorenzo says to her:

> You have a noble and a true conceit
> Of godlike amity, which appears most strongly
> In bearing thus the absence of your lord;

that is, she has a correct opinion of the classical idea of male friendship. Her answer is that Antonio must be like Bassanio, so in helping the friend she is helping her husband:

> I never did repent for doing good,
> Nor shall not now. For in companions
> That do converse and waste the time together,
> Whose souls do bear an equal yoke of love,
> There must be needs a like proportion
> Of lineaments, of manners, and of spirit;
> Which makes me think that this Antonio,
> Being the bosom lover of my lord,
> Must needs be like my lord. If it be so,
> How little is the cost I have bestowed

> In purchasing the semblance of my soul
> From out the state of hellish misery!

In such a mood it is easy for her to make convincing her lie that she will spend the time until Bassanio returns in prayer and contemplation at a nearby monastery. How far this is from her real mood is quickly evident in the spirited playfulness with which she discloses to Nerissa the plan to go to Venice in disguise. She even catches the opportunity for a dirty joke:

> NERISSA: Why, shall we turn to men?
> PORTIA: Fie, what a question's that,
>   If thou wert near a lewd interpreter!

And so we come to the famous Trial scene, and to the essential question about Portia. Was she just playing with Shylock, as a cat with a mouse, before she pounced to destroy him? In order to avoid this conclusion, some productions have shown Portia as receiving a brilliant flash of illumination about the law just in time to save Antonio's life. This last-minute rescue is a stock device of the crudest melodramas and reduces the stature of the scene; and what is more, it misses the whole point of the play. Portia had her trump card before she arrived at the Court; it was contained in the notes she received from Doctor Bellario. Then why does she not play it immediately and save Antonio and thus relieve her husband's agony? Because she must first try to save the soul of Shylock, to exorcize the demon which inhabits his body. Before her arrival, the Duke has pleaded with Shylock to show mercy on general humanitarian grounds, but Portia's plea is very different; it is that mercy benefits the giver as much as the receiver, and it is the benefit to Shylock, the giver, she is concerned with, since she knows that Antonio can be saved by a legal technicality. She warns Shylock of the danger of using the law as a cover for malicious intent:

> Though justice be thy plea, consider this:
> That in the course of justice none of us
> Should see salvation. . . .

Though this is generally received in its religious implications, it has a specific relevance to what happens in the trial, which seems to illustrate a profound truth: He that lives by the letter of the law shall perish by the letter of the law. The relation between ethics and legality is an abiding problem, which is memorably stated in a dialogue between Bassanio and Portia. Bassanio puts the humane point of view:

> . . . I beseech you
> Wrest once the law to your authority.
> To do a great right, do a little wrong.

But Portia defends the inviolability of the law:

> It must not be. There is no power in Venice
> Can alter a decree established.
> 'Twill be recorded for a precedent,
> And many an error, by the same example,
> Will rush into the state. It cannot be.

For his own sake, Portia presses Shylock for some show of mercy as long as she can. After he has rejected her major plea, she later bids him:

> . . . Be merciful;
> Take thrice thy money; bid me tear the bond.

And later still, in a last plea for some sign of saving grace, she says:

> Have by some surgeon, Shylock, on your charge,
> To stop his wounds, lest he do bleed to death.

Here it is Shylock's life that is in danger, because, if he refuses the request, as he does, it is obvious that his intent is murderous,

> And the offender's life lies in the mercy
> Of the Duke only, 'gainst all other voice.

As we have previously seen, Portia's wit and playfulness never desert her, even in her most serious moments, nor do they now. As, in disguise, she hears her husband say to Antonio:

> Antonio, I am married to a wife
> Which is as dear to me as life itself;
> But life itself, my wife, and all the world,
> Are not with me esteemed above thy life.
> I would lose all, aye, sacrifice them all
> Here to this devil, to deliver you,

she cannot refrain from commenting:

> Your wife would give you little thanks for that,
> If she were by, to hear you make the offer.

Once Shylock has himself been trapped by the letter of the law, Portia with complete consistency calls upon the Duke and Antonio to show mercy, and they both do. Shylock is subject to the penalty of death and the confiscation of all his goods. The Duke spares his life and reduces the state's claim on half his property to a fine. Antonio merely takes the other half in trust for Lorenzo and Jessica and insists that Shylock make a will leaving all his property to them.

With the conclusion of the trial, Portia's mischievousness immediately returns. As a token of appreciation for saving Antonio's life, she begs the ring she had given Bassanio, instead of the proffered three thousand ducats, as a fee. She says, quite rightly:

> An if your wife be not a madwoman,
> And know how well I have deserved this ring,
> She would not hold out enemy for ever,
> For giving it me. . . .

Even so, Bassanio will not part with the ring, and Portia leaves in a pretended huff. It is Antonio who persuades him to send the ring after her, and, after Antonio has been willing to give his life for Bassanio, how can he be refused?

Shakespeare does not lead us immediately to the comedic untangling of the ring complication. He prefaces the return to the joys of Belmont with a passage of exquisite lyricism in praise of moonlight and music, and, having established this atmosphere for Portia's return, he uses it to reveal the wise and serious ob-

server of life before we again see the merry prankster. As she
sees from afar the lighted candle in her hall, she says:

> How far that little candle throws his beams!
> So shines a good deed in a naughty world.

That is far from a reflection of rosy-cheeked optimism; it is a
rather sad and mature reflection on the ratio of good and evil in
the world. When Nerissa points out, "When the moon shone, we
did not see the candle," Portia does not modify her former
thought, but starts a new train of thought, and, when she hears
music, she reflects, "Methinks it sounds much sweeter than by
day," and moves on to consider how much our appreciation of
things is conditioned by circumstances:

> The crow doth sing as sweetly as the lark
> When neither is attended, and I think
> The nightingale, if she should sing by day,
> When every goose is cackling, would be thought
> No better a musician than the wren.
> How many things by season seasoned are
> To their right praise and true perfection!

Shakespeare felt it necessary to remind us of the natural philosopher in Portia to balance our final view of her as the teasing
wife, who is as quick-witted as she was in our very first view of
her. When Bassanio says:

> I swear to thee, even by thine own fair eyes,
> Wherein I see myself—

she immediately picks it up with

> Mark you but that!
> In both my eyes he doubly sees himself,
> In each eye, one. Swear by your double self,
> And there's an oath of credit.

To sum up, Jessica speaks for me when she answers Lorenzo's
question, "How dost thou like the Lord Bassanio's wife?" She
says:

Past all expressing. It is very meet
The Lord Bassanio live an upright life;
For, having such a blessing in his lady,
He finds the joys of heaven here on earth;
And if on earth he do not merit them,
In reason he should never come to heaven.
Why, if two gods should play some heavenly match
And on the wager lay two earthly women,
And Portia one, there must be something else
Pawned with the other; for the poor rude world
Hath not her fellow.

9   Shylock

T HE CARDINAL POINT about Shakespeare's Shylock is that he was a usurer and a man to whom money was all; he also happened to be a Jew, and this was an exotic fact which Shakespeare probed for its human significance.

Officially there were no Jews in Elizabethan England, though there is evidence that they were there clandestinely, or under cover of being converted to Christianity. In the year 1600 the Bishop of Exeter complained that in his diocese, "Jewism also aboundeth, twenty factions in one city." It is probable that the Jews in Devonshire, the Bishop's county, had come there by sea after their expulsion from Spain and Portugal in the year in which Columbus discovered the New World.

To the Elizabethan a Jew was a mysterious and alien being, probably regarded in much the same way as some simple-minded Americans today think of a "Commie." When men feel menaced by difference, be it of color, race, religion, or ideology, they see only the difference and deliberately blind their eyes to the common humanity that all share; Shakespeare looks for and finds the man.

Then there is the question of usury, which originally meant the simple lending of money for profit, without the connotation of exorbitant interest. Since for centuries it had been forbidden by the Church, reinforced by Aristotle, and since the leaders of medieval Europe had often been in dire and urgent need of large funds, the Jewish money-lender had become an economic necessity, but he led his life in constant terror since it was at the mercy of the very men who owed him money. The Jewish religion also forbade usury, but the same text from the Book of Deuteronomy on which the prohibition was based could also be interpreted to allow Jews to lend money at interest to Christians; the passage in the King James version reads thus: "Thou shalt not lend upon usury to thy brother . . . unto a stranger thou mayest lend upon usury; but unto thy brother thou shalt not lend upon usury." With the rapid expansion of trade in the fifteenth and sixteenth centuries, borrowed capital became such a widely needed commodity that religious and ethical scruples were conveniently ignored and money-lending gradually ceased to be a Jewish monopoly. But many Elizabethans, and among them Shakespeare, still had great doubts about the practice; his hero, Antonio, is a merchant who will not touch usury, but his villain, Shylock, makes it his means of livelihood. Since, as I believe, in *The Merchant of Venice* Shakespeare was examining the whole relation of man to money, usury was a symbol of a dangerous value because to breed from a "barren metal" was unnatural.

Much has been made of linking *The Merchant of Venice* with a Roderigo Lopez, a Portuguese Jew who was a physician to the Queen and who was executed on June 7, 1594, for complicity in a Spanish plot to poison her. The whole story of Lopez is a fascinating and ambiguous one. There is evidence that he was a counterspy, and was largely the victim of the enmity of the Earl of Essex. It is certain that the Queen was reluctant to believe him guilty, that she delayed his execution, that he died protesting his innocence and that the Queen in the following year arranged the return of his confiscated property to his widow and children.

It has often been suggested that the trial and execution of Lopez unleashed an anti-Jewish feeling in London and that Shakespeare wrote *The Merchant of Venice* in response to that feeling. Apart from the fact that this supposition degrades the purpose of the play, which is primarily about money and the implications of usury and not about Jews, the accepted dating of the play, largely based on its style, is at the earliest a year after the Lopez incident and more usually two years after. If there were not certain evidence that Marlowe's *The Jew of Malta* had been written four or five years before, it would assuredly have been suggested that it owed its inspiration to the Lopez case, for its spirit would certainly have fed the flames of anti-Semitism. Edward Alleyn's company took advantage of the Lopez furore to revive the play with great success.

A word needs to be said about *The Jew of Malta*. (Incidentally, it has been suggested that Shylock's reference to Barrabas in the Trial scene may be to Marlowe's Jew rather than to the murderer who, St. Luke tells us, was released to the crowd in preference to Christ, but I don't think this makes sense, as Shylock would not feel the necessary degradation in Marlowe's Barrabas that he would in the Biblical one; the quotation is:

> . . . I have a daughter.
> Would any of the stock of Barrabas
> Had been her husband rather than a Christian!)

I don't think Marlowe's play deserves to be dismissed as it often is, even by such distinguished critics as T. S. Eliot, who writes it off as a "farce," though I admit he has his own rather puzzling definition of that genre. It is, at its worst, an exciting melodrama. For our immediate purpose, two things need to be noted about the play: Marlowe did not conceive of Barabas (the spelling of the name in Marlowe, Shakespeare and the Bible all differ) as a loathsome villain; he had the same rebellious admiration for him as he did for his Tamburlaine; and the second thing to be noted is that he used his Barabas, as Shakespeare used his Shylock, to expose the hypocrisy of Christians. Here is a characteristic musing of Barabas:

> Thus trowls our fortune in by land and sea,
> And thus we are on every side enriched:
> These are the blessings promised to the Jews,
> And herein was old Abram's happiness:
> What more may Heaven do for earthly man
> Than thus to pour out plenty in their laps?
>
> .   .   .   .
>
> Who hateth me but for my happiness?
> Or who is honoured now but for his wealth?
> Rather had I a Jew be hated thus,
> Than pitied in a Christian poverty:
> For I can see no fruits in all their faith,
> But malice, falsehood, and excessive pride,
> Which methinks fits not their profession.
> Haply some hapless man hath conscience,
> And for his conscience lives in beggary.
>
> .   .   .   .
>
> I must confess we come not to be kings;
> That's not our fault; alas, our number's few,
> And crowns come either by succession,
> Or urged by force: and nothing violent
> Oft have I heard tell, can be permanent.
> Give us a peaceful rule, make Christians kings,
> That thirst so much for principality.

Stage interpretations of Shylock have varied widely, from the low comic of Thomas Doggett in 1701, through the terrifying villain of Charles Macklin in 1741 to the noble victim of Henry Irving in 1879. It is interesting to note that to make room for Doggett's comic Shylock, the intentionally comic part of Gobbo was excised, and in Irving's version, the fifth act was excised. The contemporary claim for Macklin's Shylock was that it was "the Jew that Shakespeare drew." It would be enlightening to know how the part was played in the original production, and a good key to this would be to know who played it. There is a highly dubious tradition that it was played by Burbage in a comic vein, but I believe T. W. Baldwin's conjecture is much the more likely one, that Burbage played Bassanio and that Shylock was played by Pope, who was also the original Falstaff. Twentieth-century interpretations have run the full gamut. The truth is that he is a very complicated and real human being, dominated throughout by his all-consuming obsession for money.

The first words that Shylock utters are about money: "Three thousand ducats." Bassanio has come to him for a loan to fit out his expedition to Portia, and Antonio has agreed to become his surety. The prospect is an intriguing one for Shylock. Here are these Christians who despise usury forced to come to him for money. He hesitates, not because he is doubtful about the security, but because he is savoring the unexpected situation. Antonio is his business enemy, for he has been loud in his denunciation of usury and in his contempt for the man who practices it. Shylock in pretending to weigh Antonio as a security reveals that he knows all about his enterprises and therefore his shortage of ready cash, and he also shows a subtle but biting humor. In referring to the hazards to which Antonio's ships are subject he mentions "water-thieves and land-thieves," hastily adding that he means pirates, probably because Bassanio had reacted hostilely to the obvious implication, for indeed Jews were all too subject to the seizure of their property. Bassanio needles Shylock into revealing the Jew in him by an invitation to dine. Shylock replies: "I will buy with you, sell with you, talk with you, walk with you, and so following; but I will not eat with you, drink with you, nor pray with you." It is noteworthy that now that his Jewish pride has been provoked, his first soliloquy is in verse; the language of the usurer is prose, but that of the Jew is verse. It should also be noted that Shylock does not live up to his proud words. Later he accepts an invitation to dine with Bassanio.

Shylock's first description of Antonio repays examination: "How like a fawning publican he looks!" "Publican" as a term of Jewish abuse derives from the days of the Roman occupation of Palestine, when the Romans used Jews to gather the taxes for them, so that a publican was a Jew who extorted money from his own people in the interests of the conquerors. In what sense could Antonio be compared with a publican? A publican took money from his own people, and, in the sense that Antonio and Shylock are both merchants, so does Antonio, in denying to his brother-merchant the freedom to make money by usury. But the adjective "fawning" is a strange one, not as applied to a publican, but as applied to Antonio. It can only refer to the friendly way in which Antonio greets and converses with Bassanio, for obviously an unheard colloquy must take place between them while Shylock delivers his soliloquy. As Shylock examines his attitude to Antonio, he makes it quite clear that usury is the main issue between them:

> I hate him for he is a Christian.
> But more for that in low simplicity
> He lends out money gratis, and brings down
> The rate. of usance here with us in Venice.

Shylock assumes a reciprocal hatred in Antonio, but he makes it clear that Antonio's criticism has been of his usury.

> He hates our sacred nation, and he rails,
> Even there where merchants most do congregate,
> On me, my bargains, and my well-won thrift,
> Which he calls interest. . . .

There follows a discussion between Antonio and Shylock on the subject of usury. It is provoked by Antonio's statement:

> . . . I neither lend nor borrow
> By taking nor by giving of excess.

Shylock quotes in defense of usury the trick that Jacob had played upon his uncle Laban to acquire the greater share of the new flock of lambs; the point of the story was that no theft had been involved in the ruse and Jacob had received the blessing of God; there was the additional point that Laban had not kept his original bargain with Jacob, the implication being that, since Jews were not treated fairly by Christians, they were free, with God's blessing, to use their wits to protect themselves. But Antonio does not probe the significance of the analogy; he dismisses it with "The Devil can cite Scripture for his purpose."

Shylock is courageous enough to confront Antonio with a recital of the abuse he has showered on the Jew, but it should be noted that the inexcusable treatment Antonio had meted out to Shylock was all for the usurer:

> Signior Antonio, many a time and oft
> In the Rialto you have rated me
> About my moneys and my usances.
>
> .   .   .   .
>
> You call me misbeliever, cut-throat dog,
> And spit upon my Jewish gaberdine,
> And all for use of that which is mine own.

Shylock says that after such treatment he should refuse to help, but instead is expected to bend low and

> With bated breath and whispering humbleness,
> Say this:
> "Fair sir, you spat on me on Wednesday last;
> You spurned me such a day; another time
> You called me dog; and for these courtesies
> I'll lend you thus much moneys."

Antonio is moved to anger not remorse, probably provoked by the fact that he has himself consented to become a part of the practice he so thoroughly condemns. He tells Shylock he should not regard the loan as a business transaction between friends, but rather as a hostage in a war between enemies. Then comes Shylock's great surprise; he will lend the money exactly as Antonio would, without a farthing of interest. This, in itself, is a moral victory for Shylock and completely knocks Antonio off his perch of ethical superiority; he has to confess "there is much kindness in the Jew."

Now we must examine the "merry bond" for the pound of flesh. To start with, there had to be a "consideration" to make the obligation of the loan binding, some such token as a penny; but in completely eschewing a monetary interest in the transaction, Shylock logically avoids any symbol of money. But why the pound of flesh? Shylock could, at that moment, have had no hope of collecting it. As Antonio says:

> Within these two months, that's a month before
> This bond expires, I do expect return
> Of thrice three times the value of this bond;

and, while we hear before the trial that one of his ships has been lost on the Goodwin Sands, after the trial we hear that three of his "argosies are richly come to harbour." The symbolic significance of the pound of flesh must have given great satisfaction to Shylock; the Jew's life was always at the mercy of the Christian and now the Christian's was symbolically at the mercy of the Jew. Much was to happen to Shylock which would turn the symbol into a cruel and gratifying reality. Bassanio, with a mind not so guileless as that of Antonio, is very suspicious of the apparently kind new Shylock and says, "I like not fair terms and a villain's mind."

The domestic Shylock is a miser. His servant, Launcelot Gobbo, says, "I am famished in his service;" the first adjective Shylock uses about him in the play is "unthrifty." Launcelot decides to run away, which distresses Shylock's daughter, Jessica:

> I am sorry thou wilt leave my father so.
> Our house is hell, and thou, a merry devil,
> Didst rob it of some taste of tediousness.

Launcelot weeps at leaving Jessica, whom he describes as "Most beautiful pagan, most sweet Jew!" Many a modern girl who has rebelled against her home would echo Jessica's words:

> Alack, what heinous sin is it in me
> To be ashamed to be my father's child!
> But though I am a daughter to his blood,
> I am not to his manners. . . .

Bassanio's supper invitation to Shylock is presumably motivated by the unexpected generosity of the loan, but Shylock says:

> I am not bid for love, they flatter me.
> But yet I'll go in hate, to feed upon
> The prodigal Christian. . . .

His miserly self-justification for reversing his previous high-prin-
cipled refusal to eat with Christians is that he will be feeding at
Bassanio's cost. The same argument also reconciles him to losing
Launcelot

> To one that I would have him help to waste
> His borrowed purse. . . .

The other argument for letting Launcelot go is equally miserly:

> The patch is kind enough, but a huge feeder,
> Snail-slow in profit, and he sleeps by day
> More than the wildcat. Drones hive not with me,
> Therefore I part with him. . . .

But he has an uneasy feeling about leaving the house:

> I am right loath to go.
> There is some ill abrewing toward my rest,
> For I did dream of moneybags tonight.

He is about to lose his daughter, who, it is true, will take some
gold and jewels with her, but his dream has merely warned him
of some danger to his wealth.

The dour existence that Jessica leads in the motherless house
is exampled by Shylock's injunction to shut out all sounds of the
street-masque that he hears is to take place:

> Let not the sound of shallow foppery
> Enter my sober house. . . .

"Fair" and "gentle" Jessica was a delight to Shakespeare and the
Christians in the play, and is surely sufficient proof that there was
no specifically anti-Semitic bias in the author or the characters,
but she fares badly with some people today. They see her as a

heartless and faithless wretch and a thief, who deserted and robbed her lonely old father and broke his heart by marrying a Christian and becoming one herself. The subject of mixed marriages, whether of race or faith, is one that does not vex Shakespeare; for him, true love is the paramount consideration. As for Jessica's leaving Shylock, many a girl, for much less reason, has been prompted into marriage by a desire to escape. Shakespeare reveals his attitude to her in the words of her lover:

> Beshrew me but I love her heartily,
> For she is wise, if I can judge of her,
> And fair she is, if that mine eyes be true,
> And true she is, as she hath proved herself.
> And therefore, like herself, wise, fair, and true,
> Shall she be placed in my constant soul.

A favorable wind had sprung up and Bassanio had left hurriedly, canceling all plans for the supper and the masque. Shylock, returning home to find his daughter and his ducats gone, naturally assumes that he has been deliberately duped and that Jessica is aboard Bassanio's ship. He rouses the Duke to search the ship; they arrive too late; the ship has sailed, but Antonio assures the Duke that Lorenzo and Jessica were not aboard. Shylock becomes a madman, as Salanio reports:

> I never heard a passion so confused,
> So strange, outrageous, and so variable.

Salanio further reports that Shylock's fury had been mainly prompted by his loss of the money and the jewels, for he had cried:

> My daughter! O my ducats! O my daughter!
> Fled with a Christian! O my Christian ducats!
> Justice! the law! my ducats, and my daughter!
> A sealed bag, two sealed bags of ducats,
> Of double ducats, stolen from me by my daughter!
> And jewels—two stones, two rich and precious stones,
> Stolen by my daughter! Justice! Find the girl!
> She hath the stones upon her, and the ducats!

Antonio was present during this outburst, and the sight of him must have fed Shylock's fury. As the words "Justice! the law!" came to his lips, the cruel hope of legally securing Antonio's death may have been born, especially if, as is probable, he had heard the rumor of the loss of one of the ships.

When next we see Shylock he is open about his designs on Antonio's life: "If [his flesh] will feed nothing else, it will feed my revenge." It is important to notice that, just before this, Sala-rino, in comparing Shylock with his daughter, has said: "There is more difference between thy flesh and hers than between jet and ivory, more between your bloods than there is between red wine and Rhenish." Of course, Jessica's flesh and blood are as Jewish as Shylock's, but what matters is character and disposition, and there they are a world apart. It is the miserly usurer that is detested, not the Jew. To make his cause of revenge more ad-mirable, Shylock says of Antonio that the sole cause of his atti-tude is that "I am a Jew." This launches him on the justly famous defense of the humanity of Jews, which has a universal validity, but the dramatic reason for it is to raise the desire for revenge from mere mercantile rivalry to the proud defiance of a despised and downtrodden people. There is a Marlovian ring to the end of the speech: "If a Jew wrong a Christian, what is his humility? Revenge. If a Christian wrong a Jew, what should his sufferance be by Christian example? Why, revenge. The villainy you teach me I will execute, and it shall go hard but I will better the in-struction."

The scene between Shylock and Tubal, who has been to Genoa at Shylock's grudged cost in search of Jessica, is the one upon which the comic Shylock must have been founded, for I have seen it played experimentally, using low comedy techniques, with hilarious results; but it is hard to see how the rest of the play could have been acted in such a vein without astounding distortions. The comic element in the encounter derives from the exaggeration of Shylock's mercenary values; to get his jewels and ducats back, he would willingly see his daughter dead at his feet.

And there's Tubal's expense account too! "And I know not what's spent in the search. . . . The thief gone with so much, and so much to find the thief." The report of Jessica's extravagance is the final blow: "Your daughter spent in Genoa, as I heard, in one night fourscore ducats." Shylock is hurt and appalled: "Thou stick'st a dagger in me. I shall never see my gold again. Fourscore ducats at a sitting! Fourscore ducats!" But I think that a comic reading even of this scene is an inhuman distortion of it. Granted Shylock's obsession, his reaction to his loss is completely credible, and there is a poignant hint before the scene ends that there is a man who could love buried deep within the miser. Jessica's extravagance is, of course, a natural reaction to the parsimony in which she had been reared, and she had given a ring away for a monkey. (Monkeys were the exotic pets of wealthy Elizabethans, and a monkey would be a symbol to Jessica of all she had been denied.) Shylock's comment shows that there was at least one thing that not even he would sell: "It was my turquoise; I had it of Leah when I was a bachelor. I would not have given it for a wilderness of monkeys." It is a characteristic and unexpected Shakespearean revelation of the man. But the scene ends with the Shylock we know, the usurer who gives a very practical reason for wanting to get rid of Antonio: ". . . were he out of Venice, I can make what merchandise I will."

When Salerio brings to Bassanio in Belmont the news of Antonio's plight, he says that all his ventures have failed. To a modern audience, when we hear the good news about them at the end of the play, it seems that Shakespeare has cheated, just to give Antonio a reason for being part of the happy ending, but it would not have seemed so to Shakespeare's audience. Ships disappeared for years at a time without a word, were given up for lost, and then suddenly reappeared. The certified loss of one of Antonio's ships, together with the delay and lack of news of the others, would have been enough to start a rumor, soon hardened into certainty, of total loss. Salerio also brings remarkable news

of Venetian respect for the law, even in the case of a Jew who
sought a Christian's life:

> Twenty merchants,
> The Duke himself, and the magnificoes
> Of greatest port have all persuaded with him,
> But none can drive him from the envious plea
> Of forfeiture, of justice, and his bond.

Venice was a center of international trade, and foreigners had to
be assured of law courts they could rely on. Antonio himself
makes this point subsequently:

> The Duke cannot deny the course of law;
> For the commodity that strangers have
> With us in Venice, if it be denied,
> Will much impeach the justice of the state,
> Since that the trade and profit of the city
> Consisteth of all nations. . . .

I said that I believed Shylock's thirst for Antonio's blood
became a dominant desire in him only after Jessica's flight, but
she herself seems to contradict this, for she says:

> When I was with him I have heard him swear
> To Tubal and to Chus his countrymen,
> That he would rather have Antonio's flesh
> Than twenty times the value of the sum
> That he did owe him. . . .

I can imagine the astonishment of Tubal and Chus when they
hear that Shylock is going to lend three thousand ducats for three
months to a Christian without interest, and such declaration as
Jessica heard would necessarily have been Shylock's defense, but
till the flight of Jessica, the thief, and the first news of Antonio's
loss of a ship, I believe the "merry bond" to have been but a
symbol.

Antonio, now in prison, is allowed out under guard to make
a personal appeal to Shylock, who describes him as "the fool that

lent out money gratis." Shylock will not stay to listen; he says:

> I'll not be made a soft and dull-eyed fool,
> To shake the head, relent, and sigh, and yield
> To Christian intercessors. . . .

After he has left, Antonio gives a very practical reason for Shylock's attitude:

> I oft delivered from his forfeitures
> Many that have at times made moan to me;
> Therefore he hates me.

When pressed in the trial for a reason for demanding the pound of flesh, Shylock is and must be evasive. Obviously he cannot urge the failure of a business transaction, because he refuses double and triple the amount of the loan. Nor can he openly acknowledge that he wants to kill Antonio. He says he is governed by an irrational impulse:

> So can I give no reason, nor I will not,
> More than a lodged hate and a certain loathing
> I bear Antonio, that I follow thus
> A losing suit against him. . . .

But he makes a very powerful and telling analogy based upon the immoral property rights in slaves, another exposure of the hypocrisy of Christian society:

> You have among you many a purchased slave,
> Which, like your asses and your dogs and mules,
> You use in abject and in slavish parts,
> Because you bought them. Shall I say to you,
> "Let them be free! Marry them to your heirs!
> Why sweat they under burdens? Let their beds
> Be made as soft as ours and let their palates
> Be seasoned with such viands"? You will answer,
> "The slaves are ours." So do I answer you.
> The pound of flesh, which I demand of him,
> Is dearly bought; 'tis mine and I will have it.

Shylock's confidence in the outcome enables him to maintain

an unruffled dignity in the face of Gratiano's venomous attack, and even to reply with an unsuspected wit:

> Till thou canst rail the seal from off my bond,
> Thou but offend'st thy lungs to speak so loud.
> Repair thy wit, good youth, or it will fall
> To cureless ruin. . . .

To save his life and half his wealth, Shylock says "I am content" to the conditions imposed by the Court, and one of those conditions now sticks in our craw:

> . . . that, for this favour,
> He presently become a Christian.

This, to the Elizabethans, was a deed of mercy, since the Jews were considered to be lost souls, but to us it is an intolerable cruelty. At this moment the hero becomes the villain, and the villain the victim, and Shakespeare's intention is distorted. The horrible sufferings inflicted upon Jews in our own times have made it impossible for many people not to look upon Shylock as primarily a Jew and Jessica as a despicable renegade, but this is the opposite of Shakespeare's intention, and I believe the play he wrote and the values it implied can be made acceptable today, apart from the enforced conversion; in that matter, at least, our values are finer than those of the Elizabethans. It might be pointed out that in the Book of Common Prayer of the Church of England even today a collect for Good Friday reads: "Have mercy upon all Jews, Turks, Infidels, and Hereticks, and take from them all ignorance, hardness of heart, and contempt of thy Word; and so fetch them home, blessed Lord, to thy flock, that they may be saved among the remnant of the true Israelites, and be made one fold under one shepherd." I have heard that prayer said, and so did Shakespeare. (The American version of the prayer does not particularize, but merely says: "Have mercy upon all who know thee not as thou art revealed in the Gospel of thy Son.") Judged at its best, the spirit which prompts that collect is something akin to that of the white liberal who aims at complete integration of the black man into society, an aim now vigorously opposed by large numbers of blacks, who demand equality with the full expression of their own separate identity.

Shylock leaves the court a defeated man, and we feel sorry for him, but it is a grave mistake for an actor to turn the exit into a heroic one, as Henry Irving did. If Shylock had been primarily a Jew, he would never have consented to become a Christian. I could wish that there had been something of the spirit of Marlowe's Barabas in him; that Jew had said, "No, governor, I will be no convertite," and he had died cursing his Christian enemies; but then the play would have been about Shylock, and it isn't. Shakespeare's Shylock remains true to the last to his real god—Money.

10　Jacques

JACQUES IS a pure character study. He could be easily removed from *As You Like It* without in any way affecting the development of the story. In this play Shakespeare adhered, more closely than was his wont, to the plot of *Rosalynde*, a popular prose romance written by Thomas Lodge; he simplified the action and added some characters, most notably Touchstone and Jacques.

As You Like It was probably written in 1599. The year before, Shakespeare's company had achieved a big success with the first original work of a new playwright, Ben Jonson, and Shakespeare himself had played a leading part in it, for his name leads the list of the ten "principal Comoedians" in a postscript to the play as it appears in the Ben Jonson Folio of 1616. The title of the play, *Every Man in His Humour*, indicates its intention; it is to portray types of men in their eccentricities, foibles, obsessions and affectations. The characters are to be both revealing cartoons and recognizable portraits.

Shakespeare entered the theatre quietly, reshaping what he found and discovering himself through imitation of others, but

Jonson was a self-conscious and self-proclaimed innovator. In the prologue to the play, which I believe was written after, possibly years after, its original production, for it contains an attack on the practices of Shakespeare's actors which it is hard to believe they would have spoken, Jonson impudently proclaims for himself as author:

> He rather prays, you will be pleased to see
> One such today, as other plays should be.

He says that his play will deal with

> Deeds, and language, such as men do use:
> And persons, such as comedy would choose,
> When she would show an image of the times,
> And sport with human follies, not with crimes.

He ends his prologue with the challenging assertion that, if his play causes his audience to laugh,

> . . . there's hope left then,
> You, that have so graced monsters, may like men.

The "Comedy of Humours" reflected the psychology of the day, as mechanistic as some of our own day, according to which our dispositions and temperaments are determined by the excessive or deficient activity of certain of our physical constituents. To the Elizabethans the universe was a mathematically neat one, and so the determining elements in man's body were reflections of the four natural elements: air, earth, fire, water. The corresponding bodily elements were the "humours" of blood, black bile, yellow bile, phlegm. Excess of these severally resulted in temperaments that were sanguine, melancholy, choleric and phlegmatic. The most desirable of these was, of course, the sanguine, though this, too, in overabundance could produce a lustful rowdy. The pattern was further refined by a widespread belief in astrology; thus, a melancholic was under the influence of Saturn; hence the saturnine disposition.

It was the melancholy humour that most interested Shakespeare, and Jacques is a study of it, somewhat wryly observed. Shakespeare had already given an example of it in Antonio, and was soon to give his supreme study of it in Hamlet, after dealing with it in Brutus. Orsino, in *Twelfth Night*, is another study in melancholy, that of the rejected lover, morosely in love with love; Romeo, before he meets Juliet, is suffering in much the same way. Indeed, both *Twelfth Night* and *Romeo and Juliet* could be considered as demonstrating the difference between being in love with love and being in love. But all Shakespeare's melancholics are widely different because they are seen and realized as human beings, not case histories. It seems to me that Jacques has particular relevance to today; he is the detached intellectual, who, after once taking a stand in the fight against wrong, is content thereafter to remain aloof and make rueful observations on the human comedy.

It would seem that melancholy was one of the fashionable affectations of young Englishmen around the year 1600, just as some two hundred years later the long-enduring fashion of Byronism was to start and spread throughout Europe, and as in our own day youth hurries to conform to its own expression of nonconformity. In *Every Man in His Humour* Shakespeare had met an amusingly stupid affector of melancholy, Master Stephen, who, when offered hospitality, said "Have you a stool there to be melancholy upon?" It is also highly possible that, in reading Thomas Lodge's *Rosalynde*, he had also read the same author's *Wits' Misery, and the World's Madness, discovering the devils incarnate of this age*, in which abstractions are personified, as in the old morality plays. One of these characters was Scandal and Detraction, a most undesirable gentleman, in whom there is a hint for one of Rosalind's criticisms of Jacques. Of Scandal and Detraction we learn: "Well spoken he is, and hath some languages, and hath read over the conjuration of Machiavel; in belief he is an Atheist or a counterfeit Catholic; hath been long a traveller and seen many countries, but bringeth home nothing but corruptions to disturb the peace of his own country." Rosalind says to Jacques:

> A traveller! By my faith, you have great reason to be sad.
> I fear you have sold your own lands to see other men's;
> then, to have seen much, and to have nothing, is to have
> rich eyes and poor hands. . . . Look you lisp and wear strange
> suits, disable all the benefits of your own country, be out
> of love with your nativity, and almost chide God for making
> you that countenance you are, or I will scarce think you
> have swam in a gondola.

There Rosalind was displaying a newly proud Englishman's denunciation of those who obliquely boasted of their travels abroad
by bewailing their own country's shortcomings in comparison with
the glories of other countries. But, in Jacques, Shakespeare aimed
at giving a portrait of a genuine melancholic; he says, in effect,
when a quality is affected and the affectation merits scorn, that
scorn is also likely to be poured on the heads of those in whom
the quality is genuine.

In a sense Jacques exhibits the happiness of melancholy, in
which an essentially solitary man's musings are his chief happiness,
whereas Hamlet exhibits the agony of melancholy. In the year
1621 an extraordinary book was published: *The Anatomy of
Melancholy* by Robert Burton. Much of it still makes fascinating
reading. The range of its learning is astonishing, and, though we
now find some of the detail absurd, much of it has a wisdom that
endures. Nothing makes me so wary of the ascription of certain
sources to Shakespeare as this book, for it would seem to have
inspired many passages in the plays, but it was not published until
five years after he was dead. One of Burton's prefaces to the book
is in verse and has the title: "The Author's Abstract of Melancholy." It consists of twelve eight-line verses, alternately displaying the contrary aspects of melancholy, the faces of Jacques and
Hamlet. Here is a sample of the contrast, the ninth and tenth
verses:

> Friends and companions get you gone,
> 'Tis my desire to be alone;

Ne'er well but when my thoughts and I
Do domineer in privacy.
No Gem, no treasure like to this,
'Tis my delight, my crown, my bliss.
    All my joys to this are folly,
    Naught so sweet as melancholy.
'Tis my sole plague to be alone,
I am a beast, a monster grown,
I will no light, nor company,
I find it now my misery.
The scene is turned, my joys are gone,
Fear, discontent, and sorrows come.
    All my griefs to this are jolly,
    Naught so fierce as melancholy.

We first hear of Jacques in a report of one of the lords. He has taken his stand against the world's iniquity by going into voluntary banishment with the exiled Duke, but, unlike the Duke who

> Finds tongues in trees, books in running brooks,
> Sermons in stones, and good in everything,

Jacques finds iniquity everywhere, and finds that they, the victims of usurpation, are themselves usurpers, for they have brought death to the deer, whose natural home they have invaded. The Duke himself is a considerable moralizer, but his feeling towards the deer causes only a slight and sentimental twinge of conscience, and does not stop him from hunting:

> Come, shall we go and kill us venison?
> And yet it irks me the poor dappled fools,
> Being native burghers of this desert city,
> Should in their own confines with forked heads
> Have their round haunches gored.

We hear that Jacques is characteristically alone, talking to a wounded and weeping deer by a brook. He does nothing to help the deer, or put it out of its agony; he just talks, and finds intellectual pleasure in comparing the plight of the wounded animal with that of man. The Lord reports his moralizing thus:

> First, for his weeping into the needless stream;
> "Poor deer," quoth he, "thou mak'st a testament
> As worldlings do, giving thy sum of more
> To that which had too much." Then, being there alone,
> Left and abandoned of his velvet friends,
> " 'Tis right," quoth he; "thus misery doth part
> The flux of company." Anon a careless herd,
> Full of the pasture, jumps along by him
> And never stays to greet him. "Aye," quoth Jacques,
> "Sweep on, you fat and greasy citizens;
> 'Tis just the fashion. Wherefore do you look
> Upon that poor and broken bankrupt there?"
> Thus most invectively he pierceth through
> The body of the country, city, court,
> Yea, and of this our life; swearing that we
> Are mere usurpers, tyrants, and what's worse,
> To fright the animals and to kill them up
> In their assigned and native dwelling-place.

The Duke is eager to catch Jacques in this mood, not to laugh at him but to listen to him:

> I love to cope him in these sullen fits,
> For then he's full of matter.

But Jacques is not eager to be coped, as so many amateur philosophers are, whose greatest pleasure is to display their wisdom before an appreciative and impressed audience. Jacques is his own best audience and is content with it; argument he avoids. He says, when he hears that the Duke has been looking for him all day, "And I have been all this day to avoid him. He is too disputable for my company. I think of as many matters as he; but I give Heaven thanks, and make no boast of them."

As You Like It is a comedy in the popular pastoral mode, and Shakespeare is happy in it to recreate the delights of his own Stratford countryside, but, while he puts on the rose-tinted spectacles worn by the pastoralists, he also takes them off on occasion to look on the rural truth as he knew it; Jacques and Touchstone are his two adverse commentators on the delights of the country. They have much in common; thus, when Jacques asks for a pastoral song only to parody it, Touchstone's comment on a romantic song is "I count it but time lost to hear such a foolish song;" the theme of Jacques' parody is that a man who deliberately abandons his wealth and life of ease is an ass, a sentiment which is paralleled by Touchstone when he says, "Aye, now am I in Arden, the more fool I. When I was at home, I was in a better place. But travellers must be content." So when Jacques inevitably happens upon Touchstone in the forest, he rejoices in finding a kindred spirit; for the only time in the play he "looks merrily." If Jacques owes his conception to the new Jonsonian comedy of humours, there is no doubt that Touchstone was written to suit the witty fooling of Robert Armin who had joined the company of players to replace Thomas Kemp; it is very probable that Touchstone was the first Armin part that Shakespeare wrote.

Viola in *Twelfth Night* in commenting on the foolery of Feste, another Armin part, says:

> This fellow is wise enough to play the fool,
> And to do that well craves a kind of wit.
> He must observe their mood on whom he jests,
> The quality of persons, and the time,
> And, like the haggard, check at every feather
> That comes before his eye. This is a practice
> As full of labour as a wise man's art.

Touchstone, with his skill in sensing what will please his audience, immediately moralizes when he meets Jacques, who later confesses:

> . . . I did laugh sans intermission
> An hour by his dial. Oh, noble fool!
> A worthy fool! Motley's the only wear.

It should be noticed that Jacques is being made to laugh at himself, for, in parody of his own propensity to seize upon every action as an excuse for a sermon, Touchstone just looks at his watch to tell the time and delivers a homily which would seem very much at home in Samuel Beckett's wonderful play, *Waiting for Godot*. Here is Jacques' account of the incident:

> And then he drew a dial from his poke,
> And looking on it with lacklustre eye,
> Says very wisely, "It is ten o'clock.
> Thus we may see," quoth he, "how the world wags.
> 'Tis but an hour ago since it was nine;
> And after one hour more 'twill be eleven;
> And so, from hour to hour, we ripe and ripe,
> And then, from hour to hour, we rot and rot;
> And thereby hangs a tale." . . .

That Jacques can laugh at this parody of his own melancholy is a redeeming grace; it is by this kind of touch that Shakespeare takes a type and turns it into an individual human being. Jacques goes even further and analyzes his own laughter:

> He that a fool doth very wisely hit
> Doth very foolishly, although he smart,
> Not to seem senseless of the bob. . . .

Jacques calls for the freedom of the fool:

> . . . I must have liberty
> Withal, as large a charter as the wind,
> To blow on whom I please; for so fools have;
> And they that are most galled with my folly,
> They most must laugh . . . ;

and this is how he describes the purpose of the crusading clown, the Savonarola in cap-and-bells:

> Invest me in my motley. Give me leave
> To speak my mind, and I will through and through
> Cleanse the foul body of the infected world,
> If they will patiently receive my medicine.

The Duke's reply is a profound surprise. He suggests a personal reason for Jacques' misanthropy, a disgust with his own sexual

indulgence, the "brutish sting," which has poisoned his view of
the rest of mankind:

> For thou thyself hast been a libertine,
> As sensual as the brutish sting itself;
> And all the embossed sores and headed evils
> That thou with license of free foot hast caught
> Wouldst thou disgorge into the general world.

Shakespeare does not pursue this revelation; it is not in the mood
of this sunny comedy; it belongs to the spirit of the bitter comedies, but it is a flash of lightning that illuminates a whole new
dimension in Jacques. It is as though Shakespeare for his own
satisfaction, to see more clearly the man in the type, had probed
thus deeply, but felt it inappropriate to his main purpose to develop his findings. The reply of Jacques is an evasion; he does
not refer at all to the personal criticism but says that the critic
who attacks human folly and wickedness need not have a particular person in mind; he works on the principle of "If the cap
fits, wear it."

Jacques' solitary cogitations have bred in him an admirable
imperturbability. A fierce young man enters with a drawn sword
to demand food and cries: "Forbear, and eat no more;" to which
Jacques calmly replies, "Why, I have eat none yet," and turns to
the rest of the company with "Of what kind should this cock
come of?" Then, having been told that anyone who touches the
fruit will die, he deliberately starts to eat, saying, "An you will
not be answered with reason, I must die." Here is indeed the
courageous soft answer that turneth away wrath.

Although Shakespeare did not pursue the implications of the
Duke's revelation about the former life of Jacques, it established
a more serious mood in which Orlando could speak of the idyllic
forest as "this desert inaccessible," in which he thought "that all
things had been savage," and in which the verdant trees had become "melancholy boughs," and could talk of Adam as "Oppressed with two weak evils, age and hunger." This leads the

philosophic Duke to refer to the general unhappiness of the human lot; in his lightest comedies Shakespeare never lets us forget that the bright sun casts strong shadows. The Duke says:

> Thou seest we are not all alone unhappy.
> This wide and universal theatre
> Presents more woeful pageants than the scene
> Wherein we play in,

and this serves as cue for one of the most famous of Shakespeare's speeches, beginning "All the world's a stage."

It is probable that *As You Like It* was the first new play by Shakespeare to be performed in the new Globe Theatre, and that "This wide and universal theatre" refers to the name. The text of Jacques' sermon is a free translation of the motto which the Globe displayed: "Totus mundus agit histrionem."

Jacques' version of the Seven Ages of Man is too well known to call for detailed comment, but it should be noted that the attitude is one of tolerant compassion of man's absurdity, self-absorption and self-importance, and infinite pity for his final and inevitable decay. In which of the seven ages is Jacques himself? Surely, in the fifth, for is there not a touch of amused observation of himself in "Full of wise saws and modern instances?" Later, Audrey describes him as "the old gentleman."

In next seeking for Touchstone, in whose company he now rejoices, Jacques happens upon "Signior Love," Orlando, whose company is most unwelcome, for a man in love is sickly sweet company for a man out of love with the world. They are mutually inimical, for to Jacques' "Let's meet as little as we can," Orlando replies, "I do desire we may be better strangers." But when Jacques does chance upon Touchstone, it is to find him too in love, though here the attitude of Jacques is very different, for he is certain that Touchstone's earthy desire for the country hoyden, Audrey, will have no veneer of romantic nonsense. Touchstone's subsequent account of his forthcoming marriage is the ultimate in matter-of-fact realism: "As the ox hath his bow, sir, the horse his curb, and the falcon her bells, so man hath his desires; and as pigeons bill, so wedlock will be nibbling." Jacques thoroughly enjoys, unseen, Touchstone's witty attempt at dialogue with the stupid Audrey; as the Fool says: "When a man's verses cannot be understood, nor a man's good wit seconded with the forward child, understanding, it strikes a man more dead than a great reckoning in a little room."

When Sir Oliver Martext arrives to marry the comic and ill-sorted couple, Jacques steps out from hiding to give the bride away, and we find he is conventional enough to be appalled by the unsavory priest, whose incompetence is betokened by his name, and who, from long tradition, is usually played as drunk. Jacques upholds the institution of marriage as the necessary cement for an enduring partnership, and he feels that they should find a good priest to perform the ceremony; but Touchstone has no mind for an enduring marriage, and for his purpose Sir Oliver Martext is admirable: "I am not in the mind but I were better to be married of him than of another; for he is not like to marry me well; and not being well married, it will be a good excuse for me hereafter to leave my wife." But Jacques will have none of this; he insists on their abandoning Martext, and says to Touchstone: "Let me counsel thee," but what counsel he gives is dubious, for when next we see the pair, they are still unpriested, and Touchstone is asking Audrey to have patience.

Rosalind, in the guise of the "pretty youth" Ganymede, has a scintillating wit, and so Jacques desires to be "better acquainted" with her. He is led to analyze melancholy with her as it shows itself in various people, and it may be of value to paraphrase his analysis at some length. The scholar's melancholy derives from comparing his work with that of others and lamenting how short he comes; the musician's, as that of all artists, springs from his imagination; the lawyer's is deliberately assumed for a purpose; the lady's is a stylish affectation; the lover's is, by turns, all these. In describing his own brand of melancholy Jacques says: "It is a melancholy of mine own, compounded of many simples, extracted from many objects, and indeed the sundry contemplation of my travels, in which my often rumination wraps me in a most humourous sadness." That last adjective, of course, does not mean "funny," but refers to melancholy as a "humour." He further explains that travel, which Rosalind makes fun of, has given him experience. She has a devastating comment: "And your experience makes you sad. I had rather have a fool to make me merry than experience to make me sad—and to travel for it too!" Shakespeare respects the melancholy of Jacques, but he can laugh at it too. When the love-sick Orlando arrives and addresses Ganymede as Rosalind, it is too much for Jacques, and he leaves abruptly.

As the play moves to the romantic couplings of its end, the pairing of Touchstone and Audrey provides an earthy counterpoint, as Jacques makes clear as he sees them approaching: "There is, sure, another flood toward, and these couples are coming to the ark. Here comes a pair of very strange beasts, which in all tongues are called fools." Touchstone declares his intentions about Audrey very clearly to the Duke: "I press in here, sir, amongst the rest of the country copulatives, to swear and to forswear, according as marriage binds and blood breaks. A poor virgin, sir, an ill-favoured thing, sir, but mine own." Jacques is most eager for the Duke to share his own delight in Touchstone, and the Fool obliges by putting on a brilliant display on the punctilio of courtly quarreling, a subject well chosen as appropriate to the Duke's former life and as proof of his own good breeding. Jacques is delighted to act as his "straight-man," and at the end of the performance turns to the Duke with the pride of an impresario who has discovered a brilliant talent: "Is not this a rare fellow, my lord? He's as good at anything, and yet a fool."

The news arrives that the usurping Duke Frederick has been converted by "an old religious man," and the fortunes of the two Dukes are to be reversed, but Jacques has found his only happiness in contemplative exile and decides to remain in the forest and to seek out Duke Frederick:

> . . . Out of these convertites,
> There is much matter to be heard and learned.

Shakespeare gives a final dignity to Jacques by allowing him to give a sort of benediction to each of the men; he is even gracious to Orlando whom he bequeaths to "a love that your true faith doth merit." His last words are for Touchstone:

> And you to wrangling, for thy loving voyage
> Is but for two months victualled.

Jacques will not even accept the Duke's invitation to stay for the wedding dance:

> I am for other than for dancing measures.
>
> .   .   .   .
>
> To see no pastime I. What you would have
> I'll stay to know at your abandoned cave.

To the Duke the forest had been a temporary hardship of which he had made the best, but he was eager and happy to return to the world of civilization, of action and responsibility. But Jacques could not face the world again; it was an evil place to be shunned, and its evil was to be meditated upon with the satisfaction of no longer being a part of it; a happy ending for an attractively unhappy man, who cherishes his melancholy. As he said to Ganymede: " I do love it better than laughing."

11 ❧ Malvolio

EVEN MORE than the nickname "Hotspur" is an indication of the character of Henry Percy, "Malvolio," "Ill-wisher," is a clue to that of the Lady Olivia's steward in *Twelfth Night*, and it is this very quality in him, unredeemed to the end, that has been obscured in many modern productions, which have pictured him as the undeserving victim of a cruel hoax. Shakespeare's intention in Malvolio seems to me clear and simple; he has the clarity of a character from the comedy of humours; but our view of him has been so muddied for the last hundred years, largely by sentimentality, that William Archer could write in 1884: "I confess that Malvolio has always been to me one of the most puzzling of Shakespeare's creations." I see the ill-wisher as a man of great dignity (both natural and cultivated), ability, and probity whose life is soured and embittered by the impossibility of his ambition, an impossibility determined by his birth in a society where one's social limits were fixed by one's ancestry, where everything is decided by fortune, the luck of the cradle.

As Olivia's steward, Malvolio was in an important position. The social unit of the great Elizabethan manor house was large and complicated, involving a small army of servants, and those servants were of two classes, as can be clearly seen in Shakespeare's plays. First, there were the well born, who served a sort of social apprenticeship in the house, comparable in their smaller world with the ladies- and gentlemen-in-waiting at the Queen's Court. Such is the relationship of Nerissa to Portia in *The Merchant of Venice*, Lucetta to Julia in *The Two Gentlemen of Verona*, Margaret and Ursula to Hero in *Much Ado About Nothing*, and it is this relationship which Maria in *Twelfth Night* bears to Olivia; it is a gross mistake, but a very common one, to picture her as a kitchen-wench who cleverly secures a title for herself by marrying Sir Toby. This makes quite implausible the fact that Viola cannot distinguish between Olivia and Maria when she first sees them. Fabian, too, is probably a young gentleman, possibly "the younger son of a younger son," those sad victims of primogeniture; in Olivia's presence he refers to "Toby" without the title, a sure sign of implied equality. The other kind of servant is the menial, and it is from these that Shakespeare usually gets his low comedy; Launcelot Gobbo is a good example. Malvolio, as the steward of the household, had status and power. He was essential to Olivia's life. When he seems to be losing his mind, she says: "I would not have him miscarry for the half of my dowry." He probably came from the yeoman class, which with the rising merchant class was gaining power in the country, soon to become decisive. His position in the household of Olivia was comparable on its own scale with that of Sir William Knollys, the Controller of the Queen's Household. It is interesting to note that Leslie Hotson believes that, in Malvolio, Shakespeare was guying Knollys, but I feel this is unlikely, as Sir William, who was the uncle of the Earl of Essex, was too highly regarded by the Queen.

Much has been made of Maria's line to describe Malvolio: "sometimes he is a kind of puritan." She does not say and does not mean that Malvolio is a Puritan, only that sometimes he behaves like one, as indeed he does. In her next speech she retracts her analogy with the words, "The devil a puritan that he is, or anything constantly, but a timepleaser," a description to which we shall return.

If, as seems likely, the play got its title from the fact that it was to be first performed on Twelfth Night, that is the twelfth and final night of the Christmas season and festivities, Malvolio is the Scrooge of the occasion. The tiny Maria is a bundle of merriment; as she says: "If you desire the spleen, and will laugh yourself into stitches, follow me." As opposed to the spirit of mirth, Malvolio cannot laugh; he cannot even smile. He has no sense of humor, and this is his affliction, for a sense of humor is a sense of proportion, and this he lacks.

Shakespeare is very careful to guide our sympathies. The first thing Malvolio does in the play is to discredit Feste and try to get him dismissed. Just before the trap of the letter is set, we hear that he has also tried to discredit Fabian for going to a bear-baiting, which the genteel considered a very vulgar sport. And immediately before we see him for the last time, lest our sympathies should be turning too much towards him, we unexpectedly hear of another of his malicious actions: the kindly sea-captain who had saved Viola is in prison "at Malvolio's suit."

Shakespeare paints Malvolio's character at his first entrance with unique boldness, and what we see in him then he remains throughout the play. His first speech shows with what deadly seriousness he takes life and how much he despises frivolity. After a clever syllogistic display by the professional clown, Olivia asks Malvolio: "What think you of this fool, Malvolio? Doth he not mend?" Malvolio answers: "Yes, and shall do till the pangs of death shake him. Infirmity, that decays the wise, doth ever make the better fool." A man to whom death and decay are the frames of reference for life represents values directly opposed to those of Sir Toby, whose first speech also mentions death, but with what a difference! "What a plague means my niece, to take the death of her brother thus? I am sure care's an enemy to life." Here the two attitudes which were already at war in Shakespeare's England are personified, and there was no doubt on which side

Shakespeare stood, for the Malvolio position was actively opposed to the theatre. Malvolio was to have his greatest triumph in Cromwell, but Sir Toby was to come into his own again with Charles II. The enmity of the two attitudes is still a basic constituent of the life of all English-speaking countries, and Sir Toby's challenging retort to Malvolio has an enduring relevance: "Dost thou think because thou art virtuous, there shall be no more cakes and ale?" But Malvolio is no mere Aunt Sally, set up to be knocked down. Shakespeare respects the strength and integrity of the man, however dangerously misguided he may think it to be, and it is essential that Malvolio remain unreconciled, and that he have no part in the general happiness with which the comedy ends.

Malvolio's ideological intransigence is flawed with human weakness; he is so eager to be the nonpareil in his Lady's favor that he must find fault with anybody who might challenge that position. He not only objects to fooling in general but to this particular Fool, who finds favor with Olivia, and so he goes on to criticize the quality of his wit. Olivia replies with a precise and penetrating analysis of Malvolio: "Oh, you are sick of self-love, Malvolio, and taste with a distempered appetite. To be generous, guiltless, and of free disposition is to take those things for bird bolts that you deem cannon bullets." That second sentence has little application to the immediate scene; it is a generalization which shows that Malvolio took delight in reporting the peccadillos of the household to Olivia, as he did in the case of Fabian; probably one of his most frequent utterances was: "My Lady shall know of it."

In asking Malvolio to deal with "Cesario," the disguised Viola, both before and after she has seen "him," Olivia does not treat her steward as a messenger but as an ambassador; she tells him to say "What you will," which, incidentally, is Shakespeare's alternative title to the play. Malvolio certainly takes full advantage of his license when he returns the ring to Cesario; he had had no indication at all that the ring had been "peevishly" thrown at Olivia, but it gives him an excuse for doing just that in return, thus emphasizing his superior status to a young whippersnapper who had behaved to him in a "very ill manner" when they had first met at the gate.

Malvolio's intrusion upon the rowdy midnight drinking bout of Sir Toby, Sir Andrew, and the Clown was in fulfillment of his duties and not merely an expression of his fun-hating propensities. Maria makes this quite clear: "If my lady have not called up her steward Malvolio and bid him turn you out of doors, never trust me." Again Malvolio is the ambassador of Olivia and invested with her powers, to turn even her own uncle out of doors. It is usual, and I believe fitting, for Malvolio to make his midnight entrance clad in a nightdress and a nightcap, but wearing his chain of office; his dignity may seem absurd in such a dress and such a setting, but it is as natural and necessary to him as breathing. Malvolio's deep class-consciousness is apparent in the terms with which he reviles the merrymakers; he thinks that noisy reveling is an activity befitting the lowliest artisans, tinkers and cobblers; and his basic regard for decorum is expressed in the rhetorical question, "Is there no respect of place, persons, nor time in you?" The tone and the words with which Malvolio confronts Sir Toby are not those of a servant bringing a message. Malvolio is outraged by the conduct of the drunken knight and speaks in his own voice but with the authority of Olivia:

> Sir Toby, I must be round with you. My lady bade me tell you that, though she harbours you as her kinsman, she's nothing allied to your disorders. If you can separate yourself and your misdemeanours, you are welcome to the house; if not, an it would please you to take leave of her, she is very willing to bid you farewell.

But Sir Toby is too drunk to take the hint, and he replies to Malvolio as himself and not as Olivia's steward; he knows the weapon that will give the most hurt, a social gibe; he may be a rowdy drunk but he shares Olivia's blood, and the truth of his words stings when he says, "Art any more than a steward?" He further points the gibe with, "Go, sir, rub your chain with crumbs," that chain which is at once the symbol of Malvolio's authority and his service; the reference to the polishing of the silver chain with breadcrumbs was the final indignity, for it was the function of a menial to clean the household silver. None of the others dares confront Malvolio like that; Feste in their improvised duet suggests that even Sir Toby "dare not." Maria says not a word, not even when Malvolio rebukes her for supplying the carousers with drink. On the contrary, when she sees that Sir Toby is going to defy Malvolio, she tries to restrain him. Not until Malvolio is gone, and is well out of sight and hearing, does she dare to say, "Go shake your ears."

But it is Maria who concocts the plot of the letter, which depends upon her skill in imitating Olivia's handwriting, an accomplishment which she had probably often put to use in dealing with the minutiae of her lady's correspondence. Just as Olivia gave us our first insight into Malvolio, it is now Maria who completes the picture; Shakespeare's women are almost invariably the more perceptive of the two sexes. She calls him "a timepleaser, an affectioned ass, that cons state without book and utters it by great swarths; the best persuaded of himself, so crammed, as he thinks, with excellencies, that it is his grounds of faith that all that look on him love him."

Malvolio spends his life in learning to act as the nobleman he wishes he were would act. Thus, when we next see him he will have been "yonder i' the sun practising behaviour to his own shadow this half hour." There is no man so well versed in etiquette as the social climber. He tries desperately to keep in touch with the latest vogue at Court; it is in this sense that he is a "timepleaser." To illustrate this, one production had him speak with a West Country accent, for there might have been a time, and apparently there is some evidence that there was, when the young gallants at Court wished to be mistaken for the fellow-countrymen of such idolized adventurers as Drake and Raleigh. Again, from his point of view, and with some justification, he is a paragon of excellencies, and he believes that anyone of taste and judgment would recognize this; already he knows the high regard in which Olivia holds him.

At the beginning of the Letter scene, in which Malvolio is trapped by his vanity and ambition, Sir Toby describes him as "the niggardly rascally sheep-biter." The first epithet is Sir Toby's prejudiced description of Malvolio's careful stewardship of the household purse; "rascally sheep-biter" compares his petty fault-finding and tale-carrying with the way a sheep dog nips at the sheep to prevent them from straying from the way in which they should go; "rascally" is deserved because Malvolio does get a perverse delight from his sheep-biting.

Malvolio enters intoning his theme song: "'Tis but fortune. All is fortune." This is the moan of all ambitious but lowly-born talents in a class-ridden society. We then find that he is audaciously thinking of the Lady Olivia, and so is in exactly the right mood to be caught by the letter which he will want to believe is from her. He has been too ready to misinterpret her complimentary remarks; it is certainly true that she has treated him "with a more exalted respect than anyone else that follows her," and apparently she had said, one day, as a supreme compliment, that, if she married, it would be someone of his temperament. To marry a title is the only way Malvolio can expect to acquire one. His imagination feeds full on "To be Count Malvolio!" and the aspect of noble rank which most appeals to him is not the wealth or gracious living but the exercise of social superiority, and in his fantasy he chooses to exercise this alone, "having come from a day-bed, where I have left Olivia sleeping." He sees himself in a rich velvet gown calling the household officers about him and telling them the cardinal rule of social behavior: "I know my place as I would they should do theirs." Then "Count Malvolio" calls for his "kinsman Toby;" it is very revealing of Malvolio's aspirations that in his fantasy both Olivia and her uncle have lost their titles, for he is now their social equal. "Seven of my people, with an obedient start, make out for him." "Count Malvolio" keeps a great estate with a large retinue all trained to strict obedience and eager to please him. "I frown the while,"—the aspect he most enjoys—"and perchance wind up my watch, or play with my—some rich jewel." In feeling for the imagined jewel, Malvolio touches his chain; reality has intruded upon the fantasy, only to be quickly discarded. "Toby approaches, curtsies there to me—" The unseen and onlooking Sir Toby can scarcely be restrained at that, but contents himself with "Shall this fellow live?" Malvolio is now lost in the pantomime of his fantasy: "I extend my hand to him thus, quenching my familiar smile with an austere regard of control." Smiling for Malvolio is certainly not familiar, in our sense of the word; he uses the word strictly, meaning that it is a countenance reserved for equals, and since the real Malvolio lives in a world of superiors and inferiors, a smile is never called for. When he learns in the fake letter that Olivia wants him to smile, it is to him further proof of her desire to make him an equal. The reason "Count Malvolio" wishes to see his "cousin Toby" is not surprising: "You must amend your drunkenness," and he goes on to chide him for associating with Sir Andrew Aguecheek, and, in so doing, voices a principle of the no-nonsense, work-hard, up-and-coming London merchant class, to most of whom the theatre was anathema: Don't "waste the treasure of your time."

The letter has been brilliantly concocted by Maria; it must not only have the authenticity of Olivia's phrases but Malvolio must find it credible, and he is not a stupid man. With his beliefs and attitudes, he would understand that Olivia could not declare herself openly to him, and he would approve of the device of leaving the letter for fortune to decide whether he should see it; further, it would have to be couched in riddle-like terms, in case somebody else chanced upon it.

After some teasing lines of verse, which contain such plain indications as "I may command where I adore," the first injunction is: "If this fall into thy hand, revolve." In several productions I have seen Malvolio stand and turn around at this point, which, to quote Hamlet, "though it make the unskillful laugh, cannot but make the judicious grieve," for it makes Malvolio a silly idiot. The word "revolve" here means "consider," "turn it over in your mind," "puzzle it out," a meaning which the word seems to have acquired in the fifteenth century. The letter appeals to Malvolio's belief, by referring to the stars, fate, and fortune. He is told to "be not afraid of greatness," and "greatness" to Malvolio meant only one thing: the status of the aristocracy. The letter implies that there are three ways of acquiring a title: birth, outstanding achievement, and marriage. It then counsels him to begin to act in those very ways in which we have seen him indulge in his fantasy: "Be opposite with a kinsman, surly with servants, let thy tongue tang arguments of state, put thyself into the trick of singularity." That last piece of advice has often marked those who for any reason are self-securely exceptional; they are not as other men, so they don't have to act as if they were. The letter ends with the most enticing bait: "She that would alter services with thee;" now she is his Lady, but, if he married her, he would become her Lord. As part of the necessarily unspoken wooing, he must give a sign that he has found and read the letter; he is to wear yellow stockings and cross-gartering, which must have been a stylish affectation of the moment. We imagine Malvolio as invariably sober-suited, but occasionally he must have made a bold atempt at following a courtly fashion, for the letter mentions that Olivia had commended his yellow stockings and cross-gartering; she had obviously done so out of politeness to cover his embarrassment, for we learn later " 'tis a colour she abhors, and cross-gartered, a fashion she detests." The postscript asks him to smile, an unaccustomed activity which will require much practice before a mirror.

When, obeying every injunction of the letter, Malvolio comes to woo Olivia, it is small wonder that she thinks he is suffering from a "very midsummer madness," for his dialogue largely consists of diligently learned quotations from the letter, which sound like gibberish to her. And when, in her presence, he treats Maria with the hauteur prescribed in the letter, it is further proof that he has lost his balance. Olivia hastily escapes with Maria, telling her to fetch Sir Toby to look after Malvolio. This only convinces Malvolio of the truth of the letter, for no less a person than her own uncle is to come to him so that he can start to treat him from the standpoint of his approaching status. He even misinterprets her use of the word "fellow" in reference to him, taking it literally as implying equality of rank.

Sir Toby, Fabian, and Maria approach cautiously, pretending that Malvolio is indeed mad, possessed of the Devil. They adopt a variety of approaches, but Malvolio is only concerned with the acting out of his new role, and, since they will not leave him to enjoy his privacy, he leaves them with his constant judgment on all of them and their like: "You are idle shallow things."

After Malvolio's exit, Sir Toby propounds the culmination of the plot: "Come, we'll have him in a dark room and bound. My niece is already in the belief that he's mad. We may carry it thus, for our pleasure and his penance, till our very pastime, tired out of breath, prompt us to have mercy on him." This use of the inhuman Elizabethan treatment of insanity is, of course, quite inexcusable, but it is to be noted that it was done in sportful revenge for many injuries received, that it was not to be kept up indefinitely, and that there was hope it might do Malvolio some good. Fabian, already somewhat guilt-stricken, even voices the opinion that it may "make him mad indeed;" but Maria replies flippantly, "The house will be the quieter."

It is Maria, too, who prompts the tormenting of Malvolio while he is confined in the dark; it is she who procures the clerical gown and the beard for Feste to masquerade as Sir Topas, the curate, visiting the afflicted Malvolio, though she comments later, "Thou mightst have done this without thy gown and beard. He sees thee not;" still the disguise was aimed at giving the onlookers more fun, both those on the stage and those in the audience. In a clever skit on the examination of the insane, it is the examiner that exhibits craziness. Sir Toby, who is now in bad odor with Olivia, has qualms about the trick they have played on Malvolio:

"I would we were well rid of this knavery. If he may be conveniently delivered, I would he were." But that is not going to
be so easy. How can they explain the trick to Olivia, without
incurring her wrath? He asks the Clown to go in his own person
to Malvolio; he does this and agrees to get the wherewithal for
the imprisoned man to write to Olivia, thus preparing the way for
the denouement.

Absorbed by her romantic complications and their unravel-
ing, even Olivia has forgotten about Malvolio. When she is reminded of him, she sends for him:

> . . . Fetch Malvolio hither.
> And yet, alas, now I remember me,
> They say, poor gentleman, he's much distract.
> A most extracting frenzy of mine own
> From my remembrance clearly banished his.

"They say" implies that she has received reports of Malvolio's
condition subsequent to her alarming encounter with him; those
reports have presumably come from Maria and Sir Toby. At this
point the Clown brings Olivia the letter from Malvolio, and the
perpetrators of the trick must be very worried. But the opening
of the letter seems clear proof of Malvolio's distraction, for, in
his justifiable anger, he omits all courteous address, of which the
normal Malvolio would have been a master, and begins, "By the
Lord, madam." Olivia is affronted, and is in no mood to endure
the Clown's fooling on the matter; she asks Fabian to read the
letter, which, as the Duke says, "savours not much of distraction,"
and ends, as it began, in a way deliberately uncharacteristic of
the man: "I leave my duty a little unthought-of, and speak out
of my injury. The Madly-Used Malvolio." Olivia does not ask
for an explanation but sends Fabian to fetch Malvolio so that he
can speak for himself.

When Malvolio produces the original letter, Olivia sees at
once that he has been the victim of a plot in which Maria is impli-

cated, and her judgment is as full a retribution as could be conceived:

> But when we find the grounds and authors of it,
> Thou shalt be both the plaintiff and the judge
> Of thine own cause.

It falls to Fabian to plead for the pranksters, for Sir Toby and Maria are not present; they are away somewhere celebrating their somewhat surprising marriage. Fabian, in a proper gentlemanlike manner, implicates himself, though he had but a minor role in the plotting; he also tries to take the blame as much as possible from Maria, who Olivia already knows is involved:

> Most freely I confess, myself and Toby
> Set this device against Malvolio here,
> Upon some stubborn and uncourteous parts
> We had conceived against him. Maria writ
> The letter at Sir Toby's great importance,
> In recompense whereof he hath married her.
> How with a sportful malice it was followed
> May rather pluck on laughter than revenge,
> If that the injuries be justly weighed
> That have on both sides passed.

There have indeed been injuries on both sides, but Fabian's hope that the incident would be erased in laughter is not to be fulfilled. Olivia's comment is full of compassion for Malvolio: "Alas, poor fool, how have they baffled thee!" That "poor fool" is a term of affection; it is exactly the same phrase with which Lear expresses his love for the dead Cordelia.

Fabian, probably out of consideration for the Clown's livelihood, had deliberately omitted mention of his part in the plot, but Feste himself now declares it, and reminds both Malvolio and Olivia of the way in which Malvolio had tried to get him dismissed by discrediting his power of fooling. For the Clown it had been a simple case of tit-for-tat: "And thus the whirligig of time brings in his revenges."

Malvolio waits for no more but dashes out with the vicious cry: "I'll be revenged on the whole pack of you." The whole pack; everybody shall be made to suffer by the embittered man who feels that he has been given a dirty deal, first by birth and then by society. The Duke gives the order, "Pursue him, and entreat him to a peace," but we feel that such a move will be fruitless. Malvolio cannot be a part of any social happiness; his only perverse satisfaction in life will be to live out his name, "Ill-Wisher."

12   Angelo

COLERIDGE SAID, "*Measure for Measure* is the simple exception to the delightfulness of Shakespeare's plays. It is a hateful work, although Shakespearean throughout. Our feelings of justice are grossly wounded in Angelo's escape." This, to me, is a sad misreading of the play, the title of which is ironic, for at the end of the play measure is not meted out for measure, nor an eye taken for an eye. A main theme of the play, as in *The Merchant of Venice*, is that justice must not be mechanically applied but must be tempered with mercy. Portia's great plea for mercy is echoed in a speech by Isabella:

> No ceremony that to great ones 'longs,
> Not the king's crown, nor the deputed sword,
> The marshal's truncheon, nor the judge's robe,
> Become them with one half so good a grace
> As mercy does.

Shakespeare examines the whole question much more deeply in this later play, which came some seven or eight years after *The Merchant of Venice*. He knows that there are occasions when mercy may seem to be a mistake. Thus, old Escalus dismisses the pimp, Pompey, with a warning, but Pompey shows clearly that he has been let off only to return to his former fleshly trade. He says, "I thank your worship for your good counsel; [*Aside*] but I shall follow it as the flesh and fortune shall better determine." And Escalus himself realizes that to forgive a criminal may be but to release him to further crime:

> Mercy is not itself, that oft looks so;
> Pardon is still the nurse of second woe.

Angelo at the end, with admirable integrity, pleads that the law which he has so rigorously applied shall be so applied to him:

> Immediate sentence, then, and sequent death
> Is all the grace I beg.

And later:

> I am sorry that such sorrow I procure;
> And so deep sticks it in my penitent heart
> That I crave death more willingly than mercy.
> 'Tis my deserving, and I do entreat it.

But mercy wins. In asking for Angelo's death, Coleridge is deaf to the plea of Shakespeare in the play and ranges himself with Gratiano when he wanted the death of Shylock; when Portia said, "What mercy can you render him, Antonio?" Gratiano's comment was, "A halter gratis; nothing else, for God's sake."

It is customary to say that *Measure for Measure* loses its greatness after the first three acts. Such criticism is of the same kind as that which begged Bernard Shaw to omit the Epilogue in his *Saint Joan*; in both cases the point of the play would have been missed. The quick pairing of the couples at the end of *Measure for Measure* is not just the mechanical necessity for a happy ending, as it is in some of the comedies; it is the expression of a higher justice than that of the law. In proof of this, Shakespeare brings back Barnadine, the perpetually drunken criminal to whom the prison had been a home for nine years. His reappearance at the end of the play has no relevance to the plot; he is there just to be pardoned:

> Sirrah, thou art said to have a stubborn soul
> That apprehends no further than this world,
> And squarest thy life according. Thou'rt condemned.
> But, for those earthly faults, I quit them all,
> And pray thee take this mercy to provide
> For better times to come. Friar, advise him;
> I leave him to your hand.

In this play against the background of an evil and licentious city, the torment of frustrated sexual passion expresses itself in cruelty and is opposed by a militant virtue; cynicism about life is expressed by a Friar counseling a doomed young man to wish for death as being preferable to life. It is indeed a bitter comedy, and its language is often appropriately difficult, but, in addition to the density and compression of the language, characteristic of Shakespeare at this point in his career, there are additional difficulties in parts of *Measure for Measure* due to a faultily transmitted text.

In the thesis of the difference between the letter of the law and a merciful administration of justice, the Duke and Angelo are the opposing exemplars, but, quite apart from his function in the thesis, it is Angelo the man who absorbs us. His name itself is significant:

> Oh, what may man within him hide,
> Though angel on the outward side!

He is a supreme example of the inherent duplicity of man; the cold and passionless exterior of apparent incorruptibility may cover deeps of ravenous and guilty desire, and the inhuman but correct exercise of power may be an expression of a ruthless self-discipline aimed at taming the beast within:

> He doth with holy abstinence subdue
> That in himself which he spurs on his power
> To qualify in others. . . .

Among the sonnets there is one that could have been spoken by Angelo. I feel sure that the same mood in Shakespeare which produced the character of Angelo produced the sonnet. It is the cry of a man embittered by his slavery to lust:

> The expense of spirit in a waste of shame
> Is lust in action; and till action, lust
> Is perjured, murderous, bloody, full of blame,
> Savage, extreme, rude, cruel, not to trust;
> Enjoyed no sooner but despised straight,
> Past reason hunted, and no sooner had
> Past reason hated, as a swallowed bait,
> On purpose laid to make the taker mad;
> Mad in pursuit, and in possession so;
> Had, having, and in quest to have, extreme;
> A bliss in proof, and proved, a very woe;
> Before, a joy proposed; behind, a dream.
> > All this the world well knows; yet none knows well
> > To shun the heaven that leads men to this hell.

The appearance that Angelo presents to the world has even deceived the cynical and licentious Lucio, for he describes him as:

> . . . a man whose blood
> Is very snow broth; one who never feels
> The wanton stings and motions of the sense,
> But doth rebate and blunt his natural edge
> With profits of the mind, study and fast.

The prince who disguises himself as a beggar to observe the life of his subjects is a well-worn convention in tales of many countries, and it is as such a convention that it must be accepted in *Measure for Measure*, but among the motives which determine the Duke to disguise himself as a friar it would appear that one was to test Angelo himself, for he seemed too good to be true. He describes him as "a man of stricture and firm abstinence," and later says:

> . . . Lord Angelo is precise,
> Stands at a guard with envy, [*i.e.* will take care that

> his judgments will not be influenced by ill-will]
> scarce confesses
> That his blood flows or that his appetite
> Is more to bread than stone. Hence shall we see,
> If power change purpose, what our seemers be.

In his commission to Angelo, the Duke had been careful to link mercy with the power of life-or-death:

> In our remove be thou at full ourself.
> Mortality and mercy in Vienna
> Live in thy tongue and heart. . . .

It is revealing that Angelo's first act is to revive a law, long in disuse, which made sexual indulgence outside the marriage bond punishable by death. (There are still communities, I believe, where this is the law.) The first victim of the new law is Claudio, who has got Juliet with child. They were betrothed and were only delaying marriage to ensure the goodwill of people who had control of her dowry. The sexual rights of the period between betrothal, which sometimes took place in a church, and marriage were much in question in Shakespeare's day. His own was very much a case in point. There is no record of his marriage, but there is a record that a license to marry, after only one calling of the banns, was issued by the Bishop of Worcester. The usual practice was, and still is, that the banns should be called on three successive Sundays; Shakespeare's special license was to expedite the marriage. He was nineteen at the time and Anne Hathaway was eight years older. They had obviously gone to bed together during their betrothal because, even assuming that they were married immediately after the single calling of the banns, their first daughter, Susanna, was born within six months of the marriage. So Shakespeare could sympathize with Claudio's dilemma.

Angelo makes his position about the strict administration of the law clear the first time we see him in his new office:

> We must not make a scarecrow of the law,
> Setting it up to fear [i.e. frighten] the birds of prey,

> And let it keep one shape till custom make it
> Their perch, and not their terror.

It is because of this unequivocal position that the Duke has chosen Angelo as his deputy over the more obvious choice, Escalus. If some curb was to be placed on the excesses of the city, a stern administrator of the law was needed; Escalus, as we have already seen, allows his kindly nature to pardon criminals, even though he knows that, in the interests of society, he cannot justify such a proceeding. In trying to mitigate the sterness of Angelo's attitude and to justify his own more lenient one, Escalus points out that a judge too is a potential breaker of the law, and asks

> Whether you had not sometime in your life
> Erred in this point which now you censure him,
> And pulled the law upon you.

Angelo's immediate reply is a priggish one:

> 'Tis one thing to be tempted, Escalus,
> Another thing to fall. . . .

But he goes on to point out that if law had to be administered by perfect men, there would be no law; imperfect men have to punish crime when it is disclosed; undiscovered crimes escape punishment. Here Angelo is admirably reasonable:

> . . . I not deny,
> The jury, passing on the prisoner's life,
> May in the sworn twelve have a thief or two
> Guiltier than him they try. What's open made to justice,
> That justice seizes. . . .
> .   .   .   .   .   .
> You may not so extenuate his offence
> For I have had such faults; but rather tell me,
> When I that censure him do so offend,
> Let mine own judgement pattern out my death,
> And nothing come in partial. . . .

He did not realize then that his own judgment was indeed to

pattern out his death, but, when the time came, he begged to be a victim of his own merciless interpretation of the law.

Angelo's first instinct is to punish the unsavory, hoping some legal excuse may be found for doing so. In the low-comedy scene in which the malapropisms of the clownish constable, Elbow, and the garrulousness of the accused pimp, Pompey, drag on endlessly, Angelo grows tired of it and leaves the final decision of the case to Escalus, but he has prejudged the case, for he hopes that Escalus will "find good cause to whip them all."

When the Provost comes again to Angelo to make sure that the sentence of Claudio's death is to be carried out, Angelo is angered by the suggestion that he might have been weak enough to change his mind; in his disposition of the pregnant Juliet he is cold but not cruel:

> See you the fornicatress be removed.
> Let her have needful, but not lavish, means.

Before we deal with the first of the powerful scenes between Angelo and Isabella, it is important to consider Shakespeare's conception of her character. In the accepted original of the story, the sister does agree to the condition of fornication to save her brother's life, but Shakespeare's Isabella sets a higher value on her chastity than on Claudio's life, and to give this choice more force and credibility, Shakespeare makes Isabella a novice; she is preparing herself to become a bride of Christ and not of man. To the great majority of people today, when chastity is set at low value and, if deliberately persisted in, is considered as a sick aberration, Isabella's choice is ridiculous, perverse, and heartless. They would say to Isabella as Bassanio did to the disguised Portia: "To do a great right, do a little wrong." But Isabella believed deeply what most Christians give but lip service to, that this life is but a brief moment in which to prepare for eternity; such a certainty alters the normal attitude to both life and death; it puts a higher value upon the way every moment of life is lived and takes away the terror of death. Most critics who so roundly condemn Isabella fail to notice that she would willingly give her life for her brother, and that, to her, Claudio's soul was infinitely more precious than his body. As to Isabella's cherishing of her chastity, she was only upholding the basic moral teaching of the Church, and it is with the Church that most of her critics should find fault and not with Isabella; we may not approve of her inherited values, but we must admire her logic and courage in maintaining them.

Isabella is well aware of the ambiguity in her plea to Angelo, for she condemns her brother's sin as thoroughly as does the law:

> There is a vice that most I do abhor,
> And most desire should meet the blow of justice,
> For which I would not plead but that I must,
> For which I must not plead but that I am
> At war 'twixt will and will not.

Angelo seems impervious to the arguments of the "fair maid," and is unassailable in his position as the impersonal emissary of the law:

> It is the law, not I, condemn your brother.
> Were he my kinsman, brother, or my son,
> It should be thus with him. . . .

We know that Angelo means those words. And he goes on to give the argument of all those who look upon legal punishment as a deterrent. When Isabella says that many have committed the offense, Angelo says:

> The law hath not been dead, though it hath slept.
> Those many had not dared to do that evil
> If the first that did the edict infringe
> Had answered for his deed. . . .

Then Isabella uses an argument that tells:

> . . . Go to your bosom;
> Knock there, and ask your heart what it doth know
> That's like my brother's fault. If it confess

A natural guiltiness such as is his,
Let it not sound a thought upon your tongue
Against my brother's life.

Angelo's desire for Isabella has begun to stir, and he temporizes by asking her to return on the morrow. She mentions the word "bribe," at which Angelo bridles, but he relaxes when he finds that her bribe was the spiritual one of prayers.

When he is alone, we hear the first signs of the torment that has begun to rage in him. Shakespeare shows that it bursts out of him immediately after Isabella's exit, for he completes her last sentence, "Save your honour," with the words, "From thee, even from thy virtue." He realizes that it is Isabella's glowing purity that is the essence of her attraction to him. In his first meeting with her, the loose-living and loose-tongued Lucio had said to her:

I hold you as a thing enskied and sainted,
By your renouncement, an immortal spirit,
And to be talked with in sincerity,
As with a saint;

and it is this very quality in her that Angelo is being moved to desecrate:

What dost thou, or what art thou, Angelo?
Dost thou desire her foully for those things
That make her good? Oh, let her brother live.
Thieves for their robbery have authority
When judges steal themselves. What, do I love her,
That I desire to hear her speak again
And feast upon her eyes? What is't I dream on?
O cunning enemy, that to catch a saint
With saints dost bait thy hook? Most dangerous
Is that temptation that doth goad us on
To sin in loving virtue. Never could the strumpet,
With all her double vigour, art and nature,
Once stir my temper; but this virtuous maid
Subdues me quite. Ever till now,
When men were fond, [i.e. foolish] I smiled and wondered
    how.

Angelo is in the double torment of desire and guilt. He is his own harshest judge, both as a man of integrity and as the official embodiment of that law which he is being tempted to break; at this stage there is no hint of the villainous hypocrite in him, no trace of the man who deliberately hides the face of lust with the mask of austerity.

When he awaits the coming of Isabella on the next morning, instinctively he prays, but, as in the case of Claudius in *Hamlet*, "[his] thoughts fly up, [his] words remain below." This is how Angelo puts it:

> When I would pray and think, I think and pray
> To several subjects. Heaven hath my empty words,
> Whilst my invention, hearing not my tongue,
> Anchors on Isabel. Heaven in my mouth,
> As if I did but only chew his name,
> And in my heart the strong and swelling evil
> Of my conception. . . .

He admits that he takes a sinful pride in his public image, but only now does he realize how false that image is. He had been fooled by his own mask. He is led to a bitter reflection on the power of outward forms:

> . . . O place, O form,
> How often dost thou with thy case, thy habit,
> Wrench awe from fools, and tie the wiser souls
> To thy false seeming! Blood, thou art blood.

This whole soliloquy is a most poignant revelation of a would-be good man in the throes of temptation, in which his honestly held beliefs are being battered by lust.

The announcement of the approach of Isabella quite undoes him:

> Why does my blood thus muster to my heart,
> Making both it unable for itself,
> And dispossessing all my other parts
> Of necessary fitness?

The climactic scene between Angelo and Isabella is one of astonishing brilliance and power. When Angelo castigates the sin for which Claudio must die, his words now lacerate himself, and almost everything he says has double meaning. But Isabella sees only the figure of implacable justice, and his subtle suggestions are all lost on her. In angry frustration he complains:

> Your sense pursues not mine. Either you are ignorant,
> Or seem so, craftily, and that's not good.

He is forced to say:

> . . . But mark me:
> To be received plain, I'll speak more gross.

Then, hiding his passion as best he can, he puts his proposition to her as an abstract speculation. (In this speech, there are two irritating examples of almost certain mistakes in the received text: "loss of question" and "all-building law." An eighteenth-century Shakespearean scholar, Lewis Theobald, suggested "all-binding law" for the latter. For the former, "loose of question" has been suggested, but I have the temerity to suggest "gloss of question.") Angelo says:

> Admit no other way to save his life—
> As I subscribe not that, nor any other,
> But in the gloss of question—that you, his sister,
> Finding yourself desired of such a person
> Whose credit with the judge, or own great place,
> Could fetch your brother from the manacles
> Of the all-binding law; and that there were
> No earthly mean to save him, but that either
> You must lay down the treasures of your body
> To this supposed, or else to let him suffer—
> What would you do?

Isabella, in the spirit of academic argument, bases her reply on her value that the life of the soul is immeasurably more important than the death of the body. Angelo replies in words that Isabella's critics have echoed since:

> Were not you, then, as cruel as the sentence
> That you have slandered so?

Her answer rightly puts the onus of Claudio's death upon Angelo:

> Ignomy in ransom and free pardon
> Are of two houses. Lawful mercy
> Is nothing akin to foul redemption.

Angelo now catches Isabella in a contradiction; she had played down the seriousness of Claudio's sin but now, in argument, says she would not commit the same sin to save his life. Her answer shows that she is not the prig, which she has so often been accused of being; it is an acknowledgment of human weakness:

> Oh, pardon me, my lord. It oft falls out,
> To have what we would have, we speak not what we mean.
> I something do excuse the thing I hate
> For his advantage that I dearly love.

Angelo seizes on this as the first chink in the armor, and, under cover of his answer, reveals the sad truth he has discovered about himself: "We are all frail." He is emboldened to speak more plainly, but Isabella is merely confused and says:

> . . . Gentle my lord,
> Let me entreat you speak the former language.

Angelo is forced to be completely blunt: "Plainly conceive, I love you." In the dawning horror of the intention of this robed justice, Isabella still strives to maintain the spirit of the argument:

> My brother did love Juliet,
> And you tell me that he shall die for it.

And then Angelo unambiguously states his condition:

> He shall not, Isabel, if you give me love.

In her revulsion against the truth behind the mask, Isabella echoes the words of the Duke and Angelo himself: "Seeming, seeming!"

Then quickly she believes she has found the way to save her brother's life:

> Sign me a present pardon for my brother,
> Or with an outstretched throat I'll tell the world aloud
> What man thou art.

But Angelo is safe in the power of his seeming:

> Who will believe thee, Isabel?
> My unsoiled name, the austereness of my life,
> My vouch against you, and my place i' the state,
> Will so your accusation overweigh,
> That you shall stifle in your own report
> And smell of calumny. . . .

Now the dam of his control is broken, and the murky floods overwhelm him:

> . . . Redeem thy brother
> By yielding up thy body to my will,
> Or else he must not only die the death,
> But thy unkindness shall his death draw out
> To lingering sufferance. Answer me tomorrow,
> Or, by the affection that now guides me most,
> I'll prove a tyrant to him. As for you,
> Say what you can, my false o'erweighs your true.

This threat of death by slow torture is probably as humiliating a revelation to Angelo of the depth of cruelty within him as it is a horrible one to Isabella. The words of the sonnet are fully realized:

> . . . and till action, lust
> Is perjured, murderous, bloody, full of blame,
> Savage, extreme, rude, cruel, not to trust.

It is at this point in the story that we learn a startling fact about Angelo. He too, like Claudio, was betrothed to a woman with full intention to marry her, but when her dowry was lost with her brother at sea, the ambitious Angelo, robbed of the money, had deserted his Mariana. The situations of Angelo and Claudio are parallel, with the important difference that Angelo had refrained from taking advantage of the pact to sleep with his bride-to-be.

This device of parallelism is an important element in several of Shakespeare's plays; thus, in *King Lear*, we have two old men who suffer at the hands of heartless children, and in *Hamlet* there are three sons, Hamlet, Laertes and Fortinbras, who are all burdened with the duty of avenging the death of a father. Incidentally, *Hamlet, Measure for Measure*, and *King Lear* were written at the same period of Shakespeare's development, probably within four years, and he may have become particularly aware at that time of the dramatic value of parallelism. It was at the time of the revival of the masque with its addition, with which Ben Jonson is usually credited, of the anti-masque, whose action paralleled that of the masque, usually for purposes of comic contrast. It is possible that Shakespeare was thus prompted to his own repeated use at this time of a similar device, but he used it for the very different purpose of illuminating and commenting upon one man's reaction to a situation by another man's different reaction to a similar situation. In the case of Angelo it helps to explain his harshness to Claudio, for in most men their own faults loom largest in their eyes, and so, in punishing Claudio, Angelo was punishing himself vicariously.

The substitution of Mariana for Isabella in the bed of Angelo is completely incredible and must be accepted as a plot convention —the same "bed-trick" is used in *All's Well That Ends Well*—but what matters is the truth as human beings of the characters. Shakespeare does his best to mitigate the incredibility of the substitution by making the Duke tell Isabella to impose these conditions upon Angelo: "that your stay with him may not be long, that the time may have all shadow and silence in it, and the place answer to convenience."

The irony of Angelo's public image is now at its greatest, and so Lucio's comic version of it is most telling: "They say this Angelo was not made by man and woman after this downright way of creation. . . . Some report a sea maid spawned him; some, that he was begot between two stockfishes [*i.e.* dried codfish]. But it is certain that when he makes water, his urine is congealed ice; that I know to be true."

The fact that Angelo breaks his promise after he has lain with Mariana in the supposed person of Isabella, and gives fresh order for the execution of Claudio, has given him the reputation of unredeemed villainy, for which Coleridge would have him hanged. But there is no hint of vindictive or sadistic satisfaction in Angelo as a motive for the killing of Claudio. Angelo himself gives a very practical reason for his decision:

> . . . He should have lived,
> Save that his riotous youth, with dangerous sense,
> Might in the times to come have ta'en revenge
> By so receiving a dishonoured life
> With ransom of such shame. . . .

But there is more to it than that. With Angelo's stern veneration of the law, he could not make it a scapegoat for his sin. His decision to proceed with the execution of Claudio was not an easy one:

> . . . Would yet he had lived!
> Alack, when once our grace we have forgot,
> Nothing goes right. We would, and we would not.

That Mariana still loves Angelo and persuades Isabella to join with her in begging for his life strikes some people as incredible, but love and reason often contradict each other. Furthermore, as I hope I have shown, there is much that is admirable in Angelo, and he is a man who will profit from self-chastening. Mariana says:

> They say best men are moulded out of faults,
> And, for the most, become much more the better
> For being a little bad; so may my husband.

Even Isabella, who wanted but recently "to pluck out his eyes," recognizes the good there was in Angelo before he became unbalanced by his lust for her:

> . . . I partly think
> A due sincerity governed his deeds,
> Till he did look on me. Since it is so,
> Let him not die. . . .

Angelo himself says not one word in extenuation of his fault; he merely craves his legal due of death. When he learns that his order for Claudio's death had, by an evasion, not been carried out, he expresses no relief or joy. A man so severe with himself could not have his burden of guilt lifted so easily. The Duke knows his man, and knows that, even though he benefited by it, he would not be happy that the law had been thwarted by the substitution of the head of Ragozine for that of Claudio. Most men would be infinitely grateful to the Provost for the ruse, but not Angelo, and so the Duke says:

> Forgive him, Angelo, that brought you home
> The head of Ragozine for Claudio's.
> The offence pardons itself.

In those last four words the Duke proclaims that there is a higher justice than that of measure for measure.

13   Leontes

IN RECENT DECADES, *The Winter's Tale*, like other plays of the "Final Period," "The Last Phase," has been so overladen with symbolic significance, both mythological and theological, as almost to squash the life out of it. The mythologists see it as a rehash of the wonderful Greek allegory of the cycle of the seasons, with Perdita as Persephone and Hermione as Demeter, and of course it is that. The theologians see it as an allegory of the Christian cycle: sin, repentance, redemption; and of course it is that too. Then the theatre historians see it as an example of the new Jacobean vogue of dramatic romances enlivened with elements of the masque and anti-masque (the pastoral dance and the dance of the satyrs). It is all these things and more, but my purpose is to show that, in spite of its artifice and incredibility, it contains a superb study of a jealous man. Emilia's description of jealousy in Othello is much more applicable to Leontes:

> They are not ever jealous for the cause,
> But jealous for they are jealous. 'Tis a monster
> Begot upon itself, born on itself.

Those words are not true of Othello. His jealousy was not "begot upon itself," but was the result of the devilishly clever work of Iago, but, of course, Emilia did not know this. But the words are a perfect description of the jealousy of Leontes, who needed no Iago.

The Winter's Tale has been described as a play with a broken back, or two plays in one, because the first three acts are divided from the last two by "Time" who indicates a lapse of sixteen years. So much has this division been felt as a blemish that David Garrick made a play out of the second part, calling it *Florizel and Perdita*, prefacing it with a prose resumé of the action in the first part, and Garrick's distortion held the stage for half a century. But this division is the essence of Shakespeare's intention, for the play is one of sharp contrasts: jealousy-love, age-youth, death-life, cruelty-kindness; and this contrast is typified in the double setting of the play, Sicilia-Bohemia.

Many writers have pointed out that Shakespeare inverted the action in the two countries. He took the plot from Robert Greene's *Pandosto: The Triumph of Time*, in which Pandosto (Shakespeare's Leontes) is King of Bohemia, and Egistus (Shakespeare's Polixenes) is King of Sicily. Why did Shakespeare invert the two countries? It seems to me that he had a very good reason, revelatory of his purpose in the play. One country was a setting for the dark wintry realities of courtly life, the other for the bright spring of youth and love in an idealized countryside. One country must be for this play what the Forest of Arden was in *As You Like It*, what Prospero's island was to be in *The Tempest*, a place of escape and chastening and purification, from which men return to the real world the better able to deal with its harsh realities. Sicily, well-known to Elizabethan travelers and seamen, was too real a place for this magical atmosphere; Bohemia was much more mysterious and evocative, and is so still. I am sure that if English-speaking audiences seeing the play today were questioned about the whereabouts of the two countries, the great majority would be far more sure about Sicily than about Bohemia.

Lots of people down the years have had a laugh at Shakespeare's ignorance in giving a seacoast to Bohemia. Ben Jonson started it, for his Scottish friend, William Drummond, recorded him as saying, "Sheakspear in a play brought in a number of men saying they had suffered Shipwrack in Bohemia, wher ther is no Sea neer by some 100 Miles." But Shakespeare's Bohemia is not to be found on any map, nor is it bounded by physical limitations.

Shakespeare made fundamental alterations in Greene's story, in which Pandosto is guilty of incestuous feelings towards the beautiful girl whom he does not know to be his daughter; at the end of Greene's story Pandosto commits suicide. Instead, Shakespeare invents the extraordinary scene in which the statue of the supposedly dead Hermione comes to life. Of course it can have no rational credibility, but it is a superb coup de théâtre. A similar effect in Reinhardt's production of *The Miracle*, when a statue of the Virgin Mary comes to life, will always be remembered by those who saw it as a profoundly moving experience.

Several critics have felt that Shakespeare could have made the statue device a little more credible by letting us know in advance that Hermione was not dead; but the point was that he wanted to surprise us as much as the characters in the play. There is the subtler problem of why Paulina delayed the reconciliation between Hermione and the deeply repentant Leontes. In a manuscript note of Coleridge's, he even suggests how a reason for Paulina's delay might easily have been included: "This might have been easily affected by some obscure sentence of the oracle, as *e.g.*, 'Nor shall he ever recover an heir if he have a wife before that recovery.'" But surely the reason is implicit in the last pronouncement of the Delphic Oracle: "The King shall live without an heir if that which is lost be not found." Had Leontes and Hermione been joined together again before the discovery of their daughter, their union would have been barren, which would have been a deep sorrow to both of them. As we learn from Hermione's final speech in the play, both she and Paulina interpreted the oracle as giving hope that Perdita was still alive.

Shakespeare has been criticized for what is to me one of the profound truths in the play, the complete illogicality, and therefore incredibility, of Leontes' jealousy. But this is precisely the quality of jealousy: it springs from such a sense of insecurity, which in turn springs from a guilty sense of unworthiness, that it justifies its fears by distorting what it sees. It is particularly provoked by innocence because it cannot believe in it. Leontes is not jealous because of anything that happens, as is Othello. He is jealous by nature before the play begins, and masochistically he arranges occasions on which his jealousy can feed.

In his *Anatomy of Melancholy*, Burton says that of all the passions which the melancholy of love produces, jealousy is the worst.

> 'Tis a more vehement passion, a more furious perturbation, a bitter pain, a fire, a pernicious curiosity, a gall corrupting the honey of our life, madness, vertigo, plague, hell; they are more than ordinarily disquieted, they lose "bonum pacis," as Chrysostom observes; and though they be rich, keep sumptuous tables, be nobly allied, yet . . . they are most miserable, they are more than ordinarily discontent, more sad, . . . more than ordinarily suspicious.

The dialogue at the beginning of *The Winter's Tale* is redolent of flowery ambassadorial exchanges, which probably catered to the more exclusively courtly audience of the period. Polixenes expresses his thanks for the hospitality of Leontes in this fashion, but it is significant that the host speaks briefly and simply; he is looking for food for his jealousy in the ornate words of his guest. Furthermore, he is driven to beg him to stay longer, and to get Hermione to add her persuasions to his; if she is successful, it will be proof of their clandestine affair. He moves aside while Hermione speaks to Polixenes; the jealous man must not have his jealousy impaired by the facts of innocence; he must be left free to imagine the worst from looks, smiles, gestures. But as he rejoins the group, it was probably Shakespeare's intention for him to hear Hermione's final words, which, though completely innocent, sound very suspicious:

> The offences we have made you do we'll answer,
> If you first sinned with us, and that with us
> You did continue fault, and that you slipped not
> With any but with us.

Leontes' comment on Hermione's success in getting Polixenes to stay an extra week is "At my request he would not." He goes on to torment himself that it had taken him three sour months to gain the hand of Hermione, but now, in less than three minutes, she and Polixenes had come to agreement. The words she uses about the way men should deal with women Leontes most assuredly applies to Polixenes.

> . . . You may ride's
> With one soft kiss a thousand furlongs ere
> With spur we heat an acre.

Again Leontes moves away to give his jealousy scope to work him into a fury.

> Too hot, too hot!
> To mingle friendship far is mingling bloods.
> I have tremor cordis on me; my heart dances,
> But not for joy, not joy. . . .

His reason fights for control. After all, Hermione's conduct may be merely that of a good hostess; but reason stands little chance in the struggle:

> . . . This entertainment
> May a free face put on, derive a liberty
> From heartiness, from bounty, fertile bosom,
> And well become the agent; 't may, I grant;
> But to be paddling palms and pinching fingers,
> As now they are, and making practised smiles,
> As in a looking-glass, and then to sigh, as 'twere
> The mort of the deer—oh, that is entertainment
> My bosom likes not, nor my brows! . . .

"Nor my brows." With that phrase, jealousy begins its ultimate work of destruction, for it refers to the cuckold's horns.

Doubt about the paternity of his child, as groundless as that of Leontes, drove the Captain in Strindberg's *The Father* to the straitjacket. Hermione is pregnant; Leontes suspects Polixenes of being the father. And then he looks at his beloved Mamillius, his son and heir; his eyes tell him that the boy is his, and yet . . . and yet. . . .

There follows a difficult passage, whose intricate construction and ambiguous phraseology reflect the writhings of Leontes' soul:

> Affection, thy intention stabs the centre!
> Thou dost make possible things not so held,
> Communicatest with dreams—how can this be?—
> With what's unreal thou coactive art,
> And fellow'st nothing. Then 'tis very credent
> Thou mayst cojoin with something; and thou dost,
> And that beyond commission, and I find it,
> And that to the infection of my brains
> And hardening of my brows.

All depends on the interpretation of the first word, which I have seen explained as the lust of Hermione for Polixenes. I believe Leontes is talking about himself, and my paraphrase of the speech would be: My love for Hermione, in its desire to possess her completely, pains my very heart. Then reason tries again to assert itself, only to be knocked down again: It is true that my kind of love is ready to believe things that are not there, but in this case there definitely is something, and that beyond the bounds of the permissible, and it is that undoubted evidence that has infected my brains and made me fear I have been cuckolded.

Leontes' self-torturing doubts are now apparent in his face and call forth comments from Hermione and Polixenes. Leontes covers up by saying that he had been saddened by looking at Mamillius and remembering his own boyhood. This is a brilliant stroke by Shakespeare, because it is both a regret by Leontes for

lost innocence and a reminder of the days of his boyhood friendship with Polixenes, who had described their relationship in these
words:

> We were, fair Queen,
> Two lads that thought there was no more behind
> But such a day tomorrow as today,
> And to be boy eternal.
>   .   .   .   .   .
> We were as twinned lambs that did frisk i' the sun,
> And bleat the one at the other. What we changed
> Was innocence for innocence; we knew not
> The doctrine of ill-doing, no, nor dreamed
> That any did. . . .

To torture himself still further, Leontes again takes himself
off with Mamillius, to allow Hermione to walk with Polixenes;
he even compliments himself on his cleverness:

> . . . I am angling now,
> Though you perceive me not how I give line.

His certainty of the unfaithfulness of Hermione now turns
into a general denunciation of all womankind, and the degrading
words he uses reveal his own sensuality:

> . . . There have been,
> Or I am much deceived, cuckolds ere now.
> And many a man there is, even at this present,
> Now while I speak this, holds his wife by the arm,
> That little thinks she has been sluiced in's absence
> And his pond fished by his next neighbour, by
> Sir Smile, his neighbour. Nay, there's comfort in't
> Whiles other men have gates and those gates opened,
> As mine, against their will. Should all despair
> That have revolted wives, the tenth of mankind
> Would hang themselves. Physic for't there is none.
> It is a bawdy planet, that will strike
> Where 'tis predominant; and 'tis powerful, think it,
> From east, west, north, and south. Be it concluded,
> No barricado for a belly; know't;

It will let in and out the enemy
With bag and baggage. Many thousand on's
Have the disease and feel't not. . . .

While Leontes fires his fury with this speech, Hermione and
Polixenes are out of sight, gone for a walk at Leontes' own injunction, though he had even commented adversely on the speed
with which they had disappeared. Incidentally, Nicholas Rowe's
eighteenth-century addition of "Attendants" who accompany
Hermione and Polixenes on their walk serves but to make Leontes'
suspicions unnecessarily ridiculous; there is no indication in the
Folio text of attendants anywhere in the scene, and I feel there
should be none; the more intimate the scene the better. In the
absence of Hermione and Polixenes, the imagination of Leontes
about what they may be doing runs riot.

Now he needs confirmation of his suspicions and will twist
innocence into guilt. When Camillo points out under what seems
to be casual questioning that Leontes had failed to get Polixenes
to prolong his visit but that the Queen had succeeded, jealousy
immediately jumps to the conclusion that the whole Court is
whispering that he is a cuckold. He presses Camillo for confirmation of this new suspicion and misinterprets every sentence. Thus,
when Camillo says that Polixenes had stayed

To satisfy your Highness, and the entreaties
Of our most gracious mistress,

Leontes seizes on the sexual implications of the words "satisfy"
and "mistress";

Satisfy!
The entreaties of your mistress! Satisfy!

He must get Camillo to approve his suspicions, for Camillo has
been his confidant and father-confessor:

. . . I have trusted thee, Camillo,
With all the nearest things to my heart, as well
My chamber-councils; wherein, priest-like, thou

Hast cleansed my bosom, I from thee departed
Thy penitent reformed. . . .

As Leontes reveals his suspicions about Hermione, Camillo is
shocked in disbelief:

. . . 'Shrew my heart,
You never spoke what did become you less
Than this. . . .

In his anger and frustration, for he is desperate for Camillo's support, Leontes spews forth a list of what he conceives to be sure
proofs, distorting facts in the process, and attributing thoughts to
his guilty pair:

Is whispering nothing?
Is leaning cheek to cheek? Is meeting noses?
Kissing with inside lip? Stopping the career
Of laughter with a sigh?—a note infallible
Of breaking honesty—horsing foot on foot?
Skulking in corners? Wishing clocks more swift?
Hours, minutes? Noon, midnight? And all eyes
Blind with the pin and web but theirs, theirs only,
That would unseen be wicked? Is this nothing?
Why, then the world and all that's in't is nothing,
The covering sky is nothing, Bohemia nothing,
My wife is nothing, nor nothing have these nothings,
If this be nothing.

This raving has the opposite effect upon Camillo from that which
was intended, and he says:

Good my lord, be cured
Of this diseased opinion, and betimes,
For 'tis most dangerous.

Up to this point, while condemning the Queen, Leontes has
not revealed the identity of her suspected lover; now he names
Polixenes, and calls upon Camillo to poison him. He realizes that
the passion of his outbursts has been proof to Camillo that his
mind is diseased, and he suddenly decides that he must convince

him of his sanity, and so with eminent reasonableness he says:

> Dost think I am so muddy, so unsettled,
> To appoint myself in this vexation; sully
> The purity and whiteness of my sheets,
> Which to preserve is sleep, which being spotted
> Is goads, thorns, nettles, tails of wasps;
> Give scandal to the blood o' the Prince my son,
> Who I do think is mine and love as mine,
> Without ripe moving to't? Would I do this?
> Could man so blench?

Camillo now seems to agree to the dastardly plot, but makes the provision that Leontes, for the sake of his son and to kill gossip, will resume his former relationship with the Queen. Leontes, still intent on proving that he is rational, says:

> Thou dost advise me
> Even as I mine own course have set down;
> I'll give no blemish to her honour, none.

Leontes leaves Camillo, certain that his plot on the life of Polixenes will be carried out. He encounters Polixenes and can no longer hide his feelings, for he hurries past him, avoiding his eye, but not before Polixenes has noted his hostile look.

When Camillo discloses the plot to the intended victim, Polixenes with great insight realizes the extent and danger of Leontes' obsession; a king has been betrayed by his best friend with a wife who seemed perfection:

> . . . This jealousy
> Is for a precious creature. As she's rare,
> Must it be great. And as his person's mighty,
> Must it be violent. And as he does conceive
> He is dishonoured by a man which ever
> Professed to him, why, his revenges must
> In that be made more bitter. . . .

When Leontes discovers that Camillo has escaped from the country with Polixenes, it is proof positive to him of their joint guilt, and he seizes on it with a sick joy:

> How blest am I
> In my just censure, in my true opinion!

Only then, after the eager excitement of the confirmation of his suspicions, does he realize how tragic is his joy:

> Alack, for lesser knowledge! How accursed
> In being so blest! . . .

Like Othello, he then fools himself into believing that all would have been well had he not known of his wife's faithlessness. Othello says:

> He that is robbed, not wanting what is stol'n,
> Let him not know't and he's not robbed at all.
>
> .   .   .   .
>
> I had been happy if the general camp,
> Pioners and all, had tasted her sweet body,
> So I had nothing known.

Leontes' version of the same sentiment is less direct, as befits his more involuted nature, and is clothed in a metaphor:

> . . . There may be in the cup
> A spider steeped and one may drink, depart,
> And yet partake no venom, for his knowledge
> Is not infected. But if one present
> The abhorred ingredient to his eye, make known
> How he hath drunk, he cracks his gorge, his sides,
> With violent hefts. I have drunk, and seen the spider.

What he considers to be the defection of Camillo now gives full rein to the suspicions of Leontes:

> There is a plot against my life, my crown.
> All's true that is mistrusted. . . .

When Leontes accuses the pregnant Hermione in front of his Court of adultery with Polixenes, her gentle and dignified reaction is amazing, as is her ultimate ready forgiveness of her husband. We find the same astonishing virtue in the dying Desdemona. This must not delude us into the belief that they are impossibly patient and saintly martyrs, for they are both women of spirit when occasion demands. Their forgiveness is the measure of their love for their husbands, whose ill conduct they believe to be the result of some temporary aberration. Hermione ascribes it to astrological forces:

> There's some ill planet reigns.
> I must be patient till the Heavens look
> With an aspect more favourable. . . .

Antigonus and the First Lord go to great lengths to try to get Leontes to reverse his decree of imprisonment for Hermione, but he merely accuses them of stupidity or worse. It is interesting to note that, whereas Emilia had wrongly supposed the jealousy of Othello to be "born on itself," Antigonus is equally wrong in the contrary assumption that some evil creature had been responsible for implanting jealousy in Leontes. (The speech of Antigonus contains a mystifying phrase, "land-damn," that has baffled commentators. I would suggest "loud-damn" as a possible reading.) Antigonus says to Leontes:

> You are abused, and by some putter-on
> That will be damned for't. Would I knew the villain,
> I would loud-damn him. . . .

Shakespeare makes a significant change from the original in making Leontes himself rather than Hermione appeal to the Delphic Oracle. His motive is not to confirm his suspicions for himself, but to justify them in the eyes of others:

> Though I am satisfied and need no more
> Than what I know, yet shall the oracle
> Give rest to the minds of others, such as he
> Whose ignorant credulity will not
> Come up to the truth. . . .

In spite of his certainty, Leontes cannot sleep. He despises himself for what he considers to be his weakness, but attributes it to his inability to secure full revenge:

> Nor night nor day no rest. It is but weakness
> To bear the matter thus, mere weakness. If
> The cause were not in being—part o' the cause,
> She the adultress; for the harlot King
> Is quite beyond mine arm, out of the blank
> And level of my brain, plot-proof. But she
> I can hook to me. Say that she were gone,
> Given to the fire, a moiety of my rest
> Might come to me again.

As in everything else, he completely misinterprets the sickness of Mamillius, bereft of his mother, and finds in it further confirmation of the guilt of Hermione:

> To see his nobleness!
> Conceiving the dishonour of his mother,
> He straight declined, drooped, took it deeply,
> Fastened and fixed the shame on 't in himself,
> Threw off his spirit, his appetite, his sleep,
> And downright languished.

When the forthright and fearless Paulina confronts Leontes with his prematurely born daughter, the fact that he does not answer her taunts with an order for her instant death shows that he is still not gone beyond all restraint. He himself makes this point clear:

> Out of the chamber with her! Were I a tyrant,
> Where were her life? She durst not call me so,
> If she did know me one. . . .

The intervention of Paulina does have the effect of modifying Leontes' intention about the baby. Instead of committing it to the fire, he commits it to exposure, and, in punishment of Paulina, charges her husband with the execution of his decree:

> . . . We enjoin thee,
> As thou art liegeman to us, that thou carry
> This female bastard hence, and that thou bear it
> To some remote and desert place quite out

> Of our dominions, and that there thou leave it,
> Without more mercy, to its own protection
> And favour of the climate. . . .

In bringing Hermione to public trial, Leontes is again at great pains to justify his conduct:

> . . . Let us be cleared
> Of being tyrannous, since we so openly
> Proceed in justice, which shall have due course,
> Even to the guilt or the purgation.

The freeing of Leontes from jealousy is a traumatic experience induced by his open defiance of the gods. When the oracle declares his guilt, he says:

> There is no truth at all i' the oracle,
> The sessions shall proceed. This is mere falsehood.

Immediately comes the news of the death of Mamillius, and Leontes sees it as a punishment:

> Apollo's angry, and the heavens themselves
> Do strike at my injustice.

When Paulina brings the news of the apparent death of Hermione, he meekly endures her well-deserved berating:

> Go on, go on;
> Thou canst not speak too much. I have deserved
> All tongues to talk their bitterest.

Paulina is immediately contrite on seeing the change in him, but his comment is:

> Thou didst speak but well
> When most the truth; which I receive much better
> Than to be pitied of thee. . . .

At the opening of the second half of the play, divided from the first by sixteen years, we learn that Leontes in guilty sorrow has shut himself up; he has sent for Camillo to return, but the old man has made himself indispensable to Polixenes, who urges him to stay in Bohemia. Cleomenes describes the penance which Leontes has imposed upon himself:

> Sir, you have done enough, and have performed
> A saintlike sorrow. No fault could you make
> Which you have not redeemed; indeed, paid down
> More penitence than done trespass. At the last,
> Do as the Heavens have done, forget your evil;
> With them forgive yourself.

In the final scene, Camillo, happily reunited with his King, bears similar testimony:

> My lord, your sorrow was too sore laid on,
> Which sixteen winters cannot blow away,
> So many summers dry. Scarce any joy
> Did ever so long live; no sorrow
> But killed itself much sooner.

It has often been remarked that Shakespeare deliberately leaves the reunion of Leontes with Hermione wordless in order to enhance the meeting of mother and daughter, but surely his motive is a more positive one; the very silence of the reconciliation of husband and wife is infinitely more moving and meaningful than words could be. Shakespeare, the master of words, knows the power of silence. The sorrow of Macduff when he hears of the death of his wife and children is too deep for words, as is the joy of Leontes and Hermione. In the theatre, the moment in which Hermione embraces the husband she had loved and lost is profoundly affecting; indeed, the words with which Hermione greets her daughter come as a relaxing of the highly-charged moment.

The sixteen years of Leontes' penance does much to suggest the quality of the man with whom Hermione originally fell in love. We do not, as in the case of Othello, see the man before he was poisoned by jealousy. The fact that all the people whom

Leontes injured strive hard to make him forget their injuries must be our guarantee that he is worthy of the love of Hermione.

Dryden said that jealousy is the jaundice of the soul, and Blake that it has a human face. In Leontes, Shakespeare reveals both with unique power.

🙥 14 🙧   Prospero

THE TEMPEST is the *King Lear* of the Comedies in that it is rich in multi-faceted significance. It is a true poetic creation in that it stirs the imagination to endless speculation. Prospero and Lear have much in common, though the effect upon them of the action of the plays is opposite in shape: Prospero proceeds from turmoil of spirit to peace, while Lear moves from sanity and peace to madness and confusion. At the beginning of his play Lear renounces his power, to prepare himself for death, which is exactly what Prospero does at the end of *The Tempest*. Lear's words,

> . . . 'tis our fast intent
> To shake all cares and business from our age,
> Conferring them on younger strengths, while we
> Unburdened crawl toward death,

are paralleled by Prospero's

> And thence retire me to my Milan, where
> Every third thought shall be my grave.

No single source has been found for *The Tempest*. It is "compounded of many simples, extracted from many objects,"

as Jacques described the sources of his melancholy. But it was undoubtedly influenced by the excitement occasioned in London by
the movement to colonize the New World. The first landing of
the would-be settlers in Jamestown had taken place in 1607, and
many tales and more rumors had circulated in London before
The Tempest came to be written in 1611. In particular, the extraordinary adventure of Sir Thomas Gates had become known the
year before. He had been in charge of a relief fleet of eight ships
(some accounts say nine), and in a storm his flagship, on board
which were also the two other leaders of the expedition, was separated from the fleet and driven ashore in the Bermudas, Shakespeare's "still-vexed Bermoothes." There they and the crew and
passengers came safely to land and maintained themselves for ten
months, during which time they were believed to have been lost.
They made for themselves two new ships and in them sailed safely
to Jamestown. The news of their miraculous survival caused a
great stir in London. The situation is similar in *The Tempest;*
only one ship is caught by the storm; the rest of the fleet sail
safely home. It should also be noted that a contemporary account
of the Sir Thomas Gates adventure described the Bermudas as
"of all nations said and supposed to be enchanted and inhabited
with witches and devils, which grew by reason of accustomed
monstrous thunder, storm, and tempest, near unto those islands."
They were such islands as might be the natural abode of supernatural creatures like Caliban, Sycorax and Ariel. Travelers
brought back strange tales and strange objects, which were ex-
hibited in sideshows. As Trinculo says: "Any strange beast there
makes a man [*i.e.* makes his fortune]. When they will not give a
doit to relieve a lame beggar, they will lay out ten to see a dead
Indian."

For purposes of the plot, Prospero's island is set in the Mediterranean, but many of its qualities are drawn from the New
World. From this point of view, the play can be seen as an in-
vestigation of the problems and possibilities of colonization. The
departure of the first three ships for Virginia in 1606 had been

celebrated by Michael Drayton in a ballad in which he describes the new colony as "Earth's only Paradise." It is this spirit which Gonzalo expresses in his account of how he would govern the newly discovered island so that it would "excel the Golden Age." The relationship between Prospero and Caliban, thus considered, may be seen as the uneasy relationship between the colonists and the savage natives.

But Prospero has magic powers, and has acquired control over nature by means of a life devoted to study. With this the center of our thinking about the play, it takes on a different significance. Now Prospero, like Dr. Faustus, personifies the dilemma of modern man, whose power over nature grows daily, but it is a power which can be directed towards life or death.

Like *Cymbeline* and *The Winter's Tale*, *The Tempest* is a dramatic romance, but, unlike them, it contains no violence or death. It is a quiet and profoundly beautiful coda to the group of plays, and to Shakespeare's career as a whole. It is possible, and has often been suggested, that Prospero's farewell to his magic powers is consciously Shakespeare's farewell to the theatre, but this can be a dangerous assumption in dealing with the character of Prospero. It robs him of the dynamic quality so necessary to give full life to the play. It has resulted in many a Prospero's becoming a pompous bore.

We have already noted that in *The Winter's Tale* Shakespeare made his most drastic breach of the unities. As if to compensate for that, and possibly to show the critical Ben Jonson that he could do it, he adhered more strictly than ever before to the classical unities in his next and last play, *The Tempest*. (He was involved in one more play, *Henry VIII*, some two years later, but he was probably not its sole author.)

The editors of the First Folio chose to open their volume with *The Tempest*, probably because the text they had was exceptionally good, and because it contained an unusual number of stage directions which would have made its visualization easier for the reader; it is also possible that at the time of publication it was still a popular play in the theatre. One of the reasons for its popularity was the excuse it gave for increasingly demanded stage-effects, an element in the play that was to become a curse, for no play stands less in need of elaborate stage decoration, which tends to obscure the exquisite beauty of its poetry. Its storm, its masque, its magic banquet, its music in the air, have been sore temptations to elaborate productions. For two hundred years a version of the play by William Davenant and John Dryden, with the alternative title of *The Enchanted Island*, held the stage in various editions; in it the inhabitants of the island were multiplied, and they included a sister for Caliban, Sycorax, and one for Miranda, Dorinda. In all its distortions and mutilations the play was always popular.

The play begins with a storm at sea, and it is interesting to speculate on the reason for its inclusion, for it can be omitted without affecting the intelligibility of the play. (This is just as well because in some productions the noise of the storm overwhelms the dialogue, and one is tempted to change the Boatswain's line to "What cares these roarers for the name of Shakespeare?") The scene has good theatrical and poetic justifications. It is a realistic attention-getter in sharp contrast with the static expositionary first scene on the island, but it is also a symbolic presentation of the storm in Prospero's mind, and it is from that storm that the whole impulse of the play derives. The storm in *King Lear* has a somewhat similar symbolic significance.

The Prospero we see at the beginning of the play is at the moment in his life for which he has worked and waited for twelve years, a moment of revenge. Fortune has brought his enemies within the range of his magic power, but it is not enough to destroy them; they must be brought face to face with their victim turned judge. It is the moment, too, to reveal his ducal identity and the story of his expulsion from Milan to his daughter. He has often been tempted to do so, as Miranda tells us:

> You have often
> Begun to tell me what I am, but stopped,

> And left me to a bootless inquisition,
> Concluding, "Stay, not yet."

It would have been cruel to tell Miranda of her true status until the opportunity arose to restore her to it. It is sometimes objected that, as a piece of play construction, this scene is an obligatory, crude and tedious piece of exposition, such as, for example, Orlando's opening speech in *As You Like It* where he recounts to Adam events and facts well known to the old man. But it seems to me that this scene in *The Tempest* is very different, and is indeed as much a revelation of Prospero as of his story. For twelve years he has kept silent, and now the story bursts out of him. Although he starts by telling the story for Miranda's sake he soon gets lost in it for his own satisfaction; this accounts for his frequent stops to ensure that Miranda is listening. As she says, "Your tale, sir, would cure deafness." Almost gloatingly Prospero recounts the details he has chewed on in silence for years. At last he might say, as he does later,

> Now does my project gather to a head.
> My charms crack not; my spirits obey; and Time
> Goes upright with his carriage.

With his story told, Prospero prepares for the next step and must summon Ariel, the spirit through whom he works his magic. To this Miranda must not be a witness, and so he puts her to sleep. (I have seen productions in which Prospero has had to prod her into wakefulness throughout the scene, a betrayal of its whole exciting purpose, but sometimes the Prospero has been so orotund and solemn that members of the audience have also needed his prodding.)

It is only his excited absorption with the culmination of his plans that can account for Prospero's harsh words to Ariel, when the spirit reminds him of his promise of liberty. He calls Ariel "malignant thing," "dull thing," epithets sharply at odds with the more usual "my brave spirit," "my Ariel, chick," "my tricksy spirit," "my dainty Ariel," "my quaint Ariel." This unusual anger towards Ariel is in itself proof of Prospero's high-keyed mood in the scene, for it is very human to be irritated by a routine request at a moment of climactic intensity. Also, it should be noted that Prospero, in the manner of many parents, affects a language of anger in excess of his true feeling. Thus, later, when he pretends to be angry with Miranda, he says:

> Silence! One word more
> Shall make me chide thee, if not hate thee.

But Miranda is well aware of this trait in her father, for she tells Ferdinand:

> My father's of a better nature, sir,
> Than he appears by speech. . . .

Just as Ariel is essential to Prospero's magic, Caliban is necessary to his survival on the otherwise uninhabited island. When Caliban offers his services to Stephano, we learn in what ways he has served Prospero:

> I'll show thee every fertile inch o' th' island.
> .   .   .   .
> I'll show thee the best springs, I'll pluck thee berries,
> I'll fish for thee, I'll get thee wood enough.
> .   .   .   .
> I prithee let me bring thee where crabs [*i.e.* crab apples]
>   grow,
> And I with my long nails will dig thee pignuts,
> Show thee a jay's nest, and instruct thee how
> To snare the nimble marmoset. I'll bring thee
> To clustering filberts, and sometimes I'll get thee
> Young scamels [probably seagulls] from the rock.

Prospero acknowledges to Miranda:

> We cannot miss him. He does make our fire,
> Fetch in our wood, and serves in offices
> That profit us. . . .

Prospero rules both Ariel and Caliban by fear of punishment.

In the case of Ariel he threatens to return him to the imprisonment from which he had released him, and for the same duration:

> If thou more murmur'st, I will rend an oak
> And peg thee in his knotty entrails till
> Thou hast howled away twelve winters.

In the beginning Prospero had treated Caliban kindly, and the
creature in return had been friendly. Here is Caliban's account
of the initial relationship:

> . . . When thou camest first,
> Thou strokedst me, and madest much of me, wouldst give me
> Water with berries in't. And teach me how
> To name the bigger light, and how the less,
> That burn by day and night. And then I loved thee,
> And showed thee all the qualities o' th' isle,
> The fresh springs, brine pits, barren place and fertile.

And here is Prospero's account of the same process:

> . . . I pitied thee,
> Took pains to make thee speak, taught thee each hour
> One thing or other. When thou didst not, savage,
> Know thine own meaning, but wouldst gabble like
> A thing most brutish, I endowed thy purposes
> With words that made them known.

Prospero even allowed Caliban to share the same shelter with him
and Miranda. What went wrong? Caliban could not but behave
like the animal he was. What more dared Prospero expect from
a creature sired by a devil upon a witch? Caliban sought sex with
Miranda, and from that moment Prospero took away his liberty
and made him a slave, and in slavery Caliban came to realize that
he had lost his birthright to the island:

> This island's mine, by Sycorax my mother,
> Which thou tak'st from me. . . .

Prospero accounts for the change in the relationship thus:

> . . . I have used thee,

Filth as thou art, with human care, and lodged thee
In mine own cell till thou didst seek to violate
The honour of my child.

   .   .   .   .   .   .

                        Abhorred slave,
Which any print of goodness wilt not take,
Being capable of all ill! . . .
. . . thy vile race,
Though thou didst learn, had that in't which good natures
Could not abide to be with. Therefore wast thou
Deservedly confined into this rock,
Who hadst deserved more than a prison.

A later judgment of Prospero on Caliban is:

A devil, a born devil, on whose nature
Nurture can never stick; on whom my pains,
Humanely taken, all, all lost, quite lost.
And as with age his body uglier grows,
So his mind cankers. . . .

If this relationship is considered as an allegory of colonialism,
Caliban's final summation of it reveals the widespread result:

You taught me language, and my profit on't
Is I know how to curse. . . .

In further pursuit of the allegory, Stephano's treatment of Caliban represents colonialism at its worst, for he gains his service by making him drunk on liquor.

Considered as a human being rather than as a symbol, Prospero had to woo and tame Caliban as an aid to survival; his instinct was paternal towards the strange creature until his particular paternal instinct towards his young daughter—she was only three when they were first cast on the island—was outraged, and from that moment to protect her from Caliban was his dominant concern. This was easy because Caliban's parentage predisposed him to belief in Prospero's magic powers. Even when Prospero was not present, he believed him to be watching and listening:

> I must obey. His art is of such power
> It would control my dam's god, Setebos,
> And make a vassal of him.

Prospero has a twofold purpose: to unmask the twelve-year-old villainy, and to secure the future of his daughter. Miranda has been robbed of her rightful place in Milan, so, to compensate for those lost years, she shall not only be restored to her place in Milan, but ultimately become Queen of Naples. To accomplish this last purpose, Prospero uses Ariel to bring together Ferdinand, the heir to the kingdom of Naples, and Miranda, trusting to love to do the rest, as it does at first sight. That this is Prospero's intention is clear from his first comment on their meeting:

> It goes on, I see,
> As my soul prompts it. . . .

All future barriers he puts in the way of the lovers are merely to test the young man's worthiness:

> . . . But this swift business
> I must uneasy make, lest too light winning
> Make the prize light. . . .

He goes quickly to the extreme of accusing Ferdinand of being a traitor and a spy, and decreeing harsh punishment:

> . . . Come,
> I'll manacle thy neck and feet together.
> Sea water shalt thou drink; thy food shall be
> The fresh-brook mussels, withered roots, and husks
> Wherein the acorn cradled. . . .

Ferdinand naturally draws his sword to resist, and "is charmed from moving;" but the young man passes his first test superbly:

> My father's loss, the weakness which I feel,
> The wreck of all my friends, nor this man's threats,
> To whom I am subdued, are but light to me,
> Might I but through my prison once a day

> Behold this maid. All corners else o' th' earth
> Let liberty make use of; space enough
> Have I in such a prison.

Small wonder that Prospero's private comment is, "It works." Ferdinand's later judgment on Prospero is "He's composed of harshness."

At the same time, Prospero is using Ariel for another test, to find out if time has worked any reformation in Antonio, the villainous brother who had usurped his dukedom. Given the opportunity by Ariel, Antonio runs true to his old form, and persuades the king's brother that they together should kill the sleeping King and Gonzalo, who are only saved by Ariel's agency.

Prospero spies upon Ferdinand and Miranda when they think him at study. He has set a test for Miranda too, for he has forbidden her to chatter with Ferdinand and to tell him her name. Her love cannot obey such behests, and the father approves. Prospero's ambiguous comment on the lovers is that of all fathers about to lose a beloved only daughter in marriage:

> So glad of this as they I cannot be,
> . . . but my rejoicing
> At nothing can be more. . . .

For the first confrontation with the villains, Prospero uses Ariel, while he watches unseen, and gives a display of his magic powers. It is already clear that he is not contemplating revenge; he hopes to bring home to them such a sense of guilt that they will repent, and the better to persuade them he threatens them with lingering death. He even lets Alonso believe that his son has been drowned as a punishment of the father. Ariel, speaking for him, says:

> . . . You three
> From Milan did supplant good Prospero,
> Exposed unto the sea, which hath requit it,
> Him and his innocent child. For which foul deed
> The powers, delaying not forgetting, have
> Incensed the seas and shores—yea, all the creatures—

Against your peace. Thee of thy son, Alonso,
They have bereft, and do pronounce by me
Lingering perdition—worse than any death
Can be at once—shall step by step attend
You and your ways. Whose wrath to guard you from—
Which here, in this most desolate isle, else falls
Upon your heads—is nothing but heart sorrow
And a clear life ensuing.

When Prospero reveals to Ferdinand that all his hardships
had been but trials of his love, he is next at pains to ensure that
the betrothal does not give rights to the marriage-bed. It is probable that, by the time *The Tempest* was written, the practice, of
which Shakespeare himself had taken advantage, was generally
frowned upon. Again, as in all his relationships, Prospero to ensure
his will makes threats of condign punishment. (Is it possible that
Shakespeare was drawing upon the unhappy experience of his own
marriage?) Prospero says;

If thou dost break her virgin knot before
All sanctimonious ceremonies may
With full and holy rite be ministered,
No sweet aspersion shall the Heavens let fall
To make this contract grow; but barren hate,
Sour-eyed disdain, and discord shall bestrew
The union of your bed with weeds so loathly
That you shall hate it both. . . .

And later he warns Ferdinand:

. . . Do not give dalliance
Too much the rein. The strongest oaths are straw
To the fire i' the blood. Be more abstemious,
Or else, good night your vow!

Prospero puts on an elaborate masque to celebrate the betrothal. It has been suggested that this was a later interpolation
for a performance of the play which was part of the betrothal
and marriage festivities of the Princess Elizabeth and the Elector
Palatine, and that, to accommodate it, some part of the original

text was cut. I prefer to believe that the masque was an integral part of the original conception of the play. If Prospero would put on a magic display to frighten his enemies, why not one to bless his daughter's betrothal? We have a similar ceremony in *As You Like It*, when there was no magician to provide it. It is hardly likely that Shakespeare would miss the opportunity for such a beautiful spectacle in a play which abounds in the spectacular. And the text, as we have it, contains a delightfully human touch. Prospero, in giving orders to Ariel for the masque, says:

> . . . I must
> Bestow upon the eyes of this young couple
> Some vanity of mine art. It is my promise,
> And they expect it from me.

We certainly haven't heard him make such a promise, and I like to think that he is just rationalizing a desire to impress his son-in-law-to-be with an exhibition of his powers. Such simple vanity is all the more forgivable in a man who is soon to divest himself of all the powers he has spent a lifetime of study in acquiring. Ferdinand reacts to the masque with words that must have endeared him to Prospero:

> This is a most majestic vision, and
> Harmonious charmingly. . . .
> .   .   .   .
> Let me live here ever.
> So rare a wondered father and a wise
> Makes this place Paradise.

But Prospero breaks off the masque abruptly when he remembers that an attempt is to be made upon his life by Stephano, prompted by Caliban. He must use his magic to deal with hatred as well as love. Anger overtakes him, and he apologizes to Ferdinand:

> . . . Sir, I am vexed.
> Bear with my weakness; my old brain is troubled.
> Be not disturbed with my infirmity.

Prospero divides offenders into those in whom some betterment of life may be expected and those, like Caliban and his new companions, whose natures are beyond reclamation. On these latter he lets loose dogs, and says:

> Go charge my goblins that they grind their joints
> With dry convulsions. Shorten up their sinews
> With aged cramps, and more pinch-spotted make them
> Than pard or cat o' mountain.

Now Prospero approaches the climax of his life:

> . . . At this hour
> Lie at my mercy all mine enemies.

His twelve-year pent-up fury has in a few hours given way to mercy and forgiveness. He has come to see the futility of vengeance. His future is dominated by two considerations, both of which will profit from his virtuous magnanimity: his daughter's marriage, for one of his enemies will become her father-in-law, and his own preparation for death. He expresses his decision thus:

> Though with their high wrongs I am struck to the quick,
> Yet with my nobler reason 'gainst my fury
> Do I take part. The rarer action is
> In virtue than in vengeance. They being penitent,
> The sole drift of my purpose doth extend
> Not a frown further. . . .

Repentance is made the prerequisite for forgiveness, and Alonso voices his remorse with moving sincerity, for the future Queen of his kingdom had been one of his victims. Antonio and Sebastian do not voice their penitence, even though Prospero is particularly considerate of them in that he does not disclose their plot against the King, but he makes it quite clear to them he knows about it:

> I here could pluck His Highness' frown upon you,
> And justify you traitors. At this time
> I will tell no tales.

There is an implied threat in "at this time," which Prospero uses to guarantee their future good conduct. Sebastian, to whom all magic is black, ascribes, in an aside, Prospero's knowledge of their evil intentions to the Devil. Prospero's next word is a simple "No." This can, of course, be a continuation of the above-quoted speech, but I prefer to consider it as a comment on the aside which he should not have heard. It is a pitying rebuke to Sebastian, who cannot believe in white magic. The distinction is made throughout the play: Prospero derives his power from beneficent spirits, symbolized by Ariel, but Caliban's witch-mother, Sycorax, had called upon evil spirits; she had imprisoned Ariel for refusing to obey "her earthy and abhorred commands."

In renouncing his "rough magic," Prospero describes how he has used it:

> . . . I have bedimmed
> The noontide sun, called forth the mutinous winds,
> And 'twixt the green sea and the azured vault
> Set roaring war. To the dread rattling thunder
> Have I given fire, and rifted Jove's stout oak
> With his own bolt. The strong-based promontory
> Have I made shake, and by the spurs plucked up
> The pine and cedar. Graves at my command
> Have waked their sleepers, oped, and let 'em forth
> By my so potent art. But this rough magic
> I here abjure . . .
> .   .   .   .
> . . . I'll break my staff,
> Bury it certain fathoms in the earth,
> And deeper than did ever plummet sound
> I'll drown my book.

Why did Prospero renounce the powers to whose acquisition he had devoted his life? Originally his studies had been completely altruistic; he had sought knowledge for its own sake, and had indeed neglected the governing of his dukedom. He was born to be a scholar, not a ruler. It was this absorption in study that had given Antonio both the desire and the opportunity to supplant his brother, as Prospero testifies:

I, thus neglecting worldly ends, all dedicated
To closeness and the bettering of my mind
With that which, but by being so retired,
O'erprized all popular rate, in my false brother
Awaked an evil nature. . . .

The good Gonzalo, foolishly entrusted with the task of setting
Prospero and the three-year-old Miranda adrift in a rotten boat,
had provided them with many things, among which,

Knowing I loved my books, he furnished me
From mine own library with volumes that
I prize above my dukedom.

Incidentally, Prospero's vulnerable humanity is further shown
when he sees Gonzalo again, standing charmed in the magic circle:

Holy Gonzalo, honourable man,
Mine eyes, even sociable to the show of thine,
Fall fellowly drops. . . .

With his books on the desolate island, Prospero is enabled to
continue his studies, and now they have an all-absorbing aim,
to bring his enemies within his power. This he accomplishes only
to forgo vengeance on which his hope had fed. He has no further
use for rough magic, but he says that he will miss his Ariel. Now
he will return to his Milan, to live quietly in the happiness of his
daughter, and to prepare for death.

Prospero, to me, is a very human figure, capable of fury, bad
temper, vanity, role-playing, kindness and tears. As do many men,
he lived the years of his greatest power dedicated to an end he
found to be empty, but, unlike most men, he also found, before
it was too late, better values and practiced them. His is a story
of conversion and renunciation, of the use of power to create
happiness, and then the sacrifice of power in pursuit of serenity.
The play is well called *The Tempest*, but the more important
tempest is the one within the soul of Prospero, and it is this which
gives vitality to the play, and it is this storm which is at last stilled.
His promise to his enemies of "calm seas, auspicious gales" will
characterize the rest of his own life.

PART III

INTRODUCTION TO

THE *Tragedies*

I SHALL NOT SPEND time in trying to define tragedy. All the famous definitions will leave some plays, which are felt and accepted to be tragedies, outside their limitations. Thus, Aristotle, whose definition is the one from which all other considerations spring and which is still the most stimulating and provocative, drew most of his arguments from consideration of *Oedipus Tyrannus;* he would have had to exclude some of the other extant tragedies of Sophocles because they do not have unhappy endings. Does the fact that the Biblical story of *Job* has a happy ending, thought by some scholars to be a factitious addition, inhibit us from sensing it as a supreme example of a tragic dramatic poem?

Why is it that tragedy is felt to be a more profound experience than comedy? The same materials can be used for both; thus, in a Western movie, the frequent deaths can provoke laughter as readily as tears, if the aim of the film is comedy. The treatment, the point of view towards human experience, determines our reaction to the work. If Ben Jonson had written *Timon of Athens*, we might have had another *Volpone*. The tragic point of view is concerned with the mysteries of existence, the deep and hidden roots of life, the unanswerable questions; comedy is more concerned with the finite appearances of life. Tragedy sees man in the context of eternity; comedy sees him in the context of time.

The tragic playwright may not have a consistent or even conscious philosophy, but, in exposing the height and depth of human experience, he challenges theologians and philosophers for answers to the enigmas of life in this world. Unlike Milton, who in *Paradise Lost* set out "to justify the ways of God to man," Shakespeare has no didactic purpose. He shows us life as he saw and felt it, in all its complexity of misery and magic, good and evil, but he attempts no explanation. His tragedies raise for all time the abiding questions, to which religions and philosophies provide varying and contradictory answers.

Two of the abiding questions, which every religion and philosophy must face or find a good reason for not facing, are the evil in man and the suffering in humanity. The one results in what Coleridge called the "motiveless malignity" of Iago, and the other produces the cry from Gloucester:

> As flies to wanton boys are we to the gods;
> They kill us for their sport.

The suffering caused to humanity by forces outside its control —Nature, the gods, Fate, God—is a particular dilemma for Christianity, whose belief is that God is both almighty and beneficent, Almighty God and Father. It is easy to see God in a beautiful sunset and a lovely rose, but what about an earthquake and a cancer cell? These two springs of man's unhappiness, man's villainy and remorseless Fate, result in two different emphases in tragedies. The one, man's inhumanity to man, is predominant in plays like *Othello* and *Macbeth;* the other, the suffering caused by forces outside man's control, is predominant in plays like *Romeo and Juliet;* but there is a sense of both forces in most tragedies. In a supreme work like *King Lear* they seem conjoined to work man's destruction.

The Elizabethan age was one in which the individual was

paramount. The Renaissance had made man aware of his infinite potentialities. Medieval certainties were giving way to modern questions raised by man's discoveries. The future was exciting and was to be dominated by man. Courage and defiance in the face of evil and suffering were the most admired virtues. It is therefor natural to expect man rather than Fate to be at the center of a typical Shakespearean tragedy. The characteristic attitude is:

> The fault, dear Brutus, is not in our stars,
> But in ourselves. . . .

It is the weaker Gloucester, not Lear, that makes the plaint about the gods, and when he attributes all evils in the world to the stars, the symbols of Fate, Edmund's comment is, I think, characteristic of the best of the age:

> This is the excellent foppery of the world, that when we are sick in fortune—often the surfeit of our own behaviour—we make guilty of our disasters the sun, the moon, and the stars as if we were villains by necessity, fools by heavenly compulsion; knaves, thieves, and treachers by spherical predominance; drunkards, liars, and adulterers by an enforced obedience of planetary influence; and all that we are evil in, by a divine thrusting on—an admirable evasion of whoremaster man, to lay his goatish disposition to the charge of a star!

From the point of view of man's responsibility for his destiny, *Macbeth* is the perfect tragedy. In *King Lear* there are agencies of evil in Goneril, Regan and Edmund; in *Hamlet* there is Claudius; in *Othello* there is Iago; but in *Macbeth* there is only Macbeth. (We shall consider the significance of the Witches and Lady Macbeth in Chapter Nineteen.)

It is this emphasis on the individual that, of necessity, makes the tragic hero a man of stature, and in nothing is his stature more apparent than in the way he reacts to misfortune. All men suffer and die, but not all men suffer and die with courage, defiance, dignity, and nobility. Malcolm's praise of Cawdor in death might be applied to Macbeth himself:

> . . . Nothing in his life
> Became him like the leaving it. He died
> As one that had been studied in his death
> To throw away the dearest thing he owed
> As 'twere a careless trifle.

Macbeth speaks for all tragic heroes at the approach of defeat and death:

> . . . Blow, wind! Come, wrack!
> At least we'll die with harness on our back.

It has been pointed out that it seems to be impossible for aestheticians, philosophers, and literary critics to propound a succinct formula which will serve as a measure for all tragedies, but it is not fundamentally an important question. What matters is the experience of each individual play. It has often been said that our times cannot produce tragedies. On the one hand evil and potential suffering have become too enormous to be personalized, and on the other hand modern man is too dwarfed by social forces to be truly heroic. But playwrights will always continue to present man in his ultimate confrontations with the mysteries of life, within him and without. That Aristotle would not recognize as tragedies the modern plays which result from this preoccupation does not invalidate them. The play's the thing, not the label. Although *The Death of a Salesman* does not measure up to some classical criteria of tragedy, there are many Americans whose experience of it has moved them to such an awareness and examination of their life's values and impulses that it, for them, is a true tragedy. Again, although we laugh at *Waiting for Godot*, Samuel Beckett in that play is concerned with presenting the human dilemma, just as Shakespeare and Sophocles were; Beckett calls his play a tragicomedy. If the term had existed then, it would have been a perfect description of Shakespeare's *Troilus and Cressida;* its merits as a play are in no way altered because Shakespeare's editors called it a tragedy and we now call it a comedy.

It is usual to consider ten of Shakespeare's plays as tragedies, and they in themselves are so varied that it would be almost impossible to find one formula that would cover them all. As in the Histories and Comedies, we find the same kind of development, from imitation through lyricism to full maturity, and then through a fierce bitterness to a beautiful close.

His first tragedy, *Titus Andronicus*, was an apprentice play written in the fashion of Thomas Kyd's *The Spanish Tragedy*. For a long time it was felt to be such a distasteful amalgam of blood and cruelty that certain scholars made desperate attempts to prove that Shakespeare did not write it. There is really no doubt that it is his and also that it was popular. Within recent years, and dating particularly from Peter Brook's remarkable production in 1955 with Laurence Olivier as Titus and Vivien Leigh as Lavinia, the play has been given a new theatrical lease on life; a world that has become acquainted with cruelty on a colossal scale no longer finds *Titus Andronicus* absurd. And it must be remembered that stage representations of blood and torture, which the Elizabethan audience seems to have demanded, are an element in Shakespeare's greatest tragedies, *e.g.*, the blinding of Gloucester, the severed head of Macbeth. We should not feel too superior to this crude taste: many of us feel cheated when a circus aerialist works with a safety net; heavyweight fights are more popular than lightweight fights, because the fighters are likely to draw more blood and cause more damage; in a bullfight there is not only the spectacle of the killing of the bull but also the exciting possibility that the matador may be gored.

In *Titus Andronicus*, revenge is the theme and horror the manner. *Hamlet*, too, is a revenge play, and it is the specificity of the Biblical formula that causes one of Hamlet's harrowing dilemmas: "And if any mischief follow, then shalt thou give life for life, eye for eye, tooth for tooth, hand for hand, foot for foot, burning for burning, wound for wound, stripe for stripe."

It is the vitality of the characters in *Titus Andronicus* that announces the advent of Shakespeare's genius; in some ways he never surpassed the vigorous enjoyment of evil which he achieved in Aaron, the Moor, the beloved of that ultimate Queen of Revenge, Tamora. Here is Aaron's final utterance, after he has been condemned to be set breast-deep in earth and starved to death:

> I am no baby, I, that with base prayers
> I should repent the evils I have done.
> Ten thousand worse than ever yet I did
> Would I perform if I might have my will.
> If one good deed in all my life I did,
> I do repent it from my very soul.

Tamora bears a son by Aaron, and, when her legitimate sons seek to destroy the baby, the Moor defies them and gives the "Black is beautiful" theme memorable expression:

> What, what, ye sanguine, shallow-hearted boys!
> Ye white-limed walls! Ye alehouse painted signs!
> Coal-black is better than another hue
> In that it scorns to bear another hue;
> For all the waters in the ocean
> Can never turn the swan's black legs to white,
> Although she lave them hourly in the flood.

It is interesting to note that just as Shakespeare's first History, *Henry VI, Part 1*, seemed to foretell the last of the series, *Henry V*, so does his first tragedy, *Titus Andronicus*, seem to foretell his last, *Coriolanus*. Aemilius tells us:

> They hither march amain, under conduct
> Of Lucius, son to old Andronicus,
> Who threats, in course of his revenge, to do
> As much as ever Coriolanus did.

Some eighteen years later, Shakespeare was to tell the story of that Coriolanus.

Romeo and Juliet is an exquisitely sad and beautiful tale but seems to lack the stature of true tragedy because Shakespeare is not yet in the tragic mood. Accident and chance dominate the plot and yet they do not dominate the feeling of the play; Shakespeare is not deeply questioning Destiny, though from the outset he sees his protagonists as "a pair of star-crossed lovers." The implications of the play are simply moralistic, as the Prince makes clear at the end:

> . . . Capulet! Montague!
> See what a scourge is laid upon your hate,
> That Heaven finds means to kill your joys with love.
> And I, for winking at your discords too,
> Have lost a brace of kinsman. All are punished.

Julius Caesar heralds the great tragic period. Within some four or five years we were to be given *Hamlet, Othello, King Lear,* and *Macbeth.* These five plays all introduce an element that Aristotle found essential in the tragic hero: "hamartia," which is usually considered as the "tragic flaw," though that has been variously considered as a moral weakness or an error in judgment. Hamlet himself gives us a description of it, attributing its source either to man's innate character or to Fate:

> So oft it chances in particular men,
> That for some vicious mole of nature in them,
> As in their birth—wherein they are not guilty.
> Since nature cannot choose his origin—
> By the o'ergrowth of some complexion,
> Oft breaking down the pales and forts of reason,
> Or by some habit that too much o'erleavens
> The form of plausive manners, that these men,
> Carrying, I say, the stamp of one defect,
> Being Nature's livery, or Fortune's star—
> Their virtues else—be they as pure as grace,
> As infinite as man may undergo—
> Shall in the general censure take corruption
> From that particular fault. . . .

It is not always easy, as we shall see, particularly in Hamlet's own case, to determine what the "particular fault" is. In the case of Brutus, the first of this group of tragic heroes, his fault is really an excessive virtue, an uncompromising idealism, which ill fits him for the practical conduct of public affairs. The conspirators had needed his well-known incorruptibility to mask, in the public eye, their own less worthy motives, but their troubles began when Brutus was not content to be a figurehead. Every decision he imposed upon the conspirators was an ideal one and led to their inevitable downfall. Thus, he overrules the plan to forestall the revenge of Mark Antony by murdering him:

> Our course will seem too bloody, Caius Cassius,
> To cut the head off and then hack the limbs,
> Like wrath in death and envy afterwards;
> For Antony is but a limb of Caesar.
> Let's be sacrificers, but not butchers, Caius.
> We all stand up against the spirit of Caesar,
> And in the spirit of men there is no blood;
> O, that we then could come by Caesar's spirit,
> And not dismember Caesar! . . .

Brutus is so naïve in his idealism that, after the assassination of Caesar, he even believes that Antony can be persuaded of the rightness of the crime:

> Our reasons are so full of good regard
> That were you, Antony, the son of Caesar,
> You should be satisfied. . . .

With Brutus safely dead, Antony, his opposite in every way, can afford to praise his unique altruism:

> This was the noblest Roman of them all.
> All the conspirators, save only he,
> Did that they did in envy of great Caesar;
> He only, in a general honest thought
> And common good to all, made one of them.
> His life was gentle, and the elements
> So mixed in him that Nature might stand up
> And say to all the world, "This was a man!"

In Plutarch's *Life of Marcus Brutus* there is a hint which most playwrights would have seized on:

> It is said that Caesar had so great a regard for him that he
> ordered his commanders by no means to kill Brutus in the

battle, but to spare him, if possible, and bring him safe to
him, if he would willingly surrender himself; but if he made
any resistance, to suffer him to escape rather than do him
any violence.

The battle referred to is that of Pharsalia, in which Caesar had
defeated Pompey, prior to the action of the play. Plutarch continues:

And this he is believed to have done out of a tenderness to
Servilia, the mother of Brutus; for Caesar had, it seems, in
his youth been very intimate with her, and she passionately
in love with him; and, considering that Brutus was born about
that time in which their loves were at the highest, Caesar
had a belief that he was his own child.

It must have been a sore temptation to Shakespeare to use and
develop this element in the relationship between Caesar and Brutus, but he resisted it because it would have complicated the
simple issue of Brutus's idealism as the sole motive for his involvement in the conspiracy.

The year 1607 seems to have been the year of transition for
Shakespeare: *Pericles* was the bridge from the bitter comedies to
the three dramatic romances, and *Timon of Athens* the bridge
from the four great tragedies to the final two, *Antony and Cleopatra* and *Coriolanus*.

Timon of Athens is an unsatisfactory play, but consideration
of its weakness illuminates the nature of the greatness of better
plays. It was obviously considered to be an inferior play from
the beginning, for Heminge and Condell were reluctant to include
it in the First Folio, where its text is much mangled. Nor is there
any evidence of its being performed in Shakespeare's time. Modern scholarship tends to regard it as an unfinished work of his.
That certainly may be true because it bears the marks of having
been written in a white heat of fury and never having been sub-
mitted to that process of shaping and chastening to which every
artist must submit his work. Timon is a crudely characterized
mouthpiece for invective. He lacks the necessary stature and hu-

manity to engage our sympathy and invoke our pity, and yet it is not without effectiveness in the theatre.

High among the vices of mankind Shakespeare rated ingratitude. It is an important element in *King Lear*, and even in the sunny comedy, *As You Like It*, it finds notable expression:

> Blow, blow, thou winter wind;
> Thou art not so unkind
>   As man's ingratitude;
> Thy tooth is not so keen,
> Because thou art not seen,
>   Although thy breath be rude.
>
> .   .   .   .
>
> Freeze, freeze, thou bitter sky;
> Thou dost not bite so nigh
>   As benefits forgot;
> Though thou the waters warp,
> Thy sting is not so sharp
>   As friend remembered not.

Timon of Athens is Shakespeare's ultimate outcry against ingratitude. The voice of the cursing cynic, Thersites, in *Troilus and Cressida*, is but a minor one and redeemed by wit; but Timon's voice dominates his play, and it is harsh and ranting. Yet even in the black world of *Timon of Athens* there is a bright ray of light. His loyal steward, Flavius, seeks him out in his misery only to be sent away with a reward of gold and this advice:

> Hate all, curse all, show charity to none,
> But let the famished flesh slide from the bone
> Ere thou relieve the beggar. Give to dogs
> What thou deniest to men. Let prisons swallow 'em,
> Debt wither 'em to nothing. Be men like blasted woods,
> And may diseases lick up their false bloods!

The last two tragedies, *Antony and Cleopatra* and *Coriolanus*, are worthy to be ranked with the greatest. The ill-considered fury of *Timon of Athens* is quite burnt out, and it has been replaced with a new detachment, in which the divine compassion of Shakespeare is again apparent. Alcibiades called Timon "noble," a quality in which he is conspicuously lacking; but in the last two tragedies nobility is restored, and it finds its expression in some of Shakespeare's greatest poetry.

In Shakespeare's tragedies we see and feel man at his most noble and his most evil, and we are moved to awe and terror by the revelation. The tragic heroes and villains transcend ordinary men in stature but they share their essence; in them we recognize ourselves in the ultimate confrontations of our lives, and they speak to our most secret selves.

 15

Romeo

IN TWO WAYS *Romeo and Juliet* is unique among Shakespeare's tragedies: it is the most Fate-ridden and the most lyrical. Yet we are hardly moved to awe by the contemplation of the unseen forces that determine men's lives and deaths, and sometimes the lyricism degenerates into tiresome verbal quibbles. But the total effect of the play, one of Shakespeare's most popular from the beginning, is that of a compelling tale told with brilliance and beauty.

From the outset Shakespeare sees the doom of the lovers as both determined by Fate and the result of their parents' hatred:

> From forth the fatal loins of these two foes
> A pair of star-crossed lovers take their life,
> Whose misadventured piteous overthrows
> Do with their death bury their parents' strife.
> The fearful passage of their death-marked love,
> And the continuance of their parents' rage,
> Which, but their children's end, naught could remove,
> Is now the two hours' traffic of our stage.

Whether the play was ever acomplished in two hours or not in the theatre, it should certainly give an impression of headlong speed. (I have seen an important production in which one third of the text was cut and yet the elaborate performance lasted for over three hours!) Shakespeare used as his source a long poem by Arthur Brooke, called *The Tragicall Historye of Romeus and Juliet*, in which the action covers some nine months; Shakespeare compresses it into five days, and in so doing achieves an exciting momentum from the shared bed to the shared tomb.

Fate does not dominate the play in the sense in which it does that of Oedipus, whose downfall is inevitable from the beginning. The sad end of *Romeo and Juliet* is the result of a tissue of chance and accident. Thus, if only the plague had not delayed Friar John's journey to Romeo, if only Friar Laurence had arrived a few minutes sooner at the tomb, if only . . . and so on. Nor is the hatred of the families a very real force. It is dutiful rather than vital. Only in Tybalt is it a dominating passion. When Capulet learns from him that Romeo has gate-crashed the party, he restrains Tybalt and praises Romeo.

As for the lyricism of the play, it is so over-abundant that, when Shakespeare needs to heighten it for the first meeting of Romeo and Juliet, he has recourse to a formal sonnet. In this play such a beautiful and detachable aria as Mercutio's famous Queen Mab speech is quite at home. The play is full of dazzling metaphors, cleverly pursued. The first quarto of the play, which is in itself an intriguing puzzle since much of its text is too accurate to have been pirated and the rest of it too inaccurate to have been authorized, has as its title: *An Excellent Conceited Tragedie of Romeo and Juliet*. It is noteworthy that "conceited" was the adjective chosen to arouse the potential reader's interest, the word being used in the sense of containing verbal and poetic artifice. We shall see later that the dramatist on occasion skillfully uses the poet's delight in verbal conceits, but he is also capable of such elaboration of a pun, even in moments of great emotional impact, as to rob the character of the necessary sincerity and directness of utterance. Thus, any actress is going to have great difficulty with this speech, in which Juliet expresses her fear that Romeo may have been killed:

> Hath Romeo slain himself? Say thou but "I,"
> And that bare vowel "I" shall poison more
> Than the death-darting eye of cockatrice.
> I am not I, if there be such an I,
> Or those eyes shut, that make thee answer "I."

Three of those "I's" should be printed "Aye," but I preferred to keep them as they appear in the First Folio, because it seems to emphasize the artificiality of the speech. In no play of Shakespeare's is Samuel Johnson's criticism more deserved:

> A quibble is to Shakespeare what luminous vapours are to the traveller; he follows it at all adventures; it is sure to lead him out of his way, and sure to engulf him in the mire. It has some malignant power over his mind, and its fascinations are irresistible. . . . A quibble is the golden apple for which he will always turn aside from his career, or stoop from his elevation. A quibble, poor and barren as it is, gave him such delight, that he was content to purchase it, by the sacrifice of reason, propriety and truth. A quibble was to him the fatal Cleopatra for which he lost the world, and was content to lose it.

All this is to say that in *Romeo and Juliet* the man in Shakespeare as yet lacked the experience of life and the maturity of outlook for great tragedy, and the dramatist in him did not yet have the poet firmly on the leash. But this is not to belittle the play, for it has abundant compensations. It is unsurpassed as a paean to young love, in whose service the greatest powers of the lyric poet were called forth. As in the case of the companion plays, *Richard II* and *A Midsummer Night's Dream*, the subject was unerringly chosen to display Shakespeare's greatest powers at that time of his life and career.

Such considerations should prepare us to find that Romeo lacks the stature of a great tragic hero; he is a study of a headstrong young man in love. When he cries, "I defy you, stars," it lacks the depth of defiance of a Macbeth.

Most actors consider Romeo a poor part compared with others in the tragic canon of Shakespeare; down the years many leading players have chosen to play Mercutio; there is a well-worn witticism that Shakespeare had to kill off Mercutio halfway through the play to stop him from stealing the whole of it. With the exception of a few of his scenes, there is a tendency to dismiss Romeo as a bore in love and a hysteric in grief. But I believe this judgment to derive from a misconception of Shakespeare's purpose in the play, which is to expose the difference between the affectation of love and the true experience. From this point of view Romeo is a fascinating character, and his development an exciting challenge to any actor.

In the Elizabethan Age the sad sickness of rejected love was a courtly vogue, in much the same fashion as the world-weariness some three hundred years later of Byron imitators or the suicidal sentimentality of the apers of Goethe's Werther. Burton devoted much more space to Love-Melancholy than to any other kind in his *Anatomy*. Orsino in *Twelfth Night* is a notable example of the melancholy rejected lover, happily unhappy in his love of love, and Romeo, at the beginning of *Romeo and Juliet*, is another. Such a love-sick swain ostentatiously sought solitude and, following the fashion of Petrarch in his bittersweet devotion to Laura, wrote sonnets to his disdainful mistress, often a creature more of fantasy than reality. As Mercutio says of Romeo, "Now is he for the numbers that Petrarch flowed in. Laura to his lady was but a kitchen wench."

We first hear of Romeo that he avoided the company of his friend, Benvolio, by stealing into a wood. His father says that it has become Romeo's custom to seek seclusion:

> Many a morning hath he there been seen,
> With tears augmenting the fresh morning's dew,
> Adding to clouds more clouds with his deep sighs.
> But all so soon as the all-cheering sun

Should in the farthest east begin to draw
The shady curtains from Aurora's bed,
Away from light steals home my heavy son,
And private in his chamber pens himself,
Shuts up his windows, locks fair daylight out,
And makes himself an artificial night.

Romeo's first entrance is wonderfully in key with the idea
of a young man who has fooled himself into suffering the pangs
of despised love; he plays the role superbly, only half aware that
it is a pose. When Benvolio bids him "Good morrow," he replies,
"Is the day so young? . . . Sad hours seem long." Romeo now
indulges in the artificial wordplay so characteristic of the vogue
of melancholy love. Surely Shakespeare means us to smile at this,
for such mechanical antitheses are as easy as they are shallow:

Why then, O brawling love! O loving hate!
O anything, of nothing first create!
O heavy lightness! Serious vanity!
Misshapen chaos of well-seeming forms!
Feather of lead, bright smoke, cold fire, sick health!
Still-waking sleep, that is not what it is!
This love feel I, that feel no love in this.
Dost thou not laugh?

Any man of sense would answer "Yes," for this empty rhetoric is
not far removed from Pyramus's "O night, which ever art when
day is not," but Benvolio is too much like Romeo to have the
necessary detachment to laugh; he too had gone walking with a
"troubled mind" and, when Romeo had avoided him, had "gladly
shunned who gladly fled from me." Romeo goes on to develop
pretty conceits about love, like a literary exercise:

Love is a smoke raised with the fume of sighs;
Being purged, a fire sparkling in lovers' eyes;
Being vexed, a sea nourished with lovers' tears.
What is it else? A madness most discreet,
A choking gall and a preserving sweet.

This is the language of the sonneteers and in no time at all Romeo is speaking in rhyme, even picking one up from Benvolio:

ROMEO: Oh, she is rich in beauty, only poor
That, when she dies, with beauty dies her store.
BENVOLIO: Then she hath sworn that she will still live chaste?
ROMEO: She hath, and in that sparing makes huge waste;
For beauty, starved with her severity,
Cuts beauty off from all posterity.
She is too fair, too wise, wisely too fair,
To merit bliss by making me despair.
She hath forsworn to love, and in that vow
Do I live dead, that live to tell it now.

Next we are introduced to Juliet, and much of the scene is devoted to establishing, with iteration and emphasis, that she is not yet fourteen; she dies before her birthday. Rarely does Shakespeare insist on the age of his characters, and nowhere more than here. What is more, she is sixteen in Brooke's poem. Why does Shakespeare change her age and make a point of it? I think that herein lies the essence of the relationship between Romeo and Juliet.

By way of parenthesis, the comment of Juliet's mother should be noted when she first introduces to Juliet the subject of marriage to Paris:

Well, think of marriage now. Younger than you
Here in Verona, ladies of esteem,
Are made already mothers. By my count,
I was your mother much upon these years
That you are now a maid. . . .

This would make Lady Capulet a mere twenty-eight, but we must think of her as belonging to an older generation. Both maturity and death came much sooner to the average Elizabethan than to us. Furthermore, in no play is the unbridgeable generation gap between parents and children a more important element. Shakespeare stresses the age gap in the case of Juliet's father, who we find had given up dancing thirty years earlier.

Many words have been written to deal with the apparent

anomaly of Lady Capulet's age. One ingenious suggestion which I have seen is that the phrase "your mother" is a printer's error for "a mother," and that Lady Capulet had had other children than Juliet, possibly by a previous marriage. Alternatively, if Capulet had been her only husband, the other children had died. I feel that such a patent printer's error, if it were one, would have been corrected somewhere along the line in the nine versions we have of the text, five Quartos and four Folios. I prefer to accept the existing text. As in the case of Lady Macbeth's hypothetical children, to which we shall refer in due course, Shakespeare uses two apparently contradictory and separated facts to reinforce the argument of the moment; the young age of her mother is used as a precedent to justify Juliet's early marriage, and later the old age of her father is used to emphasize the generation gap. All that matters is that father and mother are as one in their relation to their daughter. Even if Lady Capulet is only twenty-eight, it is an Elizabethan twenty-eight, and we should not find her lack of sympathy surprising when in our own time many young people set thirty as the age beyond which sympathetic understanding of youth is impossible.

Juliet is very knowledgeable about courtship, marriage and sex, for she has been brought up with many a bawdy leer by her delectably earthy Nurse in preparation to be a wife and mother. In particular, she knows all the rules of the intricate game of courtship. She knows all, but has experienced nothing, and this Shakespeare's reduction of her age emphasizes.

Romeo, on the other hand, is a sophisticate, mooning about his Rosaline in the fashion of the young gallants of his day. How old is Romeo? It is highly probable that he was first played by Richard Burbage after he had memorably created the part of Richard III. He is a mature and experienced young man. Why is Mercutio the witty and sophisticated cynic that he is? His sole purpose in the plot is to be killed so that Romeo may be incensed to the point of revengefully killing Juliet's kinsman; any amiable character would have served that purpose. He is strikingly delineated in order to reveal the essential Romeo, for when Romeo is freed from his moody thralldom to Rosaline the two friends have a battle of wits and it is the clever Mercutio who is beaten and cries quits, and welcomes Romeo back to the sophisticated companionship of the young men-about-town with "Now art thou sociable; now art thou Romeo; now art thou what thou art, by art as well as nature." Much of their ribald dialogue centers around the word "goose," which was an Elizabethan euphemism for a whore, and I believe that Romeo's line, "Thou wast never with me for anything when thou wast not there for the goose," means that they had gone awhoring together.

Thus then, my interpretation of the relationship between the two lovers is that it is the result of an encounter between sophistication and knowledgeable but essentially guileless innocence. Romeo's confrontation with Juliet's ardent fragility is an overwhelming experience which shatters his preconceptions of the love-game and has something of the effect upon him of a religious conversion; it is surely not without significance that the sonnet which expresses their first reaction to each other is based upon a religious figure of speech, in which she is the saint and he the pilgrim.

Romeo is persuaded to go without invitation to the Capulet party because his beloved Rosaline will be there. It was apparently the custom for a party of masked revelers to seek uninvited admission to a party by presenting their request in the person of one of their number disguised as blind Cupid, but Benvolio prompts them to dispense with such an old-fashioned practice. Just before their entry Mercutio tries to dispel Romeo's love-melancholy with a scintillating display of his wit, but all the response he gets is

> Peace, peace, Mercutio, peace!
> Thou talk'st of nothing.

Just before their entrance into the Capulet house, Romeo expresses a warning of disaster. His mood in the whole scene has been more truly somber and less artificial than that in his first scene with Benvolio, though his companions assume it to be still an expression of his melancholy love for Rosaline. Romeo says that his heart-heaviness derives from a dream, but Mercutio does not allow him to enlarge upon this; he takes it as another affectation and uses it as a cue for his brilliant improvisation on the theme of the causer of dreams, Queen Mab. Romeo reluctantly agrees to accompany the maskers, of which the stage direction says there are eight or nine, but not before he has voiced his deep misgiving:

> . . . For my mind misgives
> Some consequence, yet hanging in the stars,
> Shall bitterly begin his fearful date
> With this night's revels, and expire the term
> Of a despised life closed in my breast
> By some vile forfeit of untimely death.

By whom was Romeo's life "despised?" By Rosaline, himself, or Fate? This very ambiguity is a bridge between the artificiality of the Romeo we have seen and the Romeo we are about to see. The sense of doom in a romantically forlorn lover provokes a smile, but not that of a young man who has a sudden feeling of tragic destiny.

Capulet is delighted by the invasion of the masked young men; he says, "this unlooked-for sport comes well." When Tybalt recognizes the voice of "that villain, Romeo," and is prevented from causing a disturbance, Capulet praises the son of his enemy:

> He bears him like a portly gentleman.
> And, to say truth, Verona brags of him
> To be a virtuous and well-governed youth.

In the delightful first exchange between Romeo and Juliet, his sincerity is countered by a playfulness in her. She has certainly learned the rules of dalliance well. In her inexperience she cannot yet tell the genuine from the artificial, and tells him, "You kiss by the book." But when she is alone with the Nurse, we learn that she has been as deeply affected as Romeo. They severally learn the other's identity from the Nurse, and are immediately confronted by the barrier of their families' hostility.

As a background for the famous Balcony scene, two facts should be noted: Romeo is in the garden at considerable risk, and he is there just to be near his beloved; that his courage in daring discovery by members of the Capulet household (it is clear from the opening scene of the play that the servants of the two families nursed the feud violently) would be rewarded by seeing and speaking with Juliet is a slender hope rather than a confident expectation. The ribald and bawdy comments of Mercutio who is searching for him must have sounded like impious desecration to Romeo, who listens to them unseen.

The stage direction, "Juliet appears above at a window," added by Nicholas Rowe in the early eighteenth century is, I think, misplaced. All Romeo sees at first is a light. He prays that it may be Juliet's and that she will appear on her balcony. The scansion of the line, "It is my lady, oh, it is my love!" with the stressed accent on the repeated "is" shows that it is at that point that Juliet emerges, as if in answer to his prayer. Why does not Romeo immediately reveal himself? He cannot as yet know that she reciprocates his love, and she might react dangerously to the voice of an unseen stranger. His speech as he watches her is inspired by a true poetic feeling, unlike the artificiality which Rosaline had prompted; it is as decorated as before, but costume jewelry has been replaced with priceless gems. When he hears her speak wistfully of Romeo, he can scarce contain himself, and when she finally says to the night,

> . . . Romeo, doff thy name,
> And for thy name, which is no part of thee,
> Take all myself,

he steps out from cover and speaks. He addresses her as "dear saint" and "fair saint," thereby recalling their first brief meeting. When she has recovered from her wondrous surprise, her immediate concern is for his safety:

How camest thou hither, tell me, and wherefore?
The orchard walls are high and hard to climb,
And the place death, considering who thou art,
If any of my kinsman find thee here.

He tries to brush this aside, but she persists: "If they do see thee, they will murder thee." Again he tries to make light of her fears, but again she counters with: "I would not for the world they saw thee here." She continues to be practical in her fear, and wants to know how he found the place. Again he is fanciful in his reply, and finally turns her concern for his safety to blushes at his praise with the magic of

I am no pilot, yet wert thou as far
As that vast shore washed with the farthest sea,
I would adventure for such merchandise.

She then becomes aware of the fact that he has already overheard her express her love for him, and by that very fact all she had learned about the love-game has gone overboard. Then she remembers she must be suspicious of a lover's vows; also that he may think her too easily won. The confusion between the remembered warnings and actual experience gushes out of her:

Fain would I dwell on form, fain, fain deny
What I have spoke. But farewell compliment!
Dost thou love me? I know thou wilt say "Aye,"
And I will take thy word. Yet if thou swear'st
Thou mayst prove false. At lovers' perjuries
They say Jove laughs. O gentle Romeo,
If thou dost love, pronounce it faithfully;
Or, if thou think'st I am too quickly won,
I'll frown and be perverse and say thee nay,
So thou wilt woo; but else, not for the world.
In truth, fair Montague, I am too fond,
And therefore thou mayst think my 'haviour light.
But trust me, gentleman, I'll prove more true
Than those that have more cunning to be strange.
I should have been more strange, I must confess,
But that thou overheard'st, ere I was ware,

> My true love's passion. Therefore pardon me,
> And not impute this yielding to light love,
> Which the dark night hath so discovered.

Romeo tries to interpose, but her excitement, embarrassment, love, doubt, and fear force her to rush on. The thought of the impossibility of it all pulls her up:

> I have no joy of this contract tonight.
> It is too rash, too unadvised, too sudden,
> Too like the lightning, which doth cease to be
> Ere one can say, "It lightens." . . .

She tries to leave, but cannot, and when she is called by the Nurse, she says to Romeo: "Stay but a little; I will come again." When she does so, in the impetuosity of her love, she breaks the final rule of the game by herself proposing marriage:

> If that thy bent of love be honourable,
> Thy purpose marriage, send me word tomorrow
> By one that I'll procure to come to thee,
> Where and what time thou wilt perform the rite,
> And all my fortunes at thy foot I'll lay,
> And follow thee my lord throughout the world.

In a daze of disbelief at a miracle, Romeo begins to leave but is called back again by Juliet, who speaks for all lovers the reluctance of their good-nights. Romeo is content to stand and listen, but when she says her final good-night, he leaves to go straightway to his Father Confessor.

Friar Laurence is a delightful, kindly, and garrulous old man, who does ill in striving to do good. Withal, he has a worldly shrewdness. When he learns that Romeo has not been to bed, he immediately assumes, "God pardon sin!" that he has spent the night with Rosaline. He also surmises that Rosaline's coldness to Romeo was due to her realization that his protestations of love were hollow, though not consciously so:

> Oh, she knew well
> Thy love did read by rote and could not spell.

His first reaction to the news about Juliet is not, as might be expected, the danger and difficulty of the relationship, but the fact that it might have a good result:

> For this alliance may so happy prove,
> To turn your households' rancour to pure love;

and so indeed it might have turned out, had it not been for Tybalt, who has already sent a letter, assumed by Mercutio to be a challenge, to the Capulet house, a challenge which Benvolio is certain Romeo will answer.

When Romeo comes upon his friends, Mercutio and Benvolio, he is a changed man from the love-melancholic who had given them the slip the night before. He is an ecstatically happy man, and overwhelms Mercutio with his exuberant play upon words, so much so that the delighted Mercutio cries, "Nay, if thy wits run the wild-goose chase, I have done; for thou hast more of the wild goose in one of thy wits than, I am sure, I have in my whole five."

When the Nurse comes to seek out Romeo for his message to Juliet there is no sign of concern in her about the danger of the marriage, any more than there was in Friar Laurence. She is only worried that Romeo may be attempting a plain seduction, a fear natural to her and one reinforced by the bawdy encounter with Mercutio. The whole spirit of their scene is that of the brightest comedy, as is that in which the Nurse returns to Juliet with the news of the arrangements for the marriage. It is as though Shakespeare wanted to picture the fairest summer day before it is lost in a sudden thunderstorm. In his mature tragedies, the sense of the impending storm is always present. The possibility of the storm is hinted at by Romeo to the Friar, as they await the arrival of Juliet for the marriage:

> . . . But come what sorrow can,
> It cannot countervail the exchange of joy
> That one short minute gives me in her sight.

Do thou but close our hands with holy words,
Then love-devouring death do what he dare,
It is enough I may but call her mine.

There follows the exciting scene which, with the deaths of Mercutio and Tybalt, starts the rush of events which leads pell-mell to the double suicide in the tomb. When Tybalt makes his public challenge, Romeo is faced with a truly tragic dilemma: in refusing to fight he will be dubbed a coward, the basest insult to an Elizabethan, and in fighting he may hurt or even kill a relative of his new wife. He chooses what the infuriated Mercutio calls "calm, dishonourable, vile submission!" From that moment, all goes wrong. In interposing between Tybalt and Mercutio, he enables his enemy to give a mortal wound to his friend:

My very friend hath got his mortal hurt
In my behalf, my reputation stained
With Tybalt's slander—Tybalt, that an hour
Hath been my kinsman. O sweet Juliet,
Thy beauty hath made me effeminate,
And in my temper softened valour's steel.

We now become aware of an unsuspected element in Romeo's character, one which he shares with Hamlet: a desperate, fiery impetuosity. As he sees Tybalt again, fury captures him:

Away to Heaven, respective lenity,
And fire-eyed fury be my conduct now.

His mad attack overwhelms the schooled skill of the duelist, and he kills Tybalt. With the death, Romeo himself becomes subject to the death penalty, and is urged by Benvolio to flee. As he does so, he utters the cry which is the essence of this kind of tragedy: "Oh, I am fortune's fool!" (It is interesting to note that Malvolio makes a similar comment: " 'Tis but fortune; all is fortune." A sense of sour destiny can make a comedy as well as a tragedy.)

It is the Lady Capulet who, upon seeing the corpse of her nephew, demands revenge. She cannot believe Benvolio's story that Tybalt, the famed swordsman, was slain by Romeo:

He is a kinsman to the Montague;
Affection makes him false; he speaks not true.
Some twenty of them fought in this black strife,
And all those twenty could but kill one life.
I beg for justice, which thou, Prince, must give.
Romeo slew Tybalt, Romeo must not live.

Romeo is exiled, under pain of death.

Romeo, in hiding in the Friar's cell, awaits news of the Prince's judgment. When he hears the dread word "Banishment," the same wildness that enabled him to kill Tybalt is now turned upon himself, for the sentence means that he will never see Juliet again. The Friar tries in vain to argue with the "madman," but to no avail. Even in his desperation, Romeo uses an argument which seems potent against the celibate Friar:

Thou canst not speak of that thou dost not feel.
Wert thou as young as I, Juliet thy love,
An hour but married, Tybalt murdered,
Doting like me, and like me banished, ·
Then mightst thou speak, then mightst thou tear thy hair
And fall upon the ground, as I do now,
Taking the measure of an unmade grave.

The coming of the Nurse with her description of Juliet's grief drives Romeo in guilty fury to attempt suicide, but this provokes the Friar to a surprising and effective display of anger:

Hold thy desperate hand.
Art thou a man? Thy form cries out thou art.
Thy tears are womanish; thy wild acts denote
The unreasonable fury of a beast.
Unseemly woman in a seeming man!
Or ill-seeming beast in seeming both!
Thou hast amazed me. By my holy order,
I thought thy disposition better tempered.

The Friar's calmer counsels prevail, especially when he promises that Romeo shall spend the night with Juliet, and furthers that with what seems a feasible plan for ultimate happiness:

> Go, get thee to thy love, as was decreed;
> Ascend her chamber; hence and comfort her.
> But look thou stay not till the watch be set,
> For then thou canst not pass to Mantua,
> Where thou shalt live till we can find a time
> To blaze your marriage, reconcile your friends,
> Beg pardon of the Prince, and call thee back
> With twenty hundred thousand times more joy
> Than thou went'st forth in lamentation.

Romeo's despair is changed to a prospect of a "joy past joys."

We are immediately informed of a new barrier to that joy; her father's arrangements for Juliet's marriage to Paris. But in happy ignorance of this, Romeo and Juliet spend their marriage night; yet with the dawn Romeo must hurry away. Their reluctant yet hasty leave-taking is to be their last view of each other alive. As she looks down from the balcony upon Romeo below, the almost morbidly impressionable Juliet sees an omen of disaster:

> Oh God! I have an ill-divining soul.
> Methinks I see thee, now thou art below,
> As one dead in the bottom of a tomb.

Romeo, who has been trying to cheer her up, cannot help echoing her mood: "Dry sorrow drinks our blood."

With Romeo in Mantua, the story now concentrates on the Friar's daring scheme of the potion which makes sleep look like death, and which will enable Juliet to avoid the imminent marriage to Paris. Again it seems eminently feasible and a happy end is assured:

> In the meantime, against thou shalt awake,
> Shall Romeo by my letters know our drift,
> And hither shall he come, and he and I
> Will watch thy waking, and that very night
> Shall Romeo bear thee hence to Mantua;
> And this shall free thee from this present shame.

But again the Friar's scheme is to be frustrated, for his messenger to Romeo will be delayed en route by an outbreak of plague, and the news of the apparent death of Juliet will get first to Romeo by his own servant, Balthasar.

As Romeo in Mantua awaits news, he has another dream, and this one almost foretells the direful truth about to happen, but his happy mood gives it a happy ending:

> I dreamed my lady came and found me dead—
> Strange dream, that gives a dead man leave to think!—
> And breathed such life with kisses in my lips
> That I revived and was an emperor.

When Romeo receives the news of Juliet's death from Balthasar, he is not lost in a wild paroxysm of grief as one might expect after his previous reaction to the news of banishment. Immediately he makes the decision to return to Verona and die in the tomb with Juliet. To this end, although his "looks are pale and wild," his instructions to his servant are detailed and practical. There is a coldness of resolution in him. He recalls the particulars of the apothecary and his shop with extraordinary detachment. In face of a lover's ultimate sorrow, the death of the beloved, an almost frightening strength has replaced extravagant grief. Here Romeo begins to achieve true tragic stature. He can even comment on the evil power of money, as he pays the apothecary for the poison:

> There is thy gold, worse poison to men's souls,
> Doing more murder in this loathsome world
> That these poor compounds that thou mayst not sell.
> I sell thee poison; thou hast sold me none.

When Romeo arrives at the tomb with Balthasar, he gives him the suicide letter for his father and warns him to be gone. To emphasize his threat to Balthasar not to stay and spy on him, he describes his mood:

> The time and my intents are savage-wild,
> More fierce and more inexorable far
> Than empty tigers or the roaring sea;

but now his wildness is controlled and steely, and so all the more impressive.

When he finds Paris, whom he does not recognize, in the tomb, he calls him "Good gentle youth," an evidence of Romeo's new maturity. He tries to avoid fighting him:

> . . . I beseech thee, youth,
> Put not another sin upon my head,
> By urging me to fury. Oh, be gone!

There is a foretaste of Macbeth in this, who, in his reluctance to fight with Macduff, says:

> But get thee back; my soul is too much charged
> With blood of thine already.

In his beautiful death speech, Romeo achieves a moving dignity. He begs forgiveness of Tybalt and his farewell to his doomed life has the ring of tragic maturity:

> . . . Oh, here
> Will I set up my everlasting rest,
> And shake the yoke of inauspicious stars
> From this world-wearied flesh. . . .

His last words remind us of those of Othello, who said:

> No way but this,
> Killing myself, to die upon a kiss.

Romeo's dying words are: "Thus with a kiss I die."

I have already described Richard II and King Lear as characters who achieve purification through suffering. Romeo achieves maturity through suffering, and he presents a rewarding challenge to an actor. We must see the young gallant in love with love who experiences true love as an ecstatically elevating experience. We must see the bright wit and happy lover suddenly confronted with a tragic dilemma. Then is revealed the essentially violent man, who kills in anger, and whose violence then turns in upon himself. Finally we see his fury controlled until he achieves at last the stature of a true tragic hero. I have yet to see this Romeo played.

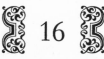 16   Hamlet

J u s t a s every actor is supposed to want to play Hamlet, it
would seem that every author wants to write about him. He has
received more performances in the theatre and more explication
on the printed page than any other character of Shakespeare.
Theatregoers collect Hamlets as philatelists do stamps, and in both
cases, it would seem, the rarer and stranger the specimen the more
it is cherished.

Since every actor is unique, no two performances of any role
will be exactly alike, not even when an understudy strives, or is
made to strive, hard to copy his principal, but it is particularly
true that all Hamlets are different. More than once in the history
of the play, four separate productions have been offered to the
public in one city in one year. Hamlet is such an all-encompassing
human phenomenon that it will absorb and be illuminated by
actors of quite contrary qualities. It is a particularly naked part,
and no actor will succeed in it who tries to hide himself, and no
actor will completely fail who is content to let Hamlet take hold
of him rather than he of Hamlet.

Just as every actor's Hamlet is himself, so is every writer's.

He sees in the character what his personality, predilections, prejudices, beliefs lead him to see. And so do I. In what follows I am prompted by two considerations: to contradict Goethe's conception of Hamlet and the many subsequent versions of it, and to provide for an actor a blueprint of the character as I see it, always remembering that a blueprint is not the building.

To begin with, a brief quotation from Carlyle's translation of *William Meister's Apprenticeship*, which gives the essence of Goethe's conception of Hamlet: "A lovely, pure, noble, and most moral nature, without the strength of nerve which forms a hero, sinks beneath a burden it cannot bear and must not cast away. All duties are holy for him; the present is too hard. Impossibilities have been required of him; not in themselves impossibilities, but such for him." "Without the strength of nerve which forms a hero." If that is true, Hamlet, and with him the play, lacks true tragic stature. Coleridge's Hamlet, while more impressive as a tragic figure than Goethe's, is from a similar mold: "He is a man living in meditation, called upon to act by every motive human and divine, but the great object of his life is defeated by continually resolving to do, yet doing nothing but resolve." These conceptions of an ineffectual saint are much better descriptions of Shakespeare's Henry VI than his Hamlet. In arriving at the "lovely, pure, noble, and most moral nature" concept, one feels that Goethe must have completely missed Hamlet's gross obscenities, and Coleridge's "doing nothing but resolve" seems to ignore the fact that Hamlet has an extraordinary record of slaughter; in the course of the play he willfully causes the death of five people, one on impulse, two in anger, and two by diabolical cleverness; this spineless wretch is the first to jump aboard in an attack on a pirate ship. It is, of course, true that the whole action of the play derives from Hamlet's hesitation in killing Claudius, but I think the hesitation to be that of a strong man, not a weak one.

Before we proceed to trace Hamlet's character as he is revealed in the play, we must consider his age. Shakespeare's use of time is poetic and dramatic rather than chronometric. To quote what I have said elsewhere:

> How old is Hamlet? There is only one clear indication, and that is in the graveyard scene, after his return from England, when we learn by implication that he is thirty years old. But he is a student in the university at the beginning of the play, and in Elizabethan days students usually left the university at the age at which they now enter; we are to think of him as a very young man. The action of the play occupies but a few months and yet in that time Hamlet has aged ten years. This, I think, is precisely what Shakespeare intends; the Hamlet who returns from England is a much more mature man than the one who left Denmark.

Just before the play begins, Hamlet had been a student at Wittenberg, separated from Elsinore and the Court by a journey of some weeks, and so any news he receives from home is already old. He hears that his father has died suddenly of a snakebite; furthermore, his uncle is now king, and, most incredible of all, has married the widowed queen.

The fact that Claudius has become king is not really surprising. Only late in the play does Hamlet complain that his uncle had "popped in between the election and my hopes." The country had been in a nervous state expecting an invasion by young Fortinbras, at the head of a lawless band of adventurers, in revenge for his father's death at the hands of King Hamlet. A strong new king was immediately needed; the election of Claudius, particularly in the absence of Hamlet, was inevitable. What is more, it was immediately justified, because Claudius manages to dispel the threat of invasion by appealing to the King of Norway to curb his nephew, Fortinbras; the ambitious young soldier was the more ready to cancel the projected invasion because the object of his revenge, Hamlet's father, was now dead, and in return he received free passage through Denmark to fight against Poland.

There are grounds for believing that Hamlet was antipathetic to his uncle prior to the marriage, for he saw in him the opposite of those qualities for which he admired his father. Hamlet sums up the difference in "Hyperion to a satyr." The contrast is clear in their attitude to drinking in the Court; King Hamlet had forbidden it while King Claudius encouraged it. Hamlet approved and, to some extent inherited, his father's values. The fact that Gertrude could marry, and so soon, a man so opposite to her son's father was a natural shock to Hamlet. The truth probably was that Gertrude found the sensuality of Claudius more congenial than the austerity of his brother.

The first action of Hamlet in the play is one of overt defiance. The period of royal mourning has been declared over, much sooner than the normal custom, but at a ceremonial meeting of the Court, with everybody in colorful costume and regalia, the Prince deliberately appears in solemn black. Hamlet's first words, an aside, reveal his mordant wit; he says that Claudius is "A little more than kin and less than kind." The word "kind," of course, is used as in the phrase "not my kind." From Hamlet's point of view, he would have been less than kind in any case, but the marriage has made his detested uncle his step-father too. The new King behaves to the Prince impeccably; publicly he proclaims him his heir and begs him not to return to Wittenberg. The Queen adds her entreaties and Hamlet makes it clear, in acquiescing, that it is her plea he is responding to. The King deliberately ignores this slight by describing the response as "a loving and a fair reply," and a "gentle and unforced accord." The ceremony is over and Hamlet is left alone.

No other character in Shakespeare is so much left alone on stage. His solitary self-communings are so characteristic that to many people they have become the total picture of the man, a misanthropic world-weary melancholic, the courageous man of action completely forgotten. Yet every soliloquy has a dramatic as well as a psychological significance.

To me, Hamlet's first soliloquy is the expression of an internal struggle to overcome a deep sense of guilt. His suit of mourning has been a visible and public protest against the royal marriage, a protest in which he is completely alone, and in which he has hurt his mother and been gently rebuked by the generosity and consideration of his uncle. At this stage, he has small logical grounds for disapproval, for everybody else rejoices in the new king and the new marriage. All he has to object to is that the marriage has taken place too soon and that it is incestuous. To deal first with the second point: To describe the marriage as incestuous was not the product of a sick imagination, but a legal fact. It was not until 1907 that such a marriage was allowed in England. To the Elizabethans, as to Hamlet, the marriage was incestuous, and this was an important issue to them, for their own Queen Elizabeth owed her throne to the fact that Henry VIII's marriage to Katharine of Aragon was incestuous in exactly the same way as that of Gertrude to Claudius, in that Katharine had been the widow of Henry's brother, Arthur; it was on this ground that the marriage had been annulled.

Of course, Hamlet would have objected to his mother's marriage if it had taken place after the official period of mourning was over and if the detested man had not been his uncle, but it will be a long time before he will openly acknowledge that. Now he makes much in a crescendo of repetition of the unseemly haste of the marriage, but nobody shares his disgust, so he must hold his tongue.

In this first soliloquy we find his tendency to unpack his heart with words in full spate. His wrath is turned not only against the frailty of women as shown in his mother's marriage but against the corruption of the society that can approve it. His wish for death and threat of suicide are, to me, characteristically violent expressions of his disgust, guilt, and frustration, of the kind that violent men often express with angry shouts of "I wish I was dead!" The "To be, or not to be" soliloquy is a very different matter.

The lonely outburst is followed by the appearance of Horatio, Marcellus, and Bernardo, who have come to tell Hamlet about the Ghost. Hamlet's joyous surprise at seeing his good friend and fellow student, Horatio, is a wonderful relief after the solitary distress of the soliloquy. Horatio had made the journey from Wittenberg to be present at King Hamlet's funeral. We can assume from this that he, like the young Prince, admired and shared the values of the dead monarch, but he is careful not to echo Hamlet's disapproval of the o'er hasty marriage.

Horatio is Hamlet's Rock of Gibraltar throughout the play. He confides in him alone, he submits his suspicions to the confirmation of Horatio's judgment and finally dies in his arms, entrusting him with the justification of his acts to posterity. The first thing we hear of Horatio is that he is a scholar, and this intellectual bent he shares with Hamlet, but temperamentally they are opposites. Hamlet praises Horatio for the qualities that he himself conspicuously lacks. Horatio is not "passion's slave;" he has an imperturbability of mind and spirit that nothing can shake. Hamlet, when he is about to test Horatio's friendship and judgment, says:

> Since my dear soul was mis⁺ress of her choice
> And could of men distinguish, her election
> Hath sealed thee for herself for thou hast been
> As one, in suffering all, that suffers nothing,
> A man that Fortune's buffets and rewards
> Hath ta'en with equal thanks; and blest are those
> Whose blood and judgement are so well commingled
> That they are not a pipe for Fortune's finger
> To sound what stop she please. Give me that man
> That is not passion's slave, and I will wear him
> In my heart's core—aye, in my heart of heart,
> As I do thee. . . .

But now Horatio has brought news of the Ghost. Since this is at the heart of Hamlet's subsequent dilemma, some preliminary consideration must be given to it. Horatio's reaction, when he was first told of the Ghost, was that which most people today would have had:

> Horatio says 'tis but our fantasy,
> And will not let belief take hold of him.

When he does see the Ghost himself, Horatio does not assume it is the spirit of the dead king, even though it looks like him. Instead of treating the apparition as though it were indeed the king, Horatio challenges it to declare its nature, and later charges it to stay and speak, if it can. He addresses it as "illusion."

Ghosts, still a matter of controversy, were particularly so in Shakespeare's day. The growing appeal to reason made supernatural phenomena subject to much skepticism. The official denial by the new Church of England of the doctrine of Purgatory, which many had assumed to be the abode of restless spirits, complicated the issue, and made people more ready to believe that apparitions were evil in origin. Upon mature consideration, Hamlet shares Horatio's skepticism:

> The spirit that I have seen
> May be the Devil, and the Devil hath power
> To assume a pleasing shape. Yea, and perhaps
> Out of my weakness and my melancholy,
> As he is very potent with such spirits,
> Abuses me to damn me. . . .

Even before he has seen the Ghost, Hamlet assumes that it is probably an emanation of Hell:

> If it assume my noble father's person,
> I'll speak to it though Hell itself should gape
> And bid me hold my peace. . . .

But Hamlet is eager for communication with the Ghost, whatever it is. He is oppressed in spirit to an extent which the marriage seems hardly enough to justify. Both he and Horatio feel that the apparition bodes ill; Horatio thinks it foretells "some strange eruption to our state," but Hamlet's expectation is much more specific and personal: "I doubt [*i.e.* suspect] some foul play." Maybe his melancholy is justified beyond his knowledge.

It is this which makes him cry out later that his soul had been prophetic; it had known more than his mind.

At his first sight of the Ghost, Hamlet instinctively prays to Heaven for protection. In addressing the apparition, he immediately states his doubts about its origin, whether it be an agency of God or the Devil:

> Be thou a spirit of health or goblin damned,
> Bring with thee airs from Heaven or blasts from Hell,
> Be thy intents wicked or charitable,
> Thou comest in such a questionable shape, [*i.e.* seeming to
>   invite questions]
> That I will speak to thee. . . .

But Hamlet wants to believe it is the spirit of his dead father, for he yearns for some knowledge which will explain and justify his feelings.

When the Ghost beckons Hamlet to follow it, Horatio's first reaction is to assume evil intent, and he and Marcellus strive to restrain Hamlet forcibly, but he throws them both off; Hamlet is no physical weakling. He even threatens to kill them. Horatio says, "He waxes desperate with imagination;" Hamlet, unlike Horatio, was always subject to impulsive and irrational action.

= The first thing the Ghost tells Hamlet is that he has come from Hell where he is suffering the torments of the damned,

> Till the foul crimes done in my days of nature
> Are burnt and purged away. . . .

He goes on to suggest, though he is forbidden to describe, the horrors of Hell.

> . . . But that I am forbid
> To tell the secrets of my prison house,
> I could a tale unfold whose lightest word
> Would harrow up thy soul, freeze thy young blood,
> Make thy two eyes, like stars, start from their spheres,
> Thy knotted and combined locks to part
> And each particular hair to stand on end
> Like quills upon the fretful porpentine.

This emphasis of the Ghost on his torments is very important and is the reason for Hamlet's sparing Claudius when he finds him at prayer. The theology of the day believed that King Hamlet was enduring the torments of Hell because he died without having a chance to make his peace with God. Yet he was a good man, but all men are sinners. Claudius was a murderer, but he might in prayer be confessing his sin and seeking the forgiveness of God. Never would he be more ready to die, and thus Hamlet would not fulfill the obligations of revenge, for if the good king went to Hell, so much more must the wicked one. Even after the account of the murder, the Ghost again emphasizes that he had no chance to secure the last rites of the Church:

> Thus was I, sleeping, by a brother's hand
> Of life, of crown, of Queen, at once dispatched;
> Cut off even in the blossoms of my sin,
> Unhouseled, disappointed, unaneled,
> No reckoning made, but sent to my account
> With all my imperfections on my head.

Hamlet has learned not only of the murder of his father, but also of the previous adultery of his mother. In describing this, the Ghost has used imagery which will remain with Hamlet:

> . . . Lust, though to a radiant angel linked,
> Will sate itself in a celestial bed
> And prey on garbage.

But the Ghost lays all the blame upon "that adulterate beast," Claudius, who had seduced Gertrude with his "wicked wit and gifts," and he commands Hamlet:

> Taint not thy mind, nor let thy soul contrive
> Against thy mother aught. Leave her to Heaven,
> And to those thorns that in her bosom lodge
> To prick and sting her. . . .

Hamlet is so overwhelmed by the revelations of the Ghost that, again "desperate with imagination," he can scarcely refrain from collapsing physically. And then a wild ecstasy dominates him. He had been right all along, and all the others had been wrong. "Oh, wonderful!" Then suddenly he becomes cautious. He cannot tell what he has heard, not even to Horatio. He has just sworn, on the evidence of an apparition, that he will commit the ultimate crime of killing a king. It will be sure proof to Horatio that the Ghost came from the Devil. What was more, if Hamlet persisted in believing the Ghost, it would be Horatio's bounden duty to reveal the story to the King; loyalty to the throne was a paramount duty to all good Elizabethans. No king was more aware of his divine authority than Claudius:

> There's such divinity doth hedge a king
> That treason can but peep to what it would,
> Acts little of his will.

And so Hamlet must hide his purposes even from Horatio. He resorts to "wild and whirling words," still exalted by his new justification. In this spirit he says:

> . . . Touching this vision here,
> It is an honest ghost, that let me tell you.

When calmness returns, doubts about the ghost will return too. Now Hamlet hears the Ghost again, insisting that he make his companions swear to tell nothing of what they have seen. But only Hamlet can hear the Ghost; and so, when he talks to an unseen presence, the others assume that he has become unbalanced. (Gertrude has exactly the same reaction in the Closet scene, when she can neither see nor hear the Ghost.) Sensing their reaction to his strangeness, Hamlet immediately turns it to good account. He has a solitary, difficult, and dreadful task to perform; he will need a cover perhaps to allow him greater freedom:

> . . . I perchance hereafter shall think meet
> To put an antic disposition on.

Having got them to swear to secrecy, Hamlet decides he cannot leave them with no explanation at all. They would naturally assume that the supernatural visitation had been an omen of some ill to come. Indeed, both of them at separate times had so interpreted it. Hamlet now, his ecstasy spent, confirms them in that belief:

> The time is out of joint. Oh, cursed spite,
> That ever I was born to set it right.

This, to Horatio and Marcellus, is an innocent formula; Hamlet has been called upon to perform some great national duty. They still stand apart from him, but he assures them that he is his normal self and their friend again with, "Nay, come, let's go together."

The play is nearly half over before we see Hamlet and Ophelia together, and yet the relationship and its problems have been well established by that time. We first hear of it when her brother and then her father warn her against Hamlet, who, however much he professes to love her, cannot marry her, because he is of the royal blood and she is not. (One of the great ironies of the play is that they were wrong in this matter, for at Ophelia's burial, the Queen says:

> I hoped thou should'st have been my Hamlet's wife;
> I thought thy bride bed to have decked, sweet maid,
> And not have strewed thy grave.)

Polonius and Laertes were genuinely solicitous of Ophelia's wellbeing. I have pointed out elsewhere the evidence for believing that father and son were lasciviously inclined, and judged Hamlet's intentions from their own in such a case. To protect her from what he thinks will be the inevitable outcome, Polonius forbids Ophelia to see or correspond with Hamlet, and, as a dutiful and trusting daughter, she obeys.

We next hear of Hamlet's forcing himself into her room and behaving like a conventional madman. She rushes to her father in terror to describe it:

> My lord, as I was sewing in my closet,
> Lord Hamlet, with his doublet all unbraced,

> No hat upon his head, his stockings fouled,
> Ungartered and down-gyved to his ankle,
> Pale as his shirt, his knees knocking each other,
> And with a look so piteous in purport
> As if he had been loosed out of Hell
> To speak of horrors, he comes before me.

It helps to understand this passage if we compare it with Rosalind's description in *As You Like It* of a man, mad for love:

> A lean cheek . . . a blue eye and sunken [i.e. eyes heavy with dark shadows] . . . an unquestionable spirit [i.e. beyond words, and wanting none; Hamlet's only sound is a heavy sigh in the reported scene with Ophelia] . . . a beard neglected . . . Then your hose should be ungartered, your bonnet unbanded, your sleeve unbuttoned, your shoe untied, and everything about you demonstrating a careless desolation.

Small wonder that Polonius's immediate reaction is "Mad for thy love?" Ophelia says that, in obedience to her father, she has refused to see Hamlet or to accept his letters.

What is Hamlet's motive in this strange episode? Two things have happened since we last saw him: he has begun to play the madman, and he has suddenly found his beloved Ophelia barred from him. He must know that Ophelia is acting in obedience to her father, whose values he despises. In assuming the disguise of the mad lover, he is doing two things: telling Ophelia how much he loves her and yet protecting his new identity, for he knows that Ophelia will report the scene to her father, who will in turn report it to the King. But alas! Ophelia is not moved to compassion, but to terror. She has disappointed him a second time; the first was when her love for him was less than her respect for her father.

Polonius hurries to the King with his explanation of what Claudius describes as "Hamlet's transformation," but the King has made his own arrangements to find out what is wrong. He has sent for Rosencrantz and Guildenstern, two of Hamlet's boyhood

friends, to sound him out. I feel that Rosencrantz and Guildenstern are two gentlemen spies, as Marlowe was.

It is probable that Marlowe's death before he was thirty was
connected with espionage. When he was a student at Cambridge
he had long and unexplained absences, but the university au-
thorities were pacified, or at least silenced, by the Queen's Privy
Council, which declared: "he had behaved himself orderly and
discreetly, whereby he had done Her Majesty good service, and
deserved to be rewarded for his faithful dealings . . . . it was not
Her Majesty's pleasure that anyone employed as he had been in
matters touching the benefit of his country should be defamed by
those who are ignorant in the affairs he went about." Plot and
counter-plot were such constant elements in the life of Elizabeth
and her country that espionage was an inevitable part of the body
politic. Rosencrantz and Guildenstern were secret emissaries of
their King in much the same way that Marlowe was of his Queen,
but Gertrude sees them merely as friends of her son; the King's
relationship with them is very different when the Queen is not
present. I believe their honest motivation is loyalty to the throne
and protection of the monarch. It is Rosencrantz who gives memorable expression to the significance of the death of a king,

> . . . upon whose weal depends and rests
> The lives of many. The cease of majesty
> Dies not alone, but like a gulf doth draw
> What's near it with it. . . .
> .   .   .   .
> . . . Never alone
> Did the King sigh, but with a general groan.

Rosencrantz and Guildenstern are only villains from Hamlet's
point of view. Had his father lived, they would have remained
friends, for their loyalty and service is to the throne, not to a
person.

Polonius, who is far more than Hamlet's "tedious old fool,"

uses spying as a natural source of knowledge; he even employs it against his own son and daughter, whom he loves. He has extracted from Ophelia the details of Hamlet's "solicitings," and proudly reads to the King a love-letter, which he treats like a captured document. The King is not convinced that Hamlet's madness is due to love, and so Polonius sets up a trap by which he and the King will spy upon a meeting between the two lovers. But first Polonius will encounter Hamlet himself in an attempt to discover the reasons for his strange behavior.

In the scene with the wily Lord Chamberlain Hamlet delivers some shrewd thrusts under cover of his distraction. As Polonius says, "Though this be madness, yet there is method in't." Particularly does he make it clear by implication that he understands why Polonius has forbidden Ophelia to see him, and that he despises him for holding the values which prompted him to it. He makes conception sound loathsome, as he pretends to endorse Polonius's decision to separate Ophelia from him. "For if the sun breed maggots in a dead dog, being a god kissing carrion —Have you a daughter? . . . Let her not walk i' the sun. Conception is a blessing, but not as your daughter may conceive." Polonius misses the point of this, merely seizing on the mention of "daughter" as a confirmation of his diagnosis of Hamlet's trouble, and he leaves to effect the meeting with Ophelia which will afford the King final proof that frustrated love has driven the Prince mad.

Rosencrantz and Guildenstern now enter to fulfill their mission to probe Hamlet, who greets them with the open delight with which he had previously welcomed Horatio. In no time at all they are indulging in bawdy chit-chat. Then the spies begin their work. Just as Polonius from his sensual predilections had assumed frustrated sex to be the answer to the Hamlet problem, Rosencrantz and Guildenstern with their preoccupation with kingship and power assume the answer to lie in frustrated ambition, for Hamlet's expectation of the throne had been at least and quite unexpectedly postponed. This immediately puts Hamlet on the alert, for this must surely be what the King suspects. (At this stage, Claudius can have no inkling of Hamlet's knowledge of the truth, for no one could possibly know of his crime, least of all Hamlet, who had been hundreds of miles away at the time.) Hamlet senses that the presence of Rosencrantz and Guildenstern at Court is not a "free invitation" and he presses them until they are forced to confess that they were sent for. His attitude to them changes; they are yet another example of the perfidy of men. He tells them that he does not know the reason for his melancholy, and goes on to describe his sadness at the gulf between actual man and his infinite capacity. Rosencrantz and Guildenstern are quick to change the subject and tell Hamlet of the approach of the players. With a carefully calculated double entendre, to assure the emissaries of the King of his dutiful regard for him, he says, "He that plays the King shall be welcome. His Majesty shall have tribute of me."

The interpolation about the boy-players is often dismissed as mere topical coloring and an opportunity for Shakespeare to make a hostile comment on behalf of his fellow players; although that element is undoubtedly in it, Shakespeare is primarily a playwright and uses the story for a very telling analogy. Just as the players have been dispossessed by the children and forced to travel, and just as their patrons have proved fickle in their loyalty, so Claudius has dispossessed King Hamlet, and the people have proved likewise fickle. ". . . my uncle is King of Denmark, and those that would make mows at him while my father lived, give twenty, forty, fifty, a hundred ducats apiece for his picture in little."

Hamlet's final comment to Rosencrantz and Guildenstern before Polonius enters to herald the players has been the subject of much speculation: "But my uncle-father and aunt-mother are deceived . . . I am but mad north-north-west. When the wind is southerly, I know a hawk from a handsaw." The amusing description of Claudius and Gertrude covers the bitterness that not only has his hated uncle become his father but his beloved mother has become merely his aunt. He seeks to assure them that they should not be too worried about him, for he is only a few degrees away from the true north of sanity. The last sentence is ambiguous, depending upon whether "hawk" and "handsaw" are considered as birds or tools. I prefer to regard them as birds, the handsaw being a heron. Then the sentence has a very subtle meaning, the heron being much larger than the hawk but less deadly. The south wind was the dangerous one, bringing plague and disease. (Caliban's curse on Prospero was: "A southwest blow on ye,/And blister you all o'er!") So it seems to me that Hamlet is saying, "In times of unseen danger, I can tell a foe from a friend, even though the foe looks the more innocent of the two." This, like many of the cryptic utterances of his "antic disposition," deliberately veiled a truth which he had great personal satisfaction in uttering; only he knew that he was describing Rosencrantz and Guildenstern. In their later report to the King and Queen, Guildenstern says that Hamlet

> . . . with a crafty madness, keeps aloof
> When we would bring him to some confession
> Of his true state.

With a similar "crafty madness" Hamlet compares Polonius with the Biblical Jephthah, but all Polonius got from it was another reference to "daughter," completely missing the implication that Jephthah had unwittingly sacrificed his daughter for a political purpose, and she had died an unwilling virgin because she was an obedient daughter.

Hamlet is a friend of the actors and a very knowledgeable critic of acting. He immediately calls upon the leading player for a sample of his wares, choosing a description of the death of old Priam by the sword of young Pyrrhus, a passage Hamlet himself knows by heart. There is one part of the extract which has particular significance for Hamlet. Pyrrhus, wounded in the collapse of the building, is temporarily halted in his vengeful slaying, but only to resume his dread work with more fury:

So as a painted tyrant, Pyrrhus stood,
And like a neutral to his will and matter
Did nothing.
But, as we often see, against some storm
A silence in the heavens, the rack stand still,
The bold winds speechless and the orb below
As hush as death, anon the dreadful Thunder
Doth rend the region; so after Pyrrhus' pause
Aroused vengeance sets him new awork;
And never did the Cyclops' hammers fall
On Mars's armour, forged for proof eterne,
With less remorse than Pyrrhus' bleeding sword
Now falls on Priam.

That pause of Pyrrhus will torment Hamlet as soon as he is alone. He is pausing too; but why? Can it possibly be cowardice, the basest of failings? He vents his fury in words against himself, and then against Claudius. He gives way to an uncontrolled verbal paroxysm, and then pulls himself up sharply, despising himself for such weakness:

Why, what an ass am I! This is most brave,
That I, the son of a dear father murdered,
Prompted to my revenge by Heaven and Hell,
Must, like a whore, unpack my heart with words,
And fall acursing, like a very drab,
A scullion!
Fie upon't! Foh! About, my brain! . . .

And never again does Hamlet unpack his heart with words. When he hears Laertes doing so over Ophelia's grave, he mocks him with imitation, saying,

. . . Nay, an thou'lt mouth,
I'll rant as well as thou.

Hamlet knows very well why he does not sweep to his revenge. He must first be assured that the Ghost is honest, for no one is more aware than he of the enormity of what he is called upon to do, and the coming of the players has inspired him with a plan to test Claudius's guilt. Before he indulged in his passionate soliloquy, he had already arranged with the players to play *The Murder of Gonzago* before the King, with "a speech of some dozen or sixteen lines which I would set down and insert in't," such lines, of course, being to make certain that Claudius could not miss the parallel with his own crime.

The famous "To be or not to be" soliloquy has, I think, been largely misinterpreted in its dramatic significance. Hamlet is really not contemplating suicide in it at all. It is concerned with "enterprises of great pitch and moment" which assuredly means the revenge-killing of the King, and not Hamlet's suicide. Again, he is considering the reasons for his delay, but now he does not accuse himself of cowardice. He says that just as one rightly hesitates at suicide because of "the dread of something after death," no matter how unbearable life is, so does he hesitate at his task of revenge, and with equally good reason.

The physical act of killing the King would be as easy to Hamlet as that of committing suicide, but in both cases the unknown consequences to the soul give him pause. In this he is very different from Macbeth, who, believing as does Hamlet in an afterlife, would, in pursuit of his purpose in this world, "jump the life to come." In puzzling out the reasons for his instinctive hesitance to kill the King, he finds a parallel in the natural human reluctance to commit suicide, even when death seems preferable to life; it is a commendable reluctance because God has set "his canon 'gainst self-slaughter." Similarly, Hamlet would jeopardize his soul if he committed the murder of "God's annointed" unless he was quite certain that in doing so he was an instrument of God's justice.

A crucial point in the confrontation with Ophelia is whether Hamlet is aware of the "lawful espials," Claudius and Polonius. In most productions he is made so aware, but Shakespeare never leaves us in doubt about such matters, and so I prefer to assume that he does not know they are there. If he did, his natural impetuosity, particularly in the fury with which he ends the scene, would have led him to disclose the hidden men. Furthermore, I feel certain that he cannot even suspect the presence of the King, or he would never so prematurely reveal his intention with "Those that are married already, all but one, shall live."

This is the first time Hamlet has seen Ophelia since his intrusion upon her in his assumed madness. At the first sight of her, reading a devotional book, his old love wells up in him. Her greeting of him has an almost studied formality:

> Good my lord,
> How does your Honour for this many a day?

He answers with an equal formality: "I humbly thank you, well, well, well." The repetition of "well" is a cover for suspicious consideration. The whole occasion is suddenly suspect. If she has been kept from him, why is she now seeing him? She then offers to return his gifts to her, which implies that she expected to see him. Is the same scheming hand behind this as first separated them? Is his adored Ophelia allowing herself to be a cat's-paw to entrap the man she pretended to love? And under the cover of praying too? Small wonder that his tone changes to "Ha, ha! Are you honest?" His disgust that his "most dear lady" should be a perfidious wretch makes him lash out in a crescendo of vicious, hurtful words. If she is false, there is no virtue in man. "We are arrant knaves all." Repeatedly he tells her to go to a nunnery, a gibe which has lost its force today. Its surface meaning is that such a pious prayerbook-carrying maid should escape from the wicked world and preserve her chastity in a convent, but to the Elizabethans the word "nunnery" also meant a brothel, a meaning it had acquired from the anti-monastic zeal of the Reformation. Convinced that Polonius is responsible for Ophelia's charade, Hamlet suddenly says, "Where's your father?" It is probable that the master of spying is lurking somewhere within earshot. Frightened and tormented Ophelia, who could not have anticipated this question, blurts out, "At home, my lord," but she is not a good liar, and her tone confirms Hamlet's angry suspicions and also his fury that she should lie to him. His words make clear that he does not believe her: "Let the doors be shut upon him, that he may play the fool nowhere but in's own house." His final denunciation, in which "thou" changes to "you," is of all female hypocrisy, of which Ophelia has just given him the supreme example:

> I have heard of your paintings too, well enough. God hath given you one face and you make yourselves another. You jig, you amble, and you lisp, and nickname God's creatures, and make your wantonness your ignorance [*i.e.* cover your loose and lewd behavior with a mask of innocence]. Go to; I'll no more on 't. It hath made me mad.

Poor Ophelia, in her distraction, her first step to insanity, laments the loss of the perfect being she once knew and loved, a Hamlet who occasionally peeps out from the tormented being we see in the play:

> Oh, what a noble mind is here o'erthrown!
> The courtier's, soldier's, scholar's, eye, tongue, sword;
> The expectancy and rose of the fair state,
> The glass of fashion and the mould of form,
> The observed of all observers, quite, quite down!

She is convinced that Hamlet is indeed mad.

The King is now certain that Polonius is wrong; there is something more than frustrated love disturbing Hamlet. He had overheard the threat, "all but one shall live." The very percipient Claudius says:

> Love! His affections [*i.e.* his emotional state] do not that
>   way tend;
> Nor what he spake, though it lacked form a little,
> Was not like madness. There's something in his soul
> O'er which his melancholy sits on brood,
> And I do doubt the hatch and the disclose
> Will be some danger. . . .

The King decides to remove the potential danger by sending

Hamlet to England to collect "neglected tribute." (This reference to Danegeld, extorted from the English by the invading Danes, would put the action in the tenth century. It might be interesting to see a production set in that period, but nobody would be more surprised by it than Shakespeare himself; to him Hamlet was very much his contemporary.) Polonius still sticks to his "neglected love" theory, and persuades the King to postpone his decision until Hamlet has been subjected to one more trap, a meeting with his mother with Polonius as eavesdropper.

The presentation of *The Murder of Gonzago*, which Hamlet renames *The Mousetrap* to suit his private purpose, is a turning-point in the action, for it resolves Hamlet's doubts and establishes the authenticity of the Ghost. In preparation for it, we have Hamlet's brilliant discourse on the art of acting. In it Shakespeare has an opportunity to contrast the more natural playing of his own company with the broader style of Edward Alleyn and the Admiral's Men, but it has an immediate dramatic purpose too: Hamlet is particularly concerned that the interpolated speech, which he has written, shall be a convincing reconstruction of Claudius's crime; it must shock him into a revelation of his guilt, and, to do this, the acting must have immediacy and verisimilitude.

Hamlet, conscious that his judgment may be warped by passion, tells his plan to the dispassionate Horatio—we hear that he has already told him the Ghost's story—and secures him as an additional witness.

As he comes to see the play, the King greets Hamlet with "How fares our cousin Hamlet?" In reply he receives another cryptic riddle, but, although the King pretends not to understand it, he must be aware of its implication. In order to avoid any suspicion of the truth, Hamlet shrewdly hints that his trouble is what the King's spies had thought it to be: frustrated ambition. He does not want to dull the surprise of the play, and says, "I eat the air, promise-crammed."

The Queen invites Hamlet to sit by her, but this would not have given him a position of vantage from which to rivet his eyes to the King's face. Instead he chooses to sit at Ophelia's feet, which Polonius seizes on as further proof that his love theory is right. The conversation between Hamlet and Ophelia is private, and at some distance from the King and Queen. In a cruelly bantering mood, a fit sequel to his last conversation with her, Hamlet degrades Ophelia with obscene innuendo.

The play is given twice, first in pantomime and then with dialogue. This, too, has a dramatic purpose. In Claudius, Hamlet has a worthy opponent. He is clever, subtle, and courageous. The dumb-show leaves him quite unmoved. He is so certain that no one can possibly know his secret that it is going to take much to make him see the play as more than a coincidence; and, even when he begins to suspect the purpose of the performance, he will strive hard not to betray his guilt. There is no evidence in the text that even Gertrude knew of the murder, and I believe her to be innocent of the knowledge. Hamlet, in his nervous anxiety, cannot leave well enough alone; he goes to the royal couple to make certain that they have not missed the point. Among the interpolated words in the play was undoubtedly the couplet, spoken by the Player Queen:

> In second husband let me be accurst!
> None wed the second but who killed the first.

Hamlet's private comment on this had been, "Wormwood, wormwood!" As soon as he speaks to the Queen, the King challenges him with "Have you heard the argument? Is there no offence in't?" Claudius begins to suspect that, in some incredible way, Hamlet knows the truth. As the tension mounts, Hamlet cannot keep still; he returns to Ophelia for another obscenity, cries out against the over-acting of the villain in the play, for Claudius must see himself in that villain, and rushes back to hammer guilt into the King's ear. The King rises in fright and hurries from the room calling for lights; anything can happen in the dimly lit spectators' part of the chamber. Hamlet has succeeded in his purpose, but in his impetuosity he has also revealed his knowledge to the King, and has thus put him on his guard; in uncovering the King's secret, Hamlet has also uncovered his own.

Hamlet's immediate reaction is one of wild ecstasy, as it had been when he first learned from the Ghost that his melancholy was justified. He gets the confirmation he needs from Horatio, and then turns to deal in his madly happy mood with Rosencrantz and Guildenstern, who have come to rebuke him for angering the King, and to say that his mother wants to see him. The tone of the two spies is now openly hostile, but they restrain themselves once more in an attempt to probe Hamlet, and again he tells them that his strange behavior is due to the fact that he lacks advancement. Rosencrantz counters with "How can that be when you have the voice of the King himself for your succession in Denmark?" Hamlet's reply is that his ambition is impatient; he half-quotes the proverb, "While the grass grows, the horse starves." He then chastises his erstwhile friends for their lying and hypocrisy, aimed at plucking out the heart of his mystery. That phrase has been often quoted as though it referred to the universal mystery of human life, but in context it is merely the description of the object of two spies, commissioned to discover the reason for his strange conduct.

In preparing for his meeting with his mother, Hamlet cautions himself, knowing that his all-too-ready passion may get out of control when he thinks of her guilt. Apart from his natural feeling for her, the Ghost had warned him to take no revenge against his mother. It is going to be difficult, for he is in a dangerous mood:

> . . . Now could I drink hot blood,
> And do such bitter business as the day
> Would quake to look on. . . .

The Mousetrap has indeed caught Claudius and provoked two reactions in him: a confirmation of his plan to send Hamlet to England, and a deep religious sense of guilt. He strives to pray for forgiveness, but

> That cannot be, since I am still possessed
> Of those effects for which I did the murder:
> My crown, mine own ambition, and my Queen.

Hamlet comes upon the King at prayer, and his failure to take the easy opportunity to kill him is often adduced as the ultimate proof of his essential weakness, which is the result of the conflict between his conscience and his duty. But I have already pointed out that to kill the King at prayer would have been evading the obligations of the primitive revenge code. It took strength, not weakness, to stay Hamlet's hand. Critics have accused Hamlet of being barbaric in his reasoning, but it is the code, not Hamlet, which is barbaric; as well accuse every American who fights in Vietnam of being warlike. It should also be remembered that Hamlet's restraint at this point leads to a much finer discharge of his duty to his dead father; in the end, the guilt of Claudius will be patent and public, and his death no secret act of private vengeance.

As he approaches his mother's room, Hamlet calls out to her. This is an indication that, in spite of his warning to himself, he is emotionally highly charged, which becomes evident in the initial stichomythic dialogue. In preventing his angry mother from leaving the room and forcing her to sit down, his keyed-up state makes him use unnecessary violence; Gertrude is frightened and cries out; the hidden Polonius adds his own cries and Hamlet, beside himself, thrusts through the arras, and kills the unseen eavesdropper. Hamlet cries out, "Is it the King?" A moment's reflection would tell him that it couldn't be, because he has just seen the King at prayer, but Hamlet's most notable weakness is that his brilliant brain is often overwhelmed by his fiery impetuosity; he lacks Horatio's calm.

Still in his almost hysterical state, he blurts out his suspicion of his mother:

> A bloody deed! Almost as bad, good mother,
> As kill a king and marry with his brother.

There is no justification whatsoever for the first part of Hamlet's suspicion, and Gertrude is understandably appalled and mystified by it; it is but another proof of Hamlet's madness. Nowhere does the Ghost suggest that the Queen was a party to his murder. All he accuses her of is adultery, and even this he blames upon the seductive powers of Claudius. The Ghost still loves his Queen, and is solicitous of her. Nor does Hamlet, in striving to make her acknowledge her guilt in the marriage, again suggest her guilt in the murder; it was a black suspicion which spewed out of his irrational depths. But as he contrasts the two kings, Gertrude's guilt in the marriage is tapped, and she cries out:

> O Hamlet, speak no more!
> Thou turn'st mine eyes into my very soul,
> And there I see such black and grained spots
> As will not leave their tinct.
>
> .   .   .   .   .   .
>
> Oh, speak to me no more!
> These words like daggers enter in my ears.
> No more, sweet Hamlet.

At this moment, Hamlet is all too sane for Gertrude's comfort, but then the Ghost appears and does not reveal his presence to her, and, as Hamlet speaks to it, seeming to address the empty air, she is brought back to the purpose of the meeting, which was to probe Hamlet's madness. His conduct now leaves no doubt that he is mad. The Ghost says,

> Do not forget. This visitation
> Is but to whet thy almost blunted purpose.

I believe this to be a comment on the specific scene, rather than a general injunction to Hamlet; he had been told to leave his mother to Heaven, and here he is torturing her. All his efforts of revenge should be centered on Claudius. It is Hamlet who assumes that the Ghost has come to chide him because Claudius still lives. The Ghost bids Hamlet to calm his mother. The bad, pirated First Quarto of the play has an occasional revealing gleam, and in this scene there is such a one, probably the record of an observed performance. It contains the stage direction: "Enter the Ghost in his night gown." This domestic touch again suggests that the Ghost is more concerned with the Queen in this scene than with Hamlet. The last look the Ghost gives is one of compassion, not anger or stern command; compassion for his sinful wife and tormented son. Hamlet's comment is:

> Do not look upon me,
> Lest with this piteous action you convert
> My stern effects; then what I have to do
> Will want true colour, tears perchance for blood.

After the Ghost has vanished, and taking advantage of Hamlet's kinder attitude to her, Gertrude tries to show him that his speaking to nothing is proof of madness. Here is a new danger for Hamlet; his reproof of his mother will be dismissed as coming from a madman; he has put the antic disposition on too well:

> Mother, for love of grace,
> Lay not that flattering unction to your soul,
> That not your trespass but my madness speaks.

He again returns to his accusations, now turned to pleas that she will no longer share the bed of Claudius. When she says, "O Hamlet, thou hast cleft my heart in twain," it is not clear whether it expresses distress about Hamlet's condition or guilt for her marriage; perhaps both.

It is probable that the scene was originally meant to end with the couplet:

> I must be cruel only to be kind.
> Thus bad begins, and worse remains behind.

But the reason for the afterthought, both in Shakespeare and Hamlet, seems clear. The sweep of the play depends upon the Hamlet-Claudius action; from this point of view the Gertrude scene has been a digression, and the main drive of the play must be resumed before the scene ends. But for Hamlet too there is a similar purpose. What will Gertrude tell Claudius? Above all, the King must not be warned that the madness is a cloak for some nefarious purpose. He warns the Queen in a most roundabout way, even hinting in a story about an ape who breaks his neck in trying to fly, that she might do herself harm unwittingly. She gets the point and says:

> Be thou assured if words be made of breath
> And breath of life, I have no life to breathe
> What thou hast said to me.

And she keeps her word, for all she reports to the King is the death of Polonius, which she ascribes to Hamlet's madness, and adds the plea that "He weeps for what is done." She even keeps quiet about Hamlet's disclosure that he has a plan to get rid of Rosencrantz and Guildenstern.

The death of Polonius is Claudius's final argument for the dispatch of Hamlet to England, an argument cogent even for his mother:

> His liberty is full of threats to all,
> To you yourself, to us, to everyone.
> Alas, how shall this bloody deed be answered?
> It will be laid to us, whose providence
> Should have kept short, restrained, and out of haunt
> This mad young man. But so much was our love,
> We would not understand what was most fit.

The "so much was our love" is, of course, a sop to Gertrude. Claudius speaks very differently when she is not there: "How dangerous is it that this man goes loose!" We then hear of Hamlet's popularity, an echo of Ophelia's account of him:

> Yet must not we put the strong law on him.
> He's loved of the distracted multitude,
> Who like not in their judgement, but their eyes.

But Claudius maintains the pretense of solicitude in telling Hamlet why he must leave the country:

> Hamlet, this deed, for thine especial safety,
> Which we do tender, as we dearly grieve
> For that which thou hast done, must send thee hence
> With fiery quickness. . . .

Hamlet, whose attitude in this confrontation has been mordantly witty and insolent, replies to the King's protestation of good intentions with the cryptic, "I see a cherub that sees them."

The First Folio and far too many productions omit the wonderful soliloquy beginning: "How all occasions do inform against me." Any pruning of the text to bring a production within normal playing time does a disservice to Shakespeare; thus it has been normal in the past completely to omit the character of Fortinbras, so losing a vivid dramatic contrast to Hamlet. Fortinbras too had felt he had been saddled with the obligation of revenge, and to fulfill it he had been ready to lay waste a whole country; his enemy had been King Hamlet, who had slain his father in a fair fight. Now Fortinbras is passing through Denmark, by agreement, to fight against Poland. He is a man who will always find a reason for war. There had been no grounds of even wild justice in his original intention to invade Denmark. But Hamlet's obligation is as much to punish evil as to revenge a murder. In contrasting himself with Fortinbras, Hamlet again ponders whether cowardice is what really is holding him back, though he knows that there is the wisdom of scrupulous justice in the delay. Only the brave man can contemplate the possibility of cowardice in himself; the coward must justify his conduct by magnifying any scrap of bravery he can find in himself. Hamlet knows that impetuous violence is easy for him, but it is not enough. It is not enough that justice should be done, but that it should be seen to be done, as it finally will be. His reason and his blood must work in harmony, but the sight of the single-minded Fortinbras makes him long for such simplicity:

> . . . How stand I then,
> That have a father killed, a mother stained,
> Excitements of my reason and my blood,

And let all sleep while to my shame I see
The imminent death of twenty thousand men,
That for a fantasy and trick of fame
Go to their graves like beds, fight for a plot
Whereon the numbers cannot try the cause,
Which is not tomb enough and continent
To hide the slain? Oh, from this time forth,
My thoughts be bloody or be nothing worth!

Not once in this scene does Hamlet lament the fact that he is being taken away from the object of his revenge. Had he really had any cowardly reluctance to kill Claudius, he would have welcomed this intervention of Fate. But he knows that somehow or other he will get back to Denmark and his task. The unforeseen adventure of the pirate ship affords him the opportunity.

In his letter to the King, telling him of his imminent return to Denmark, Hamlet is at pains to raise no suspicion. He was given a royal commission and has failed to carry it out. "Tomorrow shall I beg leave to see your kingly eyes, when I shall, first asking your pardon thereunto, recount the occasion of my sudden and more strange return." On receipt of the letter, the King and Laertes concoct their dastardly plans for the certain death of Hamlet. Claudius has already said that it is his consuming love for Gertrude that makes it impossible for him to move openly against Hamlet, for she "lives almost by his looks," but their plans are such that

. . . for his death no wind of blame shall breathe,
But even his mother shall uncharge the practice
And call it accident.

We next see Hamlet with Horatio in the churchyard, and there is a new maturity in him, as he makes his observations on the great mocker, Death. Jacques would find him as good company as he did Touchstone, as he moralizes on how Death makes naught of the skills and aspirations of the politician, the courtier, the lawyer, the jester, and the emperor.

The freshly acquired maturity in Hamlet is seen in his en-

counter with Laertes at the grave of Ophelia. In his new contempt for unpacking the heart with words he out-rants Laertes.
When Laertes attacks him, he says something which is only now
true of him: "I am not splenitive and rash." When he does his
mock-ranting, his mother pleads for him on the old grounds:

> This is mere madness,
> And thus awhile the fit will work on him.
> Anon, as patient as the female dove,
> When that her golden couplets are disclosed,
> His silence will sit drooping.

As if to prove her point, Hamlet says gently to Laertes:

> Hear you, sir.
> What is the reason that you use me thus?
> I loved you ever. . . .

In his later talks with Horatio, in which he tells him of how
he had substituted for the King's orders, aimed at securing his
own death, orders to secure the death of Rosencrantz and Guildenstern, Hamlet has a sense that God is using his impetuosity for
His own purposes; this alone would account for the strangeness
of his return to Denmark.

> . . . Rashly—
> And praised be rashness for it; let us know,
> Our indiscretion sometime serves us well
> When our deep plots do pall; and that should learn us
> There's a divinity that shapes our ends,
> Rough-hew them how we will.

After his mocking exchange with the "water-fly," Osric, who
has come to invite him to a rapier match with Laertes, his serious
mood returns again, but this time he has a sense of his own approaching death. His meditations on death in the churchyard and
his new awareness of an overruling destiny are joined in the ultimate reflection: "There's a special providence in the fall of a
sparrow. If it be now, 'tis not to come; if it be not to come, it

will be now; if it be not now, yet it will come; the readiness is all."

There is no sense, as the climax approaches, that Hamlet is about to achieve his purpose. It is as though Shakespeare wanted to lull the audience into a temporary forgetfulness so that the inevitable may yet come as a surprise. All our thoughts are on Hamlet's Fate, for we know he cannot escape the poisons of Laertes and Claudius. It is this which lends a moving irony to Hamlet's plea for forgiveness to Laertes. Previously he had pointed out to Horatio the similarity of their causes:

> But I am very sorry, good Horatio,
> That to Laertes I forgot myself,
> For by the image of my cause I see
> The portraiture of his. . . .

It seems as if destiny does indeed determine the end. To begin with, Hamlet surprises everybody by surpassing in swordsmanship the much-vaunted Laertes, who is forced to wound Hamlet with the poisoned point during a moment of rest. This knavery releases the old fury in Hamlet which sweeps everything before him. Then it is the Queen who drinks from the poisoned cup. Finally, in total justification of Hamlet's delay, the guilt of the King is publicly proclaimed by the Queen and Laertes, who says:

> . . . The King, the King's to blame.
> .   .   .   .
> He is justly served.
> It is a poison tempered by himself.
> Exchange forgiveness with me, noble Hamlet.
> Mine and my father's death come not upon thee,
> Nor thine on me.

As death approaches Hamlet it is "felicity" and he leaves a "harsh world." Horatio is left to report his cause aright and to declare his voice for Fortinbras in the election to the vacant throne of Denmark, but in his first report this upright, loyal friend says of Rosencrantz and Guildenstern whose deaths are reported from England, "He never gave commandment for their death." In such a man as Horatio, who knows that they had died as a result of Hamlet's counter-scheme, this can only mean that he honestly feels that Hamlet is not morally responsible for their deaths. He remembers Hamlet's own words:

> Why, man, they did make love to this employment.
> They are not near my conscience; their defeat
> Does by their own insinuation grow.

Fortinbras, whose home is the battlefield and whose values are a soldier's, gives his highest praise to Hamlet:

> Let four captains
> Bear Hamlet, like a soldier, to the stage;
> For he was likely, had he been put on,
> To have proved most royally. . . .

Through the ages Hamlet has been and will continue to be the "observed of all observers." Briefly—and yet at more than twice the length I have given to most of the other characters—this one observer has outlined a blueprint for his conception of Hamlet. Others have seen and will see him differently, and all will see their own truth in this quintessential man, the most fascinating of all Shakespeare's characters.

 17   Othello

OTHELLO, THE MOOR OF VENICE. In trying to understand the character of Othello, much depends on what the two
nouns in the subtitle meant to Shakespeare. It is certain that
"Moor" did not mean to him what "Negro" means to us. (Not
that a Negro actor should not play the part; a deep otherness is
the essence of the situation.) Othello is called "black" in the play,
but the meaning in Shakespeare is usually much nearer "dark" or
"brunette"; thus, he calls his beloved lady of the sonnets "black":

> Then will I swear beauty herself is black,
> And all they foul that thy complexion lack.

To the Elizabethans, to be fair was to be beautiful, so that "fair"
came to mean "beautiful." All ladies shunned the sun, for sunburn
was the sign of a peasant. And the opposite to "fair" was "black."

The Moslem world had made a centuries-long two-pronged
invasion of Europe, the North African Moors through Spain and
the Asian Turks through the Balkans. Their reputation for valor
in battle was buried deep in European consciousness. The Moors
in Spain had received their final defeat in 1492, but they were

not completely expelled from Spain until a few years after *Othello* was written. The Turks had been stopped at the gates of Vienna in 1529 and had suffered a total naval defeat at the Battle of Lepanto in 1571, when Shakespeare was seven years old. All these were events that Shakespeare would have grown up to know. The Turks did not lose their hold on the Balkans until the nineteenth century. The fact that the Moors and Turks were of different racial origins was an anthropological distinction to be made some centuries after Shakespeare; it was enough to the Elizabethans that they were both pagan Moslems.

But England had had a direct contact with the Ottomans in the Crusades, and folk-memory had given an aura of craftiness, unpredictability, strangeness, and mystery to the "Pagan," and withal an awed respect. Perhaps the traditional sense of the difference is illustrated in Sir Walter Scott's *The Talisman* in the contrast between the Christian hero, Richard the Lion-Heart, and Saladin, the Pagan hero; Richard split a steel mace with his two-handed sword, but Saladin deftly cut in two a cushion of silk and down with his scimitar. More than one hundred years after the last Crusade, Shakespeare's Henry IV was intent on trying to capture Jerusalem from the Turks.

As to Venice, we must not think of it in its present form at all. It was a powerful state with extensive territories on the mainland and along the eastern Aegean coast; it also ruled the islands of Crete, Rhodes, and Cyprus. The shrunken Venice of today was the work of Napoleon.

Why was a Moor the general of the Venetian forces? The answer is found in the enemy, the Turk. It was thought that no Christian could outwit the wily Ottoman, so a brilliant mercenary from a kindred race is brought in, just as early American settlers looked for friendly Indians to help them outwit unfriendly ones. It is interesting to note that when Richard the Lion-Heart wanted to send an effective emissary to Saladin he chose a Moorish nobleman who had long been a prisoner.

So Othello is a first-class mercenary general, a stranger from a different civilization in a sophisticated city with values different from his. To the Venetians, as to Shakespeare and his audience, there is an air of ancient mystery about him. He has been to strange places and seen strange sights. This mystery is summed up by Shakespeare in the handkerchief. It is a ridiculous belittling of Othello to believe, as some people do, that he is making up the strange tale about the handkerchief, and altogether pretending to make a great fuss about very little. The handkerchief is the symbol of the whole mystery of his different background. For Shakespeare, for Othello, the following description is literally true:

> . . . That handkerchief
> Did an Egyptian to my mother give.
> She was a charmer, and could almost read
> The thoughts of people. She told her, while she kept it,
> 'Twould make her amiable and subdue my father
> Entirely to her love; but if she lost it
> Or made a gift of it, my father's eye
> Should hold her loathed, and his spirit should hunt
> After new fancies. She dying gave it me,
> And bid me, when my fate would have me wive,
> To give it her. I did so. And take heed on't,
> Make it a darling like your precious eye.
> To lose't or give't away were such perdition
> As nothing else could match.
> .   .   .   .
> . . . There's magic in the web of it.
> A sibyl that had numbered in the world
> The sun to course two hundred compasses
> In her prophetic fury sewed the work.
> The worms were hallowed that bid breed the silk,
> And it was dyed in mummy which the skilful
> Conserved of maidens' hearts.

There was another quality the mysterious Moor and Turk were thought to have, and this is also in Othello; beneath the impassive exterior slept the fury of a volcano, far more fierce than the anger of a Christian. The actor playing Othello must portray both the awesome nobility and the frightening fury. Very few have succeeded in both qualities; far more actors have made a reputation with Iago than with Othello.

Before we consider the Moor, we must briefly consider two other characters: his extraordinary antagonist, Iago, and his beautiful wife, Desdemona. Iago was Shakespeare's most complete embodiment of the evil in the heart of man. Other villains, like Richard III and Edmund, show remorse for their deeds, but not Iago. Coleridge found in his soliloquies "the motive-hunting of motiveless malignity." In the beginning he certainly had a legitimate reason for wanting some revenge on Othello, but the revenge he wreaked was out of all proportion to the grievance. He, a soldier with battle experience, had been passed over for promotion in favor of a man who had learned his soldiering from books; the feeling between him and Cassio was that between many a senior sergeant and junior lieutenant. As Iago began to scheme against Othello, his success gave him a sense of power in the manipulation of men's lives; his appetite for power grew and his plans grew more and more complicated as opportunity for destruction offered itself; he became an obsessed improviser. He began to feel the power of God and the pleasure of the Devil. Men were clay to be molded because they trusted him. He was every man's best friend so that he could be his worst enemy.

Desdemona is an intriguing complex of almost contradictory qualities. Having fallen completely under the spell of Othello's strangeness, she secretly marries him in defiance of her father's wishes. (Ophelia's fate derives from filial obedience, Desdemona's from filial disobedience.) Thereafter, in her boundless and unquestioning love of her husband she reveals an astonishing naïveté, made all the sharper by contrast with Emilia's sophistication. A major irony of the play is that she shares Othello's strict sexual code of honor, for an apparent breach of which she dies. Her function in the original Italian story on which the play is based —no English version has been discovered—was to illustrate the moral of filial obedience; in it she says something to the effect of, "Let me be an example to all young women not to marry against the wishes of their parents. Young ladies of Venice should learn from me not to marry a man made different from them by God and way of life."

We first hear of Othello from Iago, and a word of warning is immediately necessary. Unlike Richard III, for instance, who never lies to himself, Iago is a victim of his own fantasies, which are necessary to justify his actions to himself. His account to the gullible Roderigo of Othello's choice of Cassio for his lieutenant is very farfetched:

> . . . Three great ones of the city,
> In personal suit to make me his Lieutenant,
> Off-capped to him. And, by the faith of man,
> I know my price; I am worth no worse a place.
> But he, as loving his own pride and purposes,
> Evades them, with a bombast circumstance
> Horribly stuffed with epithets of war.

"Bombast" is not a quality we are going to find in Othello, and that three important civilians would interfere about a minor military promotion is absurdly unlikely; only Roderigo would believe it. Some critics have found it incredible that Iago would make the simple-minded Roderigo a party to his scheming; it was too dangerous. But apart from the fact that Roderigo was a source of money, Iago's manipulation of him was a satisfying exercise in what was to prove his greatest joy. As Iago himself says:

> For I mine own gained knowledge should profane
> If I would time expend with such a snipe
> But for my sport and profit, . . .

and sport comes before profit.

Iago, having aroused Brabantio, under cover of night, with obscene speeches about his daughter's coupling with the Moor, hurries to Othello and tries to arouse him against Brabantio, but to no avail. When Iago makes much of Brabantio's power in Venice, we hear that Othello is not at all conscious of social inferiority; on the contrary, he is of royal blood. When Iago counsels him to avoid meeting Brabantio and his hostile party, Othello is completely secure and unafraid:

> Not I; I must be found.
> My parts, my title, and my perfect soul [*i.e.* clear conscience]
> Shall manifest me rightly. . . .

When Brabantio's group confronts Othello's, the Moor is quick to interpose and prevent a clash, which he does merely by his natural authority, even displaying a gentle sense of humor: "Keep up your bright swords, for the dew will rust them." The quality which is paramount in this first sight of Othello is his forbearance and imperturbability. Brabantio insults him grossly and orders his arrest; another clash seems imminent, and again the simple presence of unquestioned authority prevents it:

> Hold your hands,
> Both you of my inclining and the rest.
> Were it my cue to fight, I should have known it
> Without a prompter. . . .

It is significant that Brabantio immediately assumes that Desdemona has been seduced by magic, and this is going to be the grounds of his plea for the annulment of the marriage. The Moor comes from a strange world where magic is a natural element. Brabantio calls him "a practicer of arts inhibited and out of warrant."

The Duke takes Brabantio's accusation of magic seriously, and says:

> Whoe'er he be that in this foul proceeding
> Hath thus beguiled your daughter of herself
> And you of her, the bloody book of law
> You shall yourself read in the bitter letter
> After your own sense—yea, though our proper son
> Stood in your action.

In Othello's dignified defense we learn much about him. He is the complete soldier, having known no other life since he was

seven years old. At one time he had been captured by "the insolent foe and sold to slavery." Brabantio had enjoyed his company
and frequently invited him to the house to hear him tell his lifetime of strange adventures; Desdemona had been captivated by
his tales:

> She loved me for the dangers I had passed,
> And I loved her that she did pity them.
> This only is the witchcraft I have used.

Desdemona completely defeats Brabantio's case by publicly
preferring her duty as wife to that as daughter, which reduces
her father to the bitterness of "I had rather to adopt a child than
get it."

The Duke, in dispatching Othello immediately to Cyprus,
which is under threat of a Turkish invasion, states the general
opinion of Othello's soldierly superiority: "Though we have there
a substitute of most allowed sufficiency, yet opinion, a sovereign
mistress of effects, throws a more safer voice on you." Again
Othello proclaims the battlefield his natural world, and this it is
that unfits him later to deal with the subtleties of the city:

> The tyrant custom, most grave Senators,
> Hath made the flinty and steel couch of war
> My thrice-driven bed of down. . . .

While Othello is in Cyprus, the Duke suggests that Desdemona should return home to her father, but Brabantio is the
first to say, "I'll not have it so," and Othello and Desdemona immediately add, "Nor I." Desdemona pleads to be allowed to accompany Othello, and uses some surprising words:

> That I did love the Moor to live with him,
> My downright violence and storm of fortunes
> May trumpet to the world. . . .

"Violence," "storm," "trumpet," are evidence of Desdemona's
strong-willed acknowledgment of the implications of her marriage
to Othello. He, in adding his plea that she may be allowed to

accompany him, surprises us by saying that he is past the time of strong sexual appetite:

> . . . I therefore beg it not
> To please the palate of my appetite,
> Nor to comply with heat—the young affects
> In me defunct—and proper satisfaction,
> But to be free and bounteous to her mind.

This fact of Othello's being much older than Desdemona is going to present itself as a reason to him later that she may find the younger Cassio more attractive. As Iago says in persuading Roderigo to disguise himself with a beard and follow them to Cyprus, "She must change for youth." Incidentally, we learn in the same scene that Iago is twenty-eight years of age. Cassio, Iago, Desdemona, and Emilia are all of one generation, Othello of another.

Montano, Othello's predecessor in Cyprus, shows no disgruntlement at being superseded; on the contrary, he praises Othello highly:

> I am glad on't. 'Tis a worthy governor.
> .   .   .   .
> . . . I have served him, and the man commands
> Like a full soldier. . . .

The storm that has destroyed the Turkish fleet has scattered the three Venetian ships so that they arrive separately. Othello's is the last to arrive, and while the other voyagers, particularly Desdemona, anxiously await his arrival, Iago beguiles the time with witty improvisations on various kinds of women. Desdemona, while not approving of his conclusions, still encourages his tongue to wag; she obviously is used to this flippant kind of social chit-chat, which is a foreign and distasteful language to Othello. His is of quite a different kind, as in his greeting of Desdemona:

> . . . If it were now to die,
> 'Twere now to be most happy, for I fear
> My soul hath her content so absolute

> That not another comfort like to this
> Succeeds in unknown fate.

Iago is completely incapable of distinguishing love from lust. He feels that every man must lust after every desirable woman. Cassio must "love" Emilia, as it is likely she does him; it is probable that Othello has slept with Emilia, and possibly Cassio has done so too. He even admits that he himself "loves" Desdemona,

> Not out of absolute lust, though peradventure
> I stand accountant for as great a sin,
> But partly led to diet my revenge
> For that I do suspect the Moor
> Hath leaped into my seat. . . .

Already the initial grudge is being supplanted by other reasons for revenge, all bred of fantasy.

Othello gives order for a joint celebration to mark the destruction of the Turkish fleet and his own marriage, but he warns Cassio not to let the festivities get out of hand. In retiring with Desdemona, he playfully makes it clear that his maturity and dignity are not such as to spoil his wedding night:

> Come, my dear love,
> The purchase made, the fruits are to ensue;
> That profit's yet to come 'tween me and you.

There is evidence in the play that Shakespeare considered Othello to be Christian. In quelling the disturbance which Iago had skillfully engendered from the festivities, Othello says:

> Are we turned Turks, and to ourselves do that
> Which Heaven hath forbid the Ottomites?
> For Christian shame, put by this barbarous brawl.

And in his final speech in the play, he refers to a Turk whom he had killed as "the circumcised dog." We know that he had lived in a soldier's world since he was seven years old. It may well be that from an early age he had been brought up by Moorish mercenaries who had fought for Christians and had thus missed the pubertial circumcision of his people and had gradually acquired Christianity. There is no doubt that Brabantio considers him a "pagan," and it is clear that as the play progresses we have a sense in him of a reversion to older codes and ancient passions.

In his exasperation at the reluctance of the culprits to confess the cause of the disturbance, Othello begins to show signs of the volcano which is to erupt with such terrifying force in the second half of the play:

> Now, by Heaven,
> My blood begins my safer guides to rule,
> And passion, having my best judgment collied,
> Assays to lead the way. If I once stir,
> Or do but lift this arm, the best of you
> Shall sink in my rebuke. . . .

When Iago, with seeming reluctance, puts the blame on Cassio, Othello's justice is summary:

> . . . Cassio, I love thee,
> But never more be officer of mine.

It is now time to examine closely the process by which Iago transforms Othello from a doting husband to a ravening monster. I have previously said that, to me, Leontes is a study of a truly jealous man. Othello is not jealous by nature; it required the genius of Iago to turn his trust to suspicion. Othello correctly describes himself at the end of the play as

> . . . one not easily jealous, but, being wrought,
> Perplexed in the extreme. . . .

All Iago had to go on in the beginning was that Cassio had often taken Othello's courtship messages to Desdemona, and now she was being persistent in restoring him to Othello's favor. In his pretended reluctance to share his thoughts with the General, Iago skillfully discredits himself as a witness:

> I do beseech you—
> Though I perchance am vicious in my guess,
> As, I confess, it is my nature's plague
> To spy into abuses, and oft my jealousy
> Shapes faults that are not—that your wisdom yet,
> From one that so imperfectly conceits,
> Would take no notice, nor build yourself a trouble
> Out of his scattering and unsure observance.

Iago torments Othello with dark hints of his own suspicions and refusal to voice them. But when he warns Othello of the horrors of jealousy, Othello is forthright in showing the difference between his nature and that of a constitutionally jealous husband, to whom his wife's pleasure in the company of any other man is bitter food:

> Think'st thou I'd make a life of jealousy,
> To follow still the changes of the moon
> With fresh suspicions? No, to be once in doubt
> Is once to be resolved. Exchange me for a goat
> When I shall turn the business of my soul
> To such exsufflicate and blown surmises,
> Matching thy inference. 'Tis not to make me jealous
> To say my wife is fair, feeds well, loves company,
> Is free of speech, sings, plays, and dances well.
> Where virtue is, these are more virtuous.
> Nor from mine own weak merits will I draw
> The smallest fear or doubt of her revolt,
> For she had eyes, and chose me. No, Iago,
> I'll see before I doubt; when I doubt, prove;
> And on the proof, there is no more but this:
> Away at once with love or jealousy!

At this time Iago has no seed of proof, so he must bend his energies to tilling the ground in preparation for such scant seed as may come to hand. He begins by showing that Othello is ignorant of the hypocritical morality of Venetian society:

> I know our country disposition well.
> In Venice they do let Heaven see the pranks

> They dare not show their husbands. Their best conscience
> Is not to leave't undone, but keep't unknown.

It must be remembered that Desdemona's first reaction to Othello's strangeness seems to have been one of fear. Brabantio had told the Duke that only witchcraft could have made her "fall in love with what she feared to look on!" Iago now makes much of this and her disobedience to her father:

> She did deceive her father, marrying you,
> And when she seemed to shake and fear your looks,
> She loved them most.
> .   .   .   .   .
>   Why, go to then.
> She that so young could give out such a seeming,
> To seel her father's eyes up close as oak—
> He thought 'twas witchcraft—but I am much to blame.
> I humbly do beseech you of your pardon
> For too much loving you.

Seeing that he has begun to shake Othello, though Othello denies it, he ventures further:

> . . . to be bold with you—
> Not to affect many proposed matches
> Of her own clime, complexion, and degree,
> Whereto we see in all things nature tends—
> Foh! one may smell in such a will most rank,
> Foul disproportion, thoughts unnatural.

Iago has gone a bit too far, and quickly modifies it:

> But pardon me. I do not in position
> Distinctly speak of her; though I may fear
> Her will, recoiling to her better judgement,
> May fail to match you with her country forms,
> And happily repent.

Iago leaves to let his poison work in Othello. His manner has left two vivid impressions: he knows much more than he has said, and he has been solely motivated by his high regard for Othello.

Everybody in the play is impressed by Iago's patent honesty; even the sophisticated Emilia has no idea of the monster whose bed she shares. Left to himself, Othello chews the cud of Iago's words:

> This fellow's of exceeding honesty,
> And knows all qualities, with a learned spirit,
> Of human dealings. . . .
>
> . . . .
>
> . . . Haply, for I am black
> And have not those soft parts of conversation
> That chamberers have, or for I am declined
> Into the vale of years—yet that's not much—
> She's gone, I am abused, and my relief
> Must be to loathe her.

The sight of Desdemona seems to dispel Othello's suspicions:

> If she be false, O, then heaven mocks itself!
> I'll not believe't.

Then Iago comes by the seed of proof which he will cultivate into a mighty oak, the handkerchief. It is obvious that he had planned to use it, because he had "a hundred times" begged Emilia to steal it.

> I will in Cassio's lodging lose this napkin,
> And let him find it. Trifles light as air
> Are to the jealous confirmations strong
> As proofs of holy writ; this may do something.
> The Moor already changes with my poison.
> Dangerous conceits are in their nature poisons,
> Which at the first are scarce found to distaste,
> But with a little act upon the blood
> Burn like the mines of sulphur. . . .

But Othello is not ready for the handkerchief yet; his suspicion must first be turned to near certainty. When Othello returns, he has clearly lost his judgment; so much so that he believes that he would have preferred to be ignorant of Desdemona's guilt. His growing passion begins to find expression in wild words:

> I had been happy if the general camp,
> Pioners and all, had tasted her sweet body,
> So I had nothing known. . . .

Never again will he have the tranquil mind necessary to authority, so his "occupation's gone." His fury vents itself on Iago, whom he commands to furnish such proof as will

> . . . bear no hinge nor loop
> To hang doubt on, or woe upon thy life!
> .　.　.　.　.　.　.　.
> If thou dost slander her and torture me,
> Never pray more; abandon all remorse;
> On horror's head horrors accumulate;
> Do deeds to make heaven weep, all earth amazed;
> For nothing canst thou to damnation add
> Greater than that.

Iago is righteously indignant:

> . . . Take note, take note, O world;
> To be direct and honest is not safe.
> I thank you for this profit, and from hence
> I'll love no friend, sith love breeds such offence.

Othello demands proof. Iago says that the only sure proof would be to catch them together, but in saying this Iago uses such sensual imagery as further to torment the distraught Othello:

> Would you, the supervisor, grossly gape on?
> Behold her topped?
> .　.　.　.　.
> It were a tedious difficulty, I think,
> To bring them to that prospect . . .
> .　.　.　.　.　.　.
> It is impossible you should see this,
> Were they as prime as goats, as hot as monkeys,
> As salt as wolves in pride, and fools as gross
> As ignorance made drunk. . . .

Now Othello is ripe for a gross lie of "imputation and strong circumstances":

. . . I lay with Cassio lately,
And being troubled with a raging tooth,
I could not sleep.
There are a kind of men so loose of soul
That in their sleep will mutter their affairs.
One of this kind is Cassio.
In sleep I heard him say, "Sweet Desdemona,
Let us be wary, let us hide our loves;"
And then, sir, would he gripe and wring my hand,
Cry, "O sweet creature!" and then kiss me hard,
As if he plucked up kisses by the roots
That grew upon my lips. Then laid his leg
Over my thigh, and sighed and kissed, and then
Cried, "Cursed fate that gave thee to the Moor!"

Believing Iago to be the soul of honesty, Othello needs no further proof, and now the handkerchief serves to make the lie of Cassio's dream absolute truth; Iago says he had seen Cassio wipe his beard with the handkerchief. Such sacrilege, for so it must appear to Othello, serves to push him into the abyss of wild revenge:

Arise, black vengeance, from thy hollow hell!
Yield up, O love, thy crown and hearted throne
To tyrannous hate! Swell, bosom, with thy fraught,
For 'tis of aspics' tongues!
.   .   .   .   .   .
Oh, blood, blood, blood!

Iago, knowing how binding an oath is to Othello, gets him to make a solemn vow not to change his purpose, and with equal solemnity makes his own vow of service to him. Othello gives Iago three days in which to report the death of Cassio, while he himself will find "some swift means of death" for Desdemona. The astonishing scene ends with a notable irony: Iago is promoted to the lieutenancy which had first prompted his scheming, but now it is scarcely noticed; Iago is reaping much more exciting rewards than a mere lieutenancy.

Desdemona has discovered her loss of the handkerchief; she

realizes its significance for Othello:

> Believe me, I had rather have lost my purse
> Full of crusadoes; and, but my noble Moor
> Is true of mind and made of no such baseness
> As jealous creatures are, it were enough
> To put him to ill thinking.

Emilia asks, "Is he not jealous?" She cannot, at this stage, mean anything specific by this question. As her husband believes all men lustful, she believes all men jealous; in their cynicism they are well matched.

Othello enters to Desdemona and finds it increasingly difficult to dissemble, for she admits that she does not know where the handkerchief is and then goes on to plead anew for Cassio! Emilia's caustic comment on Othello's anger is

> 'Tis not a year or two shows us a man.
> They are all but stomachs, and we all but food;
> They eat us hungerly, and when they are full
> They belch us. . . .

But Desdemona, in thinking over the scene, thinks she was wrong in "arraigning his unkindness," for he must be deeply disturbed about some secret affair of state,

> . . . And in such cases
> Men's natures wrangle with inferior things,
> Though great ones are their object. . . .

She cannot possibly suspect the truth since she believes Othello incapable of jealousy, in addition to which she has given him no cause.

Iago is not content to let his poison work; he must sadistically administer fresh doses. He tells Othello that Cassio has boasted of lying with Desdemona, and works the Moor to such a passion that he has an epileptic fit. Now Iago improvises brilliantly to make good his latest lie, and further feed the Moor's "unbookish [*i.e.* unsophisticated] jealousy." After Othello has recovered, he places him to overhear a conversation with Cassio, whom he questions about a whore Bianca, who is desperately in love with him; Othello is led to believe that they are talking about Desdemona. He hears Cassio say such things as, "I think, i' faith, she loves me. . . . She haunts me in every place. I was the other day talking on the sea bank with certain Venetians, and thither comes the bauble, and, by this hand, she falls me thus about my neck; . . . so hangs and lolls and weeps upon me. . . . Ha, ha, ha!"

Now Iago's villainy earns an unexpected bonus. Bianca comes to Cassius with the handkerchief which he had found in his lodgings and asked Bianca to copy because he was sure it would be reclaimed. But Bianca has done some wondering about the handkerchief, and now Othello hears her say this: "A likely piece of work that you should find it in your chamber and not know who left it there! This is some minx's token. . . . There; give it your hobbyhorse."

Now Othello has received ample proof but he is still tormented by his love for the seeming perfection of Desdemona. He alternates wildly between "Let her rot, and perish, and be damned tonight, for she shall not live," and "Oh, the world hath not a sweeter creature. She might lie by an emperor's side, and command him tasks." But Iago points out that her fair appearance makes her ugly truth all the worse. Othello had determined on poison as her mode of death, but death at this remove would be too easy to satisfy Iago's desire to make Othello suffer to the uttermost: "Do it not with poison; strangle her in her bed, even the bed she hath contaminated."

Lodovico arrives from Venice with instructions for the recall of Othello, now that danger from the Turks is past; Cassio is to take Othello's place. As the Moor half-reads the letter, he listens to the conversation of Desdemona with Lodovico, who is related to her. Desdemona is asking Lodovico to intercede with Othello on behalf of Cassio, and he hears her say:

> . . . I would do much
> To atone them, for the love I bear to Cassio.

Othello's anger bursts his restraint and he strikes Desdemona, and strides out, leaving Lodovico dumbfounded and Desdemona in tears. Lodovico's comment is: "I am sorry that I am deceived in him."

Othello questions Emilia about the meetings of Desdemona and Cassio, but cannot believe her testimony that she was always present at their meetings. He sends for Desdemona. In his scene with her, he bitterly laments his state of cuckoldry but never once mentions Cassio so that Desdemona is completely at a loss how to answer him. Othello alternates between self-pity and gross abuse of Desdemona, "that cunning whore of Venice." His distress of soul finds moving expression in a Job-like lament:

> Had it pleased Heaven
> To try me with affliction, had they rained
> All kinds of sores and shames on my bare head,
> Steeped me in poverty to the very lips,
> Given to captivity me and my utmost hopes,
> I should have found in some place of my soul
> A drop of patience. But, alas, to make me
> A fixed figure for the time of scorn
> To point his slow unmoving finger at!
> Yet could I bear that too, well, very well;
> But there where I have garnered up my heart,
> Where either I must live, or bear no life,
> The fountain from the which my current runs
> Or else dries up; to be discarded thence!
> Or keep it as a cistern for foul toads
> To knot and gender in!

The next time we see Othello he seems a changed man. It is after the welcoming banquet for Lodovico. Othello's anger has gone; his old dignity has returned. He even speaks gently to Desdemona. His torment is over, his mind made up. His purpose now is to cast anger from him so that his killing of Desdemona will be an act of justice, not anger. By his inherited code the punishment for adultery is death, but he has learned from Iago that it is not so regarded in the Venetian code, so he must be judge, priest, and executioner. All this is behind his opening words as he enters the bedchamber, where Desdemona is asleep:

> It is the cause, it is the cause, my soul.
> Let me not name it to you, you chaste stars!
> It is the cause. . . .

He cannot refrain from kissing Desdemona:

> Oh, balmy breath, that dost almost persuade
> Justice to break her sword! One more, one more.
> Be thus when thou art dead, and I will kill thee,
> And love thee after. One more, and this the last.
> So sweet was ne'er so fatal. I must weep,
> But they are cruel tears. This sorrow's heavenly;
> It strikes where it doth love. . . .

When Desdemona wakes, he bids her prepare herself for death:

> I would not kill thy unprepared spirit.
> No, Heaven forfend! I would not kill thy soul.

Finally Othello accuses Desdemona of adultery with Cassio, citing the handkerchief and Iago's lines as evidence. As Desdemona protests her innocence, Othello's fury begins to replace his judicial calm:

> O perjured woman! Thou dost stone my heart,
> And makest me call what I intend to do
> A murder, which I thought a sacrifice.

After the murder, among the welter of emotions in which Othello flounders, he is aware of a void in his life:

> Oh, insupportable! Oh, heavy hour!
> Methinks it should be now a huge eclipse
> Of sun and moon, and that the affrighted globe
> Should yawn at alteration.

As Desdemona's dying words to Emilia exonerate Othello from her murder, his need for justification is so great that he uses the words as proof that she is an inveterate liar:

> She's like a liar gone to burning hell:
> 'Twas I that killed her.

In the general confrontation scene which ends the play, Othello is unmanned by his overwhelming sense of guilt; now his occupation is indeed gone:

> I am not valiant neither,
> But every puny whipster gets my sword.
> But why should honour outlive honesty?
> Let it go all.

Now his wild torment is turned upon himself:

> Whip me, ye devils,
> From the possession of this heavenly sight!
> Blow me about in winds! Roast me in sulphur!
> Wash me in steep-down gulfs of liquid fire!
> O Desdemona! Desdemona! Dead!
> Oh! Oh! Oh!

Othello manages to pull himself together as he secretly prepares for his suicide; the others in the room think he is unarmed. When he had tried, but failed, to kill Iago, he had said:

> I am not sorry neither. I'd have thee live,
> For, in my sense, 'tis happiness to die.

In his point-of-death attempt to explain himself, he says:

> Speak of me as I am; nothing extenuate,
> Nor set down aught in malice. Then must you speak
> Of one that loved not wisely but too well,
> Of one not easily jealous, but, being wrought,
> Perplexed in the extreme, of one whose hand,
> Like the base Indian, threw a pearl away
> Richer than all his tribe, of one whose subdued eyes,
> Albeit unused to the melting mood,
> Drop tears as fast as the Arabian trees
> Their medicinal gum.

Three of Shakespeare's tragic heroes—Romeo, Othello, Antony—are destroyed as a result of their great love of a woman, and all three commit suicide. This may be morally wrong but it is artistically right. When their loved one is lost, so are they. Their tragedy is intensely personal and private and so must be their end. The intrusion of the state with its considerations of social and political justice would be inappropriate. To try Othello for murder would be to reduce his story to a sordid and humdrum crime of passion. There is an essential nobility in the man which is fully restored at the moment of his death; he kills himself with the detachment of justice.

Othello is the most domestic of all Shakespeare's mature tragedies and the easiest to make effective and compelling in the theatre. Some critics have found it lacking in cosmic significance. I think this is possibly true in regard to Othello himself, but never was there a more terrifying presentation of the evil in the heart of man than in Iago, and the dimension of this defies explanation and poses one of the fundamental questions of human existence. Othello is the victim, made vulnerable by his noble simplicity; it is this vulnerability of guileless greatness to determined villainy that creates in us a sense of awed terror; it is the very dimension of both the nobility and the villainy that raises the play from thrilling melodrama to truly great tragedy.

 18 # King Lear

WE WISH that we could pass this play over, and say nothing about it. All that we can say must fall far short of the subject; or even of what we ourselves conceive of it. To attempt to give a description of the play itself, or of its effect upon the mind, is mere impertinence: yet we must say something. It is then the best of all Shakespeare's plays, for it is the one in which he was most in earnest.

So wrote William Hazlitt about *King Lear* in 1817. A. C. Bradley commenting on it in the next century said: "*King Lear*, as a whole, is imperfectly dramatic, and there is something in its very essence which is at war with the senses, and demands a purely imaginative realization. It is therefore Shakespeare's greatest work, but it is not what Hazlitt called it, the best of his plays." The implication in "demands a purely imaginative realization" is that it is a huge work belittled by presentation in the theatre. Charles Lamb, writing a few years before Hazlitt, gave memorable expression to that point of view: "The Lear of Shakespeare cannot be acted. The contemptible machinery by which they mimic the storm which he goes out in, is not more inadequate to represent the horrors of the real elements, than any actor can be to represent Lear." And Charles Lamb was not a bookish academic who believed that Shakespeare's rightful home was the study; he loved theatre. It has often been noted by defenders of the theatre that Lamb never saw Shakespeare's play on the stage; for 150 years its place had been taken by variant corruptions of the play based upon a version by Nahum Tate which was first presented in 1681 and in which the Fool is completely removed and a happy ending is contrived involving the restoration of Lear to the throne and the marriage of Edgar and Cordelia; my own feeling is that Lamb's stricture would have been even stronger if he had seen Shakespeare's own text presented on the stage. But I believe that a play which cannot, or should not, be presented in a theatre is not really a play, just as a symphony which cannot be played is not a symphony. It is true that no one production of *King Lear* can plumb its meaning and significance; nor can one critic. Many actors must play the part, many directors must direct the play, many critics must write about it; all will reveal some of the riches, but none will reveal all.

Never was there a play in which this first question to a critic was more necessary: "What went ye out for to see?" With equal ardor and conviction commentators on the play have seen in it the ultimate expression of two absolutely opposite philosophies: existential pessimism and Christian optimism. Those espousing the pessimistic concentrate on the pointless and total suffering in the play, and find its meaning in Gloucester's cry:

> As flies to wanton boys are we to the gods:
> They kill us for their sport.

The optimists point out that Gloucester later appealed to "You ever-gentle gods," that the evil in the play is counterbalanced with self-sacrificing loyalty and goodness, and that Edgar says, "The gods are just." The sum total of the play is as profound and mysterious as life itself, and we will see in it what we see in life, and that will be determined by our faith or skepticism.

One thing is certain. The tragic end to the story is Shakespeare's, but so is the loyalty of Kent and the devotion of the Fool. The story was well known to Shakespeare's audience; there was even a previous play on the subject; but in all other versions of it there had been a happy ending, with evil put to rout and Lear restored to his throne. Whatever Shakespeare's intention was in the play, the surest indication of it must be found in the changes he made in the sources he used.

The meaning of the play is not my concern in this chapter. I shall limit myself to some account of the character of Lear as a human being, and to those considerations which an actor must have as he essays the part: who is Lear, what does he do, and why does he do it? An actor should not be concerned with the significance of a character, only its truth. (After his brilliant performance in *Waiting for Godot*, Bert Lahr once asked me to explain to him what it was all about.)

We must begin with Lear's age. When Charles Lamb saw him in the theatre he saw "nothing but corporal infirmities and weakness . . . an old man tottering about the stage with a walking-stick." Small wonder that he found this to be a gross diminution of the play. Here I shall quote what I have written elsewhere on this point:

> What of King Lear's "four score and upward?" This precision is Shakespeare's; Holinshed, his source for the story, mentions only Lear's "great yeres," and that he reigned "fortie yeeres." But Holinshed does set the story in ancient biblical times, "in the year of the world 3105, at what time Joas reigned in Juda," and Shakespeare takes the hint. Antiquarianism is a comparatively recent study—neither Shakespeare nor his audience found anything amiss in having in ancient Rome clocks that struck the hour—but he does strive to set *King Lear* in pre-Christian and pagan Britain; thus he carefully avoids the use of the word "God" in favor of "the gods." Eighty was a phenomenal age to the Elizabethans, and they would regard it as a mythical longevity, in much the same way as we regard Methuselah's nine hundred years.

Lear is not a doddering old man; minutes before his death he carries onstage a fully grown woman, and sets her down gently, which most actors find more difficult than carrying her on. He is a gigantic Job, except that he brings his sufferings upon himself; in his madness he achieves true wisdom and acquires the stature of an Old Testament prophet.

The whole action of the play springs from the opening scene, and many people have found it incredible that the King should divide his kingdom between his three daughters according to their competitive protestations of love. But this is not the situation at all. The King had no male heir, and Shakespeare's audience would have been well aware of the dangers in this situation, and would have applauded Lear's purpose in dividing the kingdom: "that future strife may be prevented now." The plan was skillful: the Scottish north was to be separated from the Cornish south by a midland kingdom, where Lear, still retaining "the name and all the additions to a king," would spend the rest of his days with his beloved Cordelia, and, while he yet lived and was still King, the new tri-partite division of the realm would settle down peacefully to its new status. It is clear from the opening lines of the play that the details of the scheme have already been decided upon and made known, and that Lear has been scrupulous in apportioning the northern and southern territories. The midland is "more opulent" by its nature, and is without a duke since Cordelia is unmarried, but it will be the abode of the King himself.

The opening scene is not a competition of filial love but a ritual of state, a ceremony in which the new form of government will be officially instituted. The King sees the occasion as a happy one, not as a sad and solemn one, and this is made the more so by the presence of two suitors for Cordelia's hand, one noble and one royal, the Duke of Burgundy and the King of France, who were traditional enemies. (It seems clear that Lear favors Burgundy. To give the King of France any claim to the throne of England would be dangerous. Indeed, he does invade England at the end of the play.) The King asks his daughters for a public declaration of their love for him in much the same spirit that an adult says to a child before handing over a lollipop which he is going to give anyway, "Tell me how much you love me." But this hides a fairly universal need: it is not enough to be loved; we must be told how much we are loved.

Why does Cordelia not go along with the innocent game? Because it masks the truth of which she is aware, but her father isn't. She knows her sisters and her father doesn't. She knows they can't wait for him to die, and their fulsome protestations are more than she can stand. Yet she refrains from exposing her sisters to their father. "What shall Cordelia do? Love, and be silent." Of course, she is also irritated by her father's too ready blindness; she tries to point out the absurdity of the situation:

> Why have my sisters husbands if they say
> They love you all? Haply, when I shall wed,
> That lord whose hand must take my plight shall carry
> Half my love with him, half my care and duty.
> Sure, I shall never marry like my sisters,
> To love my father all.

Lear has been made a fool of, by having his childish game shattered, in the last great ceremonial occasion of his life, and he overreacts; he has the pride of a king whose actions must never be called in question, and the violent and instantaneous fury of hitherto unquestioned authority. Both Lear and Cordelia are to blame, he for his initial weakness in prompting the empty charade and for the subsequent violence of his reaction, and she for her uncompromising attitude and her cold formulation of the truth; both of them display strength, he in his frightening and angry authority, she in her unflinching championship of truth; neither of them can give way. Lear ascribes her attitude to pride, a quality which ironically he himself personifies; she was too proud to declare her love for him in public: "Let pride, which she calls plainness, marry her."

Aggressively honest Kent understands and sympathizes with

Cordelia's action, and his dismay at the King's decree in disowning Cordelia sweeps away all considerations of ceremonious duty:

> . . . Be Kent unmannerly
> When Lear is mad. What wouldst thou do, old man?
> Think'st thou that duty shall have dread to speak
> When power to flattery bows? To plainness honour's bound
> When majesty stoops to folly. . . .

In using the word "mad," Kent has been unwittingly prescient, for there are the seeds of madness in uncontrolled anger. Shakespeare has foreshadowed the downfall of Lear.

In banishing Kent, Lear accuses him of pride, as he had Cordelia, and in so doing exhibits his own overweening pride, for he says that neither as man nor king could he ever go back on his word, and yet that word had been uttered in anger, not judgment:

> Since thou hast sought to make us break our vow,
> Which we durst never yet, and with strained pride
> To come betwixt our sentence and our power,
> Which nor our nature nor our place can bear,
> Our potency made good, take thy reward.

Cordelia, in defending herself before the King of France, is as stubborn as her father; she maintains her position stoutly in begging Lear to tell France the truth:

> I yet beseech your Majesty—
> If for I want that glib and oily art
> To speak and purpose not, since what I well intend
> I'll do't before I speak—that you make known
> It is no vicious blot, murder, or foulness,
> No unchaste action or dishonoured step
> That hath deprived me of your grace and favour;
> But even for want of that for which I am richer,
> A still-soliciting eye, and such a tongue
> As I am glad I have not, though not to have it
> Hath lost me in your liking.

The King of France is moved to admiration for Cordelia's stand and finds his regard for her increased thereby, even though she is now dowerless:

> Fairest Cordelia, that art most rich being poor,
> Most choice forsaken, and most loved despised,
> Thee and thy virtues here I seize upon,
> Be it lawful I take up what's castaway.
> Gods, gods! 'Tis strange that from their cold'st neglect
> My love should kindle to inflamed respect.

Lear is checked by this rebuke. His anger changes to the cold authority of dismissal:

> Thou hast her, France. Let her be thine, for we
> Have no such daughter, nor shall ever see
> That face of hers again. Therefore be gone,
> Without our grace, our love, our benison.

And so from the clash of stubborn prides is born the cataclysm that shall engulf them all. Both were self-righteously correct and neither was capable of relenting. How could Lear who in the extremity of madness still retained the consciousness that he was "every inch a king" rescind a decree made at a public ceremony? How could the strong-willed Cordelia deny the patent truth of what she had said? It seems to me that the seeds which were to bear such appalling fruit are firmly set in this oft-maligned scene.

Once Lear has left, Cordelia, in her farewell to her sisters, is able to speak plainly and with a sturdy sarcasm, very much at odds with the milk-and-water creature often presented in her name on the stage:

> The jewels of our father, with washed eyes
> Cordelia leaves you. I know you what you are;
> And like a sister am most loath to call
> Your faults as they are named. Love well our father;
> To your professed bosoms I commit him;
> But yet, alas, stood I within his grace,
> I would prefer him to a better place.

Goneril and Regan left to themselves make cautious moves. The territory that was to separate them is now divided between them; they will be two power-hungry neighbors, but it will pay them to "hit together" for they have a common problem, their father. Goneril comments on the "poor judgement" he has shown in disowning Cordelia and Regan adds that "he hath ever but slenderly known himself," a remark full of meaning: the king in Lear has blinded himself to the man in him, and also he is so impetuous that he never knows what he will do. Goneril sums up their problem: "Then must we look to receive from his age not alone the imperfections of long-ingrafted condition, but therewithal the unruly waywardness that infirm and choleric years bring with them." They are not so much happy in the unexpected acquisition of new territory as fearful that they may not be allowed to enjoy it to the full: "If our father carry authority with such disposition as he bears, this last surrender of his will but offend us." Sisters though they are in blood and villainy, Goneril and Regan are very different: Goneril is much the more forthright and direct, while Regan hides a heart of sadistic cruelty beneath a surface of sugar-sweetness.

Lear has had to change his cherished plan of living with Cordelia into spending alternate months with Goneril and Regan. He starts with Goneril and the inevitable clash begins at once; he is still the King in name, but now to Goneril he has dwindled to a difficult old man:

> By day and night he wrongs me. Every hour
> He flashes into one gross crime or other
> That sets us all at odds. I'll not endure it.
> His knights grow riotous, and himself upbraids us
> On every trifle. . . .
> .　　.　　.　　.　　.
> 　　　　　　　　　　. . . Idle old man,
> That still would manage those authorities
> That he hath given away! . . .

Kent seeks, in disguise, to reenter the service of his king, and knows how best to flatter Lear in order to do so. He tells him: "You have that in your countenance which I would fain call master—authority." When Lear is told by one of his knights, "Your Highness is not entertained with that ceremonious affection as you were wont," we are surprised to learn that he had noted it but had not reacted to it with the vigorous resentment we should have expected; he had actually begun to check his proud impulses: "I have perceived a most faint neglect of late, which I have rather blamed as mine own jealous curiosity [*i.e.* oversensitive suspicion] than as a very pretence and purpose of unkindness." Lear immediately puts the situation to the test. He asks Goneril's toadying steward, Oswald, to tell him who he is, expecting the answer, "the King." Oswald, in the spirit of his mistress's instructions, answers, "My lady's father." Lear strikes him and Kent also punishes him.

To make his altered status quite clear to Lear is now the function of the Fool in his first appearance in the play; he has been hiding away in sorrow since Cordelia's banishment. The Fool is a wonderful creation, capable of many interpretations. He seems to me to be Shakespeare's primitive version of the later courtly fool, a "natural" whose insight comes from mysterious sources, who combines the wisdom of an inspired prophet with a childlike innocence, who has the loyalty and timidity of an often chastised domestic animal; he never knows what to expect from his master, a pat or a kick, and always stands nervously ready for either. He must tell Lear the truth, though he knows it will hurt him and probably earn a kick.

> FOOL: Prithee, nuncle, keep a schoolmaster that can teach thy fool to lie. I would fain learn to lie.
> LEAR: An you lie, sirrah, we'll have you whipped.
> FOOL: I marvel what kin thou and thy daughters are. They'll have me whipped for speaking true, thou'lt have me whipped for lying; and sometimes I am whipped for holding my peace. I had rather be any kind o' thing than a fool; and yet I would not be thee, nuncle. Thou

has pared thy wit o' both sides and left nothing i' the middle.

Goneril comes to the showdown with her father in fresh anger from the treatment of Oswald, and her anger is exacerbated by such comments of the Fool as:

For, you know, nuncle,
    The hedge-sparrow fed the cuckoo so long,
    That it had it head bit off by it young.
So out went the candle, and we were left darkling.

Goneril accuses Lear of encouraging his retinue in their "rank and not to be endured riots." She talks of "censure" and "redress" and threatens such reprisals as, though unbecoming in a daughter to a father, nevertheless "necessity will call discreet proceeding."

Lear cannot believe his ears, and says sarcastically, "Your name, fair gentlewoman?" Goneril is now explicit in her demands and threats:

. . . Be then desired
By her, that else will take the thing she begs,
A little to disquantity your train;
And the remainders that shall still depend
To be such men as may besort your age,
Which know themselves and you.

Lear's characteristic fury breaks forth, and he gives immediate order to leave Goneril's Albany for Regan's Cornwall. Now he realizes the folly of his treatment of Cordelia:

. . . O most small fault,
How ugly didst thou in Cordelia show!
Which, like an engine, wrenched my frame of nature
From the fixed place, drew from my heart all love
And added to the gall. O Lear, Lear, Lear!
Beat at this gate, [*striking his head*] that let thy folly in
And thy dear judgement out! . . .

In a terrible curse, which is a considered sublimation of his anger, Lear calls upon Nature to make Goneril sterile, or, if she must bear a child, to make it such a child to its mother as she has become to her father:

> . . . If she must teem,
> Create her child of spleen, that it may live
> And be a thwart disnatured torment to her.
> Let it stamp wrinkles in her brow of youth,
> With cadent tears fret channels in her cheeks,
> Turn all her mother's pains and benefits
> To laughter and contempt, that she may feel
> How sharper than a serpent's tooth it is
> To have a thankless child! . . .

And cadent tears stain his own cheeks, and turn his fury against his own human weakness:

> . . . Life and death! I am ashamed
> That thou hast power to shake my manhood thus;
> That these hot tears, which break from me perforce,
> Should make thee worth them. . . .

Lear, whose pride has blinded him to the truth in men, for he sees in them only what he needs to feed his own ego, is completely gulled by the superficial sweetness of Regan, and he now turns to her:

> . . . Yet have I left a daughter
> Who I am sure is kind and comfortable.
> When she shall hear this of thee, with her nails
> She'll flay thy wolvish visage. . . .

The Fool, with his instinctive sensitivity about the true nature of people, is much wiser about Regan: "She will taste as like this as a crab does to a crab." Lear, in reflecting on his conduct, is aware of the danger that lies ahead; he has a flash of understanding about himself, but not about Regan:

> O, let me not be mad, not mad, sweet Heaven!
> Keep me in temper; I would not be mad!

While Lear makes his journey to Regan, who with her husband, the Duke of Cornwall, has left home to visit the Duke of Gloucester, we hear further evidence of the wisdom of Lear's original division of the kingdom to create a buffer state between the two rival dukes. An expository character, Curan, asks Edmund: "Have you heard of no likely wars toward 'twixt the Duke of Cornwall and Albany?" But such inevitable conflict is postponed while Goneril and Regan make common cause against a common nuisance, their father. It is as a result of a letter she has received from Goneril warning her of the coming of Lear and his entourage that Regan has deliberately left home.

Lear, having found Regan suddenly not at home, follows her to Gloucester's castle, and there finds his messenger, the disguised Kent, in the stocks. This insult to his majesty arouses his old passion, and he strives hard to subdue it lest he prejudge Regan. But when he hears that Cornwall and Regan are tired from their journey and cannot see him, his anger gives way; he manages to restrain himself again and tells himself that Cornwall may be ill, but the sight of Kent in the stocks persuades him that their action is deliberate and he cries:

> . . . Bid them come forth and hear me,
> Or at their chamber door I'll beat the drum
> Till it cry sleep to death!
>
> .   .   .   .   .   .
>
> O me, my heart, my rising heart! But down!

Regan's greeting, "I am glad to see your Highness," for a moment enables Lear to believe she is the daughter he expects her to be:

> Regan, I think you are; I know what reason
> I have to think so. If thou shouldst not be glad,
> I would divorce me from thy mother's tomb,
> Sepulchring an adultress. . . .
>
> .   .   .   .   .   .
>
> . . . Beloved Regan,
> Thy sister's naught. O Regan, she hath tied
> Sharp-toothed unkindness, like a vulture, here.

[*Lays his hand on his breast*]
I can scarce speak to thee; thou'lt not believe
With how depraved a quality—O Regan!

But Regan defends Goneril and suggests that Lear should return to ask her forgiveness. This prompts him to a sarcastic charade:

"Dear daughter, I confess that I am old.
Age is unnecessary. On my knees I beg
That you'll vouchsafe me raiment, bed, and food."

When Regan dismisses this as "unsightly tricks," Lear, still believing in her love, curses Goneril with frightening vehemence. Regan is moved to say:

Oh, the blest gods! So will you wish on me
When the rash mood is on.

But the blind Lear quickly reassures her:

No, Regan, thou shalt never have my curse.
Thy tender-hefted nature shall not give
Thee o'er to harshness. Her eyes are fierce, but thine
Do comfort and not burn. 'Tis not in thee
To grudge my pleasures, to cut off my train,
To bandy hasty words, to scant my sizes,
And in conclusion to oppose the bolt
Against my coming in. Thou better know'st
The offices of nature, bond of childhood,
Effects of courtesy, dues of gratitude.
Thy half o' the kingdom hast thou not forgot,
Wherein I thee endowed.

Regan's cold "Good sir, to the purpose" begins Lear's slow and reluctant reassessment of her; this, coupled with a renewed sight of Kent in the stocks. Then the cursed Goneril arrives and is greeted affectionately by Regan. But still Lear clings to his last hope in Regan, especially when it is her husband who assumes the responsibility for having stocked Kent. Regan, with smooth words, begs Lear to keep to the original arrangement and return to finish his month's sojourn with Goneril. He refuses, and manfully fights to restrain his anger against his eldest daughter:

> . . . But I'll not chide thee.
> Let shame come when it will, I do not call it.
> I do not bid the thunderbearer shoot,
> Nor tell tales of thee to high-judging Jove.
> Mend when thou canst, be better at thy leisure.
> I can be patient; I can stay with Regan,
> I and my hundred knights.

Gradually Regan reveals herself even to the blind Lear as being one with Goneril, worse in that she hides her cruelty beneath a mask of filial concern. Lear's retinue becomes the issue; the daughters argue that it is not necessary, dwindling it down until Regan finally says, "What need one?"

Under this onslaught of cold cruelty, Lear begins his final crack-up. His desire for revenge dissolves in frustration. He alternates between anger and tears; he realizes the imminence of his mental breakdown and yet begins to show signs of that transcendent wisdom which will be his when he loses his sanity. In reply to Regan he says:

> O, reason not the need! Our basest beggars
> Are in the poorest thing superfluous.
> Allow not nature more than nature needs,
> Man's life is cheap as beast's . . .
> . . . But for true need—
> You Heavens, give me that patience, patience I need!
> You see me here, you gods, a poor old man,
> As full of grief as age, wretched in both.
> If it be you that stirs these daughers' hearts
> Against their father, fool me not so much
> To bear it tamely; touch me with noble anger,
> And let not women's weapons, water drops,
> Stain my man's cheeks! No, you unnatural hags,
> I will have such revenges on you both
> That all the world shall—I will do such things—
> What they are, yet I know not; but they shall be

> The terrors of the earth. You think I'll weep.
> No, I'll not weep.
> I have full cause of weeping, but this heart
> Shall break into a hundred thousand flaws
> Or ere I'll weep. O fool, I shall go mad!

The storm in Lear's mind has already begun; Gloucester reports that another storm is imminent:

> Alack, the night comes on, and the bleak winds
> Do sorely ruffle. For many miles about
> There's scarce a bush.

But Regan merely comments that Lear must be taught a lesson:

> O sir, to wilful men
> The injuries that they themselves procure
> Must be their schoolmasters. Shut up your doors.

In his confrontation with the storm, Lear is magnificent. He

> Strives in his little world of man to out-scorn
> The to-and-fro-conflicting wind and rain.

His attitude to the furious elements varies as his mind changes. In his bitter disillusionment, he calls upon the storm to destroy the world and all mankind:

> . . . And thou, all-shaking thunder,
> Smite flat the thick rotundity o' the world!
> Crack nature's moulds, all germens spill at once
> That makes ingrateful man!

Then he contrasts the elements with his daughters:

> I tax not you, you elements, with unkindness.
> I never gave you kingdom, called you children.

But the elements are doing the will of his daughters:

> But yet I call you servile ministers,
> That will with two pernicious daughters join
> Your high-engendered battles 'gainst a head
> So old and white as this. . . .

His final attitude to the storm is one of stoic endurance:

> No, I will be the pattern of all patience;
> I will say nothing.

When Kent finds Lear and the Fool, his testimony to the storm makes Lear's defiance of it all the greater:

> . . . Since I was man,
> Such sheets of fire, such bursts of horrid thunder,
> Such groans of roaring wind and rain, I never
> Remember to have heard. Man's nature cannot carry
> The affliction nor the fear.

Now Lear becomes the voice of the storm as an instrument of divine justice, which cannot be deceived by appearances as can the justice of man:

> . . . Tremble, thou wretch,
> That hast within thee undivulged crimes
> Unwhipped of justice. Hide thee, thou bloody hand,
> Thou perjured, and thou simular [i.e. apparent] man of virtue
> That art incestuous. Caitiff, to pieces shake,
> That under covert and convenient seeming
> Hast practised on man's life. Close pent-up guilts,
> Rive your concealing continents and cry
> These dreadful summoners grace. . . .

Then he turns the eye of justice upon himself and concludes:

> . . . I am a man
> More sinned against than sinning.

This reminder of his own plight brings him back to himself, and he has a period of lucidity in which he also becomes aware of Kent, who is urging him to come to shelter, and the Fool, who has suffered the storm with him:

> My wits begin to turn.
> Come on, my boy. How dost, my boy? Art cold?
> I am cold myself. Where is this straw, my fellow?
> The art of our necessities is strange,
> That can make vile things precious. Come, your hovel.

> Poor fool and knave, I have one part in my heart
> That's sorry yet for thee.

Lear's solicitude for the Fool is the first sign of a new consideration in him for the poor ones of the world. Wisdom, a sense of
divine justice, compassion; all these are qualities which will grow
in the stricken king. His compassion for the Fool extends to all
in need:

> Poor naked wretches, wheresoe'er you are,
> That bide the pelting of this pitiless storm,
> How shall your houseless heads and unfed sides,
> Your looped and windowed raggedness, defend you
> From seasons such as these? O, I have ta'en
> Too little care of this! Take physic, pomp;
> Expose thyself to feel what wretches feel,
> That thou mayst shake the superflux to them,
> And show the heavens more just.

When Lear encounters Edgar disguised as mad Tom, his reaction is one that is becoming characteristic of him; immediately
he assumes that poor Tom's naked wretchedness is due to "unkind
daughters," but then he proceeds to consider man's existential
plight:

> Is man no more than this? Consider him well. Thou owest
> the worm no silk, the beast no hide, the sheep no wool, the
> cat no perfume. Ha! here's three on 's are sophisticated. Thou
> art the thing itself: unaccommodated man is no more but
> such a poor, bare, forked animal as thou art.

Then, with the logic of a madman, Lear tries to tear off his
clothes; we are reminded in an original stage direction that
the storm still rages. By the same logic, Lear addresses Tom as
"learned Theban" and "noble philosopher," for in his nakedness
he has achieved the ultimate wisdom of dependence upon neither
man nor beast. And it is this logic which marks his final descent
into insanity. When next we see him, Kent says, "All the power

of his wits have given way to his impatience [*i.e.* his inability to bear his suffering]."

In his mad fantasy, Lear arraigns Goneril and Regan, his fellow justices being mad Tom and the Fool, whom he describes respectively as "most learned justicer" and "sapient sir." Again Lear moves from the particular to the general, ending the lunatic trial with the unanswerable question, "Is there any cause in nature that makes these hard hearts?" He is persuaded by the disguised Kent to rest; he does so with the crazy statement, "We'll go to supper i' the morning," which the Fool picks up with "And I'll go to bed at noon."

That is the last we see or hear of the Fool, and his unexplained disappearance from the play has caused much speculation. Dramatically he is no longer necessary; his function had been to sense the implications of Lear's folly and to warn him. Now Lear has passed beyond the reach of even the Fool's peculiar wisdom; he is in a world of his own, beyond communication. In a production of the play I once directed, I gave the actor who played the Fool a motivation which isolated him and made him aware, like a faithful dog, that he was being rejected; mad Tom gradually took his place by Lear's side—"I will keep still with my philosopher"—and the Fool languished like a forlorn animal.

Cordelia and the French forces have landed in England to restore Lear to the throne, though the French King himself has had to return to France to deal with something of "fear and danger." We learn from Kent that, in his lucid moments, Lear refuses to see Cordelia because he is overwhelmed by shame for his treatment of her:

> . . . These things sting
> His mind so venomously that burning shame
> Detains him from Cordelia.

But Cordelia has sent to find him as he wanders abroad,

> As mad as the vexed sea, singing aloud,

> Crowned with rank fumiter and furrow weeds,
> With burdocks, hemlocks, nettles, cuckoo flowers,
> Darnel, and all the idle weeds that grow
> In our sustaining corn. . . .

She promises all her "outward worth" if the doctor can restore his mind.

When we next see Lear he is as Cordelia has described him. Now his obsessive fantasy is of his kingship, of his privilege of coining, of his soldiers, of his old delight in archery. But even this gives way to a new wisdom:

> To say "aye" and "no" to everything that I said "aye" and "no" to was no good divinity. When the rain came to wet me once and the wind to make me chatter, when the thunder would not peace at my bidding, there I found 'em, there I smelt 'em out. Go to, they are not men o' their words: they told me I was everything; 'tis a lie; I am not ague-proof.

When addressed by the blinded Gloucester, Lear resumes his royal fantasy. Now he is Justice, and he pardons an adulterer, because all nature is adulterous:

> But to the girdle do the gods inherit;
> Beneath is all the fiends'.

Gloucester offers to kiss his hand and Lear, even in his imagined enjoyment of kingship, is aware of the transitoriness of life and power. He says, "Let me wipe it first; it smells of mortality." In the dialogue with Gloucester, Lear reveals the view of the world, sub specie aeternitatis, which he has achieved in his madness; it is "reason in madness," which unmasks the hypocrisy of human justice:

> A man may see how this world goes with no eyes. Look with thine ears. See how yond justice rails upon yond simple thief. Hark, in thine ear: change places, and, handy-dandy, which is the justice, which is the thief? Thou hast seen a farmer's dog bark at a beggar? . . . And the creature run from the

cur? There thou mightst behold the great image of authority:
a dog's obeyed in office.
Thou rascal beadle, hold thy bloody hand!
Why dost thou lash that whore? Strip thine own back.
Thou hotly lust'st to use her in that kind
For which thou whip'st her. The usurer hangs the cozener.
Through tattered clothes small vices do appear;
Robes and furred gowns hide all. . . .

In a fleeting moment of sanity Lear recognizes Gloucester, and attempts to comfort him with the reflection that suffering is the human lot:

Thou must be patient; we came crying hither.
Thou know'st, the first time that we smell the air,
We wawl and cry. . . .

But even this reflection takes on a bitter and ironic connotation:

When we are born, we cry that we are come
To this great stage of fools. . . .

Lear finally comes under Cordelia's care and the doctor induces sleep in him:

Our foster nurse of nature is repose,
The which he lacks. That to provoke in him
Are many simples operative, whose power
Will close the eye of anguish.

In the exquisite scene of Lear's awakening, to the soothing accompaniment of music, his gradual awareness of his surroundings and Cordelia is most moving. At first he thinks he has died and become a soul in torment, watched over by Cordelia, who is "a soul in bliss." A pin prick proves to him that he is still alive. As he struggles to remember, his daughters return to his mind, and he says to the weeping Cordelia:

If you have poison for me, I will drink it.
I know you do not love me; for your sisters
Have, as I do remember, done me wrong.
You have some cause; they have not.

The doctor feels that the scene should not be prolonged; as he is borne out, Lear says to Cordelia:

> You must bear with me. Pray you now, forget and forgive.
> I am old and foolish.

The forces of Cordelia are defeated and she and Lear taken prisoner, but in the defeat Lear finds true happiness, for he and Cordelia are fully reconciled, and his newfound wisdom has put a new valuation on earthly power:

> . . . Come, let's away to prison.
> We two alone will sing like birds i' the cage.
> When thou dost ask me blessing, I'll kneel down
> And ask of thee forgiveness. So we'll live,
> And pray, and sing, and tell old tales, and laugh
> At gilded butterflies, and hear poor rogues
> Talk of court news; and we'll talk with them too,
> Who loses and who wins, who's in, who's out;
> And take upon 's the mystery of things,
> As if we were God's spies. . . .

But the interlude of happiness is to be brief. Edmund, at point of death, repents of his evil plan:

> . . . Some good I mean to do,
> Despite of mine own nature. Quickly send,
> Be brief in it, to the castle; for my writ
> Is on the life of Lear and on Cordelia.
> Nay, send in time.

But it is too late; Cordelia is already hanged. Lear, in a sudden access of his old soldierly valor, kills the man who hanged her. Then, in a paroxysm of grief, he carries her body in. The sad sight causes the onlookers to compare the moment to Doomsday, "or image of that horror." Kent makes himself known to Lear and tries to explain how he has served him in disguise, but Lear has thought for nothing but Cordelia. Albany says:

> He knows not what he says, and vain is it
> That we present us to him.

At the last moment Lear's grief is turned to joy, for he thinks he detects life in Cordelia. In fantasy he gained wisdom and now it brings him a happy death. Gloucester too had died "smilingly." Both at the last had been reconciled to the loyal and loving child they had rejected. But this is not a happy ending; it is but a flicker of light at Doomsday.

It has already been pointed out that every man finds his own significance in *King Lear*. Shakespeare did not write it to exemplify a philosophy. It is life in all its vastness and mystery as he saw and felt it at that moment in his own life: an amalgam of loyalty and treachery, love and hate, joy and suffering, sanity and madness. He attempts no answer to the Why? of it all. It is his picture of the dark mystery of this world at its most profound, and his Lear bestrides that world in the majesty of his suffering.

 19 Macbeth

A DESIRE TO please King James the Sixth of Scotland and First of England motivated the writing of *Macbeth*. Two elements in the story, which was an amalgam from Holinshed of events in the reigns of two Scottish kings, made it an appropriate subject: James was a direct descendant of Banquo and he was also a self-proclaimed expert on witchcraft. To make the first of these elements fit, Shakespeare had to change the story, for, in Holinshed, Banquo had been a party to the murder of Duncan. As for the second, in 1597 James had written a book, *Demonology*, as a counter-blast to a skeptical work on the subject written by a Reginald Scot in 1584 under the title, *The Discovery of Witchcraft;* an only slightly less skeptical account had been published in 1593 by a George Gifford in the form of *A Dialogue Concerning Witches and Witchcraft.*

King James felt that he had himself been the victim of witchcraft in Scotland; Bothwell had more than once invoked the aid of witches to bring about his death, once by the supernatural raising of a storm at sea, which had in fact occurred. When James came to the throne of England in 1603 there were some ardent witch-hunters in the entourage he brought with him from Scotland. One of his first acts was to introduce much harsher legislation against witches, and to order the burning of all copies of Scot's book. In fairness to James it must be added that he later became much more skeptical on the subject, though it is among the lesser ironies of history that his book remained a textbook for puritanical witch-hunters.

Macbeth opens with a scene of witches and it is important to examine what Shakespeare meant their function to be. In Holinshed he had read:

> there met them three women in strange and wild apparel, resembling creatures of elder world . . . afterward the common opinion was that these women were either the weird sisters, that is (as ye would say) the goddesses of destiny, or else some nymphs or fairies, imbued with knowledge of prophecy by their necromantical science, because everything came to pass as they had spoken.

There we have two very different points of view. Were they, to Shakespeare, the Fates or fortune-tellers? Did they determine Macbeth's destiny or merely foretell it? There are those who believe this play to be "a tragedy of fate." I cannot subscribe to this. To me, Macbeth's life would have been the same had there been no witches. They merely told him what he wanted to hear and encouraged him to quell his doubts. They are a personification of the evil in men's hearts, always tempting and teasing. Never once do they foretell Macbeth's evil deeds; only the wished-for consequences of them.

Of course, there is an inexorability in the play, but it is not that of the predestined crimes of Oedipus. Rather it is the inevitable working of a moral law, in which Macbeth himself firmly believed. He hesitates to murder Duncan because he believes that such a crime is bound to be punished, and in this world:

> . . . But in these cases
> We still have judgement here; that we but teach
> Bloody instructions, which being taught return

> To plague the inventor. This even-handed justice
> Commends the ingredients of our poisoned chalice
> To our own lips. . . .

Believing this, Macbeth still chooses the assassination, because he assures himself, as do all criminals, that he will be the exception that will evade justice and the law. It is this egotistical sense of difference that is dramatized in the specious assurances of the witches.

Although he degenerates into a monster of iniquity, Macbeth is not essentially a villain, like Iago or Richard III. He is a man of potential nobility. He is a tormented man because he is composed of conflicting qualities: he is as soldierly as Coriolanus but as imaginative as Juliet; he is as power-hungry as Richard III but as scrupulous in conscience as Hamlet.

A dominant quality in Macbeth is his unquenchable courage. (Just as Hamlet taunts himself with accusations of cowardice, so does Lady Macbeth taunt Macbeth; to both men it is a most despicable trait.) The first epithet applied to him in the play, and by a sergeant, "a good and hardy soldier," is "brave." And that same courage remains with him to the end:

> Ring the alarum-bell! Blow, wind! Come, wrack!
> At least we'll die with harness on our back.

Sensing that Macduff is to be the instrument of Nemesis, he yet cries:

> I will not yield
>
> .   .   .   .   .
>
> Yet I will try the last. Before my body
> I throw my warlike shield. Lay on, Macduff,
> And damned be him that first cries, "Hold, enough!"

Yet though he is "Bellona's bridegroom," *i.e.* married to the goddess of war, he is the most imaginative of all Shakespeare's tragic heroes. He is cursed with the kind of imagination which tends to paralyze the will to act. In his first soliloquy he says,

> . . . Present fears
> Are less than horrible imaginings.

In this he is the opposite of Lady Macbeth. Her plaint might
be:

> . . . Present fears
> Are less than horrible rememberings.

She is not impeded from an evil deed by thinking of it in advance,
but once it has been done she can never forget it. Macbeth can
describe in gory detail the sight of the man he has murdered.
Lady Macbeth would not have been affected had she not seen it,
but she had seen it and so she fainted. Macbeth can look on horrors but not contemplate them, she can contemplate but not look;
she prays for the cover of darkness that she see not, while he
longs for the bell that will release him to action.

The witches open the play with an atmosphere of brooding
evil as they wait for Macbeth. Their chant, "Fair is foul, and
foul is fair," with the implication that there is no distinction between good and evil, is going to be at the heart of their temptation to him, and it is surely significant that his first words in the
play echo the witches before he has even seen them: "So foul
and fair a day I have not seen."

The sergeant's description of Macbeth's action in killing the
rebel, "merciless Macdonwald," is eloquent of his extraordinary
strength and bravery upon the field of battle:

> For brave Macbeth—well he deserves that name—
> Disdaining fortune, with his brandished steel,
> Which smoked with bloody execution,
> Like valour's minion carved out his passage
> Till he faced the slave;
> Which ne'er shook hands, nor bade farewell to him,
> Till he unseamed him from the nave to the chops,
> And fixed his head upon our battlements.

It is clear that the witches did not plant the thought of the
throne in Macbeth's mind; they merely read what was already

there. As soon as they hail him "King hereafter," he starts guiltily and prompts Banquo to say,

> Good sir, why do you start, and seem to fear
> Things that do sound so fair? . . .

We even hear that he has thought of murder as a way to the throne, and the witches' prophecy has revealed in him the moral confusion which cannot tell good from ill, or what is from what is not:

> This supernatural soliciting
> Cannot be ill, cannot be good. If ill,
> Why hath it given me earnest of success,
> Commencing in a truth? I am Thane of Cawdor.
> If good, why do I yield to that suggestion
> Whose horrid image doth unfix my hair
> And make my seated heart knock at my ribs,
> Against the use of nature? Present fears
> Are less than horrible imaginings.
> My thought, whose murder yet is but fantastical,
> Shakes so my single state of man that function
> Is smothered in surmise, and nothing is
> But what is not.

He quickly takes comfort from the fact that, somehow or other, he may legally become king:

> If chance will have me King, why, chance may crown me
> Without my stir.

But this hope is soon dashed, for Duncan creates his eldest son, Malcolm, Prince of Cumberland and heir to the throne. Again Macbeth's thoughts are filled with prospective violence:

> . . . Stars, hide your fires;
> Let not light see my black and deep desires;
> The eye wink at the hand; yet let that be
> Which the eye fears, when it is done, to see.

Many critics have been upset by the sudden appearance of Lady Macbeth, but I believe it to be a brilliant coup de théâtre.

The text of the play as a whole has led to endless speculation and controversy. It is the shortest of the tragedies, and this, coupled with what are believed to be internal evidences, has caused widespread theories about missing scenes. For myself, I am happy to accept the text as we have it as being Shakespeare's complete work, with the possible exception of Hecate, which looks like a later interpolation, probably by Thomas Middleton, to add some spectacle and song and dance. As for Lady Macbeth, no actress would want to spoil her wonderful first solo entrance by having to play some previous scene.

In his letter, Macbeth describes his Lady as "my dearest partner of greatness." This is the simple truth; they are as one in their ambition. Too often Lady Macbeth is presented as having a giant will which manipulates Macbeth for her own purposes. It is true that she wants to be Queen, but only as a corollary of his being King. To me it is significant that she is given no name of her own; she is merely Macbeth's "Lady," the adjunct of her lord. (What was her name as Queen?) She knows that he is consumed by a desire to reign over Scotland, and it is her function to help him to fulfill that desire, and to remove the obstacles, the chief of which is in himself. Nobody knows him as well as she does; she is well aware of the complexities and conflicts in her man:

> . . . Yet do I fear thy nature.
> It is too full o' the milk of human kindness
> To catch the nearest way. Thou wouldst be great,
> Art not without ambition, but without
> The illness [*i.e.* wickedness] should attend it. What thou
>   wouldst highly
> That wouldst thou holily; wouldst not play false,
> And yet wouldst wrongly win. . . .

Excited by the witches' prophecy, she is eager to do battle with Macbeth's scruples:

> . . . Hie thee hither,
> That I may pour my spirits in thine ear,
> And chastise with the valour of my tongue

> All that impedes thee from the golden round
> Which fate and metaphysical aid doth seem
> To have thee crowned withal.

As if in response to her exaltation comes the surprising news,
"The King comes here tonight." Shakespeare's audience would
have been very conscious of the unexpectedness of this announcement, because they would have known of the elaborate arrangements necessary for a royal visit. Kings do not drop in casually;
months are needed for the preparations. Lady Macbeth's reaction
is a natural one:

> Thou'rt mad to say it!
> Is not thy master with him? who, were't so,
> Would have informed for preparation.

But in the mood induced by the letter, Lady Macbeth sees Duncan's coming as a fate-given opportunity to secure the fulfillment
of the prophecy; Duncan must be assassinated that night. Yet she
is fully aware of the enormity of the task; the crime itself is so
monstrous that even the raven, the messenger of death, will be
unable to give it tongue. She realizes too that the burden of the
task is hers, for scruples will abound in Macbeth. She knows also
that she will feel a natural compunction, which she must stifle;
Macbeth will seize on any sign of human weakness in her. With
the solemnity of a prayer, she calls upon the spirits of evil to unsex
her. Though the dagger must be wielded by Macbeth, it will be
her determined purpose that will direct it, and so she refers to the
murdering weapon as "my keen knife."

When Macbeth arrives, his Lady goes straight to the purpose.
It is clear that he has thought of the murderous possibilities of
the night; she speaks in riddles and tells him to leave everything
to her:

> Your face, my Thane, is as a book where men
> May read strange matters. To beguile the time,
> Look like the time; bear welcome in your eye,
> Your hand, your tongue; look like the innocent flower,

> But be the serpent under't. He that's coming
> Must be provided for; and you shall put
> This night's great business into my dispatch,
> Which shall to all our nights and days to come
> Give solely sovereign sway and masterdom.

But Macbeth lacks her single-minded certainty; he temporizes: "We will speak further."

Lady Macbeth greets the King alone, a strange dereliction of a host's duty. Duncan naturally asks, "Where's the Thane of Cawdor?" honoring Macbeth with his new title, but the question receives no answer; Macbeth is already secluded in private torment.

There is the sound and bustle of royal salutes and feasting, and then Macbeth appears. He has left the dining chamber, where the King is being entertained; he cannot wear the hypocritical mask of host to a man he wants to murder. He argues against the deed. First, he uses the pragmatic argument that he won't get away with it; "even-handed justice" will see to that; he even says he would risk everlasting damnation for it, if he could only be sure of succeeding in this world. Then comes the horror of treachery—the act itself of killing is nothing to Macbeth—and treachery against a good man:

> . . . He's here in double trust:
> First, as I am his kinsman and his subject,
> Strong both against the deed; then, as his host,
> Who should against his murderer shut the door,
> Not bear the knife myself. Besides, this Duncan
> Hath borne his faculties so meek, hath been
> So clear in his great office, that his virtues
> Will plead like angels trumpet-tongued against
> The deep damnation of his taking off.

In natural exasperation Lady Macbeth comes looking for her husband; again Duncan has questioned the strange behavior of his host. But she is greeted with the flat assertion: "We will proceed no further in this business."

This is the crucial test for Lady Macbeth. If the valor of her tongue fails now, all is lost. She chastises him with being faint-hearted:

> . . . Art thou afeard
> To be the same in thine own act and valour
> As thou art in desire? Wouldst thou have that
> Which thou esteem'st the ornament of life
> And live a coward in thine own esteem,
> Letting "I dare not" wait upon "I would,"
> Like the poor cat i' the adage? [*viz.* "The cat would eat fish
>   but would not wet her feet."]

Macbeth rightly replies that circumstances determine whether courage is a virtue:

> Prithee, peace.
> I dare do all that may become a man;
> Who dares do more is none.

Now Lady Macbeth refers to previous conversations they had had, when it seems that it was Macbeth who had first broached the possibility of murdering Duncan, though without a specific plan:

> . . . Nor time nor place
> Did then adhere, and yet you would make both.
> They have made themselves, and that their fitness now
> Does unmake you. . . .

She accuses him of having broken a pledge, a major accusation, and to reinforce her taunt of perfidy she indulges in a horrifying piece of bravado:

> . . . I have given suck, and know
> How tender 'tis to love the babe that milks me.
> I would, while it was smiling in my face,
> Have plucked my nipple from his boneless gums
> And dashed the brains out, had I so sworn as you
> Have done to this.

(Later we hear from Macduff that Macbeth has no children. It is an inconsistency not unusual in Shakespeare, and of the kind that generally passes unnoticed in a theatrical performance. Here it is necessary for Lady Macbeth's argument that she has had a child; it is equally necessary for Macduff to be cheated of complete revenge because Macbeth has no children. If the reader, viewer or actor is worried by this inconsistency, let him assume that the Macbeth child or children died in infancy, a fairly common fate for babies in Shakespeare's day.)

Macbeth now shifts his ground to the practical—"If we should fail?"—and Lady Macbeth knows that her battle is won, for she has already worked out a foolproof plan, and she subtly suggests that Macbeth will not be alone even in the deed itself:

> What cannot you and I perform upon
> The unguarded Duncan? . . .

Macbeth is won, "I am settled," and so much are their minds now in harmony that he echoes the very advice she had given him in their first scene together:

> Away, and mock the time with fairest show.
> False face must hide what the false heart doth know.

Macbeth is indeed settled now. Not even the news from Banquo of fresh kindness from the King can shake him:

> He hath been in unusual pleasure, and
> Sent forth great largess to your offices.
> This diamond he greets your wife withal,
> By the name of most kind hostess. . . .

Banquo says he has been dreaming about the three weird sisters; he is obviously worried about the implications of the prophecy; he has had "cursed thoughts." Macbeth does not receive this as a warning of Banquo's inevitable later suspicions, but only as prompting a future conference to their mutual advantage:

> If you shall cleave to my consent, when 'tis,
> It shall make honour for you.

The implications of Banquo's reply are unequivocal: he will be party to no treachery:

> So I lose none
> In seeking to augment it, but still keep
> My bosom franchised and allegiance clear,
> I shall be counselled.

And now Macbeth is alone, waiting for the bell which will be the signal that Duncan's guards are drugged asleep. This is the time of agony for the over-imaginative Macbeth. His "heat-oppressed brain" sees a dagger moving in the air towards Duncan's chamber, and later reappearing, after completing its mission, covered with "gouts of blood." He becomes aware of the silence and the dark; throughout the play there is a prevailing sense of darkness. As the storm in the elements mirrored the storm in Lear's mind, so does the darkness mirror the darkness in the mind of Macbeth. He thinks of the witches and wolves, for the night is their natural time. He longs for the sound of the bell which will deliver him from the torment of his thoughts: "Words to the heat of deeds too cold breath gives." At last the bell, and his relief is expressed in the abrupt practicality of his words: "I go, and it is done. The bell invites me."

But once the deed is done, Macbeth goes to pieces. This is somewhat surprising in him, and he will soon recover a remarkable mask of equanimity, but for the moment the horror of the regicide suffuses him with guilt so that he cries out in terror, and feels that never again will he have peace of mind or sleep of body. His ever active imagination had made him hear a voice that cried, "Sleep no more." Lady Macbeth, with an extraordinary effort of will, appears calm and practical—what she really went through at this moment will only become apparent when she reenacts it in the sleepwalking scene—and she begs Macbeth to "consider it not so deeply." She warns him:

> These deeds must not be thought
> After these ways. So, it will make us mad.

When he persists in his fantasy about the voice, she challenges him with "Who was it that thus cried?" and tries, but gently, to get him to assert his manhood:

> . . . Why, worthy Thane,
> You do unbend your noble strength to think
> So brainsickly of things. . . .

Her attention is drawn to his bloody hands and she sees the daggers. The danger makes her quickly practical:

> . . . Go get some water
> And wash this filthy witness from your hand.
> Why did you bring these daggers from the place?
> They must lie there. Go, carry them, and smear
> The sleepy grooms with blood.

But Macbeth is still incapable of this; in his horror he can even confess to fear:

> I'll go no more.
> I am afraid to think what I have done;
> Look on't again I dare not.

And so Lady Macbeth herself must add the grisly postscript to the murder. It is her own courage she now bolsters with the reflection:

> . . . The sleeping and the dead
> Are but as pictures. 'Tis the eye of childhood
> That fears a painted devil. . . .

Macbeth, left alone, is frightened by a knocking on the door. Nemesis is entering before the murder has even been discovered; "this even-handed justice" is quick. Macbeth cannot recognize himself in his fear: "How is't with me when every noise appals me?"

Lady Macbeth returns with bloody hands. The memory of Duncan's corpse and his blood on her hands will haunt her dreams, but now, by a superhuman effort, she offsets Macbeth's terror with a brave show. Again she tries to stir him into action, now of self-preservation, with an accusation of cowardice:

> My hands are of your colour, but I shame
> To wear a heart so white. . . . I hear a knocking
> At the south entry. Retire we to our chamber.
> A little water clears us of this deed.
> How easy is it then! Your constancy
> Hath left you unattended. . . . Hark! more knocking.
> Get on your nightgown, lest occasion call us
> And show us to be watchers. Be not lost
> So poorly in your thoughts.

But while she gets Macbeth to move, she cannot remove his burden of remorse: "Wake Duncan with thy knocking! I would thou couldst."

Shortly afterwards Macbeth reenters to greet Macduff and Lennox, and he is transformed. He is now the bold man on whom his wife had counted. He is now so much the gracious host that he can reply politely to Macduff's compliments on the King's reception, and when Lennox describes the unruly night,

> Lamentings heard i' the air, strange screams of death,
> And prophesying with accents terrible
> Of dire combustion and confused events
> New hatched to the woeful time . . . ,

Macbeth can reply laconically, " 'Twas a rough night."

Both the Macbeths react with appropriate horror when Macduff discovers the murder and arouses the household. Macbeth hurries to see for himself, and now, very much the self-possessed man of action, in righteous indignation he kills the suspected grooms. The gibbering victim of remorse has turned into a monster of evil. His lament at the death of Duncan is worthy of Richard III:

> Had I but died an hour before this chance,
> I had lived a blessed time; for from this instant
> There's nothing serious in mortality.
> All is but toys; renown and grace is dead;

> The wine of life is drawn, and the mere lees
> Is left this vault to brag of.

When Macduff questions his wisdom in killing the grooms, the thought of Duncan's blood no longer shakes him:

> Who can be wise, amazed, temperate and furious,
> Loyal and neutral, in a moment? No man.
> The expedition of my violent love
> Outrun the pauser, reason. Here lay Duncan,
> His silver skin laced with his golden blood,
> And his gashed stabs looked like a breach in nature
> For ruin's wasteful entrance. There, the murderers,
> Steeped in the colours of their trade, their daggers
> Unmannerly breeched with gore. Who could refrain,
> That had a heart to love, and in that heart
> Courage to make 's love known?

Macbeth's "constancy" has certainly returned, and so the woman in his Lady can afford to assert itself; as Macbeth daringly describes the death chamber, her memory of it overcomes her and she faints. The suggestion has been made that this fainting is a distracting sham, but there is no suggestion of this in the text. Rather is it the inevitable reaction of the Lady Macbeth I see; it is the first working in her of that remorse which will drive her to guilty suicide.

Banquo, who had vague suspicions of Macbeth even before the murder, is not satisfied that the grooms are solely to blame for it; there is some further secret treason to unravel:

> . . . Fears and scruples shake us.
> In the great hand of God I stand, and thence
> Against the undivulged pretence I fight
> Of treasonous malice.

Macbeth brazenly suggests that they should all confer about it.

Duncan's sons seem now to play into Macbeth's hands, for, fearful for their own safety, they fly the country:

> This murderous shaft that's shot
> Hath not yet lighted, and our safest way
> Is to avoid the aim. . . .

This both draws suspicion upon them, though it is hard to find their motive, and leaves the way to the throne open for Macbeth. But already there is an uneasiness in Macduff's mind, for he decides to absent himself from the coronation; he has doubts about the future, for he says to Ross, who is going to Scone for the coronation,

> Well, may you see things well done there—adieu!
> Lest our old robes sit easier than our new!

Just before the Macbeths make their first entrance as King and Queen, Banquo voices his firming suspicions:

> Thou hast it now: King, Cawdor, Glamis, all,
> As the weird women promised, and I fear
> Thou play'dst most foully for't. . . .

But Macbeth has been fully invested and enthroned, and Banquo has no choice but to pay him due obeisance. As soon as he is alone, Macbeth speaks his fears of Banquo:

> . . . Our fears in Banquo
> Stick deep, and in his royalty of nature
> Reigns that which would be feared. 'Tis much he dares,
> And, to that dauntless temper of his mind,
> He hath a wisdom that doth guide his valour
> To act in safety. . . .

There is more too. Macbeth must seek to frustrate the prophecy of the witches that Banquo's issue should succeed to the throne. In commenting on this, Macbeth faces the fact that to gain the throne he has damned his soul. In contemplating the murder he had been prepared to pay this price—"we'd jump the life to come" —and now he has paid it, and his

> . . . eternal jewel
> Given to the common enemy of man.

In planning the murder of Banquo and his son, King Macbeth takes his next step in infamy; from now on he must employ agents to commit his murders, a process which will multiply until his whole kingdom will live in secret terror from spies and sudden death. In recruiting his first murderers, Macbeth chooses two disaffected men and persuades them that their ill fortune has been due to Banquo. He also gives them the reason for his need of them:

> . . . And though I could
> With barefaced power sweep him from my sight
> And bid my will avouch it, yet I must not,
> For certain friends that are both his and mine,
> Whose loves I may not drop, but wail his fall
> Who I myself struck down. And thence it is
> That I to your assistance do make love,
> Masking the business from the common eye
> For sundry weighty reasons.

The new Queen is worried by her royal partner's obvious disquiet. She says to herself:

> 'Tis safer to be that which we destroy
> Than by destruction dwell in doubtful joy.

He echoes this to her a minute later:

> . . . Better be with the dead,
> Whom we, to gain our peace, have sent to peace,
> Than on the torture of the mind to lie
> In restless ecstacy. . . .

Again they are at one in mind, but now, instead of prodding him to murder, it is her function to make him forget it:

> Come on,
> Gentle my lord, sleek o'er your rugged looks;
> Be bright and jovial among your guests tonight.

When he speaks of Banquo and asks her to pay him special honor, again, as in the case of Duncan, urging the use of a mask to their real feelings,

> . . . we
> Must lave our honours in these flattering streams,
> And make our faces vizards to our hearts,
> Disguising what they are,

she demurs with "You must leave this." He hints at "a deed of dreadful note," but when she asks fearfully "What's to be done?" he replies,

> Be innocent of the knowledge, dearest chuck,
> Till thou applaud the deed. . . .

This is a watershed in their relationship. From now on they drift further apart; no longer does he share his evil plans with her. Did she not faint? Is she not now incapable of understanding that Banquo must die? Henceforth he will be alone in his villainy and she in her secret distress. As he longs for the night, which for him will signal the death of Banquo and his son, her puzzled look causes him to say, "Thou marvell'st at my words."

When the two murderers prepare for their task, we find that they have been joined by a third, and his identity has aroused incredible explanations. Worthy scholars have been convinced that it is Macbeth himself, in spite of his obviously honest dismay when he learns later that Fleance has escaped; others have even suggested that it is a "supernatural agent." James Thurber added amusingly to the theories in his *Macbeth Murder Mystery* when his American lady devotee of whodunits proudly proclaims Macduff as her candidate for the post, and this to me is little less absurd than the other theories. The Second Murderer clearly states Macbeth's motive in employing a third henchman: "He needs not our mistrust." Macbeth can no longer trust anybody; he is bent on the course that will soon lead him to say,

> There's not a one of them but in his house
> I keep a servant fee'd. . . .

While Macbeth plays host at the royal feast, he leaves the table to hear the First Murderer's report. When he hears that

Fleance, Banquo's son, has escaped, he is again tormented:

> . . . now I am cabined, cribbed, confined, bound in
> To saucy doubts and fears. . . .

In that word "saucy" is the sense that he is being paltered with,
laughed at, a sense that will be climaxed when he discovers that
Macduff was unnaturally born and so escapes the interdiction of
the witches.

Much speculation has arisen as to the reality of Banquo's
ghost at the feast. Was it, like the dagger, an "unreal mockery"
as Macbeth, prompted by his Queen, tries to believe it to be? I
think not. The fact that no one else saw it means nothing; Gertrude had not seen the ghost of her husband as Hamlet spoke
to it; it was part of the lore of ghosts that they could choose
those who could see and hear them. There is a rare and interesting account of the scene in a very early production. A Dr. Simon
Forman saw the play at the Globe Theatre on April 20, 1611,
and wrote a description of the play, in which this occurs:

> The next night, being at supper with his noblemen whom he
> had bidden to a feast, to the which also Banquo should have
> come, he began to speak of noble Banquo and to wish that
> he were there. And as he thus did, standing up to drink a
> carouse to him, the ghost of Banquo came and sat down in
> his chair behind him. And he turning about to sit down again,
> saw the ghost of Banquo, which fronted him so that he fell
> into a great passion of fear and fury, uttering many words
> about his murder, by which, when they heard that Banquo
> was murdered, they suspected Macbeth.

Lady Macbeth is confronted with two problems by Macbeth's reaction to the ghost: to still his fears and to explain his
strange conduct to the disturbed guests, who rise in their con-
sternation. She bids them

> Sit, worthy friends. My lord is often thus,
> And hath been from his youth. Pray you, keep seat.
> The fit is momentary; upon a thought
> He will again be well. If much you note him,

> You shall offend him and extend his passion.
> Feed, and regard him not. . . .

Convinced that Macbeth sees nothing but the "painting" of his fear, the Queen employs her usual device of accusing him of cowardice: "Shame itself . . . quite unmanned in folly . . . Fie, for shame!" She succeeds temporarily to such an extent that, when the ghost disappears, Macbeth is able to resume his role as host, and even to make an ironic reference to Banquo:

> Do not muse at me, my most worthy friends;
> I have a strange infirmity, which is nothing
> To those that know me. Come, love and health to all;
> Then I'll sit down. Give me some wine; fill full.
> I drink to the general joy o' the whole table,
> And to our dear friend Banquo, whom we miss.
> Would he were here! . . .

But the reappearance of the ghost shatters his hard-won equanimity. The Queen sets to work on Macbeth again, but to such little avail that finally she has to get rid of her guests quickly:

> I pray you, speak not; he grows worse and worse;
> Question enrages him. At once, good night.
> Stand not upon the order of your going,
> But go at once.

As soon as the guests have gone, Macbeth is again plagued by the thought of "even-handed justice": "It will have blood. They say blood will have blood." Who will be Nemesis? Immediately Macduff comes to his mind:

> How say'st thou that Macduff denies his person
> At our great bidding?

He must know more; his spies multiply, but he determines to seek out the weird sisters again, for they know the future, though he acknowledges they are "the worst means." He realizes now that he is irrevocably committed to a life of murder upon murder:

> . . . I will tomorrow,

And betimes I will, to the weird sisters.
More shall they speak, for now I am bent to know,
By the worst means, the worst. For mine own good
All causes shall give way. I am in blood
Stepped in so far that, should I wade no more,
Returning were as tedious as go o'er.

Lady Macbeth unwittingly reminds us of the voice which cried
"Sleep no more," when she says to Macbeth, who is lost in his
black plans, "You lack the season of all natures, sleep."

While Macbeth prepares to go to the witches, we learn from
a private colloquy of lords, who openly describe Macbeth as
"tyrant," that the kingdom aches for deliverance, that

. . . we may again
Give to our tables meat, sleep to our nights,
Free from our feasts and banquets bloody knives,
Do faithful homage and receive free honours;
All which we pine for now. . . .

But deliverance is in being; Macduff is at the English court of
Edward the Confessor to enlist aid,

. . . that a swift blessing
May soon return to this our suffering country
Under a hand accursed!

In his conjuration of the witches, Macbeth is defiantly aware
that he is calling upon the dreadful powers of evil that can bring
destruction upon all mankind:

. . . though the treasure
Of nature's germens tumble all together,
Even till destruction sicken, answer me
To what I ask you.

In the first apparition, which the witches present at Macbeth's
request, he finds his suspicion of Macduff confirmed. Later when
he learns that Macduff has escaped to England, it is an argument
for the next step in his tyranny, immediate action upon mere suspicion:

> The flighty purpose never is o'ertook
> Unless the deed goes with it. From this moment
> The very firstlings of my heart shall be
> The firstlings of my hand. . . .

The witches give Macbeth false assurances, as every man who acts against his conscience strives to give himself, but Macbeth demands with bold insistence that he be told the truth about Banquo's line inheriting the throne:

> I will be satisfied. Deny me this,
> And an eternal curse fall on you!

The witches obey, and "show his eyes, and grieve his heart;" they do not deceive him in this final truth, nor could he deceive himself at the end. His summation of this scene which he had sought is:

> . . . Let this pernicious hour
> Stand aye accursed in the calendar!

In the scene at the English Court, in which Malcolm tests the loyalty of Macduff, we learn that Macbeth's machinations have even traveled there. Malcolm explains his doubt of Macduff by saying,

> . . . Devilish Macbeth
> By many of these trains [*i.e.* devices] hath sought to win me
> Into his power. . . .

Malcolm also gives the public picture of the monster into which Macbeth has now degenerated:

> I grant him bloody,
> Luxurious, [*i.e.* lecherous] avaricious, false, deceitful,
> Sudden, malicious, smacking of every sin
> That has a name. . . .

And Ross, who brings to Macduff the terrible news of the slaughter of his family, gives a memorable description of the direful state of Scotland:

> Alas, poor country!

> Almost afraid to know itself! It cannot
> Be called our mother, but our grave. . . .
> .   .   .   .
> . . . The dead man's knell
> Is there scarce asked for who; and good men's lives
> Expire before the flowers in their caps,
> Dying or ere they sicken.

As the hostile forces mount and march against him, Macbeth takes refuge in the castle of Dunsinane, which he strongly fortifies. One of his rebellious nobles says of him:

> Some say he's mad. Others, that lesser hate him,
> Do call it valiant fury. . . .

Our judgment must be "valiant fury," the desperation of a cornered animal, who knows his end is near. The disillusioned man longs for it, but the brave soldier will fight to avoid it. In moving words he describes his utter loneliness and despair:

> I have lived long enough. My way of life
> Is fall'n into the sear, the yellow leaf;
> And that which should accompany old age,
> As honour, love, obedience, troops of friends,
> I must not look to have; but, in their stead,
> Curses, not loud but deep, mouth-honour, breath
> Which the poor heart would fain deny, and dare not.

And yet the courageous soldier adds, "I'll fight till from my bones my flesh be hacked."

He inquires about the Queen, and the doctor, who has witnessed her guilty sleepwalking, says,

> Not so sick, my lord,
> As she is troubled with thick-coming fancies
> That keep her from her rest.

Macbeth comments, "Cure her of that," and then he adds, surely speaking of himself as much as of his Queen,

> Canst thou not minister to a mind diseased,
> Pluck from the memory a rooted sorrow,

> Raze out the written troubles of the brain,
> And with some sweet oblivious antidote
> Cleanse the stuffed bosom of that perilous stuff
> Which weighs upon the heart?

Then, after another soldierly outburst, he is moved to consider the sickness to which the land has been reduced by his rule:

> . . . If thou couldst, Doctor, cast
> The water of my land, find her disease
> And purge it to a sound and pristine health,
> I would applaud thee to the very echo,
> That should applaud again. . . .

As Macbeth sits secure in his castle, whose "strength will laugh a siege to scorn," he is startled by a cry, and he says:

> I have almost forgot the taste of fears.
> The time has been my senses would have cooled
> To hear a night-shriek, and my fell of hair
> Would at a dismal treatise rouse and stir
> As life were in't. I have supped full with horrors.
> Direness, familiar to my slaughterous thoughts,
> Cannot once start me.

An essential part of Macbeth has already died: his imagination. Then comes the news that the Queen is dead. (Later we learn that she is thought to have committed suicide.) Macbeth's famous reaction to the news is capable of various interpretations: philosophical reflection, bitter despair, lonely sorrow, mounting fury. My own feeling is towards the last; Macbeth is so maddened by the fact that this untimely sorrow is added to the already overwhelming burden that he feels the whole of life is a pointless cheat, and he angrily denounces it in a cry that builds to the ultimate expression of existential despair:

> . . . It is a tale
> Told by an idiot, full of sound and fury,
> Signifying nothing.

This angry world-weariness makes him turn upon the messenger who brings the strange news that Birnam Wood seems to be moving, and ends with the conflicting moods of submission and defiance:

> I 'gin to be aweary of the sun,
> And wish the estate o' the world were now undone.
> Ring the alarum bell! Blow, wind! Come, wrack!
> At least we'll die with harness on our back.

When Macbeth finally faces Macduff, he is reluctant to fight, even before Macduff reveals the nature of his birth, because he is moved by remorse:

> . . . my soul is too much charged
> With blood of thine already.

When he hears the trick of the "juggling fiends" he is momentarily frightened—"it hath cowed my better part of man!" but the one word "coward" again awakes the brave soldier, and he dies fighting. The man proclaimed in the beginning of the play as "Bellona's bridegroom" receives as his last appellation, "dead butcher." But Macbeth is a true tragic hero because of the powerful forces for good and evil which produce the torment in his soul.

As a postscript to consideration of this play, it is interesting to note that it has long been regarded in the theatre with superstitious dread. This is probably because it is such a frightening compound of witchcraft, darkness and blood. It is considered bad luck to quote it, or even mention it by name, in the theatre. The superstitious refer to it as "the Scottish play." There is a long record of accidents and disasters associated with it: injuries to players, fire in the theatre, death in the cast. In New York in 1849, twenty-two people lost their lives in riots between the supporters of the American, Edwin Forrest, and the Englishman, William Charles Macready; both actors were playing Macbeth at the time.

⚉ 20 ⚉   Cleopatra

"Of all perhaps of Shakespeare's plays the most wonderful is the *Antony and Cleopatra.*" Such was Coleridge's judgment. And of Shakespeare's Cleopatra Swinburne wrote, "here only once for all he has given us the perfect and the everlasting woman."

Shakespeare took the play with much more than usual fidelity from Plutarch. (Typical enrichments of the material were the character of Enobarbus, and the Messenger scene, and a significant omission is that of any mention of the children Antony had by Fulvia and Octavia.) But there is a great difference in the purposes of Plutarch and Shakespeare. Plutarch was a stern moralist. Having commented on Antony's susceptibility to flattery, he goes on to introduce the story of their love:

> Antonius being thus inclined, the last and extremest mischiefs of all other (to wit, the love of Cleopatra) lighted on him, who did waken and stir up many vices yet hidden in him, and were never seen to any. And if any spark of goodness or hope of rising were left him, Cleopatra quenched it straight, and made it worse than before.

Shakespeare's Cleopatra foresees how their story will be degraded in the theatre to become a sordid affair between a drunkard and a whore:

> . . . the quick comedians
> Extemporally will stage us and present
> Our Alexandrian revels. Antony
> Shall be brought drunken forth, and I shall see
> Some squeaking Cleopatra boy my greatness
> I' the posture of a whore.

In those lines Shakespeare foresaw the inadequacy of many future productions of his play, long after his Cleopatra had ceased to be "boyed" and was played by an actress, and he also foreshadowed much of the critical assessment of the play. Thus Bernard Shaw, who acknowledged himself to be a Puritan in his attitude towards art, wrote:

> Shakespear's *Antony and Cleopatra* must needs be as intolerable to the true Puritan as it is vaguely distressing to the ordinary healthy citizen, because, after giving a faithful picture of the soldier broken down by debauchery, and the typical wanton in whose arms such men perish, Shakespear finally strains all his huge command of rhetoric and stage pathos to give a theatrical sublimity to the wretched end of the business, and to persuade foolish spectators that the world was well lost by the twain. Such falsehood is not to be borne except by the real Cleopatras and Antonys (They are to be found in every public house) who would no doubt be glad enough to be transfigured by some poet as immortal lovers.

That facetious reference to a public house reveals the essence of the error of such a judgment of the play; as well say that every old, demanding, and unwanted father is a Lear. Whole kingdoms are at stake in this passion of Antony and Cleopatra, both of whom are power-hungry people. Caroline Spurgeon has pointed out that in no other play of Shakespeare's is the vastness of the canvas so insisted upon in the imagery; to impress upon us the scale of the action, the word "world" is used forty-two times, more than twice as often as in any other of the plays. The conflict in the lovers between their sexual passion and their passion for empire is as truly tragic as that between Macbeth's conscience and his ambition. In strong contrast to this conflict we have the single-minded drive to power of the young Octavius Caesar, he who was destined to become the first Roman Emperor, and to lend his imperial name, Augustus, to a month and an age.

At the opening of the play the Roman world has been divided between the three triumvirs, Antony, Octavius, and Lepidus; to Antony had fallen the Eastern realm, and with it the suzerainty of Egypt and its queen. He commands her to come to him to Cilicia, near the city of Adana in modern Turkey. With the object of preserving her power she sets out to dazzle Antony with herself and her setting. Plutarch gave Shakespeare this account:

> Antonius, going to make war with the Parthians, sent to command Cleopatra to appear personally before him when he came into Cilicia, to answer unto such accusations as were laid against her, being this: that she had aided Cassius and Brutus in their war against him. The messenger sent unto Cleopatra to make his summons unto her was called Dellius, who when he had thoroughly considered her beauty, the excellent grace and sweetness of her tongue, he nothing mistrusted that Antonius would do any hurt to so noble a lady, but rather assured himself that within a few days she should be in great favour with him. Thereupon he did her great honour, and persuaded her to come into Cilicia as honourably furnished as she could possible; and bade her not to be afraid at all of Antonius, for he was a more courteous lord than any she had ever seen. Cleopatra, on the other side, believing Dellius' words, and guessing by the former access and credit she had with Julius Caesar and Cnaeus Pompey (the son of Pompey the Great) only for her beauty, she began to have good hope that she might more easily win Antonius. For Caesar and Pompey knew her when she was but a young thing, and knew not then what the world meant; but now she went to Antonius at the age when woman's beauty is at the prime, and she also of best judgement.
>
> So she furnished herself with a world of gifts, store of gold and silver and of riches and other sumptuous ornaments,

as is credible enough she might bring from so great a house and from so wealthy and rich a realm as Egypt was. But yet she carried nothing with her wherein she trusted more than in herself, and in the charms and enchantment of her passing [*i.e.* surpassing] beauty and grace. Therefore when she was sent unto by divers letters, both from Antonius himself and also from his friends, she made so light of it and mocked Antonius so much that she disdained to set forward otherwise but to take her barge in the river Cydnus.

There follows the famous description of the barge which Shakespeare had but to render metrical. It is significant that the description of this first meeting of Antony and Cleopatra is made in the play by Enobarbus, who is a brilliant invention of Shakespeare's. In his soldierly devotion to Antony is reflected the former greatness of his General, and no one has more cause to bewail the effect that Cleopatra has had on Antony, and he has a wry cynicism with which to express it; yet it is Enobarbus who gives the memorable description of this astonishing woman:

Age cannot wither her, nor custom stale
Her infinite variety. Other women cloy
The appetites they feed, but she makes hungry
Where most she satisfies. For vilest things
Become themselves in her, that the holy priests
Bless her when she is riggish [*i.e.* wanton].

In the stage history of *Antony and Cleopatra*, disastrous failures far outnumber even comparative successes. So much is this the case that I feel Charles Lamb's judgment on the impossibility of an adequate staging of *King Lear* seems to be much more applicable to this play.

To begin with, there is the multiplicity and variety of scenes, forty-two in all. This division into scenes is the work of editors. In the First Folio, the only authority for the text, we read, "Actus Primus. Scena Prima," and after that there is no indication of even an act division; the text rushes headlong to "Finis." It is as though even the editors of the First Folio felt that nothing must stop the reader from a sense of the rush to disaster. Any production, and there have been many, which attempts a different scenic representation for each of the forty-two episodes is doomed. It is essential that the play be presented in some approximation to Shakespeare's own stage, which it fits admirably and excitingly, with episode following fast upon episode in rich contrast and profusion. Because of its much neater simplicity, Dryden's play on the same subject, *All for Love*, displaced Shakespeare's for about a hundred years in the seventeenth and eighteenth centuries. In fairness to Dryden's play, which he himself proclaimed is "written in imitation of Shakespeare's stile," it is eminently stageworthy and deserves to be seen; among its many theatrically effective scenes is a fictitious confrontation between Antony's wife, Fulvia, and Cleopatra. But theatrical effectiveness is the play's chief virtue; it is Watteau compared with Rembrandt. When in 1759 David Garrick tried to revive Shakespeare's play with the scholarly but dubious help of Edward Capell to simplify and cut the text and reduce the number of characters, presenting the result in splendid costumes and scenery, his production failed.

The magnificence and grandeur of the action of this play are mirrored in the language, which Shakespeare never surpassed, and actors who play it must be able to use to the full both the imperial and sensuous imagery and sounds, but, of course, with emotional truth. Edith Sitwell said of the play that it was one of the greatest miracles of sound that ever came into this world.

Even productions in this century that have avoided elaborate changes of scenery have very rarely scored a notable success, and it seems to me that the main problem is the character of Cleopatra herself. It is very difficult to make "infinite variety" a credible whole. She is both kitten and tigress, playful girl and mature woman, political schemer and imperious queen, an ambiguous enigma. Why does she commit suicide? Is it, like Juliet, that she cannot live without her lover? Is it from remorse that she has tricked him into suicide? Is it to avoid the degradation of being taken by Octavius in triumph to Rome? All these; even in her death she is motivated by the double loss of her sexual love and her empire. Any actress playing her must be in herself sexually desirable beyond resisting, and at the same time her presence must have a natural and imperial authority beyond denying; and she must be so secure in both qualities that her wily wit can afford to dispense with either when it suits her. Even at her most playful, she still radiates power; witness this description of her by Enobarbus:

> I saw her once
> Hop forty paces through the public street;
> And, having lost her breath, she spoke, and panted,
> That she did make defect perfection,
> And breathless, power breathe forth.

Most actresses who essay the part lack at least one of the qualities essential: sexual appeal, queenly dignity, a quick wit, a convincingly mercurial temperament, the ability to make full use of the richness of the poetry. How lamentably short must the boy who created the part have come! But the expectation would have been less, and the Elizabethan boy-actors were highly skilled by arduous training in the speaking of verse; some of the plays specially written for them are unbelievably difficult to speak. The boy Cleopatra would have displayed the wit, the magic of the words, and the temperament, but the sexual appeal, except to a minority of his audience, and the mature authority would have been lacking. As for the mercurial temperament of Cleopatra, she is by turns compassionate and cruel, scheming and direct, self-indulgent and self-sacrificing. Human motives are usually complex, and never did any playwright achieve a more exciting and intriguing portrait of human complexity than Shakespeare did in Cleopatra.

But now to attempt to limn the portrait as Shakespeare gradually reveals it in the play. The action begins when Antony is already irrevocably caught in his passion for Cleopatra, and we first hear about her from her worst critics, Antony's officers. For them "the triple pillar of the world" has been "transformed into a strumpet's fool." Immediately the lovers enter, and her first words show that she is playing one of the most elementary and silly games of love, and without any self-consciousness in the presence of other people: "If it be love indeed, tell me how much." That their great general goes along with the game must only confirm the listening soldiers in their previous judgment. An attendant enters to announce that messengers have arrived from Rome. Here, at once, we are shown a symbol of the conflict within Antony, for Rome means duty, represented by Octavius Caesar, and honor, represented by Antony's wife, Fulvia. He does not want to see the messengers, but Cleopatra is so sure of him that she teases him:

> Nay, hear them, Antony.
> Fulvia perchance is angry, or who knows
> If the scarce-bearded Caesar have not sent
> His powerful mandate to you, "Do this, or this.
> Take in that kingdom, and enfranchise that.
> Perform't, or else we damn thee."

Antony protests feebly against her teasing, but she persists. He blushes in embarrassment and finally makes the protestation for which she has been angling, and seals it with a warm embrace:

> Let Rome in Tiber melt, and the wide arch
> Of the ranged empire fall! Here is my space.
> Kingdoms are clay. Our dungy earth alike
> Feeds beast as man. The nobleness of life
> Is to do thus, when such a mutual pair
> And such a twain can do't, in which I bind,
> On pain of punishment, the world to weet [*i.e.* know]
> We stand up peerless.

There is a bravado in this utterance, obviously aimed at his disapproving fellow-soldiers. Still Cleopatra urges that Antony see the messengers, and still he refuses, in an instinctively sharp outburst which immediately softens to an eloquent caress:

> Fie, wrangling Queen!
> Whom everything becomes—to chide, to laugh,

> To weep; whose every passion fully strives
> To make itself in thee fair and admired!

In her next appearance, Cleopatra is the petulant and unpredictable mistress, but this covers a deep disquiet for "a Roman thought" has suddenly sobered Antony. She sends Enobarbus to fetch him, but the very next moment, as she sees him approach, she hurries away with "We will not look upon him." She has sensed what is at hand: bad news from Rome, which demands the return of Antony. What she cannot sense is the surprising news that Fulvia is dead. In a scene with Enobarbus, who teases him with "light answers" about the impossibility of leaving Cleopatra, Antony decides on a "quick remove from hence."

In the meantime Cleopatra is determining her strategy in dealing with the crisis which she feels is at hand, and it is the exact opposite of the obvious way of dealing with a man, which is expressed by one of her handmaidens, Charmian. Cleopatra dispatches an attendant to find Antony:

> See where he is, who's with him, what he does.
> I did not send you. If you find him sad,
> Say I am dancing; if in mirth, report
> That I am sudden sick. Quick, and return.

Charmian feels this is the way to lose a man.

CHARMIAN: Madam, methinks if you did love him dearly,
You do not hold the method to enforce
The like from him.
CLEOPATRA: What should I do, I do not?
CHARMIAN: In each thing give him way, cross him in nothing.
CLEOPATRA: Thou teachest like a fool the way to lose him.

As Antony approaches, Cleopatra reads his decision in his face and her instinct prompts her to play sick. He knows it is but a ploy, and, when he asks her "What's the matter?" her jealous possessiveness comes out frankly, but with a sad irony, since she is unaware of the death of Fulvia:

> I know, by that same eye, there's some good news.
> What says the married woman? You may go.
> Would she had never given you leave to come!
> Let her not say 'tis I that keep you here.
> I have no power upon you; hers you are.

Antony tries to interpose—he is in no mood to be harsh with her, since their parting is imminent—but she sweeps on, voicing the eternal dilemma of the mistress:

> Why should I think you can be mine and true,
> Though you in swearing shake the thronèd gods,
> Who have been false to Fulvia? . . .

Shakespeare brilliantly builds this passage for Cleopatra to words of immortal eloquence, but now his lyrical gift is so much at the command of the dramatist that she ends with a caustic taunt:

> Nay, pray you seek no colour for your going,
> But bid farewell and go. When you sued staying,
> Then was the time for words. No going then.
> Eternity was in our lips and eyes,
> Bliss in our brows' bent; none our parts so poor
> But was a race of Heaven. They are so still,
> Or thou, the greatest soldier of the world,
> Art turned the greatest liar.

Antony finally tells her the news from Rome, leaving the news of Fulvia's death to the last. Cleopatra is momentarily stunned by this, and deliberately refrains from "childishness" in her comment. All she says is, "Can Fulvia die?" An actress can choose among many colours to paint those words. My choice for her would be: what was desirable when it seemed impossible has a bitter sadness in it when it comes to pass. But in a moment Cleopatra is back to taunting Antony, now for his apparent lack of feeling for Fulvia:

> . . . Now I see, I see,
> In Fulvia's death, how mine received shall be.

Antony tries to shift the burden of decision to her, but she avoids it by her continued taunting until Antony, in spite of his deliberate forbearance, is forced to say, "You'll heat my blood. No more." Still she persists until the tormented Antony turns to leave, when her mood changes suddenly to anguished but inexpressible pleading:

> Courteous lord, one word.
> Sir, you and I must part, but that's not it.
> Sir, you and I have loved, but there's not it;
> That you know well. Something it is I would—
> O, my oblivion is a very Antony,
> And I am all forgotten.

The end of the scene is inevitable; Antony must go, and he must go with her blessing:

> . . . Your honour calls you hence;
> Therefore be deaf to my unpitied folly,
> And all the gods go with you! . . .

In the first of the three scenes in which we see Cleopatra without her Antony, her thoughts and words are all of him. Every day she sends a messenger on the long journey to him. In return, Alexas brings her a pearl and the promise of kingdoms from him. When she was in her railing mood with him, everything he did or said was deliberately misconstrued; but now, everything she hears of the "demi-Atlas of this earth" is interpreted to his praise. Thus, when she hears that he was neither sad nor merry, she says:

> He was not sad, for he would shine on those
> That make their looks by his; he was not merry,
> Which seemed to tell them his remembrance lay
> In Egypt with his joy: but between both.
> O, heavenly mingle! Be'st thou sad or merry,
> The violence of either thee becomes
> So does it no man else. . . .

When Charmian reminds her of the extravagant praise she heaped upon Julius Caesar during her affair with him, she rounds upon her handmaiden with

> By Isis, I will give thee bloody teeth
> If thou with Caesar paragon again
> My man of men;

and she excuses what she said of Caesar with

> My salad days,
> When I was green in judgement, cold in blood.

We should not forget that she had had a child by Julius Caesar. One of the supporters of Octavius Caesar reminds Enobarbus of this very coarsely:

> She made great Caesar lay his sword to bed.
> He ploughed her, and she cropped.

She is certain of her Antony, but there is another aspect of her maturity that, "delicious poison," though it is, she cannot refrain from mentioning:

> . . . Think on me,
> That am with Phoebus' amorous pinches black
> And wrinkled deep in time?

This maturity of Cleopatra is frequently noted in the play. Thus, in the next scene, Pompey speaks of her "waned lip."

In her next scene during the absence of Antony, we find her almost echoing the words and changing moods of Orsino, that connoisseur of love bereft. To while away the hours she asks for music, changes her mind to billiards, and then to fishing; this last reminds her of the time when she had a diver hang a salt fish on Antony's hook. But the remembrance of happy times with Antony is cut short by the entrance of a messenger, whose scared looks betoken bad news. She immediately jumps to the worst conclusion: Antony is dead.

> . . . If thou say so, villain,
> Thou kill'st thy mistress. But well and free,
> If thou so yield him, there is gold, and here
> My bluest veins to kiss; a hand that kings
> Have lipped, and trembled kissing.

The messenger assures her that Antony is well and has made
friends with Caesar, but delays as long as he can news of the act
that has sealed that bond of friendship: Antony has married Octavia, the sister of Octavius Caesar. The messenger's fear was well
justified, for Cleopatra takes out her fury at the news upon him;
she beats him to the ground and drags him along by his hair; finally she draws a knife upon him, at which he manages to escape
by running out. (All these actions are indicated in the unusually
full stage directions in the First Folio text of the play; in other
plays, most of the stage directions are the work of later editors.)
In spite of her imperial fury, Cleopatra is still able, in a moment
of calm, to see herself objectively:

> These hands do lack nobility, that they strike
> A meaner than myself, since I myself
> Have given myself the cause.

The messenger is persuaded to return on the promise that he will
not be hurt, but, when he is forced to repeat the news of Antony's marriage, Cleopatra can scarce forbear striking him, but
she manages to dismiss him without doing so.

After the messenger has left, Cleopatra is torn by the abiding
conflict within her: imperial power and sexual passion. Her first
thought is of her power. She assumes that Antony's marriage to
the sister of Octavius Caesar is an indication that Caesar is in the
ascendant; she has caught the wrong man:

> In praising Antony, I have dispraised Caesar.
> .   .   .   .
>   I am paid for't now.

But now the love for Antony overwhelms her; she is all natural
woman, and wants to know all about Octavia:

> Go to the fellow, good Alexas. Bid him
> Report the feature of Octavia, her years,
> Her inclination [*i.e.* her likes and dislikes]; let him not leave
>   out
> The colour of her hair.

She wishes she could forget Antony, but she cannot:

> Let him forever go—let him not—Charmian,
> Though he be painted one way like a Gorgon,
> The other way's a Mars. Bid you Alexas
> Bring me word how tall she is. Pity me, Charmian,
> But do not speak to me. . . .

Shakespeare suspends the scene at this point, and, before it is resumed, ranges over the Mediterranean world—to Misenum, on the Bay of Naples, to Syria, to Rome. First the triumvirs had made peace with Pompey, and then Antony's peace with Octavius Caesar had seemed to be cemented by the marriage with Octavia, but cynical Enobarbus, in a conversation with Menas, an adherent of Pompey, foresees that the marriage will ultimately have the opposite effect from that for which it was designed.

> ENOBARBUS: . . . you shall find the band that seems to tie their friendship together will be the very strangler of their amity. Octavia is of a very holy, cold, and still conversation.
> MENAS: Who would not have his wife so?
> ENOBARBUS: Not he that himself is not so, which is Mark Antony. He will to his Egyptian dish again. Then shall the sighs of Octavia blow the fire up in Caesar, and, as I said before, that which is the strength of their amity shall prove the immediate author of their variance.

When Cleopatra resumes her questioning of the frightened messenger, we have a light comedy scene, in which the messenger describes Octavia in a way to please Cleopatra, who decides that Antony "cannot like her long." Now the messenger receives gold and compliments:

> He's very knowing;
> I do perceive't. There's nothing in her yet.
> The fellow has good judgement.

The scene concludes with Cleopatra's assertion:

. . . All may be well enough.

Antony leaves with Octavia for Athens, and Octavius Caesar takes advantage of his absence to belittle him and arrogate to himself the power of the third triumvir, Lepidus. Poor Octavia, torn between her duty to her brother and her husband, leaves for Rome on a forlorn mission of peace-making, but, by the time she arrives after traveling in so humble a style as to give her brother a further excuse for anger against Antony, she discovers that, as soon as she had left Athens, Antony had returned to Cleopatra, who had "nodded him to her." In Egypt, we are told, Antony and Cleopatra have set up a joint Empire of the East, and called upon the tributary kings to join them in a war against Octavius Caesar. Maecenas sums up the situation for Caesar's sister thus:

Each heart in Rome does love and pity you;
Only the adulterous Antony, most large
In his abominations, turns you off,
And gives his potent regiment to a trull,
That noises it against us.

Shakespeare now feels the need to compress events in this long play and he omits any scene of the reunion of Antony and Cleopatra in Egypt—much to our regret, and, I suspect, to his. When we next see them, they are together in Greece, at Actium, on the Ionian Sea, preparing for the inevitable battle with Octavius Caesar. This time Cleopatra will not let her Antony out of her sight, in spite of Enobarbus's criticism that her presence will

Take from his heart, take from his brain, from's time
What should not then be spared. . . .

Cleopatra hotly defends her presence on political grounds:

. . . A charge we bear i' the war,
And as the president of my kingdom will
Appear there for a man. . . .

Octavius Caesar crosses the Ionian Sea with surprising speed, and at the head of a large and experienced battle fleet. Antony's strength and skill are on land, but his common sense seems to desert him. He challenges Caesar to single combat, and, when that is refused, challenges him to battle on the famous field of Pharsalia. Naturally, Caesar refuses this also, and, in his turn, challenges Antony to do battle by sea. Antony, spurred on by Cleopatra, who says, "I have sixty sails; Caesar none better," and in spite of warning from Enobarbus, foolishly accepts the challenge. Even an ordinary soldier begs Antony to think again:

> O noble Emperor, do not fight by sea;
> Trust not to rotten planks. Do you misdoubt
> This sword and these my wounds? Let the Egyptians
> And the Phoenicians go a-ducking. We
> Have used to conquer standing on the earth
> And fighting foot to foot.

Antony's lieutenant-general, Canidius, sums up the situation:

> . . . So our leader's led,
> And we are women's men.

The result is inevitable, especially since Cleopatra herself sails into battle, at the first clash of which she turns tail, and her whole fleet with her; to his shame, Antony follows her, not in fear of defeat but, as he sadly tells her later,

> Egypt, thou knew'st too well
> My heart was to thy rudder tied by the strings,
> And thou shouldst tow me after. O'er my spirit
> Thy full supremacy thou knew'st, and that
> Thy beck might from the bidding of the gods
> Command me.

As one of his followers puts it, he has indeed "kissed away kingdoms and provinces."

Depressed by the debacle which he has watched from the land, Canidius decides to yield his legions to Caesar; six of the tributary kings have already beaten him to that action. For his part, Antony tries to make some atonement to his immediate followers by giving them his gold and bidding them leave him and make their peace with Caesar; it says much for Antony that they refuse to leave him.

Antony chides Cleopatra, especially that he is forced to treat on humble terms with Caesar, whom as a soldier he holds in contempt:

> Now I must
> To the young man send humble treaties, dodge
> And palter in the shifts of lowness, who
> With half the bulk o' the world played as I pleased,
> Making and marring fortunes.

But her genuine tears melt him at once:

> Fall not a tear, I say. One of them rates
> All that is won and lost. Give me a kiss;
> Even this repays me. . . .

Caesar's terms are harsh: for Cleopatra fair promises, but for Antony nothing:

> . . . The Queen
> Of audience nor desire shall fail, so she
> From Egypt drive her all-disgraced friend,
> Or take his life there. . . .

Antony's reaction is foolish: another angry challenge to single combat. As Enobarbus comments:

> . . . That he should dream,
> Knowing all measures, the full Caesar will
> Answer his emptiness! Caesar, thou hast subdued
> His judgement too.

Caesar sends a cunningly eloquent special ambassador to Cleopatra. He suggests that Caesar does not hold Cleopatra guilty for her affair with Antony:

> He knows that you embrace not Antony
> As you did love, but as you feared him.

．　　．　　．　　．　　．　　．　　．　　．　　．　　．

> The scars upon your honour therefore he
> Does pity as constrained blemishes,
> Not as deserved.

Cleopatra, knowing that Caesar is now the new power she will have to placate in order to retain her own, cannily goes along with the suggestion:

> He is a god and knows
> What is most right. Mine honour was not yielded,
> But conquered merely.
> .   .   .   .   .   .
> Most kind messenger,
> Say to great Caesar this: in deputation
> I kiss his conquering hand. Tell him I am prompt
> To lay my crown at's feet, and there to kneel.
> Tell him from his all-obeying breath I hear
> The doom of Egypt.

Antony enters to find Caesar's ambassador kissing the hand of Cleopatra. His fury is boundless. He has the ambassador whipped, and himself whips Cleopatra with words:

> I found you as a morsel cold upon
> Dead Caesar's trencher; nay, you were a fragment
> Of Cneius Pompey's, besides what hotter hours,
> Unregistered in vulgar fame, you have
> Luxuriously picked out; for I am sure,
> Though you can guess what temperance should be,
> You know not what it is.

Cleopatra patiently awaits the subsidence of his fury, and then easily assures him of her undying love. Immediately he takes heart again and prepares to lead what is left of his army in a last desperate fight against Caesar. There's desperation in his passion too:

> . . . I'll set my teeth
> And send to darkness all that stop me. Come,
> Let's have one other gaudy night. Call to me
> All my sad captains; fill our bowls once more.
> Let's mock the midnight bell.

> . . . .
> ... Come on, my Queen,
> There's sap in't yet. The next time I do fight,
> I'll make Death love me, for I will contend
> Even with his pestilent scythe.

But Enobarbus senses the doom in the desperation:

> Now he'll outstare the lightning. To be furious
> Is to be frighted out of fear, and in that mood
> The dove will peck the estridge [*i.e.* goshawk]. And I
>   see still
> A diminution in our Captain's brain
> Restores his heart. When valour preys on reason,
> It eats the sword it fights with. I will seek
> Some way to leave him.

When faithful Enobarbus decides to leave Antony, it is a sign that all is lost. Antony himself has a sense of foreboding, for he says to the servants:

> Tend me tonight.
> Maybe it is the period of your duty.
> Haply you shall not see me more; or if,
> A mangled shadow. Perchance tomorrow
> You'll serve another master. . . .

But when he sees they are moved to tears, he changes his tune:

> ... Know, my hearts,
> I hope well of tomorrow, and will lead you
> Where rather I'll expect victorious life
> Than death and honour. . . .

Throughout this scene of preparation for the "gaudy night" Cleopatra says not one word to Antony. She and Enobarbus observe him. Both sense the approaching disaster. Enobarbus has already decided to avoid it. Cleopatra, too, must be torn between thoughts of Antony and Caesar. Both his beloved and his friend will fail Antony in his hour of need, and both will die of grief.

After his night with Cleopatra, Antony seems full of confidence for the fight, but, after he has left her with a brusque farewell, "like a man of steel," she voices her foreboding to Charmian:

> He goes forth gallantly. That he and Caesar might
> Determine this great war in single fight!
> Then Antony—but now—Well, on.

But in the first clash of arms, Antony is the victor and Cleopatra greets him as "Lord of lords!" On the next day Antony is again inveigled into a sea battle, and this time the Egyptian fleet surrenders to Caesar. As Antony watches from the shore, his fury turns against Cleopatra, and this time without due cause, for there is no indication even in Plutarch that she had arranged the surrender. She even comes to him in the hour of defeat, which she would scarcely have done had she been guilty, but she is received with the vituperative lash of Antony's tongue. She attempts no answer, but leaves, and this further incenses Antony to the point of deciding to kill her:

> . . . The witch shall die.
> To the young Roman boy she hath sold me, and I fall
> Under this plot. She dies for't. . . .

Cleopatra, now feeling that Antony's madness is beyond her power to assuage, takes Charmian's advice to lock herself in the "monument," an elaborate tomb that she had had built, and to send Antony a message that she was dead. Cleopatra adds color to Charmian's idea:

> Mardian, go tell him I have slain myself,
> Say that the last I spoke was "Antony,"
> And word it, prithee, piteously. . . .

Mardian comes upon Antony still determined that "She hath betrayed me, and shall die the death." In such a mood, the news of Cleopatra's death overwhelms him with remorse; further life is meaningless, and death will be welcome:

I will o'ertake thee, Cleopatra, and
Weep for my pardon. . . .

. . . .

. . . I come, my Queen. . . . Stay for me.
Where souls do couch on flowers, we'll hand in hand,
And with our sprightly port make the ghosts gaze.

Antony botches his own attempt to kill himself. Cleopatra, having sensed the effect her false news might have upon him, sends Diomedes to prevent it, but he arrives to find Antony grievously wounded:

. . . She had a prophesying fear
Of what hath come to pass; for when she saw—
Which never shall be found—you did suspect
She had disposed [*i.e.* come to terms] with Caesar, and that
   your rage
Would not be purged, she sent you word she was dead;
But fearing since how it might work, hath sent
Me to proclaim the truth, and I am come,
I dread, too late.

The dying Antony is carried to the foot of the monument. He calls for "Of many thousand kisses the poor last," but she is fearful of descending from the monument lest she be captured by Caesar and made a spectacular part of his triumphant return to Rome. In one of his fits of anger, Antony had savagely etched this picture of her:

. . . Let him take thee,
And hoist thee up to the shouting plebeians!
Follow his chariot, like the greatest spot
Of all thy sex; most monster-like, be shown
For poor'st diminutives, for dolts; and let
Patient Octavia plough thy visage up
With her prepared nails.

It is this speech she remembers as she tells Antony, who lies dying at the foot of the monument, why she dare not descend to him:

> I dare not, dear;
> Dear my lord, pardon; I dare not
> Lest I be taken. Not the imperious show
> Of the full-fortuned Caesar ever shall
> Be brooched with me. If knife, drugs, serpents, have
> Edge, sting, or operation, I am safe.
> Your wife Octavia, with her modest eyes
> And still conclusion [*i.e.* unspoken judgment], shall acquire
>   no honour
> Demuring upon me. . . .

Cleopatra cannot suffer to be separated from the dying Antony, and she and her handmaidens contrive to hoist the litter on which he lies up to their place in the monument. Antony begs her to make her peace with Caesar, but she assures him that she will not do so, but will take her own life. Her resolution in this never falters.

As Antony dies, Cleopatra's lamentation bears testimony to the greatness of the man rather than to the loss of the lover:

> The crown o' the earth doth melt. My lord!
> Oh, withered is the garland of the war;
> The soldier's pole is fall'n. Young boys and girls
> Are level now with men. The odds is gone,
> And there is nothing left remarkable
> Beneath the visiting moon.

Much though this sounds like a superb funeral oration, that she feels her loss as a woman is clearly shown by the fact that at the end of it she faints, and for a moment her attendants fear that she has already joined Antony in death; when she recovers, she tells them that this is indeed what she is determined to do:

> We'll bury him, and then, what's brave, what's noble,
> Let's do it after the high Roman fashion,
> And make Death proud to take us. . . .

Caesar is determined that the captured Cleopatra shall grace his triumph in Rome, but also foresees that fear of this may prompt her to suicide. He sends ambassadors to deal gently with her and assure her of his good intentions:

> . . . Go and say
> We purpose her no shame. Give her what comforts
> The quality of her passion shall require,
> Lest in her greatness by some mortal stroke
> She do defeat us, for her life in Rome
> Would be eternal in our triumph [*i.e.* the sight of her alive
>   in his triumphal procession in Rome would be a deathless
>   memory]. . . .

In her new scale of values, Cleopatra finds " 'Tis paltry to be Caesar;" her lust for imperial power has been completely replaced by her love for Antony. While she treats with the ambassadors some soldiers gain access to the monument and capture her. She tries to stab herself but is prevented. In her frustration, she angrily declares her determination to die:

> Sir, I will eat no meat; I'll not drink, sir;
> If idle talk will once be necessary,
> I'll not sleep neither; this mortal house I'll ruin,
> Do Caesar what he can. Know, sir, that I
> Will not wait pinioned at your master's court;
> Nor once be chastised with the sober eye
> Of dull Octavia. Shall they hoist me up
> And show me to the shouting varletry
> Of censuring Rome? Rather a ditch in Egypt
> Be gentle grave unto me! Rather on Nilus' mud
> Lay me stark nak'd, and let the water-flies
> Blow me into abhorring! Rather make
> My country's high pyramides my gibbet,
> And hang me up in chains!

Just before Octavius Caesar himself comes to meet with Cleopatra, she receives confirmation that, however smooth and conciliatory his words, he means to take her in triumph to Rome. She determines that her best course is to outdo his civilities and lull his suspicions. She kneels to him and confesses:

> . . . I have
> Been laden with like frailties which before
> Have often shamed our sex.

Caesar makes it clear that he is aware of the possibility of her suicide, and gives her an explicit warning, in the midst of fair promises:

> If you apply yourself to our intents,
> Which towards you are most gentle, you shall find
> A benefit in this change; but if you seek
> To lay on me a cruelty, by taking
> Antony's course, you shall bereave yourself
> Of my good purposes, and put your children
> To that destruction which I'll guard them from
> If thereon you rely. . . .

A delightful flash of the old Cleopatra now occurs. She presents Caesar with an inventory of all her valuables and calls upon her treasurer, Seleucus, to attest to its truth. He, to gain favor with Caesar, reveals that she has kept back "Enough to purchase what you have made known." Caesar, to cover her embarrassment, says that she acted wisely. She shows her old fury to Seleucus:

> Th' ingratitude of this Seleucus does
> Even make me wild. O slave, of no more trust
> Than love that's hired! What, goest thou back? Thou shalt
> Go back, I warrant thee; but I'll catch thine eyes
> Though they had wings. Slave, soulless villain, dog!
> O rarely base!

To Caesar she says that all she has reserved are some "lady trifles . . . immoment toys," and caps this with the astonishing invention that she has kept back some precious jewels to win the goodwill of Caesar's wife and Antony's widow! This is the "serpent of old Nile" in all her captivating beguilement. Caesar responds with apparent generosity:

> . . . Still be't yours;
> Bestow it at your pleasure; and believe

Caesar's no merchant, to make prize with you
Of things that merchants sold. Therefore be cheered.
Make not your thoughts your prisons; no, dear Queen;
For we intend so to dispose you as
Yourself shall give us counsel. Feed, and sleep.
Our care and pity is so much upon you
That we remain your friend. . . .

But Cleopatra is not deceived. As soon as he is gone, she says:

He words me, girls, he words me, that I should not
Be noble to myself. . . .

She has already made arrangements for her death, and her hand-maidens do not try to dissuade her. Iras says:

Finish, good lady; the bright day is done,
And we are for the dark.

As if to confirm Cleopatra's resolution, one of Caesar's officers confides to her Caesar's real intention, to send her and her children to Rome.

It is a brilliantly surprising and oddly touching stroke of Shakespeare to make the man who brings Cleopatra the poisonous snakes, hidden in a basket of figs, a part to be played by a clown; he is a garrulous, oafish, and delightful peasant, who seems to have no fear of Cleopatra, nor indeed very much respect. He merely treats her as a customer who is buying some dangerous goods, and the extraordinary thing is that she is now content to be so treated; she has finished with the niceties of royal ceremony. But she wishes to meet Death clad in all her royal robes and regalia. Even at the last, when she holds the snake to her breast, her wit does not desert her:

. . . Poor venomous fool,
Be angry, and dispatch. Oh, could'st thou speak,
That I might hear thee call great Caesar ass
Unpolicied [i.e. outmaneuvered].

Both Charmian and Iras choose to die with their queen. As

she looks at the dead Cleopatra, Charmian delivers a fitting eulogy:

> Now boast thee, Death, in thy possession lies
> A lass unparalleled. Downy windows, close;
> And golden Phoebus never be beheld
> Of eyes again so royal. . . .

There we have it: "a lass unparalleled" and, at the same time, "so royal." It has been suggested that the Cleopatra who held Shakespeare's Antony in thrall might have been inspired by his own "dark lady." It may be so, but it is more certain that the imperious queen in Cleopatra was inspired by the enshrined memory of Queen Elizabeth. Among the many wonderful portraits of women that Shakespeare painted, that of Cleopatra is unique in its richness and fascinating complexity; she is a peerless achievement.

⚜ 21 ⚜ Coriolanus

T H E R E I S N O certain proof of the year in which *Coriolanus* was written, but from internal evidence it is generally assumed to have been the last of Shakespeare's tragedies, and to have followed closely upon *Antony and Cleopatra*. Both plays were derived faithfully from Sir Thomas North's translation of Plutarch. (North, incidentally, had taken it not from the original Greek, but from a French translation.) But there is an almost bewildering difference in these last two Roman plays of Shakespeare. In the first, Shakespeare's lyrical powers are at their height; in the second, lyrical passion has been largely replaced by political and military rhetoric. In the first, we feel an intimate involvement of the author in his characters; in the second, there seems to be an unusual detachment. It is this latter quality which results in the main problem of the play. We find it difficult to identify with Coriolanus, as it seems that Shakespeare also did. We find him in many ways admirable, but he is rarely warm and likable.

Coriolanus is the most political of all Shakespeare's plays. Much of it is taken up with the struggle between the patricians and the plebs, between the haves and the have-nots. So much is this the case that Hazlitt wrote:

> *Coriolanus* is a store-house of political commonplaces. Anyone who studies it may save himself the trouble of reading Burke's *Reflections*, or Paine's *Rights of Man*, or the Debates in both Houses of Parliament since the French Revolution or our own. The argument for or against aristocracy or democracy, on the privileges of the few and the claims of the many, on liberty and slavery, power and the abuse of it, peace and war, are here very ably handled, with the spirit of a poet and the acuteness of a philosopher.

In direct opposition to this view, there are those who see the political struggle as a mere background for a study of a potentially great man warped and ruined from childhood by a dominating mother. (Frank Harris, with characteristic perversity, finds the mother-son relationship in *Coriolanus* "steeped in tenderness," and asserts that it was the expression of Shakespeare's own great love for his mother.)

I believe that both these extreme views of the play are wrongheaded. In keeping with my thesis that Shakespeare is more interested in men than ideas, *Coriolanus* is a portrait of a man of great stature who is brought low by an inflexible pride, but his main antagonist is the common people of Rome, and so they bulk large in the play, as Iago does in *Othello*, or Claudius in *Hamlet*.

The play has often been cited as proof that Shakespeare despised the common people, but we must beware of assuming the patrician view in the play to be that of Shakespeare. He is at pains to show dissenting views among the people; they try their best to argue out the truth. It is a sad fact, even more now than in Shakespeare's day, that the public is easily manipulated by persuasive politicians and molders of opinion. It seems to me that the hungry have-nots in *Coriolanus* contain admirably objective voices.

Coriolanus is the epitome of the sin of pride, a most unlikable quality, and yet we have to yield him a perhaps reluctant admiration for his unique honesty, consistency, and refusal to compromise. He is very much alone in the play. Shakespeare emphasizes this by taking away the few faithful followers that Plutarch gave him on two climactic occasions: the entrapment within the walls of Corioli, and the banishment from Rome. Even his mother, Volumnia, tries to soften his attitude to the people so that he may become Consul; he tries to follow her persuasion, but fails.

As a courageous soldier, Coriolanus is matchless, and he had a withering contempt for cowardice. Compare Henry V's exhortation to his faltering troops outside Harfleur with that of Coriolanus outside Corioli. To Henry, his men were "dear friends," "noblest English," but here is the exhortation of Coriolanus:

> All the contagion of the south light on you,
> You shames of Rome! You herd of—Boils and plagues
> Plaster you o'er, that you may be abhorred
> Farther than seen, and one infect another
> Against the wind a mile! You souls of geese,
> That bear the shapes of men, how have you run
> From slaves that apes would beat! Pluto and hell!
> All hurt behind, backs red, and faces pale
> With flight and agued fear! Mend, and charge home,
> Or, by the fires of heaven, I'll leave the foe,
> And make my wars on you. . . .

In fairness to Coriolanus, it must be pointed out that he was capable of inspiring men to follow him too, but not in the heat of battle, when he expected every man's defiance of death to equal his own. In appealing for volunteers, albeit from a different body of men, here are the words which caused every man to shout to join him:

> . . . If any such be here—
> As it were sin to doubt—that love this painting
> Wherein you see me smeared; if any fear
> Lesser his person than an ill report;

> If any think brave death outweighs bad life
> And that his country's dearer than himself;
> Let him alone, or so many so minded,
> Wave thus to express his disposition,
> And follow Marcius.

He had it in him to be a great popular hero, with a natural charm to captivate multitudes, for when he had joined forces with the Volsces, his country's enemies, he soon won their hearts from their previous leader and his inveterate antagonist, Tullus Aufidius. As Aufidius's followers report to him:

> Your native town you entered like a post,
> And had no welcome home; but he returns
> Splitting the air with noise. . . .
>   And patient fools,
> Whose children he hath slain, their base throats tear
> With giving him glory.

It must be borne in mind that all the patricians in the play share his contemptuous and hostile attitude towards the common people, but only he is honest and tactless enough to declare it to them. The others, as particularly expressed in the person of Menenius, flatter them to their faces and revile them behind their backs. Even Volumnia counsels a double-face.

The construction of *Coriolanus* is masterly. It is a play of action that never falters. Incident follows incident in logical and exciting sequence. There is not a single soliloquy in the play, and so no soul-searching or probing of motives. It is a play of action about a man of action. It must be seen to be fully appreciated, for many of its most potent effects are visual.

The seeds of the story are skillfully planted in the three opening scenes. In the first, we meet Coriolanus's enemy, the people; in the second, his antagonist in arms, Tullus Aufidius; in the third, Volumnia, the mother who has made him what he is. His first enemy drives him into the arms of his second enemy, and his mother, in her final assertion of her dominion over him, brings about his destruction.

At the outset of the play, the demagogic First Citizen clearly states the problem in stirring up the hungry people to mutiny:

> First, you know Caius Marcius is chief enemy to the people. . . . Let us kill him, and we'll have corn at our own price. [NOTE: Caius Marcius did not receive the name, "Coriolanus," until after his capture of Corioli.]

This First Citizen makes a good case for their rebellion:

> We are accounted poor citizens, the patricians good. What authority surfeits on would relieve us. If they would yield us but the superfluity while it were wholesome, we might guess they relieved us humanely; but they think we are too dear . . . our sufferance is a gain to them. Let us revenge this with our pikes, ere we become rakes; for the gods know I speak this in hunger for bread, not in thirst for revenge.

Coriolanus, famous for his open scorn for the "many-headed multitude," becomes the focus of their hostility against the patricians. Yet, even so, the Second Citizen speaks up on his behalf: "Consider you what services he has done for his country?" But the First Citizen has an answer for this, and a very shrewd one:

> Though soft-conscienced men can be content to say it was for his country, he did it to please his mother and to be partly proud; which he is, even to the altitude of his virtue [*i.e.* he is as proud as he is courageous].

This is very perceptive, and does something to prepare us for the time when the fierce pride of Coriolanus will turn him against his country. The liberal-minded Second Citizen counters this well: "What he cannot help in his nature, you account a vice in him. You must in no way say he is covetous." And that is true too; Coriolanus never uses his military success for personal aggrandizement. He never even wants his deeds and wounds referred to, though some critics find this a sign of an inverted pride. He glories in feats of derring-do for their own sake. He fights as boys wrestle, for the excitement of defeating an opponent. There is an immaturity in Coriolanus, for which his upbringing is responsible.

The final searing taunt that Tullus Aufidius will fling at him is "Boy!" It will strike a guilty chord in Coriolanus and make him as furious as the epithet, "Traitor," hurled at him in Rome by a tribune of the people, the latter an undeserved epithet which, in his anger, he sets about to earn. Both enemies know how to arouse his fury so that his unbridled tongue will destroy him.

If only Coriolanus could have learned the lesson of his smooth-tongued and delightful old mentor, Menenius Agrippa! But then he would have been a skillfully wily and successful politician, and not a tragic hero. Both the vocal citizens are agreed about Menenius, though the First grudgingly:

> SECOND CITIZEN: Worthy Menenius Agrippa, one that hath always loved the people.
> FIRST CITIZEN: He's one honest enough; would all the rest were so!

When Menenius tries to quell the disturbance by telling the people that the patricians really care for them, First Citizen is blunt:

> Care for us! True indeed! They ne'er cared for us yet: suffer us to famish, and their storehouses crammed with grain; make edicts for usury, to support usurers; repeal daily any wholesome act established against the rich, and provide more piercing statutes daily, to chain up and restrain the poor. If the wars eat us not up, they will; and there's all the love they bear us.

Any success Menenius might have had with the would-be mutineers is foiled by the appearance of Coriolanus who lashes them with his tongue. They shrink from the force of his contempt, though the First Citizen at least has the temerity for the sarcastic comment: "We have ever your good word." Typical of Coriolanus's tongue-lashing is:

> . . . What would you have, you curs,
> That like not peace nor war? The one affrights you,
> The other makes you proud. He that trusts to you,
> Where he should find you lions, finds you hares,
> Where foxes, geese. . . .

With an unconscious prescience, he says:

> With every minute you do change a mind,
> And call him noble that was now your hate,
> Him vile that was your garland. . . .

Coriolanus was to suffer both changes and from both sides, the Romans and the Volsces.

There is a particular reason for the anger of Coriolanus when he first enters the play. He has just come from an uprising of the people in another part of the city, where they have been appeased by being granted the election of five tribunes of their own choice. This, to him, is an unforgivable weakness on the part of the patricians; he fears that this is the wedge which will split the city:

> The rabble should have first unroofed the city
> Ere so prevailed with me. It will in time
> Win upon power and throw forth greater themes
> For insurrection's arguing.

Coriolanus is the unequivocal military authoritarian; as the soldier must trust and obey his general, so must the citizen those born to power. He has no sympathy even with their hunger for bread:

> . . . They say there's grain enough!
> Would the nobility lay aside their ruth,
> And let me use my sword, I'd make a quarry
> With thousands of these quartered slaves, as high
> As I could pick my lance.

So our first view of Coriolanus is of his most objectionable and even revolting quality. It will be hard to gain enough sympathy for him to make us interested in his story, but this is just what Shakespeare sets about to do. There comes the news, foretold by Coriolanus, that the Volsces are in arms. Now the whole city will need his services, but his motive is not a lofty desire to save his city; it is a personal drive to meet in combat a worthy opponent, the leader of the Volscian army, Tullus Aufidius:

> . . . He is a lion
> That I am proud to hunt.

Coriolanus cannot resist a final gibe at the people:

> The Volsces have much corn; take these rats thither
> To gnaw their garners. . . .

As the citizens "steal away," he calls after them:

> . . . Worshipful mutiners,
> Your valour puts well forth. . . .

Coriolanus's motive in the coming war is simple and uncomplicated; he is happiest in battle against a foe he respects. He quite genuinely does not seek, like Julius Caesar, the political power that can accrue to a successful general. But this the newly-elected tribunes cannot believe. Their misreading of him tends to arouse us to his defense. They even find a base motive for his willingness to serve as second-in-command to Cominius:

> . . . for what miscarries
> Shall be the general's fault, though he perform
> To the utmost of a man; and giddy censure
> Will then cry out of Marcius: "Oh, if he
> Had borne the business!"

When we see Tullus Aufidius in session with the senators of Corioli, we find him indeed to be a worthy opponent, but more mature in his judgment and motivation than Coriolanus. Yet he acknowledges the personal rivalry:

> If we and Caius Marcius chance to meet,
> 'Tis sworn between us we shall ever strike
> Till one can do no more.

In the first scene between Volumnia and Virgilia, the proud Roman mother and the loving and fearful wife of Coriolanus, we are told at once the source of his soldierly ambitions. Volumnia reproves Virgilia about her concern for her husband's safety in the war:

> If my son were my husband, I should freelier rejoice in that
> absence wherein he won honour than in the embracements

of his bed where he would show most love. When yet he was but tender-bodied, and the only son of my womb, . . . I was pleased to let him seek danger where he was like to find fame. To a cruel war I sent him; from whence he returned, his brows bound with oak. I tell thee, daughter, I sprang not more in joy at first hearing he was a man-child than now in first seeing he had proved himself a man. . . . Hear me profess sincerely: had I a dozen sons, each in my love alike, and none less dear than thine and my good Marcius, I had rather had eleven die nobly for their country than one voluptuously surfeit out of action.

When Virgilia cries, "O Jupiter, no blood!" her retort is:

> Away, you fool! It more becomes a man
> Than gilt his trophy. . . .

Volumnia's values are to modern ears monstrous, but it must be remembered that they refer to a time when war was still regarded as the chivalric encounter of equals, hand-to-hand. Even so, this play exposes the barrenness of such values, and their destruction by more basic human feelings.

When Valeria, a friend of the family, calls upon the two ladies, we learn that the son of Coriolanus is being bred as his father was. Volumnia says of him: "He had rather see the swords and hear a drum than look upon his schoolmaster." In a tale Valeria tells of the young boy, we see another aspect of his father, an uncontrollable fury:

> I saw him run after a gilded butterfly, and when he caught
> it, he let it go again; and after it again; and over and over he
> comes, and up again; catched it again; or whether his fall
> enraged him or how 'twas, he did so set his teeth and tear it.

Volumnia and Valeria approve of the boy's tearing of the butterfly, but his mother tries to dismiss it as a boyish prank. We are going to be reminded of that butterfly later in the play, when Cominius says that the Volscians follow the vengeful Coriolanus as he seeks the Romans to destroy them:

> . . . And they follow him,
> Against us brats, with no less confidence
> Than boys pursuing summer butterflies,
> Or butchers killing flies.

It pleases us that the peace-loving Virgilia is no weakling. She has a streak of commendable stubbornness, for she resolutely maintains her determination to remain indoors until her husband returns from the war.

After the capture of the city which gave him his new name, Coriolanus has a justifiable reason for his continued contempt for his soldiers: they loot everything, even worthless things:

> See here these movers [*i.e.* removers, thieves] that do prize
>   their hours
> At a cracked drachma! Cushions, leaden spoons,
> Irons of a doit, [*i.e.* worthless implements] doublets that
>   hangmen would
> Bury with those that wore them, these base slaves,
> Ere yet the fight be done, pack up. . . .

Coriolanus had had a great disappointment at the taking of Corioli; Tullus Aufidius was not there. So he speeds to join his superior, Cominius, in the hope of meeting his respected enemy face to face, leaving Titus Lartius to deal with the captured city. Stained with battle blood, Coriolanus arrives at the camp of Cominius. He disdains to give any account of his heroic deeds at Corioli, but cannot forbear another blistering reference to his cowardly army:

> But for our gentlemen,
> The common file—a plague! Tribunes for them!—
> The mouse ne'er shunned the cat as they did budge
> From rascals worse than they.

Coriolanus does meet Tullus Aufidius foot-to-foot, but some Volscians rescue their leader. This attempt at a chivalric encounter is Shakespeare's invention; in Plutarch, Cominius sends rescuers to Coriolanus, when he is surrounded by Volscians. The personalization of the conflict is essential to the conception of Coriolanus; he is the champion gladiator for whom the battlefield is the Colosseum, if the five-hundred-year anachronism may be pardcned.

At the ceremony at which Caius Marcius is invested with the addition, "Coriolanus," he behaves with becoming modesty, which is undoubtedly genuine. It is part of his heroic training that achievement is its own reward; he is always truly embarrassed by praise:

> Pray now, no more. My mother,
> Who has a charter to extol her blood,
> When she does praise me, grieves me. . . .
> . . . .
> I have some wounds upon me, and they smart
> To hear themselves remembered.

In making Coriolanus more sympathetic, Shakespeare adds a delightfully human touch. He refuses an undue proportion of the booty of battle, but makes one request:

> I sometime lay here in Corioli
> At a poor man's house; he used me kindly.
> He cried to me; I saw him prisoner.
> . . . I request you
> To give my poor host freedom.

But alas! Coriolanus cannot remember his name.

Rome, and in particular, his family and friends, eagerly awaits the return of the victorious Coriolanus. As they speculate on the possibility of his being wounded, his wife, his mother, and old Menenius show their different reactions to the scars of battle:

> MENENIUS: He was wont to come home wounded.
> VIRGILIA: Oh, no, no, no!
> VOLUMNIA: Oh, he is wounded, I thank the gods for't.
> MENENIUS: So do I too, if it be not too much.

When Coriolanus arrives, he first kneels to his mother—the glory is really hers—and then turns to his wife, who stands silent by, weeping:

> My gracious silence, hail!
> Wouldst thou have laughed had I come coffined home,
> That weep'st to see me triumph? . . .

Volumnia hints at the next development in the career of her son, that his military prowess should be rewarded with civic power, but he immediately cautions her:

> Know, good mother,
> I had rather be their servant in my way
> Than sway with them in theirs.

Coriolanus receives a tumultuous reception from patricians and plebs alike, but the hostile tribunes have no doubt that, when the time comes, they can again stir up the people's animosity against him. They must do this because, if he should become Consul,

> Then our office may,
> During his power, go sleep.

Two officials, as they prepare the Capitol for a meeting of the Senate, sagely discuss Coriolanus and his chances of being Consul:

> That's a brave fellow, but he's vengeance proud, and loves not the common people. . . . Faith, there have been many great men that flattered the people, who ne'er loved them; and there be many that they have loved, they know not wherefore; so that, if they love they know not why, they hate upon no better a ground . . . But he seeks their hate with greater devotion than they can render it him, and leaves nothing undone that may fully discover him their opposite. Now, to seem to affect the malice and displeasure of the people is as bad as that which he dislikes, to flatter them for their love.

As might be expected, Coriolanus cannot sit to hear the official speeches lauding his deeds, and he leaves the chamber. When he returns, he hears that the Senate have made him Consul, but he still has to get the approval of the people in a ceremony of public humility. He protests:

> I do beseech you,
> Let me o'erleap that custom, for I cannot
> Put on the gown, stand naked, and entreat them
> For my wounds' sake to give their suffrage. . . .

But he is told by one of the tribunes,

> Sir, the people
> Must have their voices; neither will they bate
> One jot of ceremony.

Urged on by Menenius, Coriolanus undergoes what is to him the humiliation of begging the voices of the people as they pass him, one by one. For their part, the people want to elect him as a reward for his military services: "If he would incline to the people, there was never a worthier man." But Coriolanus cannot hide his scorn, even as they give him their grudging approval. To a citizen who remarks, "You have not indeed loved the common people," he replies with open sarcasm:

> You should account me the more virtuous that I have not
> been common in my love. I will, sir, flatter my sworn brother,
> the people, to earn a dearer estimation of them. 'Tis a con-
> dition they account gentle; and since the wisdom of their
> choice is rather to have my hat than my heart, I will prac-
> tise the insinuating nod, and be off to them most counter-
> feitly; that is, sir, I will counterfeit the bewitchment of some
> popular man and give it bountiful to the desirers. Therefore,
> beseech you, I may be consul.

In spite of this attitude, the people remember the many wounds he has received on their behalf, and wish him well. But, when the ceremony is over, it is easy for the tribunes, Brutus and

Sicinius, to make the people regret their approbation and determine en masse to reverse it at the moment of final confirmation:

> Say you chose him
> More after our commandment than as guided
> By your own true affections; and that your minds,
> Preoccupied with what you rather must do
> Than what you should, made you against the grain
> To voice him consul. . . .

In a brief interlude which prepares us for the second half of the play, we learn that the Volsces are in arms again, and Tullus Aufidius, now in Antium, is eager to wipe out the disgrace of Corioli. The heart of Coriolanus is in Antium with Aufidius:

> I wish I had cause to seek him there,
> To oppose his hatred fully. . . .

When the tribunes warn Coriolanus of the new hostility of the people his fierce anger breaks out in a wholesale condemnation of democracy. Ever-placating Menenius ascribes it to his choler, but Coriolanus quite truthfully replies:

> Choler!
> Were I as patient as the midnight sleep,
> By Jove, 'twould be my mind.

Coriolanus is the ultimate spokesman for all honest rightists; he believes in aristarchy as the best guarantee of disinterested public service:

> . . . I say again,
> In soothing them, we nourish 'gainst our Senate
> The cockle of rebellion, insolence, sedition,
> Which we ourselves have ploughed for, sowed and scattered
> By mingling them with us, the honoured number,
> Who lack not virtue, no, nor power, but that
> Which they have given to beggars.

The tribunes have an easy reply, both against Coriolanus himself and his political philosophy:

> You speak o' the people
> As if you were a god to punish, not
> A man of their infirmity.
>
> .   .   .   .   .   .
> What is the city but the people?

They feel they have provoked Coriolanus to such utterances as to demand his death for treason, and they order his arrest. This releases Coriolanus into his natural element, for he draws his sword and drives out his enemies. He is persuaded to be gone before they return in strength. Poor Menenius is left to deal with the crisis, and he succeeds in preventing the mob from seeking summary justice, on the understanding that he will bring Coriolanus to trial "by a lawful form." His own attitude to Coriolanus is equivocal; he admires and deplores his inability to compromise:

> His nature is too noble for the world;
> He would not flatter Neptune for his trident,
> Or Jove for 's power to thunder. His heart's his mouth;
> What his breast forges, that his tongue must vent;
> And, being angry, does forget that ever
> He heard the name of death.
>
> .   .   .   .   .   .
> . . . What the vengeance!
> Could he not speak 'em fair?

Menenius has a much more difficult task in pacifying Coriolanus than the mob, but he has an unexpected ally in Volumnia. The son is amazed by what seems to him the change in his mother; there had been no place for compromise in the values she had inculcated in him. She had taught him better than she knew. As he says,

> Why did you wish me milder? Would you have me
> False to my nature? Rather say I play
> The man I am.

There is more at stake than just the safety of Coriolanus; there is a real danger that his admirers will turn upon the people and "sack great Rome with Romans." Volumnia is very skillful. Abat-

ing not one jot of her abhorrence of the people, she says that
stratagems, which he has often praised in war, are sometimes necessary in peace:

> Now this no more dishonours you at all
> Than to take in a town with gentle words,
> Which else would put you to your fortune and
> The hazard of much blood.

Gradually Coriolanus seems to succumb to his mother's arguments, but at the last moment reverts to his integrity:

> . . . I will not do't,
> Lest I surcease to honour mine own truth,
> And by my body's action teach my mind
> A most inherent baseness.

This unleashes an anger in Volumnia to equal that of her son:

> . . . Come all to ruin. Let
> Thy mother rather feel thy pride than fear
> Thy dangerous stoutness, for I mock at death
> With as big a heart as thou. Do as thou list.
> Thy valiantness was mine, thou suck'st it from me,
> But owe [*i.e.* own] thy pride thyself.

Before this onslaught Coriolanus crumbles, and agrees to stand
trial.

The tribunes rely on provoking the anger of Coriolanus, and
thereby securing his condemnation:

> . . . Being once chafed, he cannot
> Be reined again to temperance. Then he speaks
> What's in his heart, and that is there which looks
> With us to break his neck.

Coriolanus answers his accusers with controlled mildness until one
of the tribunes calls him "a traitor to the people." That word
"traitor" is the match to the powder keg:

> The fires i' the lowest hell fold in the people!
> Call me their traitor! Thou injurious tribune!

Within thine eyes sat twenty thousand deaths,
In thy hands clutched as many millions, in
Thy lying tongue both numbers, I would say
"Thou liest" unto thee with a voice as free
As I do pray the gods.

The people shout for his death, but the tribune, Brutus, in a show of lenity in reward for Coriolanus's services as a soldier, calls for his perpetual banishment instead. Cominius tries to intercede, but the furious Coriolanus will have none of it. He calls down a curse upon his city, but little thinks then that he will come near to implementing it himself:

You common cry of curs! whose breath I hate
As reek o' the rotten fens, whose loves I prize
As the dead carcasses of unburied men
That do corrupt my air, I banish you!
. . . .
Let every feeble rumour shake your hearts!
Your enemies, with nodding of their plumes,
Fan you into despair! Have the power still
To banish your defenders, till at length
Your ignorance . . .
. . . . .
. . . deliver you as most
Abated captives to some nation
That won you without blows! . . .

In his farewell to his family, Coriolanus is almost brusque:

Come, leave your tears; a brief farewell. The beast
With many heads butts me away. . . .

Cominius offers to travel with the banished man a month, in the hope that he will be recalled. Coriolanus will have none of it, but he makes a promise:

While I remain above ground you shall
Hear from me still, and never of me aught
But what is like me formerly.

And this promise he was to keep, in his own way and according to his own values, but his fulfillment of it was to appall and terrify the people to whom he made it.

In the deadly love-hate of rivalry, Coriolanus is drawn to seek Tullus Aufidius in Antium. In revenge against Rome, he has decided to offer his services to him. Many critics find this an incredible and unmotivated change in the man, but they are looking for another man than Shakespeare's. Individual honor is his highest value, and not a selfless patriotism. He was a chivalric and romantic soldier first, and a Roman second. For him, circumstances decide loyalties, the credo of many oppressed or outcast minorities today. Coriolanus states it for himself:

> Oh world, thy slippery turns! Friends now fast sworn,
> Whose double bosoms seem to wear one heart,
> Whose hours, whose bed, whose meal and exercise
> Are still together, who twin, as 'twere, in love
> Unseparable, shall within this hour,
> On a dissension of a doit, break out
> To bitterest enmity. So, fellest foes,
> Whose passions and whose plots have broke their sleep
> To take the one the other, by some chance,
> Some trick not worth an egg, shall grow dear friends
> And interjoin their issues. So with me.
> My birthplace hate I, and my love's upon
> This enemy town. I'll enter. If he slay me,
> He does fair justice; if he give me way,
> I'll do his country service.

That phrase, "some trick not worth an egg," reminds us of Hamlet's comment on the war to which Fortinbras was leading his men, "even for an eggshell." Hamlet would not have understood Coriolanus at this juncture, but Fortinbras would.

Coriolanus, now in tattered garb, makes his way into the kitchen of the house of Tullus Aufidius, who is feasting some Volscian nobility, but is brought to the kitchen by report of a stranger's angry and haughty treatment of his servants. When Coriolanus declares his identity, he gives another reason, in addi-

tion to his banishment, for wanting to change sides. In his brooding on the event, he has come to accuse his fellow patricians of
cowardice in not supporting him, and so it is now the whole city,
and not merely the plebs, that has failed him. All he has left is
the ironic name, "Coriolanus," which should be his death warrant
to the Volsces:

> . . . Only that name remains.
> The cruelty and envy of the people,
> Permitted by our dastard nobles, who
> Have all forsook me, hath devoured the rest,
> And suffered me by th' voice of slaves to be
> Whooped out of Rome. . . .

Coriolanus is well aware that Aufidius may choose to kill him:

> . . . I will fight
> Against my cankered country with the spleen
> Of all the underfiends. But if so be
> Thou dar'st not this, and that to prove more fortune
> Thou'rt tired, then, in a word, I also am
> Longer to live most weary, and present
> My throat to thee and to thy ancient malice;
> Which not to cut would show thee but a fool,
> Since I have ever followed thee with hate,
> Drawn tuns of blood out of thy country's breast,
> And cannot live but to thy shame, unless
> It be to do thee service.

In an emotional utterance expressive of an emotional judgment,
Aufidius warmly embraces his old enemy as a newfound friend:

> . . . Know thou first,
> I loved the maid I married; never man
> Sighed truer breath; but that I see thee here,
> Thou noble thing, more dances my rapt heart
> Than when I first my wedded mistress saw
> Bestride my threshold . . .
>
> .   .   .   .
>
> . . . Worthy Marcius,
> Had we no other quarrel else to Rome but that

> Thou art thence banished, we would muster all
> From twelve to seventy, and pouring war
> Into the bowels of ungrateful Rome,
> Like a bold flood o'erbear. . . .
>
> .   .   .   .
>
> . . . A thousand welcomes!
> And more a friend than e'er an enemy;
> Yet, Marcius, that was much. . . .

Back in Rome, the tribunes seem to be fully justified in their banishment of Coriolanus, for the city prospers, free from danger of civil strife or enemy invasion. Sicinius, one of the tribunes, says:

> . . . Here do we make his friends
> Blush that the world goes well, who rather had,
> Though they themselves did suffer by't, behold
> Dissentious numbers pestering streets than see
> Our tradesmen singing in their shops and going
> About their functions friendly.

The tribunes are high in popular favor, and even Menenius "is grown most kind of late." But when the news accumulates to certainty that

> A fearful army, led by Caius Marcius
> Associated with Aufidius, rages
> Upon our territories, and have already
> O'erborne their way, consumed with fire, and took
> What lay before them,

all changes. The citizens remember that it was the tribunes who talked them into the cry for banishment. They say, quite rightly: "That we did, we did for the best; and though we willingly consented to his banishment, yet it was against our will." It should be noted that neither Cominius nor Menenius makes the slightest accusation of treachery against Coriolanus:

> . . . Who is't can blame him?
> .   .   .   .

> If he could burn us all into one coal,
> We have deserved it.

But all is not well with the Volsces. Coriolanus has supplanted Tullus Aufidius in the affection and admiration of the army. A lieutenant describes the situation to Tullus:

> I do not know what witchcraft's in him, but
> Your soldiers use him as the grace 'fore meat,
> Their talk at table, and their thanks at end;
> And you are darkened in this action, sir,
> Even by your own.

While Aufidius is determined to regain the ascendancy, he is astonishingly objective in his assessment of Coriolanus:

> . . . He bears himself more proudlier
> Even to my person, than I thought he would
> When first I did embrace him. Yet his nature
> In that's no changeling; and I must excuse
> What cannot be amended.

He is equally objective in weighing the reasons for the banishment of Coriolanus:

> . . . Whether 'twas pride,
> Which out of daily fortune ever taints
> The happy man; whether defect of judgement,
> To fail in the disposing of those chances
> Which he was lord of; or whether nature,
> Not to be other than one thing, not moving
> From the casque to the cushion [*i.e.* from soldier to senator,
>   war to peace], but commanding peace
> Even with the same austerity and garb
> As he controlled the war; but one of these—
> As he hath spices of them all, not all,
> For I dare so far free him—made him feared,
> So hated, and so banished. But he has a merit
> To choke it [*i.e.* the decree of banishment] in the utterance.
>   So our virtues
> Lie in the interpretation of the time.

But Aufidius is ruthless in his new determination:

> . . . When, Caius, Rome is thine,
> Thou are poor'st of all; then shortly art thou mine.

When Coriolanus and Tullus Aufidius are at the gates of Rome, threatening to burn it to the ground, first Cominius and then Menenius go to plead with Coriolanus to spare the city. Cominius reports:

> I offered [*i.e.* tried] to awaken his regard
> For 's private friends; his answer to me was
> He could not stay to pick them in a pile
> Of noisome musty chaff. He said 'twas folly,
> For one poor grain or two, to leave unburnt
> And still to nose the offence.

To Menenius, Coriolanus, in the presence of Aufidius, is even more explicit:

> Wife, mother, child, I know not. My affairs
> Are servanted to others. . . .

The harsh reception of Menenius is certainly colored by the presence of Aufidius, to whom Coriolanus says:

> . . . This man, Aufidius,
> Was my beloved in Rome; yet thou behold'st.

This earns the laconic reply: "You keep a constant temper." But then comes the climactic appeal: wife, mother, young son, family friend, all in mourning, and all humbly bowing. The very sight begins the conflict in Coriolanus, yet he is strengthened in his inhuman resolve by the presence of Aufidius. Menenius expects their peace mission to be as ineffective as his own, for he had said of Coriolanus: "There is no more mercy in him than milk in a male tiger." To the first greeting of his wife Coriolanus says: "These eyes are not the same I wore in Rome," but he cannot forbear taking her in his arms for a long kiss, and he is shamed when his mother kneels to him. Yet he tries to forestall his mother's pleas:

> . . . Do not bid me
> Dismiss my soldiers or capitulate
> Again with Rome's mechanics. Tell me not
> Wherein I seem unnatural. Desire not
> To allay my rages and revenges with
> Your colder reasons.

As Volumnia persists in making her plea, Coriolanus insists on the continued presence of the Volsces:

> Aufidius, and you Volsces, mark; for we'll
> Hear nought from Rome in private. . . .

Volumnia's first appeal is on the grounds of the dilemma of his family's dual loyalties, to Rome and to Coriolanus. To strengthen this argument, she is joined by Virgilia in saying that they will both commit suicide if he sacks Rome. It is noteworthy that his young son's reaction is very different. In him, his grandmother is rearing another Coriolanus:

> 'A shall not tread on me.
> I'll run away till I am bigger, but then I'll fight.

The effect on Coriolanus of the opening plea is to make him rise and attempt to leave, but he is stopped by further words from his mother. Now she shifts her ground; the matron of war becomes the ambassador of peace, which she says will benefit both Volsces and Romans. As he seems to remain adamant, anger creeps into her voice:

> Come, let us go.
> This fellow had a Volscian to his mother;
> His wife is in Corioli, and his child
> Like him by chance. Yet give us our dispatch.
> I am hushed until our city be afire,
> And then I'll speak a little.

Once before the mother's anger had succeeded in subduing the son, when her reason could not, and it succeeds again, but Coriolanus has a foreboding that this time his submission will destroy him.

> . . . Oh, my mother, mother! Oh!
> You have won a happy victory to Rome;
> But, for your son, believe it, oh, believe it,
> Most dangerously you have with him prevailed,
> If not most mortal to him. But let it come.

He puts it to Aufidius that he would have done the same in the same circumstances, and Aufidius acknowledges, "I was moved withal," but in an aside he shows he will use Coriolanus's capitulation to restore his own fortunes.

It is remarkable that Volumnia makes no comment on the new danger to her son; she says no word at all; nor does she speak again in the play, not even to acknowledge her triumphal reception in Rome. Is her silence due to the fact that she marked her son's words all too well, and knows that she has sacrificed him to save Rome? Her values would have demanded such a sacrifice, and a stoically silent acceptance of it.

Aufidius is remorseless in regaining the power he has lost to Coriolanus. Before he has a chance fully to defend his action, Aufidius denounces him to the lords and commoners:

> . . . perfidiously
> He has betrayed your business, and given up,
> For certain drops of salt, your city Rome—
> I say "your city"—to his wife and mother,
> Breaking his oath and resolution, like
> A twist of rotten silk; never admitting
> Counsel o' the war; but at his nurse's tears
> He whined and roared away his victory,
> That pages blushed at him, and men of heart
> Looked wond'ring each at others.

This, with the added epithet, "boy of tears," serves to let loose the uncontrolled fury of Coriolanus, as it was calculated to do. The tactic which produced his banishment from Rome will also ensure his death in Corioli. All tact, never notable in him, disappears and Coriolanus reminds them of his most famous deed:

> If you have writ your annals true, 'tis there
> That, like an eagle in a dovecote, I
> Fluttered your Volscians in Corioli:
> Alone I did it. "Boy!"

As Coriolanus and Menenius did in Rome, two Volscian lords try to plead for a "judicious hearing," but it is too late. The people who had adopted him as a hero now recall the deaths he had given to their families, and he is slaughtered in an outburst of public anger. It is tragically ironic that this hero of the sword should die as the defenseless victim of a pack of assassins; no other Shakespearean tragic hero has such a hapless fate. In a final display of revengeful victory, Aufidius stands upon the body, to the disgust of some Volscian lords, one of whom says:

> Bear from hence his body,
> And mourn you for him. Let him be regarded
> As the most noble corse that ever herald
> Did follow to his urn.

And Aufidius himself pays a last tribute:

> My rage is gone
> And I am struck with sorrow. Take him up.
> Help, three o' the chiefest soldiers. I'll be one.
> Beat thou the drum that it speak mournfully.
> Trail your steel pikes. Though in this city he
> Hath widowed and unchilded many a one,
> Which to this hour bewail the injury,
> Yet he shall have a noble memory.

A noble memory? Yes, for there is something admirable in the selfless and uncompromising adherence to a code of conduct, however misguided it may be; and there is something even inspiring in a man who sought glory, not power. The story of Coriolanus is a classical example of the unforgivable sin of hubris, but in his case it was not the gods he offended but the people. Yet, in his simple strength, he was a Mars among men.

Many readers of this book will be disappointed and some will be exasperated by its omissions; so many other characters deserve chapters to themselves. I myself regret these omissions, but it would have been impossible to include in one volume a chapter on every character of Shakespeare that deserved such treatment; at least, if not strictly impossible, the book would have been so gargantuan as to be impractical. The approximate size of the book was determined in advance, and this seemed to call for the present format. (Even so, the resultant text is substantially longer than it was originally intended to be.)

As to the choice of the particular twenty-one characters, I think it will be generally agreed that in most cases it was inevitable. In some of the more debatable ones, I have given my reasons for choosing them in the pertinent chapters; for others, I can only say that they are the result of much internal debate, which could quite easily have resulted in other choices; but I do not regret or apologize for the selection I ultimately made.

My conception of the characters has been drawn from many sources and shaped in many ways. There was the necessity to clarify my ideas in trying to teach actor-students how to play the characters, and in the process of teaching you always learn. Then there were the discoveries made in directing the plays; good actors always want to know why a character behaves as he does, and this leads to probing which sometimes unearths buried treasure; thus, for instance, in a production I directed of *King Lear* the actor playing the Fool wanted to know why he disappeared so suddenly in the middle of the play, and the answer I came up with, which I mentioned in the chapter on *King Lear*, enabled him to play his last scene in a way that made his disappearance inevitable. Behind my ideas, too, there is a lifetime of reading about the plays and Shakespeare's world, some memorable conversations and arguments with people whose opinions I respect, a few illuminating performances, but, above all, endless reading of Shakespeare himself. It is extraordinary how one's growing experience of life will suddenly reveal a new depth of meaning in a well-known passage; familiarity can dull one's awareness of the true significance of beloved words until life pricks one into understanding.

This process of discovery of the infinite riches of Shakespeare never ends. No one can ever know his characters with a definite completeness, any more than one can fully know another person, even those who are nearest and dearest. In a very real sense, the portraits I have attempted to draw are interim studies; they are the characters as I see them now.

November 30, 1969